MrExcel
LIBRARY

Charts and Graphs:
Microsoft® Excel® 2010

Bill Jelen

que®

800 East 96th Street,
Indianapolis, Indiana 46240
USA

Charts and Graphs: Microsoft® Excel® 2010

Copyright © 2011 by Que Publishing

ISBN-13: 978-0-789-74312-1
ISBN-10: 0-789-74312-4

Library of Congress Cataloging-in-Publication data is on file.

Printed in the United States of America

First Printing: September 2010

Trademarks

All terms mentioned in this book that are known to be trademarks or service marks have been appropriately capitalized. Que Publishing cannot attest to the accuracy of this information. Use of a term in this book should not be regarded as affecting the validity of any trademark or service mark.

Warning and Disclaimer

Bulk Sales

Que Publishing offers excellent discounts on this book when ordered in quantity for bulk purchases or special sales. For more information, please contact

U.S. Corporate and Government Sales

1-800-382-3419
corpsales@pearsontechgroup.com

For sales outside of the U.S., please contact

International Sales
international@pearsoned.com

Associate Publisher
Greg Wiegand

Acquisitions Editor
Loretta Yates

Managing Editor
Sandra Schroeder

Development Editor
Sondra Scott

Project Editor
Seth Kerney

Copy Editor
Keith Cline

Indexer
Cheryl Lenser

Proofreaders
Water Crest Publishing
Debbie Williams

Technical Editor
Bob Umlas

Publishing Coordinator
Cindy Teeters

Multimedia Developer
Dan Scherf

Interior Designer
Anne Jones

Cover Designer
Anne Jones

Page Layout
Jake McFarland

Contents

Dedication

To Robert F. Jelen

About the Author

Bill Jelen, Excel MVP and the host of MrExcel.com, has been using spreadsheets since 1985, and he launched the MrExcel.com website in 1998. Bill was a regular guest on Call for Help with Leo Laporte and has produced more than 1,200 episodes of his daily video podcast, Learn Excel from MrExcel. He is the author of 30 books about Microsoft Excel and writes the monthly Excel column for *Strategic Finance* magazine. You will most frequently find Bill taking his show on the road, doing half-day Power Excel seminars wherever he can find a room full of accountants or Excellers. Before founding MrExcel.com, Jelen spent 12 years in the trenches—working as a financial analyst for finance, marketing, accounting, and operations departments of a $500 million public company. He lives near Akron, Ohio, with his wife, Mary Ellen, and his sons, Josh and Zeke.

Acknowledgments

I wish to thank Gene Zelazny of McKinsey & Company. Gene was generous with his time and feedback. He indirectly taught me a lot about charting over a decade ago, when I did a six-month stint on a McKinsey project team. Kathy Villella and Tom Bunzel also provided advice on presentations. Mala Singh of XLSoft Consulting vetted the chapter on using VBA to create charts.

Mike Alexander, my coauthor on the *Pivot Table Data Crunching* books, helped outline the table of contents for this book and provided many ideas for Chapter 7. You can catch Mike and me twice a year teaming up for the three-day Power Analyst Boot Camp.

I enjoy the visual delight of every Edward Tufte book. I apologize in advance to E.T. for documenting all the chartjunk that Microsoft lets us add to Excel charts.

Dick DeBartolo is the Daily GizWiz and has been writing for *Mad* magazine for more than 40 years, since he was 15. The pages of *Mad* were not where I expected to find inspiration for a charting book, but why not? Thanks to John Marcinko, my son's friend who pointed me, in a random conversation, to the *Mad* charts. Thanks to Bob D'Amico for illustrating the charts à la *Mad*. The pie chart in Chapter 4 is a Dick DeBartolo original, created especially for this book. Many thanks to Dick for being a contributor.

I was visiting Keith Bradbury's office in Toronto. Keith makes the completely awesome PDF-to-Excel utility at InvestInTech.com. Between parking the car and Keith's office, I saw the most amazing store, managed by David Michaelides. SWIPE is a bookstore dedicated to art and design. This is a beautiful store to browse, and if you go in and reveal that you work in Excel all day, they will sympathetically be very nice to you. In a clash of worlds, David has the original 1984 Mac way up above his cash register because it was the start of desktop publishing. I pointed out that the Mac was where Excel 1.0 got its start in 1985, so we had a common thread in our respective backgrounds. Stop by 477 Richmond Street West (two blocks west of Spadina) to take a look the next time you are in Toronto.

Thanks to Dan Bricklin and Bob Frankston for inventing the computer spreadsheet. Thanks to Mitch Kapor for Lotus 1-2-3. Thanks to David Gainer at Microsoft for guiding the Excel team through Excel 2007 and Excel 2010.

At MrExcel.com, thanks to Barb Jelen, Wei Jiang, Tracy Syrstad, Schar Oswald, and Scott Pierson. Thanks also to Josh and Zeke Jelen, who have been picking up hours after school learning how to edit and produce the MrExcel podcast.

The Microsoft MVPs for Excel are always generous with their time and ideas. Over the years, I've learned many cool charting tricks from websites maintained by John Peltier, Andy Pope, and Charley Kyd. Turn to the appendix for links to their respective websites. MVP Bob Umlas (the smartest Excel guy I know) served as a great technical editor. I still smile when I recall Bob pointing out that "9. Repeat step 9 for High, Low, and Close lines." was, in itself, a circular reference.

At Pearson, Loretta Yates is an awesome acquisitions editor. Keith Cline and Sondra Scott made this book better with their editing.

Finally, thanks to Josh Jelen, Zeke Jelen, and Mary Ellen Jelen. Writing five books simultaneously means way too many nights writing.

Introduction: Using Excel 2010 to Create Charts

Good charts should both explain and arouse curiosity. A chart can summarize thousands of data points into a single picture. The arrangement of a chart should explain the underlying data but also enable the reader to isolate trouble spots worthy of further analysis.

Excel makes it easy to create charts. Even though the improvements in Excel 2010 enable you to create a chart with only a few mouse clicks, it still takes thought to find the best way to present your data.

Choosing the Right Chart Type

Suppose you are an analyst for a chain of restaurants, and you are studying the lunch-hour sales for a restaurant in a location at a distant mall. Corporations that provide a steady lunchtime clientele during the week surround the mall. The mall does well on weekends during the holiday shopping months but lacks weekend crowds during the rest of the year.

From the data contained in the chart in Figure I.1, you can spot a periodicity in sales throughout the year. An estimated 50 spikes indicate that the periodicity might be based on the day of the week. You can also spot that there is a general improvement in sales at the end of the year, which you attribute to the holiday shopping season. However, there is an anomaly in the pattern during the summer months that needs further study.

After studying the data in Figure I.1, you might decide to plot the sales by weekday to understand the sales better. Figure I.2 shows the same data presented as seven line charts. Each line represents the sales for a particular day of the week. Friday is the dashed line. At the beginning of the year, Friday was

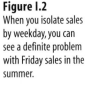

Figure I.1
This chart shows the sales trend for 365 data points.

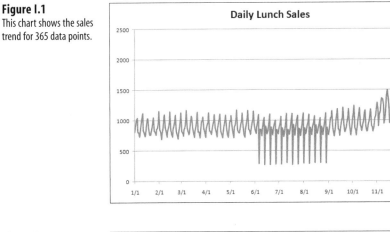

Figure I.2
When you isolate sales by weekday, you can see a definite problem with Friday sales in the summer.

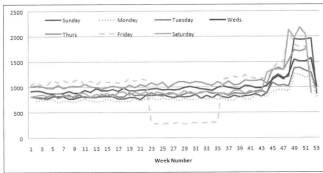

the best sales day for this particular restaurant. For some reason, around week 23, Friday sales plummeted.

The chart in Figure I.2 prompts you to make some calls to see what was happening on Fridays at this location. You might discover that the city was throwing free Friday lunchtime concerts from June through August. The restaurant manager was offered a concession at the concert location but thought it would be too much trouble. Using this pair of charts enabled you to isolate a problem and equipped you to make better decisions in the future.

Using Excel as Your Charting Canvas

Excel 2007 offered a complete rewrite of the 15-year-old charting engine from legacy versions of Excel. Excel 2007 introduced plenty of new bugs to the charting engine. Excel 2010 fixes many of those bugs, and brings back features like pattern fills that were missing from Excel 2007. Although the software offers no new charting types, Excel 2010 provides plenty of tools that allow you to make eye-catching charts. In Excel 2010, you can create better versions of the 11 existing chart types.

Creating charts in Excel 2010 basically requires these steps:

1. Set up and select your data in an Excel worksheet.

2. Choose the appropriate chart type from the Insert tab.

3. Change the chart layout or color scheme by using the Design tab.

4. Customize chart elements by using the Layout tab.

5. Micromanage formatting for individual data points by using the Format tab.

Most charts require steps 1 and 2. The remaining steps are optional and are used with decreasing frequency. It should be rare that you will need to venture to step 5. However, you are likely to customize at least a couple items in step 4.

Topics Covered in This Book

This book covers the Excel 2010 charting engine and three new types of word-sized charts called *Sparklines*. It also covers the Data Visualization and SmartArt Business diagramming tools that were introduced in Excel 2007.

Besides charts, Excel 2010 offers many other ways to display quantitative data visually. This book explains how to use the new conditional formatting features such as data bars, color scales, and icon sets to add visual elements to regular tables of numbers. In Figure I.3, conditional formatting features make it easy to see that Ontario has the largest population and that Nunavut has the largest land area. You can also add in-cell data bars such as these with a couple of mouse clicks, as described in Chapter 9, "Using Sparklines, Data Visualizations, and Other Nonchart Methods."

Figure I.3
In-cell data bars draw the eye to the largest values in each column.

	Province	Population	Area
26			
27	Province	Population	Area
28	Alberta	2974805	639987
29	British Columbia	3907740	926493
30	Manitoba	1119580	551938
31	New Brunswick	729495	71356
32	Newfound and Labrador	512930	370502
33	Northwest Territories	37360	1141108
34	Nova Scotia	908005	52917
35	Nunavut	26745	1925460
36	Ontario	11410045	907656
37	Prince Edward Island	135295	5684
38	Quebec	7237480	1357743
39	Saskatchewan	978930	586561
40	Yukon Territory	28670	474707
41			

The three new types of word-sized charts in Excel 2010 called Sparklines enable you to create tiny line charts, tiny column charts, and win/loss charts. As shown in Figure I.4, these tiny charts can show win/loss events that paint a better picture than a simple 7-3 record.

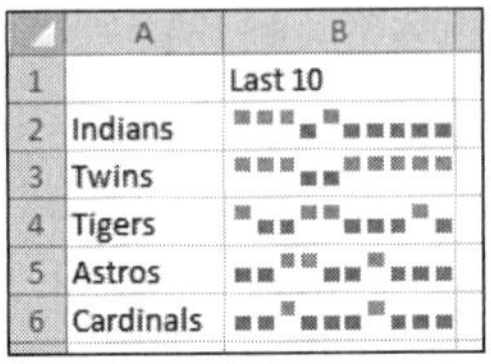

Figure I.4
The Twins baseball team made the post-season in 2009 because they won 8 of their last 10 games while the Tigers struggled.

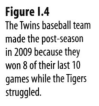

This book also takes a look at tools that you can purchase to add functionality to Excel 2010. Many vendors offer tools to create speedometer charts, supply curves, and specialized stock analysis tools. Perhaps one of the best tools is a Microsoft product called MapPoint. Using MapPoint, you can plot your Excel data in a geographic orientation on a map. See Chapter 10, "Presenting Your Excel Data on a Map Using Microsoft MapPoint," for more information about the cool tricks available with MapPoint.

This Book's Objectives

The goal of this book is to make you more efficient and effective in creating visual displays of information using Excel 2010.

In the early chapters of this book, you will learn how to use the new Excel 2010 charting interface. Chapters 3 through 6 walk you through all the built-in chart types and talk about when to use each chart type. Chapter 7 discusses creating unusual charts. Chapter 8 covers pivot charts, and Chapter 9 covers creating visual displays of information right in the worksheet. Chapter 10 covers mapping, and Chapter 11 covers the new SmartArt business graphics and Excel 2010's shape tools. Chapter 12 covers exporting charts for use outside of Excel. Chapter 13 presents macro tools you can use to automate the production of charts using Excel VBA. In Chapter 14, you will see several techniques that people can use to stretch the truth with charts. Finally, Appendix A provides a list of resources that will give you additional help with creating charts and graphs.

Versions of Excel

Excel charting was largely unchanged for the dozen years leading up to Excel 2003. This book will refer to Excel 2003 and earlier collectively as "legacy" versions of Excel.

Microsoft rewrote the charting engine for Excel 2007. Excel 2010 continues with the addition of Sparklines, improvements to data bars and SmartArt, and general fixes of bugs introduced in Excel 2007. Although this book uses screen shots from Excel 2010, most of the concepts will apply equally well to Excel 2007.

Special Elements in This Book

This book contains the following special elements:

NOTE Notes provide additional information outside the main thread of the chapter discussion that might be useful for you to know.

TIP Tips provide you with quick workarounds and timesaving techniques to help you do your work more efficiently.

CAUTION

Cautions warn you about potential pitfalls you might encounter. It is important to pay attention to Cautions because they alert you to problems that could cause hours of frustration.

CASE STUDY

Case studies provide a real-world look at topics previously introduced in the chapter.

 A video on YouTube will demonstrate how to perform one task in most chapters.

DESIGNING LIKE THE PROS

Throughout the book, several non-Excellers were asked to contribute charts unlike those found in Excel. After showing the designer's chart, you can walk through how to adjust the Excel settings to create a chart that approximates the designer's chart.

Next Steps

Chapter 1, "Introducing Charts in Excel 2010," presents the new Excel 2010 interface for creating charts. You will learn how to create your first chart and read about the various elements available in a chart.

Introducing Charts in Excel 2010

What's New in Excel 2010 Charts

Over the course of Excel 2007 and Excel 2010, the charting engine was completely rewritten. After 15 years of the same tired-looking charts, you can now create stunning charts with just a few mouse clicks.

The following list summarizes the new charting features in Excel 2010:

- To create a chart, you usually start with one of the seven new galleries on the ribbon's Insert tab. The first six galleries offer column, line, pie, bar, area, and scatter charts. The remaining chart types—stock, surface, doughnut, bubble, and radar—are grouped in the Other Charts gallery. You can display the All Charts gallery that shows all 73 chart subtypes. Select All Chart Types from the bottom of any chart drop-down menu on the Insert tab.

- Your first stop after creating a chart should be the Chart Layouts and Chart Styles galleries on the Design tab. Choose a layout and a design to select from prebuilt elements and colors. If you don't like the built-in colors, you can choose a new theme from the Page Layout ribbon, or you can head to the Format tab to change the colors for each data series.

- After choosing settings on the Design tab, you can customize individual elements of the chart by using the Layout tab. The Layout tab offers settings for the chart title, axis titles, legend, data labels, data table, axes, gridlines, plot area, chart wall, chart floor, 3-D rotation, trendline, lines, up/down bars, and error bars. In each case, a drop-down menu offers the popular choices, and a More Options choice leads to a Formatting dialog that presents all the choices.

- If you want microcontrol over the shape, fill, outline, or effects of any chart element, you can use the Format tab.

- It has always been possible to create a chart with a single keystroke—the F11 key can be used to build a default chart on a new worksheet. Excel 2010 continues to support this feature, and it also supports Alt+F1 for building a default chart embedded on the current worksheet.

- In Excel 2003, you could define custom formatting for charts by using Chart Type, Custom Types, User Defined, and Add. Excel 2010 replaces this functionality with the Manage Templates tool. Select Design, Change Chart Type, Manage Templates. The main advantage of this change is that now it is easier to move templates from one computer to another computer.

- In many galleries and formatting menus, Excel offers a Live Preview feature. You can see the effect of a change by hovering your cursor over the menu selection. You can hover over several choices until you find one that looks good, and then just click that option.

New Charting Tools and Menus

The entry point for Excel 2010 charting is the Insert tab. After you have created a chart, three new ribbon tabs appear under the Chart Tools heading: Design, Layout, and Format.

- Design offers major adjustments to the entire chart. You can switch rows/columns, choose from up to 12 built-in layouts, and choose colors and formatting effects by selecting a style.

> **NOTE**   Note that the 48 styles offered can be modified by choosing a new theme on the Page Layout tab.

- Layout offers formatting options for major elements of the chart such as title, legend, and data labels. Note that the options on the Layout tab are a small subset of available choices. It is not unusual to bypass the choices in Layout and head directly to the Format dialog.

- Format allows you to micro-manage individual items in the chart.

In general, the tabs progress from more general to more specific as you move from the Design tab on the left to the Format tab on the right. Microsoft pitched that you would progress from Design to Layout to Format in order to complete the chart. In practice, you might go from Insert to Design to Page Layout to Layout to Home to Format in order to finish a chart. Figure 1.1 shows the typical process.

Figure 1.1
Although Microsoft groups many chart settings in Design, Layout, and Format tabs, you will often have to visit Page Layout and Home tabs and the Format dialog box.

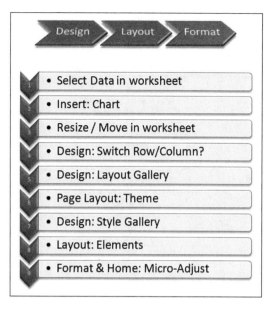

If you don't like the colors used in the Chart Styles gallery on the Design tab, you can visit the Theme drop-down on the Page Layout tab to choose a new theme color for the document.

> **NOTE** Note that changing the theme color affects all charts, shapes, and SmartArt diagrams in the workbook.

In addition, you can use many of the formatting icons on the Home tab to format titles and labels on a chart. These same icons appear on the mini toolbar when you select text within a title on a chart.

Using the Insert Tab to Select a Chart Type

As shown in Figure 1.2, the Insert tab offers seven drop-down menus in the Charts group. Each drop-down leads to a variety of chart types.

Table 1.1 describes the contents of each drop-down in the Charts group.

Figure 1.2
Five less-popular chart types are tucked under the Other Charts menu.

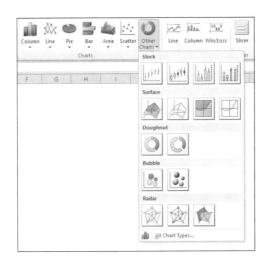

Table 1.1 Contents of Each Charts Group Drop-Down

Ribbon Icon	Contents
Column	19 types of column, cylinder, cone, and pyramid charts
Line	7 types of line charts
Pie	6 types of pie charts
Bar	15 types of bar charts
Area	6 types of area charts
Scatter	5 types of scatter charts
Other charts	4 stock charts, 4 surface charts, 2 doughnut charts, 2 bubble charts, and 3 radar charts

Using the Expand Icon to Access a Gallery of All Chart Types

A dialog launcher icon appears in the lower-right corner of some ribbon groups. This icon usually allows you to bypass the ribbon and head straight to a legacy-style dialog box.

Figure 1.3 shows the expand icon for the Charts group. Clicking this icon leads to a dialog box that shows all 73 charting types in one place.

Figure 1.3
You can click the Dialog Launcher icon to bypass the ribbon and open a charting dialog box.

Dialog Launcher Icon

Understanding the Chart Thumbnail Icons

Figure 1.4 shows the Insert Chart dialog with all 73 built-in chart types.

Figure 1.4
There are 73 chart types available in Excel 2010.

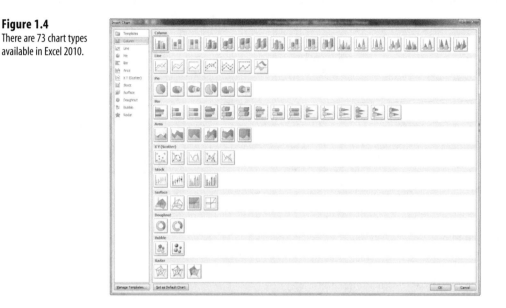

The gallery of 73 chart types might seem like a dizzying array of charts. However, in many cases, there are four variations of a given type. When you understand how Excel uses the light and dark blue icons to show these four charting types, you can quickly choose from the various thumbnails.

For example, consider the fourth through seventh icons in the Column section of Figure 1.4.

The fourth icon in the Column group of Figure 1.4 is for a 3-D clustered column chart. In this type, series 1 and series 2 are plotted next to each other. When they are plotted with different colors, it is easy to compare the height of the similar-colored bars to see how a particular value is trending. For example, the top-left chart in Figure 1.5 shows a 3-D clustered column chart. The thumbnail icon shows a light blue element and a dark blue element next to each other. Icons for clustered charts are shown in Figure 1.6.

The fifth icon in the Column group of Figure 1.4 is for a 3-D stacked column chart. In this type of chart, the values from series 2 are added to the values for series 1. This type of chart makes it easy to compare totals of all series. The lower-left chart in Figure 1.5 shows this type of chart. Although understanding how the first series is trending is straightforward, it is much harder to understand how the third series is trending. Are the West sales for April larger or smaller than those for March? It is hard to tell in a stacked chart. The icons for stacked charts always show the dark blue series on top of the light blue series, and the

Figure 1.5
Many chart subtypes offer these four variations on how the data is plotted.

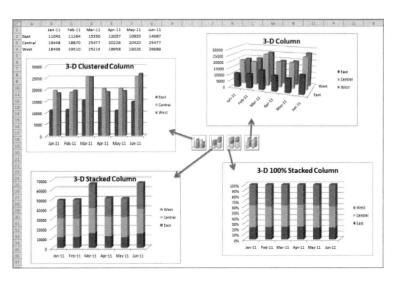

Figure 1.6
Icons for clustered charts show a dark blue and a light blue element at differing heights.

heights of the blue series vary from point to point. Icons for stacked charts are shown in Figure 1.7.

The sixth icon in the Column group of Figure 1.4 is for a 3-D 100 percent stacked column chart. These charts are similar to the stacked charts in that they plot series 2 on top of series 1. However, the total height of all series is scaled so that each data point shows 100 percent. The lower-right chart in Figure 1.5 shows a 100 percent stacked chart. This type of chart illustrates which regions are contributing to the total. The icons for 100 percent charts show the dark blue series on top of the light blue series, and the heights of all bars or points are the same. Icons for 100 percent charts are shown in Figure 1.8.

Figure 1.7
Icons for stacked charts show a dark blue element on top of a light blue element. The total height of the elements differs from category to category.

Figure 1.8
Icons for 100 percent stacked charts show a dark blue element on top of a light blue element. The total height is the same for each point.

The seventh icon in the Column group of Figure 1.4 is available only for 3-D charts. In 3-D column charts, the data for series 2 is plotted behind the data for series 1. A 3-D column chart works best when there are only a few data series. A basic problem occurs when the values in series 1 are larger than all the values in a later series. The taller bars in the front of the chart obscure the later values. Because none of the 2-D chart types offer this subtype of chart, there are fewer examples of icons that plot one series in front of the other. The six icons are shown in Figure 1.9.

Figure 1.9
Icons for 3-D charts show a dark blue element behind the light blue element.

Because there are four ways to plot multiple series, you can group 46 of the 73 chart types into 14 groups of types, as shown in Figure 1.10.

Figure 1.10
The column, line, bar, and area chart subtypes are really variations of basic types.

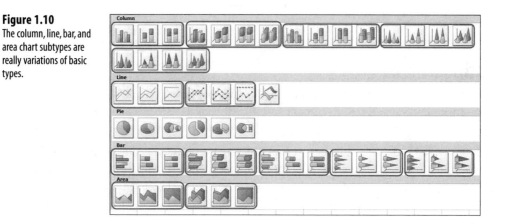

Using Gallery Controls

The charting tools tabs contain many instances of a new Office interface element known as a *gallery*. A gallery control enables you to scroll through options one row at a time or click the Open Gallery button to see all the choices at one time.

For example, the Chart Layouts gallery starts by showing three of the available icons: There are three control icons on the right side of the gallery. The up- and down-arrow icons allow you to move through the gallery one row at a time (see Figure 1.11).

Figure 1.11

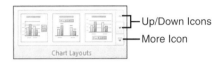

TIP   A quick trick is to use the bottom control icon, the More icon. You can click the More icon to cause the gallery to open the entire control, as shown in Figure 1.12.

Figure 1.12
When you click the More icon, you can quickly see all choices in the gallery at one time.

Creating a Chart

The first step in creating a chart is to build a worksheet that contains data to chart. Many business charts are created from summary data. If your dataset contains transactional data, consider summarizing the data using either a pivot table or formulas.

In Figure 1.13, the original dataset contained detailed transactional data. To create summary data to be used in a chart, new rows were inserted at the top of the worksheet, and a summary table was created using the new SUMIFS function. The formulas in C2:E4 create conditional sums to find the total revenue for each combination of product and year.

The formula in cell C2 in Figure 1.13 is =SUMIFS($G$9:$G$571,$B$9:$B$571,$B2, $D$9:$D$571,C$1). To use SUMIFS, specify a range to be summed (in this case, the revenue in G9:571). Then specify pairs of arguments representing a criteria range and a criteria

Figure 1.13
The new SUMIFS function simplifies creating the summary that can be used for charting

C2			▾	f_x	=SUMIFS($G$9:$G$571,$B$9:$B$571,$B2,$D$9:$D$571,C$1)			
	A	B	C	D	E	F	G	H	I
1			2009	2010	2011				
2		B447	621,845	753,547	779,730				
3		Y972	807,836	663,681	629,853				
4		Q122	966,549	742,210	710,419				
5									
6									
7									
8	Region	Product	Date		Year	Customer	Quantity	Revenue	COGS	Profi
9	West	B447	5-Jan-09		2009	Safe Aerobi	500	10475	4920	555
10	East	Q122	5-Jan-09		2009	Innovative P	900	19161	9198	996
11	East	B447	10-Jan-09		2009	Alluring Raft	500	11845	4920	692

> **NOTE**
> SUMIFS is a new function introduced in Excel 2007. It allows you to perform a SUMIF with multiple conditions. In legacy versions of Excel, you had to resort to using a SUMPRODUCT function or an array formula to perform the calculation now offered by SUMIFS.

value. The second and third arguments of the function specify that the products in B9:B571 should be compared to the product in B2. Excel sums the values in the sum range where all the criteria for that row are true.

For example, the $621,845 is the sum of all revenue in the dataset where both the product is B447 and the year is 2009. Similar logic is used to calculate all of the cells in C2:E4.

Selecting Contiguous Data to Chart

It is easiest to create charts when your data is in a contiguous rectangular block of cells. The left column of the dataset should contain the label for each series to be plotted. The first row of the dataset should contain values to be plotted along the category axis. The top-left cell should be blank. The rest of the cells in the dataset should contain values to be plotted.

In Figure 1.13, the products in B2:B4 will be plotted as individual series on the chart. The years in C1:E1 will be points along the category axis.

Selecting Noncontiguous Data to Chart

It is helpful, but not necessary, for your data to be in a contiguous range. For example, in Figure 1.14 you might want to create a pie chart that includes the category labels in Column B and the totals in Column F. Follow these steps to select data for creating a chart:

1. Click in cell B1 and drag to cell B4 to select the range of category labels.
2. While holding down the Ctrl key, click in cell F1 and drag down to cell F4 to add F1:F4 to the selection.
3. If you have additional series to plot, repeat step 2 for each additional series.

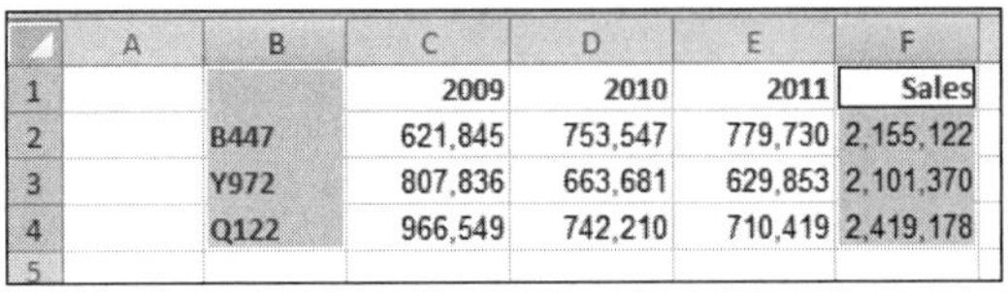

Figure 1.14
Selecting noncontiguous data requires a bit of dexterity, as you attempt to drag while holding down the Ctrl key.

◢	A	B	C	D	E	F
1			2009	2010	2011	Sales
2		B447	621,845	753,547	779,730	2,155,122
3		Y972	807,836	663,681	629,853	2,101,370
4		Q122	966,549	742,210	710,419	2,419,178
5						

NOTE Excel remembers the order in which you selected the data. Although choosing cell B1 and then individually Ctrl-clicking cells F4, F3, F2, F1, B4, B3, and B2 would lead to a selection that looks the same as Figure 1.14, it would not create an acceptable chart. You must select the category labels first and then Ctrl-click and drag to select the first series. The category labels should be the same size as the data in the first series. This is why you include the blank cell B1 in the category labels.

CAUTION
You also can create a find by using the context-sensitive menu on the menu bar. For a for view, use the Browse menu; for a worksheet view, use the Worksheet menu. Other view types have their own unique context-sensitive menu name.

Creating a Chart by Using the Insert Tab Icons

After you have selected the data to be included in a chart, click the Insert tab of the ribbon. Seven drop-down menus in the Charts group offer a total of 73 different chart subtypes. You can select one of the drop-down menus or click the dialog launcher icon in the lower-right corner of the group (refer back to Figure 1.3). Live Preview does not work when you are selecting a chart type from either the Ribbon or the Charts dialog. You have to choose one type and click to create a chart.

NOTE The ToolTips in the seven drop-downs are more descriptive than the ToolTips in the Insert Chart dialog. If you are not sure which chart subtype to use, hover your cursor over an icon in a charting drop-down to see a description of that chart subtype (see Figure 1.15).

Figure 1.15
Hover over any subtype in the ribbon drop-down menus to see a description of the subtype.

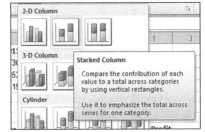

Excel charts are now automatically created as embedded charts. When you choose a chart type from the Insert tab, a chart appears somewhere in the range currently visible in the window. You will likely have to move most charts after creating them. For example, in Figure 1.16, the chart has been created in an annoying location. After moving this chart, you can resize it to fit the space by clicking to select the chart and then dragging a corner handle in or out.

Figure 1.16
Excel randomly inserts a chart somewhere in the visible range of cells. You can move and resize a chart.

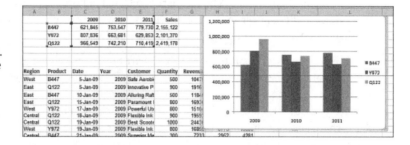

Creating a Chart with One Keystroke

Previous versions of Excel allowed you to create a chart by selecting the data and pressing the F11 key. In response, Excel created a default chart on a new sheet.

Excel 2010 still recognizes the F11 shortcut. However, it also includes an Alt+F1 shortcut that creates a default chart as a chart object embedded in the current worksheet. The Alt+F1 keystroke is a time saver when you need to create charts that match the Excel default. When Excel is installed, the default chart is a 2-D column chart. You can change the default chart type to fit the type of charts you create most often. Here's how:

1. Select an existing chart. In the Design tab, click the Change Chart Type icon. If you do not have an existing chart in your workbook, click the dialog launcher icon in the Charts group of the Insert tab.

2. Click the chart subtype that is closest to the chart type you want to create.

3. In the lower-left of the dialog, click Set as Default Chart. Then click Cancel to leave the dialog box.

After you go through this procedure, press F11 or Alt+F1 to create the selected chart type instead of the column chart.

Working with Charts

After creating a chart, you may need to rearrange the data or move the chart to a new location. The topics in this section will assist you with these tasks.

Moving a Chart Within the Current Worksheet

In the following case study, you will see that Excel had an annoying habit of locating new charts near the bottom of your dataset. With a large dataset, you may need to move the chart to the proper location thousands of rows away.

There are several ways to move a chart within the current worksheet. However, some methods are faster than others. When a chart is selected, a border appears around the chart. Eight resizing handles appear in the border. To move a chart, click the border but avoid the resizing handles. You can then drag the chart to a new location.

Because it is somewhat difficult to click a thin chart border, try clicking inside the chart to drag the chart to a new location. This approach works as long as you can click on some whitespace between the plot area and the chart border. The arrows in Figure 1.17 show areas where you can click and drag to move the entire chart. There are many areas inside the chart where clicking and dragging will have a different outcome. For example, if you click on the legend and drag, the legend within the chart area is moved. In addition, if you click anywhere inside the plot area and drag, you can nudge the plot area within the constraints of the chart area.

Figure 1.17
If you can find some whitespace outside the plot area, you can click and drag the whitespace to move the entire chart to a new location on the worksheet.

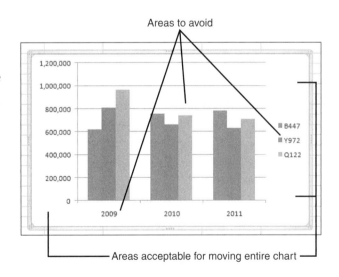

Dragging to a New Location in the Visible Window Is Easy

You can drag a chart anywhere in the visible window. However, if you try to drag the chart outside of the visible window, the mouse pointer changes to a red "no" symbol. If you release the mouse while it is the no symbol, the chart boomerangs back to its original position.

Dragging Outside of the Visible Window Is Frustrating

If you need to move a chart outside of the visible window, drag so that your cell pointer is within one-half row of the edge of the window. Excel will slowly start to scroll in the appropriate direction. As with other Windows programs, you can speed up the scroll by rapidly moving your mouse left and right. However, it is difficult to keep the mouse within the one-half row tolerance while moving left and right.

Adjust the Zoom So New Location Is Within the Visible Window

You are likely to find the scrolling action to be so slow that you will not want to use the previous technique to move the chart to a new location. Another option is to use the Zoom slider to show the worksheet at a 10 percent zoom. This has the effect of putting about 375 rows in the visible window. If you need to move a chart anywhere from 50 to 375 rows, setting the zoom to 10 percent and then dragging the chart within the visible window is a fast way to go.

Cut and Paste to Move Thousands of Rows

If your chart is created at the bottom of a 50,000-row dataset and you need to move it to the top of the dataset, cut and paste may be the fastest way to go. Follow these steps to move a chart within the current worksheet using cut and paste:

1. Select a chart.
2. Press Ctrl+X to cut the chart from the worksheet.
3. Press F5 to display the Go To dialog.
4. Type the address of the cell that you want to contain the top-left corner of the chart and click OK.
5. Press Ctrl+V to paste the chart in the new location.

Instead of completing steps 4 and 5, your favorite navigation method can be used to move to the cell that should contain the upper-left corner of the chart.

CASE STUDY: LOCATING A CHART AT THE TOP OF YOUR DATASET

Work along with this case study to build a dataset.

1. Create a blank worksheet.
2. Type **1** in cell A2.
3. With cell A2 selected, choose Home, Fill, Series.
4. Select Series in Columns. Enter a Stop Value of **3000**. Select OK to fill in the numbers from 1 to 3000 in Column A.

5. Enter the label **Result** in B1. Enter the number 1ø in B2. In B3, enter the following formula:
    =B2+RANDBETWEEN(-2,2).
6. Select cell B3. Double-click the fill handle to copy the formula down to B3001.

The goal of this case study is to create a chart of the results in A1:B3001. Follow these steps:

1. Start with the cellpointer in A1. While holding down the Shift key, press right arrow, down arrow, End, down arrow to select A1:B3001. Depending on your screen resolution, you might see Rows 2965 through 3001.
2. Select Insert, Line, 2-D Line, Line. Excel creates a chart in the center of the visible window, with the upper-left corner roughly around G2976. You now have quite a dilemma. The chart is located 2900 rows away from the proper location.

There are several ways to move the chart, including the following:

- If you grab the border of the chart, drag it to within one-half row of the top of the window, and hold it there, Excel scrolls to the proper location in 8 minutes and 47 seconds. Clearly, this is not the best solution.

- Alternatively, you can change the zoom to 10 percent. When this is done, you can drag the tiny chart to within one-half row of the top window and Excel will scroll faster, covering 2900 rows in 1 minute and 40 seconds. Adding in the time to adjust the zoom to 10 percent and then back to 100 percent, this method is 75 percent faster than scrolling at 100 percent.

- Cutting and pasting is a faster way to move the chart. With the original chart selected, press Ctrl+X to cut, Ctrl+Home to move to cell A1, click in cell D4, and press Ctrl+V to paste the chart at the top of the worksheet. This method takes about 7 seconds, depending on your manual dexterity with the keystroke combinations.

There is another, completely different method for keeping your chart at the top of the worksheet. This method involves selecting the original dataset while keeping cell A1 in view. When this is done, the created chart will be located at the top of your worksheet. Any of the following approaches will work when using this method:

- Start in cell A1. Hold down the Shift key while pressing down, End, down, right. Release the Shift key and type Ctrl+. to move to an opposite corner of the selection.

- Start in cell A2. Hold down the Ctrl+Shift keys while pressing down and then left to select the range. Press Ctrl+Backspace to bring the active cell back into view.

- Click in cell A2. Type Ctrl+* to select the current region. This will keep the visible window at the top of your dataset.

This case study is an example of how Excel 2010 offers many solutions to a problem. However, some of the solutions are dramatically faster than the obvious solution.

Reversing the Series and Categories of a Chart

Excel follows strict rules in deciding whether rows should be series or categories. Fortunately, you can reverse this decision with a single button click.

If Excel chooses the wrong orientation for the data in a chart, you can click the Switch Row/Column icon in the Design tab. When comparing the before and after charts in Figure 1.18, you will see that the years have changed from being category labels to series labels. The products have changed from being series labels to category labels.

Figure 1.18
To reverse the orientation of data in a chart, click Switch Row/Column.

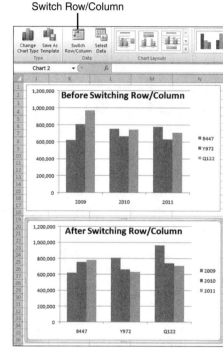

If your data has more columns of data than rows, the headings in the first row become category labels. In Figure 1.19, the eight columns of monthly data become category labels, and the three rows become series.

Figure 1.19
If your data has more columns than rows, the rows become series in the chart.

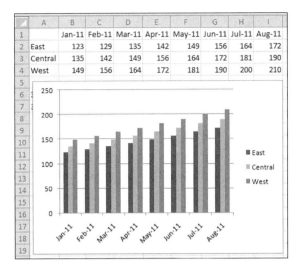

If your data has more rows than columns, the headings in the first column become category labels. In Figure 1.20, the 11 rows of city data become category labels, and the 4 columns become series.

Figure 1.20
If your data has more rows than columns, the columns become series in the chart.

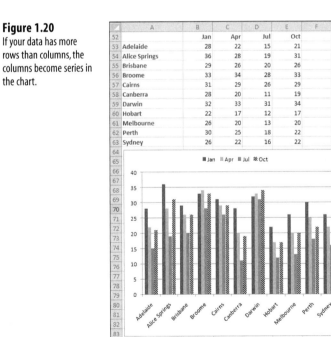

If your data has exactly the same number of rows and columns, the rows become series.

Changing the Data Sequence by Using Select Data

The Select Data icon on the Design tab allows you to change the rows and columns of your dataset. The Select Data icon also allows you to resequence the order of the series. When you click this icon, the Select Data Source dialog appears.

As shown in Figure 1.21, buttons in the Legend Entries side of the Select Data Source dialog enable you to add new series, edit a series, remove a series, or change the sequence of a series. A single Edit button on the right side of the dialog allows you to edit the range used for category labels.

When you compare Figure 1.20 to Figure 1.22, you will see that the series and categories have been reversed. The order of the cities has been resequenced from alphabetic to descending order by summer temperature. The month names have been changed to season names.

To convert the chart shown in Figure 1.20 to the chart shown in Figure 1.22, use the Select Data Source dialog as follows:

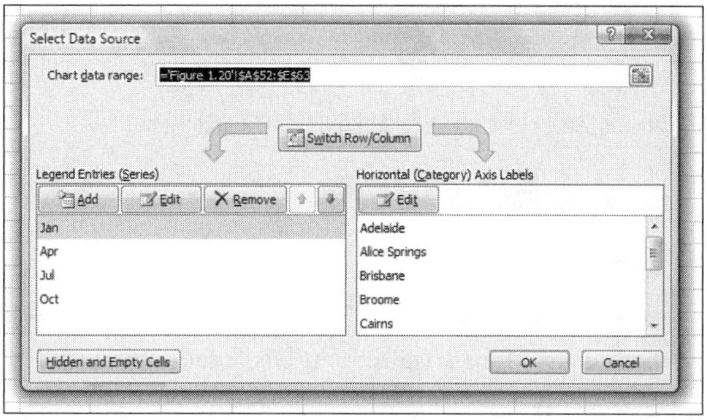

Figure 1.21
You can use the Select Data Source dialog box for more control over data series.

1. Select the chart, and then select Design, Select Data. The Select Data Source dialog displays.
2. Click Switch Rows/Columns to move the city names to the left side of the dialog.
3. Click Alice Springs on the left side and then the up-arrow button until Alice Springs is the first series.
4. Click Broome and then the up-arrow button until Broome is the second series.
5. Continue resequencing the cities until they are in the desired order.
6. On the Horizontal (Category) Axis Labels side of the dialog, click the Edit button. The data initially points to B1:E1. Change the address in the Axis Labels dialog box to an array by entering the four new labels inside curly braces:
   ```
   ={"Summer","Fall","Winter","Spring"}
   ```
7. Click OK to close the Axis Labels dialog box and return to the Select Data Source dialog box.

The modified chart in Figure 1.22 shows the cities based on the warmest summer temperatures.

Figure 1.22
Control the series order by using the Select Data icon.

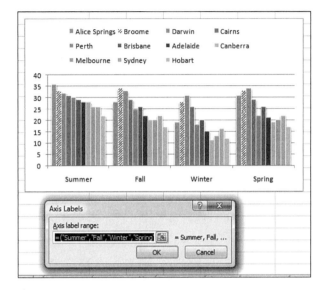

To watch a video of changing series order, search for MrExcel Charts 1 at YouTube.

Leave Top-Left Cell Blank

In the past, Excel tipsters would tell you to always leave the top-left cell of your dataset blank before creating a chart. This requirement has eased a bit with Excel 2010.

The old guideline was that if your series or category labels contained either dates or numeric labels, you should leave the top-left cell blank. In Excel 2010, if your labels contain values formatted as dates, there is no need to leave the top-left cell blank. In addition, if your data has been converted to a table, using the Format as Table icon on the Home tab, it is impossible to leave the top-left cell blank.

However, in a few instances your results improve if the top-left cell is left blank. For example, consider the data in A1:D4 of Figure 1.23. The years in B1:D1 are numeric. If you look at A1:D1, you have text in Column A, followed by three numbers in B:D. This is remarkably similar to the data in A2:D4. You have text in Column A, followed by numbers in B:D. If you create a chart from this dataset, Excel assumes that you do not have series labels and assumes that A1:A4 represent four category labels. This erroneously produces the top chart in the figure.

Cells A11:D14 in the figure contain exactly the same data as A1:D4, except the Region label was cleared from A11. In this case, Excel correctly sees three series and three categories.

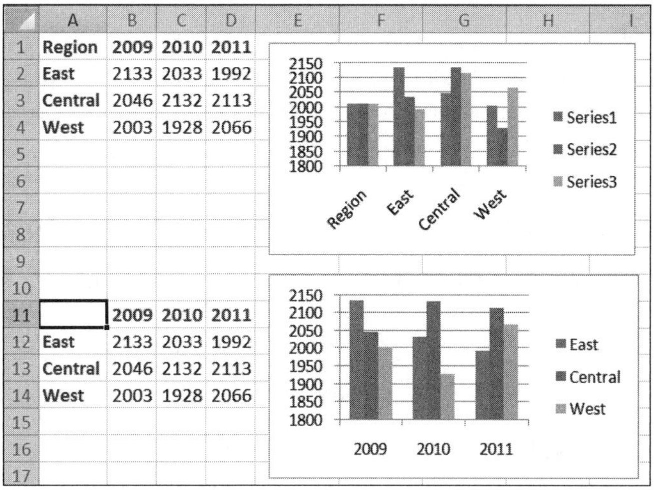

Figure 1.23
The top data is charted incorrectly because of the Region label in cell A1. The bottom data is charted correctly because cell A11 is blank.

Moving a Chart to a Different Sheet

In Excel 2010, charts always start out as objects embedded in a worksheet. However, you might want to display a chart on its own full-page chart sheet. When this occurs, there are two options for moving a chart:

- Choose the Move Chart icon at the right edge of the Design tab.
- Right-click any whitespace near the border of the chart and choose Move Chart.

Either way, the Move Chart dialog appears, offering the options New Sheet and Object In. The Object In drop-down lists all the worksheets in the current workbook. The New Sheet option allows you to specify a name for a new sheet (see Figure 1.24).

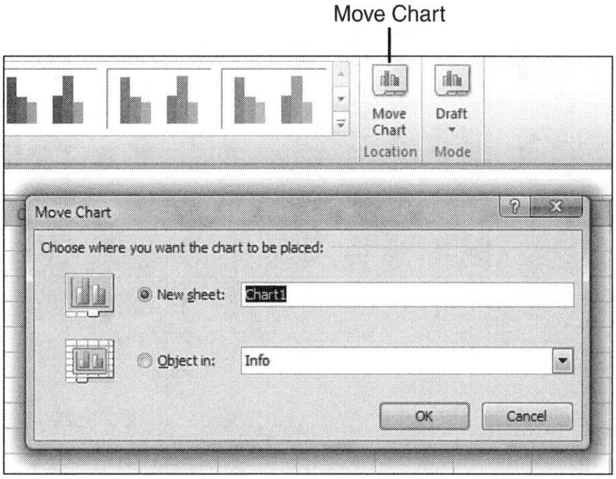

Figure 1.24
Move a chart to a different worksheet using the Move Chart dialog.

> **NOTE** When you choose to move a chart to a new sheet, the chart is located on a special sheet called a *chart sheet*. This sheet holds one chart that can be printed to fill a sheet of paper. You cannot have additional cells or formulas on a chart sheet. Figure 1.25 shows a chart that has been moved to a chart sheet.

Customizing a Chart by a Layout and Style on the Design Tab

The Design tab allows you to customize a chart with just a couple of clicks. For example, the Chart Styles gallery allows you to change the color scheme and effects for the entire chart. The Chart Layouts gallery offers professionally designed combinations of chart elements.

Choosing a Chart Layout

Depending on the chart type you have chosen, the Chart Layouts gallery offers 4 to 12 built-in combinations of chart elements. When you choose a new chart layout from the gallery, you get a predefined combination of title, layout, gridlines, and so on.

These layouts will rarely be exactly what you need. There are 780 quadrillion possible ways to configure a chart and this layout gallery offers anywhere from 4 to 12 possible layouts. The odds that your desired layout is represented exactly are slim.

Figure 1.25
A chart sheet holds one chart at full screen. There are no cells on the sheet.

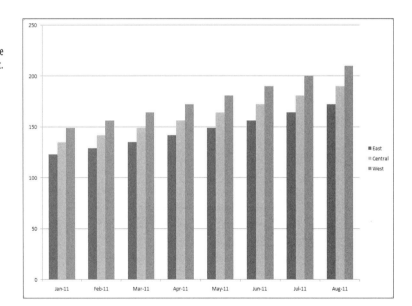

However, use the thumbnails in the layout to get close to what you want. Start with the chart title. If you do not want a chart title, then choose the 4th, 7th, or 11th layout in Figure 1.26. When you move on to the Layout tab, you will have an opportunity to fine-tune the chart.

Figure 1.26 shows 11 charts created by choosing each of the different column chart layouts from the gallery.

Figure 1.26
The Chart Layouts gallery offers up to a dozen predefined layouts for the current chart type.

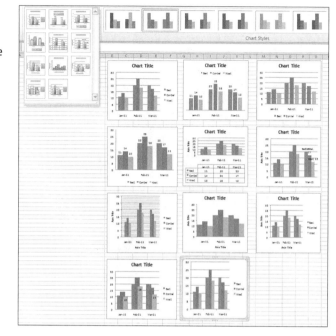

Choosing a Color Scheme

The Design tab is also home to the Chart Styles gallery that offers 48 variations of color and effects. The gallery has columns for each of the six accent colors, monochrome, and mixed colors.

Figure 1.27 shows the 48 thumbnails in the gallery and a sample of the effects available for accent color 2 in the Office theme.

As you move down the first four rows of the gallery, each style has a bit more extreme effect applied to the bars. The styles in Row 2 have a white border around the bars. The styles in Row 3 have a dark gradient. The styles in Row 4 have a glasslike surface on the bars. The styles in Row 5 have a dark border around the bars, combined with a light tint in the plot area. The final row has a dark background that is suitable if you are using the chart in a dark-themed PowerPoint presentation.

Figure 1.27
Choose from eight color schemes when using the Chart Styles gallery.

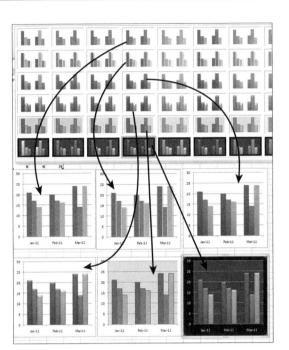

Modifying a Color Scheme by Changing the Theme

The six accent colors and the built-in effects are different in each of the 20 themes that ship with Office 2010. You can change to any of the 20 themes or create your own theme to access new colors and effects.

On the Page Layout tab, click the Themes drop-down to choose from the 20 built-in themes. If you choose a new theme from the Themes drop-down, Excel applies a new color and set of effects to all the charts in the current workbook. If you want to change only the colors or effects, use the Colors or Effects drop-down in the Themes group.

In Figure 1.28, you can see that the Opulent theme applies a jeweled effect to the columns.

> **NOTE** Some themes offer colors that are better for charting. The following themes offer a variety of colors but no one color overpowers the others: Office, Civic, Median, Paper, Technic, Trek, Urban, or Origin.

Keep the following in mind when changing a chart's theme:

- Excel, Word, and PowerPoint offer the same 20 built-in themes. If you are building a document that contains elements from more than one Office 2010 product, you should apply the same theme in all the documents.

Figure 1.28
Applying a new theme
changes the color and
built-in effects.

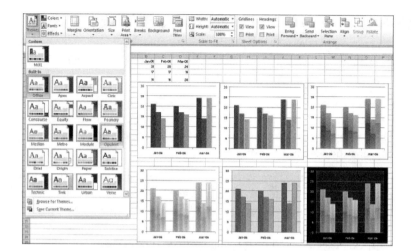

- Changing the theme affects all graphic elements in the workbook. While your Excel workbook might contain mostly numbers and one or two charts, it could make sense to change the theme to apply new colors to the chart. In Excel 2010, changing the theme also affects any SmartArt graphics in the workbook.

> **CAUTION**
>
> In PowerPoint, and to a lesser extent Word, changing the theme affects far more than the occasional chart. The chosen theme also changes the fonts used in the presentation, the slide background, and so on.

- If you want the theme to have an impact on the fonts in your workbook, use the Cell Styles drop-down in the Home tab to format your cells.
- The Effects drop-down on the Page Layout tab contains a lot of subtle information encoded in the thumbnails. See the "Choose Effects for a Custom Theme from an Existing Theme" section, later in this chapter, for details.

Create Your Own Theme

You might want to develop a special theme. This is fairly easy to do: You basically need to select two fonts and six accent colors. For example, suppose you want to create a theme to match your company's color scheme. The hardest part is probably finding six colors to represent your company, because most company logos use only two or three colors. The following subsections describe how to create a new theme and suggest resources for choosing complementary colors for your company colors.

Choose Effects for a Custom Theme from an Existing Theme

Unless you plan to edit XML files, you should reuse built-in effects from an existing theme for your new theme. The thumbnails in the Effects drop-down offer very subtle clues about the types of effects used in each theme.

The formatting galleries generally range from simple effects in the top row, moderate effects in the middle rows, and extreme effects in the bottom row. For example, if you open the Shape Styles gallery on the Format tab, the first row is simple, the fourth row is moderate, and the sixth row is extreme.

When you open the Effects drop-down on the Page Layout tab, you will see three shapes for each theme: a circle, arrow, and rectangle. The circle provides an indication of the effects used in simple formats such as from row 1 of the Shape Styles Gallery. The arrow provides an indication of the effects used in moderate formats such as from Row 4 of the Shape Styles Gallery. The rectangle provides an indication of the effects used in extreme formats such as in Row 6 of the gallery.

Figure 1.29 shows the Effects drop-down in grayscale. Please open this in your computer so that you can actually see the effects in color.

For example:

- The circle in the Civic and Equity themes show a faint line. This indicates that shapes with a simple format applied will have fainter lines when using this theme. The circles in the Module and Concourse theme have an interior reflection or glow.

- The arrow in the Trek theme has a gradient that starts out light at the top of the arrow and becomes darker at the bottom of the arrow. If you apply a moderate effect to a chart and use the Trek theme, the shapes in the chart will have a similar gradient.

Figure 1.29
The circle, arrow, and rectangle apply to simple, moderate, and intense layouts, respectively.

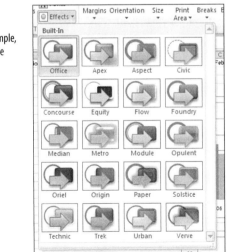

■ The rectangle in the Paper theme has a dark texture applied. The rectangle in the Metro theme has a glass or jeweled affect applied. The rectangle in the Equity theme has a thin white outline around a dark rectangle. If you format your chart with extreme effects, the shapes will have an appearance similar to the rectangle in each thumbnail.

Although you can access dialog boxes to control the font and colors in your theme, choose 1 of the 20 built-in effects as a starting point for your new custom theme. Choose any theme from the Effects drop-down to start building your custom theme.

Understanding RGB Color Codes

Colors on computer monitors are described as a mix of red (R), green (G), and blue (B). Each color channel is assigned a value from 0 to 255. For example, a color of R=255, G=0, B=0 is a bright red. As you add more blue, the red shifts toward a pink or violet color. A color of R=255, G=0, B=128 is a pinkish violet color. A color of R=0, G=0, B=0 is black. A color of R=255, G=255, B=255 is white. You can create 16.7 million different colors by using combinations of red, green, and blue.

To see a pertinent example of how this works, open your company's home page in a browser. Then, from the View menu in Internet Explorer, select Source, or, in Firefox, select View, Page Source.

You should now see the web page's underlying HTML code. You can find the colors used in the page by searching for a pound sign. A web page specifies colors in hexadecimal format, using a pound sign followed by six characters, such as #4F81BD.

Although every web page uses the hexadecimal notation for describing colors, Microsoft Excel's theme specification instead needs the RGB values for the color. As described in the following section, it is fairly easy to convert between the two.

[NOTE] The color chooser in Photoshop shows the RGB values for any hexadecimal notation.

Converting from Hexadecimal to RGB

Hexadecimal is a numbering system that has digits 0 through 9 and A through F. Including 0, there are 16 digits in the hexadecimal numbering system. In the decimal system, a 2-digit number can represent 10×10 different combinations. There are 100 numbers, from 00 to 99. In a hex system, a 2-digit number can represent 16×16 different numbers—that is, 256 numbers, from 0 to 255.

In the #123456 nomenclature, the # sign indicates that the number is in hexadecimal. The first two digits are the hex representation of the red value. The next two digits are the hex representation of the green value. The next two digits are the hex representation of the blue value.

If you don't have Photoshop or another tool that converts from a hex color to an RGB value for you automatically, you can use functions in Excel to do the conversion. For example, the worksheet in Figure 1.30 converts from a hex color in Cell B1 to the RGB values in B7:B9:

- The formulas in B2:B4 use the MID function to extract each pair of numbers from the color code. The formula for cell B2 is shown in cell C2.

- The formulas in B7:B9 use the HEX2DEC function to convert the two-digit hex number to decimal.

Figure 1.30
This quick Excel worksheet converts from a six-digit hex color code to decimal RGB values.

	A	B	C	D
1		#FF9108		
2		FF	=MID(B1,2,2)	
3		91	=MID(B1,4,2)	
4		08	=MID(B1,6,2)	
5				
6				
7	R:	255	=HEX2DEC(B2)	
8	G:	145	=HEX2DEC(B3)	
9	B:	8	=HEX2DEC(B4)	

For example, to represent the color #FF9108 in Excel, you would use R=255, G=145, B=8.

Finding Complementary Colors

If you look at your company's logo and website, you can probably identify two or three colors to use in the theme. You need to come up with a total of six accent colors for a theme.

> **TIP**
> You can use the free web-based tool at `http://colorschemedesigner.com` to find colors that look good together.

Follow these steps to find complementary colors:

1. Start with a hex representation of one of your logo colors.

2. Open `http://colorschemedesigner.com` in a browser.

3. A color wheel appears on the left. Below and to the right of the color wheel, click the RGB value to enter a new value.

4. In the window that pops up, enter the portion of the color code after the pound sign, such as FF9108.

5. Click each of the six color wheels icons across the top to review mono, complement, triad, and so on. In the Triad view, the website shows your original color, three others, and three variations of each, as shown in Figure 1.31.

6. Hover over any color to see a ToolTip showing the hex code for that color.

Figure 1.31
This web page suggests colors that complement your logo colors.

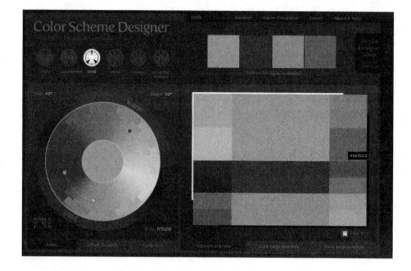

Specifying a Theme's Colors

To specify new theme colors, you follow these steps:

1. Select Page Layout, Colors, Create New Theme Colors. The Create New Theme Colors dialog appears (see Figure 1.32).

2. To change the first accent color, select the drop-down next to Accent 1. The color chooser appears.

3. From the bottom of the color chooser drop-down, select More Colors. The Colors dialog appears.

4. On the Custom tab of the Colors dialog, enter values for red, green, and blue, as shown in Figure 1.33. The New color block shows the color for the values you entered. Click OK to accept the new color.

5. Repeat steps 2–4 for each of the accent colors.

6. If you want to change the colors for Hyperlink, Followed Hyperlink, and Text, repeats steps 2–4 for any of those.

7. In the Name box, give the theme a name, such as your company name.

8. Click Preview to see the theme applied to your workbook.

9. Click Save to accept the theme.

Figure 1.32
The 12 colors in the current theme are shown here.

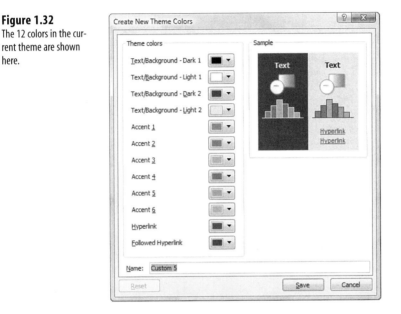

Figure 1.33
Specify the RGB values for the first color.

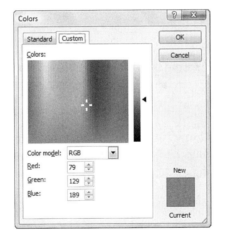

Specify Theme Fonts

Follow these steps to specify new theme fonts:

1. Select Page Layout, Fonts, Create New Theme Fonts. The Create New Theme Fonts dialog appears, as shown in Figure 1.34. Remember that a font theme contains a heading font and a body font.

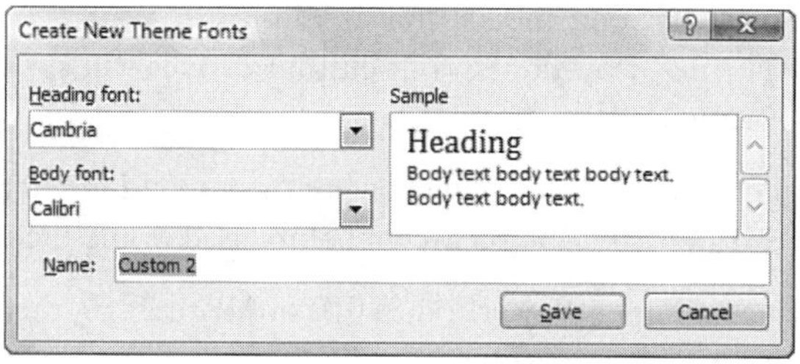

Figure 1.34
A theme is composed of two fonts.

2. Select a font from the Heading Font drop-down. If a custom font is used in your company's logo, using it might be appropriate.
3. Select a font that is easy to read from the Body Font drop-down. Avoid stylized fonts for body copy.
4. Give the theme a name. It is okay to reuse the same name from the color theme.
5. Click Save to accept the theme changes.

Saving a Custom Theme

To reuse a theme in other workbooks, you must save it. From the Page Layout tab, select Themes, Themes, Save Current Theme, as shown in Figure 1.35.

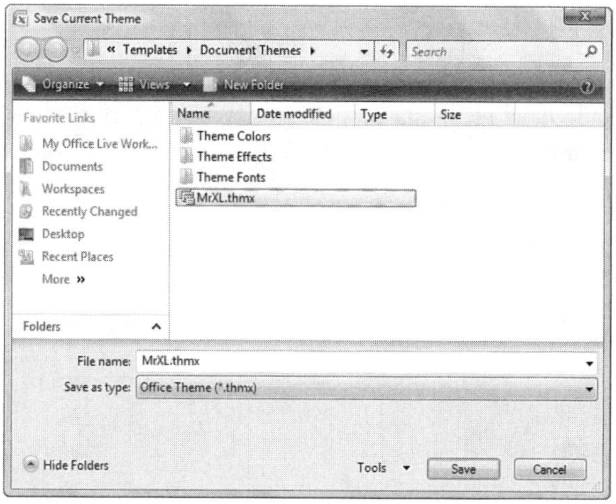

Figure 1.35
The option to save a theme is at the bottom of the Themes drop-down.

By default, themes are stored in the Document Themes folder. This folder is in %AppData%\Microsoft\Templates\Document Themes\.

Give your theme a useful name and click Save.

Using a Custom Theme on a New Document

After saving a custom theme with your company colors, fonts, and effects, the theme will be available to all workbooks, documents, and slideshows on your computer. The next time you access the Themes drop-down, your custom themes will appear first in the menu, under a heading of Custom.

Excel automatically generates a thumbnail showing the letter *A* in your headline font, the letter *a* in the body text font, and the six accent colors used in the theme.

After you save a theme and open PowerPoint 2010 or Word 2010, the new custom themes will be available in those applications, too.

Sharing a Theme with Others

If you want to share a theme with others, send them the .thmx file from %AppData%\ Microsoft\Templates\Document Themes\.

Using %AppData% in Windows Explorer is a shortcut to the application data folder in your operating system. On a Windows XP machine, this might be C:\Documents and Settings\your name\Application Data\. On a Windows Vista machine, this might be C:\ Users\Your Name\App Data\Roaming. If you just type $AppData%, Windows Explorer will navigate to the proper folder.

The people you share the theme with can either copy the .thmx file to their equivalent folder or save the .thmx file to their desktop and use the Browse for Themes option by selecting Page Layout, Themes, Themes, Browse for Themes.

Next Steps

Chapter 2, "Customizing Charts," describes how to use the Layout tab of the ribbon to toggle on or off individual elements of the chart. It also describes how you can microman-age individual elements using the Format ribbon.

Customizing Charts

Accessing Element Formatting Tools

In Chapter 1, "Introducing Charts in Excel 2010," you learned how to create a chart using the Insert tab. You also learned how to choose built-in layouts and styles on the Design tab and apply them to your chart.

In real life, you usually want to have some control over the various elements in a chart. Excel 2010 provides three additional levels of control over chart elements:

- The Layout tab contains a few popular choices for formatting 15 chart elements. In 60 percent of cases, you can use options from the drop-down menus on the Layout tab to create a perfect chart.

- The Format tab contains icons that enable you to micromanage the color, fill, outline, and effects for any individual chart element. For example, if you want to apply a soft glow, a metallic finish, and a reflection to the January data point, you can do so using the Format tab.

- For ultimate control over individual elements, the powerful Format dialog box can be used to format the currently selected element in the chart. You can access the dialog box in the following ways:

    - Select an element and press Ctrl+1.
    - Right-click a chart element and select Format.
    - Double-click any chart element,
    - Select the chart element from the first drop-down on either the Layout or Format tabs and then click the Format Selection icon under the drop-down.

2

■ Most of the drop-downs on the Layout tab lead to a More option that opens the Format dialog box.

This chapter walks you through the various chart components that can be customized. It also provides tips and tricks for creating eye-catching but meaningful results.

Identifying Chart Elements

Many elements of a chart can be customized. You rarely want to include all the available elements in a single chart because too many elements detract from the meaning of the data in the chart. Therefore, titles, axes, and gridlines should be used judiciously to help the reader understand the data presented in a chart.

Chart Labels and Axis

Figure 2.1 shows a chart that has too many elements that were included to help identify various elements in the chart.

Figure 2.1
This chart shows the various components available in a 2-D chart.

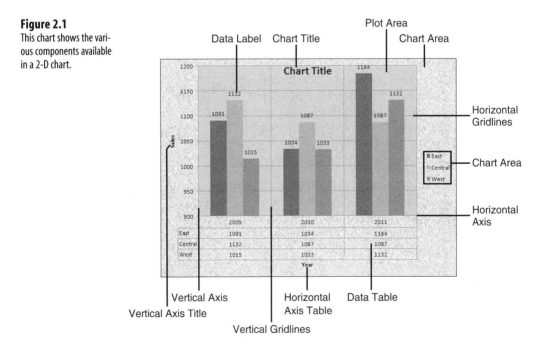

Figure 2.1 contains the following elements:

■ **Chart area**—The entire range shown in Figure 2.1, including all the area outside the plot area. The chart area is where labels and legends often appear.

■ **Plot area**—The rectangular area that includes the data series and data markers.

■ **Chart title**—Typically appears in a larger font near the top of the chart. Whereas Excel 2003 always included the chart title outside the plot area, choices in Excel 2010 encourage you to have the title overlaying the plot area.

■ **Horizontal axis title**—Identifies the type of data along the horizontal axis. In case it is not clear that "2005 2006 2010" represent years, you can add a horizontal axis title such as the one shown near number 9 in Figure 2.1.

■ **Vertical axis title**—Commonly used along the left side of a chart to identify the units along the axis. In Figure 2.1, the word "Sales" near number 12 is the vertical axis title.

■ **Legend**—Initially appears to the right of the plot area to help identify which color in the chart represents which series. The legend can be dragged anywhere in the chart area or plot area to free up space for the plot area to extend further to the right.

■ **Data label**—Option used have the actual value for each bar or point to appear on the chart. Data labels are frequently overwritten by gridlines and other charting elements. Far too often, individual data labels are nudged so they can be read.

■ **Data table**—Instead of using data labels, you can have Excel add a spreadsheet such as a data table beneath the plot area. The data table frequently takes up too much space in the chart area and reduces the size available for the plot area.

■ **Horizontal axis**—Appears along the bottom of the chart for column and line charts and along the left side for bar charts. The horizontal axis is also referred to as the category axis. Your main choice is whether the axis contains a time series. If it does, Excel varies the spacing between the points to represent actual dates.

■ **Vertical axis**—The axis along the left side of the chart in a column or line chart. In some advanced charts, you might have a second vertical axis on the right side of the chart. This axis typically contains values, and your main choice is whether you want the axis scaled in thousands, millions, and so on. This is discussed in Chapter 7, "Advanced Chart Techniques."

■ **Horizontal gridlines**—Run horizontally across the plot area and line up with each number along the vertical axis. If you do not have data labels on a chart, the horizontal gridlines are particularly useful for telling whether a particular point is just above or below a certain level. It is best to keep gridlines unobtrusive. Some of the best charts include gridlines in a faint color so they do not obscure the main message of the chart.

■ **Vertical gridlines**—Used less often than horizontal gridlines. If you are considering using them in a line chart or a surface chart, consider using drop lines instead.

Special Elements in a 3-D Chart

Some chart elements are editable only in 3-D charting styles. Figure 2.2 shows a 3-D column chart.

The following are the 3-D chart elements:

- **Back wall**—In Figure 2.2, the back wall is formatted with a texture. In legacy versions of Excel, any formatting applied to the back wall also applied to the side wall. However, in Excel 2010 these are now two separate elements.

- **Side wall**—In Figure 2.2, the side wall is formatted with a dark fill.

- **Floor**—The surface below the 3-D columns.

- **Column depth**—One of the many 3-D rotation settings you can change. In Figure 2.2, each column appears to be a deep rectangular slab. This effect is created by increasing the column depth. The chart has also been tipped forward a bit, so it appears that the viewer is at a slightly higher viewing angle.

Figure 2.2
This chart shows the various elements available in a 3-D chart.

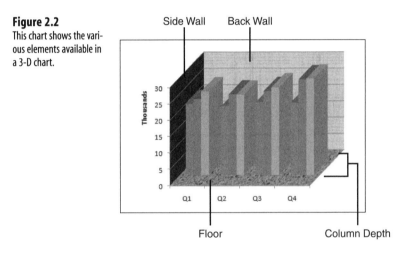

Analysis Elements

The Analysis group of elements located on the Layout tab includes elements that are of particular importance to scientists. However, some of the elements, such as the trendline, can also be useful in business charting. Figure 2.3 illustrates some of the analysis elements.

The following are the analysis elements:

- **Trendline**—If you ask for a trendline, Excel uses regression analysis to fit your existing data points to a statistical line. You can have Excel extend this line into future time-periods. In Figure 2.3, the dotted trendline shows that unless you alter the system that has been generating those actuals, you will likely miss the goal.

- **Drop lines**—The vertical lines that extend from the data point to the horizontal axis in either line or area charts. Drop lines are helpful because they enable the reader to locate the exact point where the line intersects the axis.

- **Up/down bars**—When you are plotting two series on a line chart, Excel can draw rectangles between the two lines. In Figure 2.3, when the actual exceeds the goal

Figure 2.3
This chart shows the various analysis elements.

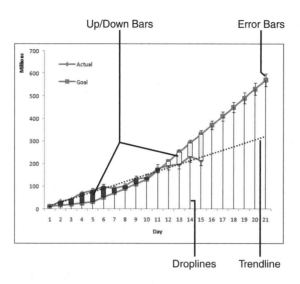

in Days 2 through 11, the up/down bars are shown in a dark color. When the goal exceeds the actual in Days 11 through 15, the up/down error bars are shown in a contrasting color. If the up/down error bars seem too wide, try using high/low lines.

- **Error bars**—This feature is popular in scientific analysis to show the error of an estimate. You might see these used in business charts to indicate the acceptable tolerance from a quality goal. For example, a quality goal might be to achieve 99.5 percent quality, with anything between 99 percent and 100 percent being acceptable. The error bars could be added to the 99.5 percent goal series to show whether the actual quality falls within the acceptable tolerance.

Formatting Chart Elements

When formatting chart elements, you generally start with some of the built-in choices available on the Layout tab. This section describes how to do this, and how to use the mini toolbar, Home tab, Format tab, or Format dialog to customize certain elements further.

Formatting a Chart Title

By default, a chart with more than one series is created without any title, as shown in the upper-right chart in Figure 2.4. To add a title, use the Chart Title drop-down on the Layout tab. Your choices are a centered overlay title or a title above the chart. When the title is added above the chart, Excel shrinks the plot area to make room for the title (see the lower-right chart in Figure 2.4). If the title fits, using a centered overlay title leaves more space for the title. However, there is the chance that the words in the title and the points plotted in the series will collide, as they do in the chart shown on the left in Figure 2.4.

Figure 2.4
Excel offers two built-in locations for chart titles.

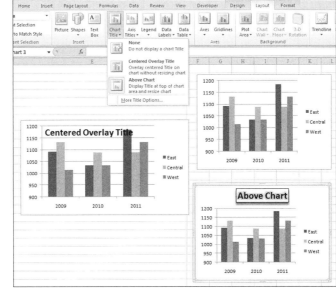

Typing and Editing a Title

After you select a title location from the drop-down, Excel adds the generic "Chart Title" placeholder text to the top of your chart. The title is selected by default, so you can immediately type the actual title, which will appear in the formula bar. When you press the Enter key, Excel replaces "Chart Title" with the words you typed.

You might prefer to edit the title in the title box instead of typing the words in the formula bar. When you initially insert a title or when you single-click a title, the title will appear with a solid box that has four handles, as shown in the top of Figure 2.5. In this selection mode, you can format the entire title and type words in the formula bar.

If you perform a second single-click inside the title, the solid box will change to a dashed box as shown in the bottom of Figure 2.5. In this mode, you can edit characters right in the title box. However, any formatting will only apply to characters that are selected within the title.

To select characters while in Edit mode, you can either drag the mouse or use the following standard Windows mouse shortcuts: Double-click in a word to select the word or triple-click to select the entire title. Note that these shortcuts only work after you have performed a single-click to select the title, and then a second single-click to enter edit mode.

To exit Edit mode, either click directly on the dotted border or just click outside the title and then back on the title.

Figure 2.5
Click inside the solid title
box to edit words directly
in the box.

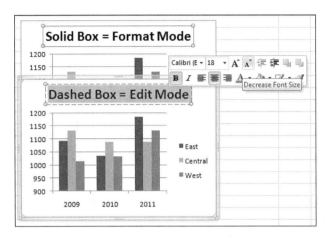

Moving a Title

To move a title, first single-click the title to select it, and then move the cursor so that it is above the outline of the title. When the cursor changes to a four-headed arrow, click and drag the title to a new location.

> **NOTE** Note that the outline contains only four handles rather than the usual eight. Therefore, you cannot use the handles to resize the title-bounding box. However, you do have some control over the size of the title-bounding box. If you press the Enter key in the middle of the title, you will force the title-bounding box to become vertically larger.

Formatting a Title with the Mini Toolbar

Once the title is in Edit mode with a dashed selection box, you can triple-click a title to select all the words in the title. When your cursor is moved slightly up and to the right, the mini toolbar appears, which allows you to select the font and other formatting to use in the title (see Figure 2.5).

If you have already moved the mouse too many pixels down and to the left, the mini toolbar may not appear. If this occurs, you can select the words and then right-click to make the mini toolbar appear.

Formatting a Title with the Home Tab

If trying to get the mini toolbar to display is too frustrating for you, you can use the Home tab instead. To do so, select characters in the title and then display the Home tab of the ribbon, and then use the icons in the Font and Alignment groups to format the title.

If you use the Orientation drop-down to angle your title, there is no setting in the drop-down to return to the original horizontal orientation. To turn off a selection such as vertical text, you have to reselect that item from the Orientation drop-down to toggle the setting to Off.

Formatting a Title with the Format Tab

Many options on the Format tab allow you to change the fill, font, and line style used in the title. The settings in the Shape Styles group affect the currently invisible rectangle that surrounds the title. A reflection cannot be added, but all the other settings are available.

To add effects to the actual words in a title, use the drop-downs in the WordArt Styles group of the Format tab (see Figure 2.6). You can control the font color, outline color of the font, shadow, reflection, and glow. Other WordArt features such as Bevel and Transforms are not available in charting titles.

Figure 2.6
Select a title and then use the three drop-downs in the WordArt Styles group to format the title.

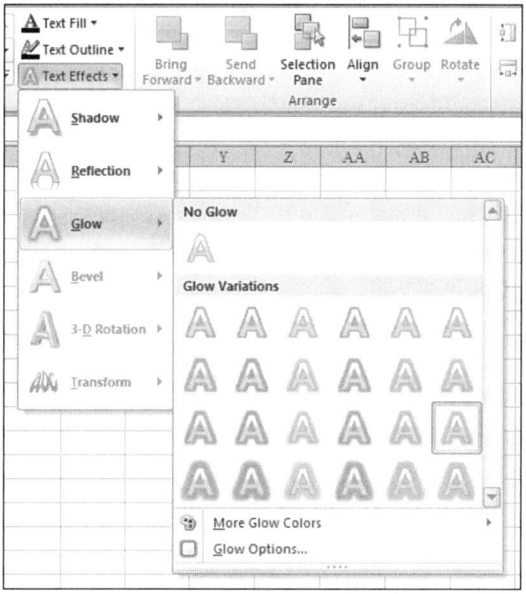

More Title Options

To access the Format dialog, right-click a title, and then select Format Chart Title. This dialog offers Fill, Border Color, Border Styles, Shadow, Glow and Soft Edges, 3-D Format, and Alignment options. The Shadow option gives you microcontrol over the shadow transparency, size, blur, angle, and distance. The Alignment tab allows you to rotate the text in 1-degree increments.

Formatting an Axis Title

Figure 2.7 shows the three built-in options for the vertical axis: Rotated Title (top left), Vertical Title (bottom left), and Horizontal Title (bottom right). In many cases, the Rotated Title option looks the best. For a horizontal axis title, the only built-in option is to turn the title on or off.

All the formatting options available for the chart title also apply to the axis titles. You can use the mini toolbar, the Home tab, or the Format tab to change the font, color, fill, and effects for the axis title.

> **TIP**
> You may see charts with "Thousands," "Millions," "Billions," and so on near the top of the vertical axis title area. These are not part of the vertical axis title. You control this setting by selecting Layout, Axes, Primary Vertical Axis, Show Axis in Thousands.

Figure 2.7
The vertical axis title can be oriented in three ways using the Axis Titles drop-down on the Layout tab.

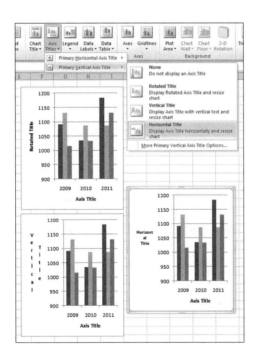

Formatting a Legend

The built-in choices for the legend include having the legend outside the left, right, bottom, or top of the plot area. If you move the legend to the top or the bottom, Excel rearranges the legend in a horizontal format, as shown in Figure 2.8.

Figure 2.8
The built-in choices include moving the legend to the top or bottom, which works well in this chart.

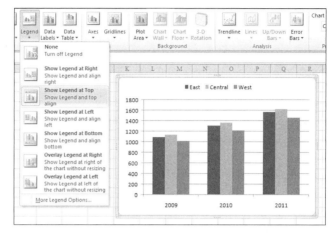

> **NOTE**
> There are two other built-in options: Overlay Legend at Right and Overlay Legend at Left. Neither of these seems to work well with column charts because the legend and the columns collide. Instead of using the Overlay options, follow the steps for floating a legend in the plot area, below.

My favorite legend trick, which is discussed in the next section, is to float a legend in an unused portion of the plot area. This can still be done in Excel 2010, but it is more difficult than in legacy versions because it takes a few more clicks now than it used to.

Floating a Legend in the Plot Area

To float a legend in the plot area, I recommend going outside the built-in legend options. Although the legend usually starts on the right side of the chart, you can often find a corner of the plot area that has whitespace. For example, due to the yearly growth of the data in Figure 2.8, there is room above the 2009 columns for the legend. Follow these steps to move the legend to that spot:

1. From the Layout tab, select the Legend drop-down, and then Overlay Legend at Right. This keeps the legend in a vertical arrangement and stretches the plot area out to the right edge of the chart.

2. Carefully click inside the legend. When the mouse pointer is a four-headed arrow, drag the mouse and drop the legend in a free spot on the chart.

> **CAUTION**
> A new problem in Excel 2010 is that the legend has a transparent fill, so the underlying gridlines may tend to show through. Step 3 will solve this problem.

3. While the legend is still selected, click the Format tab. Select Shape Fill, White to convert the transparent fill to a solid fill. The fill prevents gridlines from overwriting your legend titles.

4. Select Format, Shape Outline, Black to add a border around the legend.

Figure 2.9 shows the legend floating over a vacant area of the plot area. Notice that this allows the plot area to extend nearly to the right edge of the chart area.

Figure 2.9
Drag the legend over the chart and then format the legend so that it has a border and no transparency.

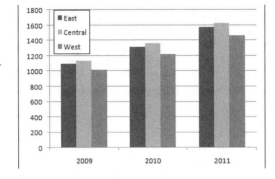

Changing the Arrangement of a Legend

A new series has been added in the top-left chart in Figure 2.10. This causes the floating legend to obscure part of the columns. To fix this problem, click the Legend to activate the resizing handles. Then drag the bottom-right corner of the legend up and out to produce a legend with the labels arranged in a 2-by-2 grid, as shown in the lower-left chart in Figure 2.10. If you keep dragging, the legend becomes a 1-by-4 arrangement, as shown in the top-right chart in the figure.

Figure 2.10
You have some control over the arrangement of the labels in the legend when you resize the legend border.

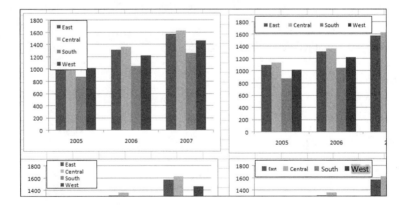

Formatting Individual Legend Entries

A feature in Excel 2010 is the ability to format or resize the individual legend entries. This proves particularly useful when one entry is longer than the other entries. To format an individual legend, follow these steps:

1. Click the legend so the entire legend is selected.

2. Click the legend entry you want to change.

3. To change the font size, right-click the text and use the options in the mini toolbar. To change anything else, use the Home tab or the Format tab.

In the chart at the bottom right of Figure 2.10, each legend entry is a different font size. You can also apply effects such as glow to the legend entries.

To remove certain legend entries, select an individual legend entry, and then press Delete. Deleting a legend is useful when you are using extra series to add elements to a chart. Several examples in Chapter 7, "Advanced Chart Techniques," utilize this method.

Using the Format Legend Dialog

To use the Format Legend dialog, select More Legend Options from the Legend drop-down on the Layout tab. This dialog allows you to change the fill color, border color, border styles, shadow, and the glow and soft edges of the legend.

Adding Data Labels to a Chart

Individuals reading your chart might be able to discern whether one adjacent column is taller than the other column. However, it is difficult to compare a column in the center of a chart that has numbers along the left axis. This is where data labels can be an advantage. This feature works best if you have only a few data points on the chart.

Traditionally, data labels for a single-series column chart appear above each column. In Excel 2010, this choice is known as Outside End. The other built-in choices on the Data Labels tab are Center, Inside End, Inside Base, and None (see Figure 2.11).

Figure 2.11
Data labels look best when placed above the bars in a column chart.

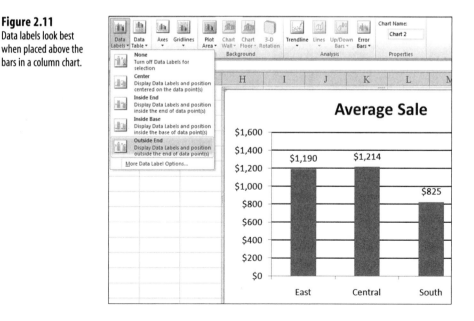

The three "inside" choices are useful when you have a stacked column chart. Rather than placing the label for the bottom column inside the top column, the inside choices keep each label inside the appropriate bar.

Figure 2.12 compares the Inside End, Inside Base, and Center options on a single chart.

Figure 2.12
When multiple series are used in a stacked column chart, you should use one of the inside locations for the data label.

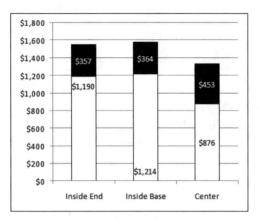

Nudging a Label to Avoid a Gridline

If your chart has dark gridlines, it may appear that the data label is crossed out by the gridline. It is a slightly tedious process to fix the labels, but doing so ensures that your data labels are readable. Complete the following steps to nudge a data label out of the way of the gridline:

1. Click a data label in the chart. Excel selects all the labels for that particular series.
2. Again, click the data label to be moved. Excel now selects just that data label (see Figure 2.13).
3. Carefully position the cursor over the border of the label. When the cursor changes to a four-headed arrow, click and drag the data label above or below the gridline.
4. Repeat steps 1-3 for any other labels that are running into the gridlines. If the next label is in the same series, you can skip step 1.

Figure 2.13
A second click selects just one data label.

Using the Format Data Labels Dialog

The Format Data Labels dialog includes nine categories in the left navigation bar. There are many important settings you can access in the various categories of the dialog to customize data labels on a chart:

■ On the Label Options category, you can change the content of the label. For example, in Figure 2.14, the pie chart is labeled with the category name and the value. For other pie charts, you might want to use the percentage instead.

■ On the Number category, you can change the number format or choose to have the format be the same as the original dataset.

Figure 2.14
Control the text in data labels by using the Format Data Labels dialog.

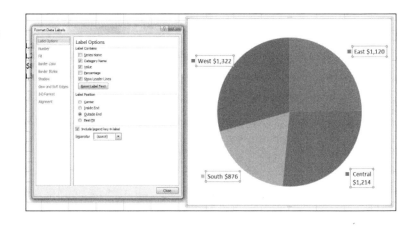

> **TIP**
>
> In all cases, the Format dialog box contains the built-in choices on the Layout tab menus, plus many more options. As I create more charts, I often head automatically to the Format dialog box so that I have full control over the format of the selected element.
>
> After you have selected an element in the chart, pressing Ctrl+1 takes you to the appropriate Format dialog box. Further, when a Format dialog box is displayed, you can click a new element in the chart. The Format dialog box will change to reflect the properties available for the newly selected element.

Adding a Data Table to a Chart

A data table is a mini-worksheet that appears below a chart. In it, Excel shows the values for each data point in the table. One advantage of a data table is that you can show the numbers that would normally be shown with data labels without adding any elements to the plot area.

There are two built-in options in the Data Table drop-down on the Layout tab: You can show the data table with legend keys or without legend keys.

The data table takes up a fair amount of space at the bottom of the chart. Putting the legend keys in the table allows you to regain some of that space by eliminating the legend element from the chart.

In the chart on the left in Figure 2.15, the legend keys appear in the chart. In the chart on the right in Figure 2.15, the data table appears without legend keys, which requires a separate legend element to appear. In this case, the legend element appears above the chart, which causes the plot area to shrink making it more difficult to interpret the data on the chart.

Figure 2.15
A data table provides a concise grid for the actual values without adding extra data to the plot area itself.

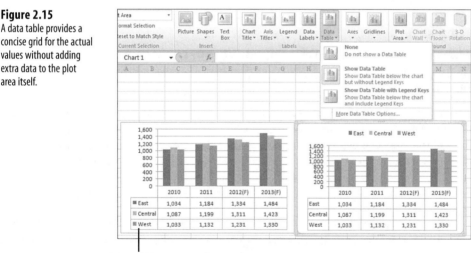

Legend Keys

Special Options for Data Tables

If you select the More Data Table options in the Data Table drop-down, you will see the usual options for fill, border color, border styles, shadow, and 3-D format, plus special data table options. You can decide to hide or show the horizontal or vertical gridlines in the table and show or hide the outline around the data table. In Figure 2.16, the outline and horizontal gridlines are turned off, which gives the data table a cleaner look.

Figure 2.16
Special options in the
Format Data Table dialog
enable you to turn on or
off various elements of a
data table.

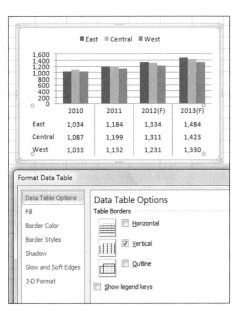

Formatting Axes

Unlike the previously described elements that are fairly cosmetic, the axis options have major ramifications. For example, axis options affect how data is displayed and whether the reader has the ability to interpret data in a chart.

The built-in choices in the Axes drop-down of the Layout tab do not begin to touch on the powerful choices in the Format Axis dialog box. For example, there are four kinds of axes, although the most you will find in a single chart is three. A pie chart actually has no axes. A radar chart has one axis. A surface chart has three axes. An X-Y chart has two axes. All other charts have two axes, with the possibility of adding an optional third axis.

> **NOTE** The category axis, which contains the category labels, appears along the bottom of the chart in column, line, area, and stock charts. It appears along the left side of the chart in bar charts. In most programs, this axis is also referred to as the x-axis. In Excel 2010, this axis is called the Horizontal (Category) Axis in all except bar charts. When you have a bar chart, the axis is called the Vertical (Category) Axis. When you switch to a bar chart, the Layout tab menu the settings move from the Primary Horizontal Axis flyout menu to the Primary Vertical Axis flyout menu.

Your most important choice for this axis is whether it should be time based or text based. In a chart with a text-based axis, the points along the axis are equally spaced. In a chart that uses a time-based axis, the points are spaced based on the relative time distance between the points. Other choices include selecting whether the data should be plotted left to right or right to left.

The vertical axis contains the scale for the numbers plotted in the chart. The primary vertical axis generally appears along the left side of the chart. In a bar chart, this axis, which appears along the bottom of the chart, is called a horizontal axis. Choices for this axis include scaling of the axis, the minimum and maximum value for the axis, and the distance between tick marks on the axis. If your data has numbers of different scales, you should specify a logarithmic axis.

In charts that have one data series that is of a vastly different order of magnitude than the others, you may want to plot that series on a secondary vertical axis. This axis has the same choices as the primary vertical axis. It usually appears along the right side of a chart or the top of a bar chart.

The depth axis is a special axis that appears in 3-D surface charts.

Built-in Axis Choices for the Horizontal Axis and Depth Axis

Excel 2010 provides a few built-in options on the Layout tab for each axis. As mentioned previously, these options are a tiny fraction of the ones available. It is interesting to note that the options chosen for the built-in menus are a few of the obscure options that you may not have discovered before.

For the horizontal axis, the built-in menu choices allow you to specify that the data should be plotted left to right or right to left. The other choice is for the horizontal axis to appear without any tick marks or labeling. This choice seems remarkably similar to the choice None (see Figure 2.17).

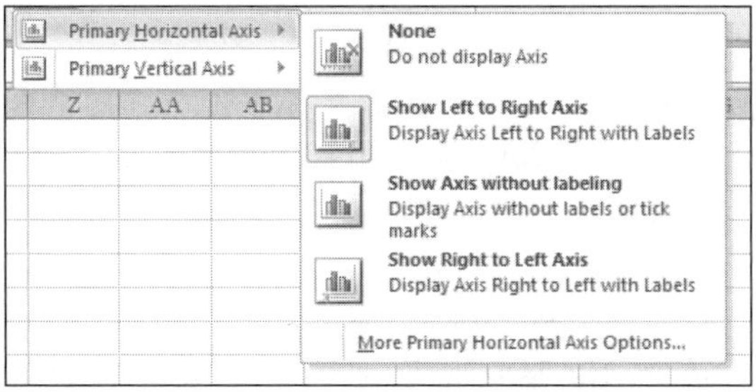

Figure 2.17
The choices in the Primary Horizontal Axis menu are interesting but obscure.

This is one of the few built-in charting menus where you can choose one item and then alter that selection by choosing another menu item. If you choose Show Right-to-Left Axis and then Show Axis Without Labeling, you get a right-to-left axis without labeling. However, if you reverse those choices, the axis labels reappear.

The choices for the depth axis in a surface chart are similar to those for the horizontal axis. However, instead of calling the choices Left-to-Right and Right-to-Left, the depth axis menu offers the options Normal Axis and Reverse Axis.

Built-in Choices for the Vertical Axis

For the vertical axis, Excel offers the choices None, Default, Thousands, Millions, Billions, and Logarithmic. The different scales are interesting and allow you to prevent having excess zeros along the vertical axis. In the bottom-left chart shown in Figure 2.18, there are so many zeros that it is difficult to figure out the numbers at a glance. In the top chart, the zeros are reduced, and a label indicates that the numbers are in billions.

Figure 2.18
Rather than fill your chart area with zeros, you can use an axis-scaling factor.

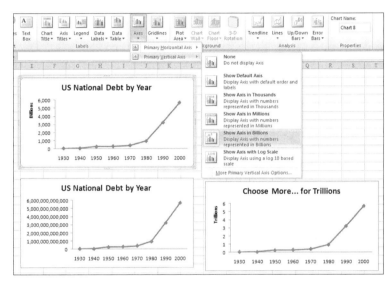

If you access the Format Axis dialog, the Display Units drop-down offers nine scaling options instead of Thousands, Millions, and Billions. You can use Hundreds, Ten Thousands, or even Trillions, as shown in the bottom-right chart in Figure 2.18.

> **NOTE**
> This effect can also be achieved by using a custom number format with commas at the end of the code. Each comma at the end of the number format divides values by 1,000. For example, a custom number format of 0,,,, would display numbers in trillions.

Logarithmic is a useful choice when you need to compare numbers of different scales along the same series. This option is described in the next section.

Using a Logarithmic Axis

While the concept of logarithmic axes sounds scary, there is a simple use for logarithmic axes.

Say that you have a series of data with both large and small data values such as sales by model line. Your company probably has high-flying models that account for 80 percent of

N O T E Scientists might say that I would be remiss for not defining a logarithm. A logarithm is the power to which a base, such as 10, must be reduced to produce a given number. Luckily, you do not have to understand that sentence in order to use this setting to improve your charts that show a wide range of magnitudes. Read on.

your revenue and then some older-model lines that are still hanging around. When you try to plot these items on a chart, Excel must make the axis scale large enough to show the sales of the best-selling products. This causes the detail for the smaller product lines to become lost because the values are a relatively small percentage of the entire scale.

In Figure 2.19, there is important data regarding the first three product lines. However, when looking at the chart, no one will be able to see if the sales of these products were near the forecast.

Figure 2.19

It is impossible to see the detail of the smaller product lines because they are relatively small compared to the largest product line.

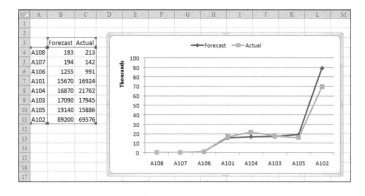

When this occurs, the solution is to convert the axis to a logarithmic axis. In a logarithmic axis, the distance from 1 to 10 is the same as the distance from 10 to 100, and so on. This allows you to see detail of the product selling a few hundred units as well as the products selling 100,000 units.

To convert to a logarithmic scale, select Layout, Axes, Primary Vertical Axis, Show Axis with Log Scale. The result is a chart such as the one in Figure 2.20. Notice that now you can see that the actual sales were lower than the forecast in the A107 and A106 product lines.

N O T E The log scale cannot be used if your data contains negative numbers. There is no way to raise 10 to a power and get a negative number. It would be helpful if Excel could actually use the log concept to show negative numbers—sort of a pseudo-log scale.

Figure 2.20
If you convert to a log scale, you can see detail for small items as well as large items.

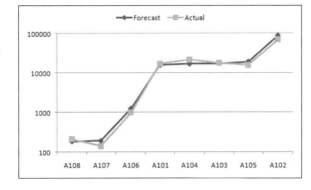

Consider Date Versus Text-Based Axes

In most Excel charts, the points along the horizontal axis are equidistant. This makes sense when you are comparing departments or regions, or even when comparing months of the year.

At times, the horizontal axis might be based on dates that have points that may not be equally spaced. Figure 2.21 shows the results of random quality control audits. For example, audits do not occur at regular periods since they are supposed to be a surprise. In the top chart, the axis uses a text-based setting that shows the points at equal distances from each other. In the bottom chart, the axis uses a date-based setting that shows certain audits happened closer to or farther away from each other.

Figure 2.21
The text-based axis in this figure shows that you can explicitly control whether the horizontal axis is equally spaced or if it is date based.

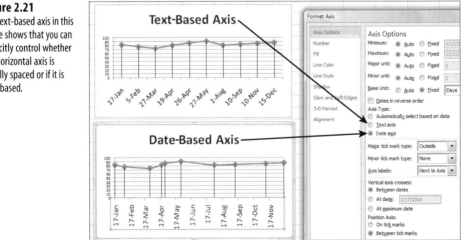

Excel often autoselects the type of axis to use. To control the axis setting, select Layout, Axes, Primary Horizontal Axis, More Primary Horizontal Axis Options, Axis Options, and then choose either Text Axis or Date Axis from the Axis Type section.

TIP   You can skip the long menu sequence by double-clicking the labels along the axis. This will immediately take you to the dialog box shown in Figure 2.21.

CASE STUDY: USING A DATE-BASED AXIS TO REPRESENT TIME

Frustratingly, Excel does not offer a time-based axis. If you wanted to plot values that occur at certain times of day, there is no automatic method for achieving this effect. To create the chart in Figure 2.22, follow these steps:

1. Convert your time values to whole numbers using =HOURS(A2)*60+MINUTES(A2). Use this column as your category values.

2. Create a line chart.

3. Change the horizontal axis to a date-based axis.

4. Using the built-in styles on the Layout tab, turn off the horizontal and vertical axes.

5. Turn on data labels for all points. Specify that the data labels should be above the point. Turn off the labels.

6. Find individual points that represent key times (for example, Figure 2.22 uses 7 a.m., noon, 5 p.m., and 10 p.m.). Click twice to select the corresponding data point. Right-click and select Add Data Label. This adds a silly label such as 459 to the point that you will fix in the next step. Repeat this step for the other three key points in the day.

7. Click a data label, and all labels are selected. Click a second time to select the individual label. Type a new value for the label, such as 7AM, and press Enter. The label changes to the text you typed.

TIP   Note that while you are typing, you cannot see the value being typed. You have to wait until you press Enter to see the value.

8. Repeat step 7 for the other visible data labels.

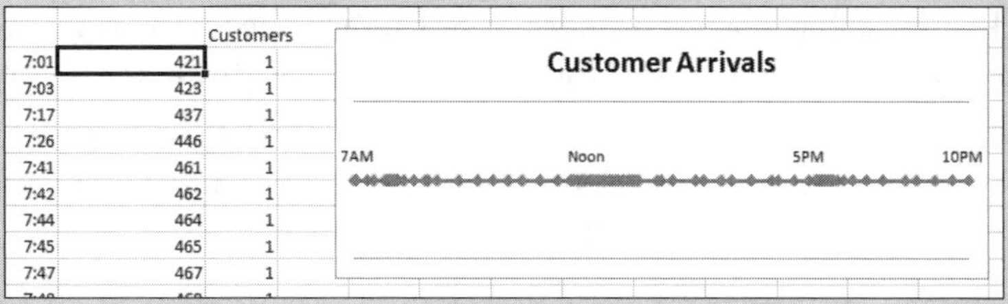

Figure 2.22
Creating a time-based axis requires a massive kluge.

	Customers	
7:01	421	1
7:03	423	1
7:17	437	1
7:26	446	1
7:41	461	1
7:42	462	1
7:44	464	1
7:45	465	1
7:47	467	1

Changing the Scale of an Axis

Typically, a chart has a vertical axis that runs from zero to a value larger than the largest value in the dataset. This is not ideal for some datasets.

The chart in Figure 2.23 shows daily changes in a measurement that typically fluctuates from 802 to 804. If you use a zero-based vertical axis, as in the top chart, you cannot make

Figure 2.23
Altering the scale of the axis allows you to see detail in certain datasets.

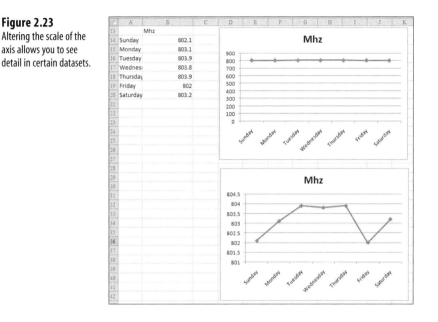

out any variability. Instead, if you change the vertical axis to run from 801 to 804.5, you can see the daily fluctuations in the value, as shown in the bottom chart in the figure.

Clearly, altering the axis in Figure 2.23 makes sense. If you didn't change the axis, the chart reader would not be able to make out the variability in a value that is fluctuating wildly within the expected range of values.

In other cases, altering the axis is a great way to mislead people. For example, the top chart in Figure 2.24 shows a 50 percent increase from 1997 to 2006. If someone wants to manipulate the reader's opinion, he or she can change the minimum and maximum values along the vertical axis. The bottom chart contains the same data as the top chart, but the increase

> **NOTE**
> The spinmeisters behind political candidates are experts at manipulating the vertical axis in order to lie or mislead with charts.

looks much more severe because the scale has been adjusted to focus on values between 5 and 9.

When you create a chart, Excel automatically decides whether the vertical axis should reach to zero. The rule is fairly simple: If the range between the lowest and highest values in the dataset is less than 20 percent of the lowest value, Excel automatically chooses a scale that is not zero based. For example, suppose are plotting data that ranges from 100 to 198. This is a range of 98. Because 98 is almost 50 percent of the lowest value, Excel automatically creates a vertical axis that extends to 0. As another example, say you are plotting data that ranges from 1,000 to 1,098. This is a range of 98. However, 98 is less than 10 percent of

Figure 2.24
Two charts of the same data paint different pictures when the range of the vertical scale is adjusted. The single vertical line between '99 and '00 is actually drawn in using Insert, Shapes.

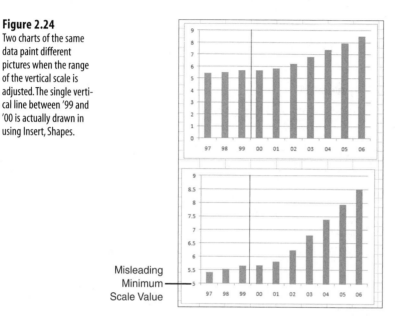

the lowest value, which means Excel will create a vertical axis that brackets the range—perhaps 950 to 1,150.

If you are not trying to use your chart to mislead the chart reader, you can usually accept Excel's decision on the vertical axis scale. However, if you need to override the setting, follow these steps:

1. Select the chart.

2. Select Layout, Axes, Primary Vertical Axis, More Primary Vertical Axis Options. Excel displays the Format Axis dialog. The axis scale options are in the Axis Options category.

3. To override the minimum value on the axis, select the Fixed option button for Minimum. You can then type a value for the minimum value to show on the axis.

Figure 2.25 shows the options that are available in the Format Axis dialog. Note the settings Major Unit and Minor Unit in Figure 2.25. These values are used to control the placement of horizontal gridlines on the chart.

Figure 2.25
Control the minimum and maximum values along the vertical axis by using this dialog.

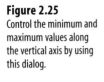

Displaying and Formatting Gridlines

Gridlines help the reader locate data on a chart. Without gridlines, it is difficult to follow the plotted points over to the vertical axis to figure out the value of a point.

Gridlines work in conjunction with the Major Unit and Minor Unit settings in the Format Axis dialog (refer to Figure 2.25). The built-in options in the Layout tab enable you to turn

Figure 2.26
The built-in choices allow you to display major gridlines, minor gridlines, both, or none.

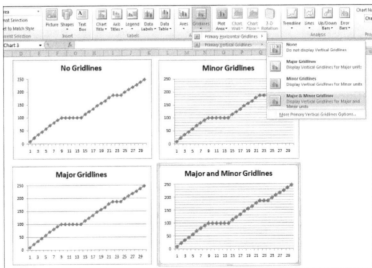

on major, minor, major and minor, or no gridlines.

Figure 2.26 shows four versions of the same chart. In this chart, the major axis unit is 50, and the minor axis unit is 10.

Choosing to display minor gridlines, as in the chart in the upper right of Figure 2.26, causes Excel to draw 25 horizontal lines on the chart. This may seem like overkill because it is difficult to follow the gridlines across the chart.

Initially, both major and minor gridlines are formatted as 0.75-point lines. This means that selecting Major & Minor Gridlines looks the same as selecting just Minor Gridlines. To make the major gridlines stand out, as in the lower-right chart in Figure 2.26, you need to

> **CAUTION**
>
> Using the More Primary Horizontal Gridline Options selection in the built-in menu on the Layout tab always leads to a dialog to format the major gridlines. This is particularly frustrating when your chart displays only the minor gridlines. For trouble-free access to the Format Minor Gridlines option, select Vertical (Value) Axis Minor Gridlines from the drop-down in the Current Selection group of the Layout tab. After you have selected the minor gridlines, click the Format Selection button, which is located immediately below the drop-down.

format the major gridlines.

Creating Unobtrusive Gridlines by Using Format Gridline

Gridlines start out as 0.75-point lines. If you plan to display major and minor gridlines on a chart, you might want to format the gridlines differently.

Each Format Gridlines dialog box has three categories in the left navigation bar:

- **Line Color**—A solid-color line can be chosen in any color, a gradient line in a variety of colors, or an automatic line. When a gradient line is chosen, Excel applies a slightly different shade to each gridline.

- **Line Style**—The width of each gridline can be controlled in 0.25-point increments. You can choose Dash Type to make the gridlines appear as dots, dashes, or various combinations.

- **Shadow**—A shadow can be added to your gridlines. Settings allow you to change the

> **TIP**
>
> The best gridlines are unobtrusive and accent your message instead of overpowering it. Using a dashed thin gridline in a subtle color allows someone to use the gridlines if necessary but makes sure that the gridlines do not overpower the message.

shadow color, transparency, size, blur, angle, and distance. Nothing shouts "chartjunk" more than a shadow on gridlines.

Figure 2.27
Make the gridlines as subtle or prominent as you want.

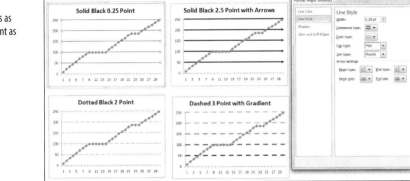

Figure 2.27 shows four varieties of horizontal gridlines and the Line Style category of the Format Gridlines dialog box.

Controlling Placement of Major and Minor Gridlines

Settings in the Format Axis dialog can be used to control the placement of major and minor gridlines. For the vertical axis, you can change the Major Unit and Minor Unit settings to control the spacing of the horizontal gridlines. Even though you are allowed to choose

Figure 2.28
By changing the units on the Format Axis dialog, you can control the spacing between horizontal gridlines.

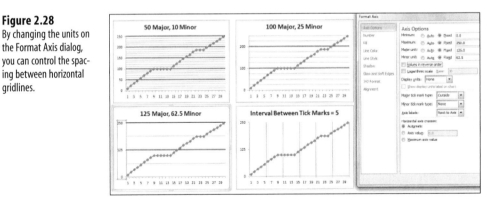

something else, for best results, the major unit should be a multiple of the minor unit.

The top and left charts in Figure 2.28 show various settings for the major and minor units and their impact on the gridlines.

To control the placement of vertical gridlines, you have to format the horizontal axis. There is a setting called Interval Between Tick Marks. In the lower-right chart shown in Figure 2.28, the interval has been increased to 5. This causes Excel to display a vertical gridline after every five points.

Formatting the Plot Area

Thankfully, Excel 2010 creates a simple white plot area as the default. In legacy versions of Excel, the plot area always started as a gray background, which looked horrible when the chart was printed on a monochrome printer.

When the plot area was gray, I almost always customized the plot area to do away with the gray. Now you can decide if you want to change the white to something a bit fancier.

The built-in choices on the Layout menu are to either turn off the plot area, resulting in a white background, or use a fill of the default color, as defined by the chart style selected on the Design tab. In many cases, this default is white, so both choices lead to the same result.

To have better control over the plot area, you need to choose the More Plot Area Options from the built-in menu. Format Plot Area allows you to choose No Fill, Solid Fill, Gradient Fill, or Picture or Texture Fill.

Some of the cool plot area options available in Excel 2010 involve changing the transparency of the plot area. This actually works in conjunction with the formatting of the chart area. If you make the plot area 90 percent transparent, you can see the formatting of the chart area. If you format the chart area to be transparent, then you see through to the spreadsheet.

Using a Gradient for the Plot Area

Setting up a simple two-color gradient has become far more difficult in Excel 2010 than it used to be. Microsoft offers many more choices for controlling the gradient, but this causes the process of setting up the gradient to be more difficult.

The first set of choices involves selecting whether the gradient should be linear, radial, or rectangular, or whether it should follow the path of the shape. Within the linear gradients, you can specify a direction such as 90 degrees for top to bottom or 180 percent for right to left. With the radial and rectangular gradients, you can specify whether the gradient radiates from the center or from a particular corner. The path type creates a gradient that is relative to the shape of the bounding object. Figure 2.29 shows a variety of gradient types.

The next choice involves the number of colors. You can choose a predefined color scheme from the Preset drop-down or you can specify your own color scheme by defining a number of gradient stops. Each stop is assigned a color, transparency, and position ranging from 0 percent to 100 percent. Excel 2010 offers an improved Gradient Stop bar that allows you to visualize the position of each stop in the gradient. Click a stop to move it or adjust the settings for that stop. Use the + or – buttons to the right of the bar to add or remove stops. You can edit only one gradient stop at a time.

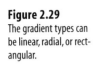

Figure 2.29
The gradient types can be linear, radial, or rectangular.

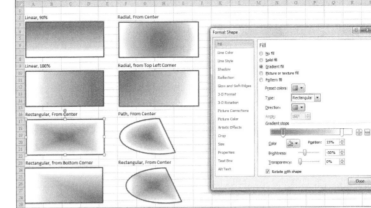

Creating a Custom Gradient

Suppose you want the plot area to contain a two-color gradient, flowing from green on the top to white on the bottom. This was simple in Excel 2003, but it is difficult to set up in Excel 2010 for the first chart. However, if you have many charts to format in the same Excel session, the settings from the first gradient will remain in the Format Plot Area dialog box, which makes it easier to format subsequent charts. You might decide that the top 5 percent of the chart should be solid green, the bottom 5 percent of the chart should be solid white, and everything in between should be a gradient from green to white.

A gradient stop consists of a position, a color, and a transparency value. The first gradient stop would indicate a color green and 5 percent as the position. The second gradient stop would indicate a color of white and 95 percent as the position. Everything from 5 percent to 95 percent would be a blend from green to white. To use a lighter color green, you can increase the transparency of the green stop.

If you have previously created a chart with a predefined gradient, you might find that the default gradient has 3 through 6 stops already defined. If this is the case, select the later stops and click Remove to remove them.

Complete the following steps to set up a two-color gradient:

1. Select a chart. From the Layout tab, select Plot Area, More Plot Area Options.

2. Change the Fill setting from Automatic to Gradient Fill.

3. Choose a Linear gradient.

4. Change the angle to 90 degrees.

5. Each chevron shape on the Gradient Stops bar indicates a gradient stop. If there are more than two stops, select the last stop and click the minus button to remove that stop. Continue removing any stops higher than Stop 2.

6. Click the first stop chevron to work with Stop 1. Choose a green color. Set the stop position at 5 percent by either using the spin button or by dragging the chevron. Set the transparency to 25 percent to make a lighter green.

7. Click the Stop 2 chevron. Choose white as the color. Set the stop position at 95 percent.

The result is a two-color gradient ranging from dark green at the top to white at the bottom. Figure 2.30 shows the gradient and the setting for Stop 1.

Figure 2.30
Creating a two-color gradient requires many more steps in Excel 2010 than in legacy versions.

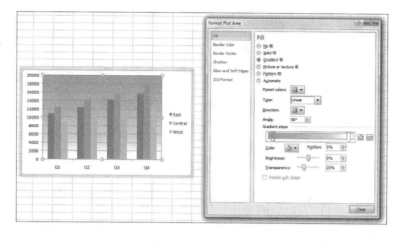

> **NOTE**
> After you have created a gradient, Excel remembers the settings and automatically applies them to future gradients that you set up.

Using a Picture or Texture for the Plot Area

You have many options available when you want to use a texture or a picture for the plot area. When choosing Picture or Texture Fill, a Texture drop-down appears, with the same two dozen textures that have been in Office for years. To use a picture instead of a texture, click the File button and browse your drives to locate a picture to insert.

When you choose a picture, it is stretched or shrunk to fill the plot area completely. This might cause your logo to be a little squashed, as shown in the top-left chart in Figure 2.31. To make your picture keep its correct aspect ratio, select the Tile Picture as Texture check box in the Format Plot Area dialog.

When you choose to tile the picture, a number of choices are available in the Tiling Options section. In the top-center chart in Figure 2.31, the Scale X and Scale Y options are set to 10 percent to create a repeating pattern of logos. The first logo is aligned with the top left of the plot area.

You can choose alternating tiles of the image to be mirror images of the first. However, this is not appropriate when using logos. Every other column can show horizontal mirror images, as in the top-right chart in Figure 2.31. You can also have every other row show vertical mirror images or turn on both horizontal and vertical mirror images, as shown in the bottom-right chart in Figure 2.31.

To lighten the picture, adjust the Transparency slider to the right. The bottom-left chart in Figure 2.31 has an 80 percent transparency.

Figure 2.31
When choose a picture, clip art, or texture, you can choose to show a single stretched image or to tile the image at various sizes.

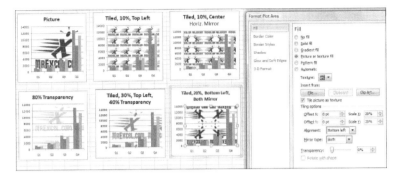

Mixing the Plot Area Color with the Chart Area Color

The Transparency slider on the Format Plot Area dialog allows you to see through the plot area to view whatever formatting has been applied to the chart area.

Notice that there is not an icon on the Layout tab for formatting the chart area. Select the chart area by clicking any whitespace just inside the border of the chart. Click Format Selection in the Layout tab, press Ctrl+1. Alternatively, select Format from the right-click menu to access the Format Chart Area dialog.

In the top three charts in Figure 2.32, the chart area includes the default opaque white formatting. If you specify that the black formatting of the plot area be 75 percent transparent, you have a plot area that is 25 percent black and 75 percent white. If you choose a black plot area that is 100 percent transparent, you see through the plot area, to the white chart area background.

Figure 2.32
Increasing the transparency of the plot area allows the formatting of the chart area to show through.

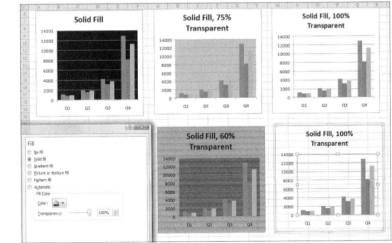

The transparency options become more interesting if you first format the chart area. In the bottom-center chart in Figure 2.32, the chart area has been formatted with a wood grain effect. This is achieved by making the plot area black with a 60 percent transparency.

In the bottom-right chart in Figure 2.32, the chart area has been formatted with the None option or using a solid color with 100 percent transparency. When the plot area is formatted as 100 percent transparent, you can see through the plot area and the chart area to the underlying cells in the spreadsheet.

Formatting the Chart Walls and Floor of a 3-D Chart

With a 3-D chart, you can format the chart wall and chart floor instead of the plot area. Drop-downs on the Layout tab offer built-in choices to turn on the formatting of either the chart wall or chart floor. Three different components can be formatted: the back wall, side wall, and chart floor.

If you use the Current Selection drop-down on the left side of the Layout tab, you can select the floor, back wall, side wall, or walls. Selecting walls is the same as selecting both the back wall and the side wall.

After you have selected an element, use the Format Selection button under the drop-down to format the element. As with the plot area, you can specify a solid fill, a gradient, a texture, or a picture.

Figure 2.33 illustrates the various elements that can be individually formatted.

Controlling 3-D Rotation in a 3-D Chart

A number of options are available for rotating a 3-D chart. Of the available options, you are most likely to change the X rotation and leave the other angles alone:

- **X rotation**—Choose a value from 0 to 359.9 degrees to rotate the floor of the chart counterclockwise. The chart at the top-right of Figure 2.34 has been rotated 50 degrees from the default rotation. This rotation forces the series names to move clockwise to the left. In some cases, it might be easier to see a short series by rotating the x-axis.

- **Y rotation**—Choose a value from –90 degrees to 90 degrees to change the height of the viewer with respect to the chart. In the default 15 percent Y rotation, it appears that the reader is slightly above the chart. For a 0-degree rotation, the view appears that the reader is at about eye level with the chart, as shown in the chart at the top left of Figure 2.35. At a 90-degree rotation, the reader appears to be looking straight down on the chart, which makes it impossible to judge the height of any columns, as shown in the chart at the bottom right of Figure 2.35. Negative rotations create a view where the reader is actually looking up at the chart from underneath a transparent floor, as shown in the bottom-left chart in Figure 2.35. For best results, you should use values from 0 to 20 degrees for the Y rotation.

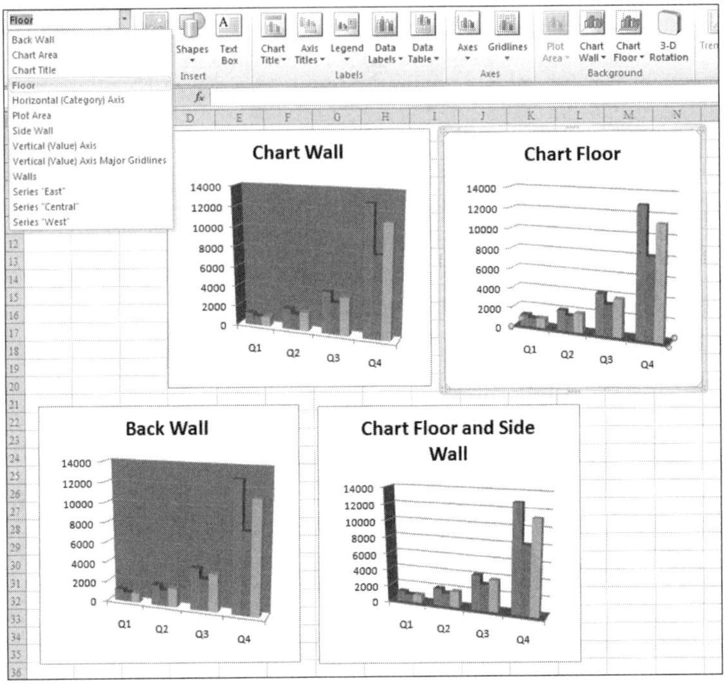

Figure 2.33
In a 3-D chart, you can format the walls individually or as a single unit.

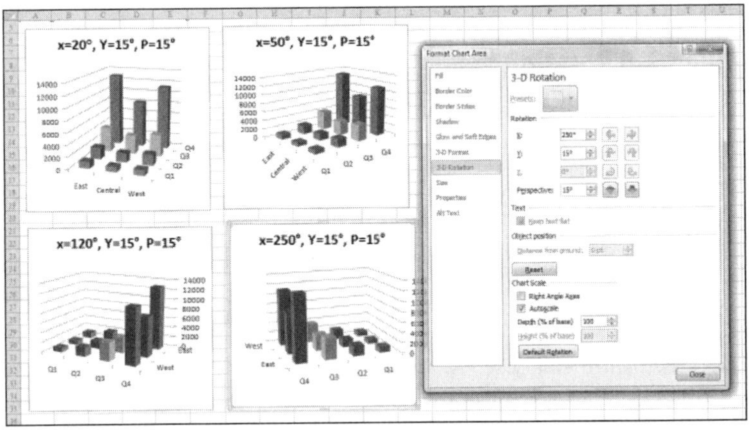

Figure 2.34
Rotating the x-axis turns the floor of the chart clockwise.

- **Perspective—**Choose a value from 0 to 120 to distort a chart further. If you have used a wide-angle lens on a camera, you might have noticed that items in the foreground appear unusually large, while items in the background appear unusually small. Increasing the perspective is similar to using a wide-angle camera. The chart at the top right of Figure 2.36 has an increased perspective. Note how the Q4 bars seem to shrink in this view.

Figure 2.35
Your angle of a view can be changed by using the Y rotation.

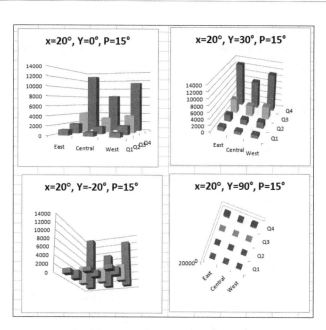

Figure 2.36
Settings for perspective, depth, and height let you twist and stretch a chart.

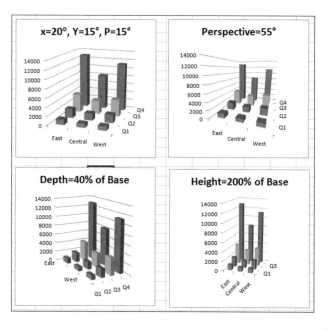

■ **Depth**—Choose a value from 0 percent to 2000 percent of the base. Decreasing the ratio of depth to the base creates a chart where the columns become wide rectangles, as shown in the chart at the lower left of Figure 2.36.

■ **Height**—Clear the Autoscale check box to enable the Height setting. You can choose a value from 0 percent to 500 percent of the base. The bottom-right chart in Figure 2.36 shows a chart with an increased height:width ratio.

Forecasting with Trendlines

A trendline attempts to fit existing data points to a formula and extend that formula into the future. When a trendline is added to a chart, Excel uses least-squares regression to find the best line to represent the data points. Excel can either draw the trendline for existing points to indicate if the points are trending up or down, or it can extend the trendline into the future to project whether you will meet a goal.

In Figure 2.37, actual progress toward a goal is tracked in Column B. Note that because the project is in process, several points in the dataset are not yet filled in.

Adding a trendline allows you to project when the project will finish if you continue working at the current pace. To add a trendline, select Layout, Trendline, Linear Trendline. Excel asks to which series it should add a trendline. If you choose the actual series, Excel adds a new virtual series to the chart. This series is plotted out to the end of the data series. In Figure 2.38, you can see that the linear trendline is projecting that you will have only 50 units complete by the 20th day.

Although creating a trendline requires only a few clicks, several trendline options are worth learning. These are described in the following subsections.

Figure 2.37
This chart shows the actual points and a goal line that indicates how much progress should be made each day in order to reach the project completion.

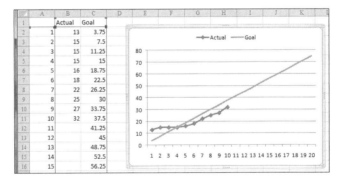

Formatting a Trendline

To format a trendline, right-click the trendline and select Format Trendline. Options in the Format Trendline dialog allow you to change the line color and the line style. I usually change the dash type on the Line Style category to show a dashed line. This indicates that it is not actual data, but a computer projection. I also change the color, often to red. When a project is falling behind schedule, the red dashed trendline becomes a call to action. The trendline says, "You need to pick up the pace of production—not just for one day, but for several sustained days."

Figure 2.38
The trendline indicates that based on your current run rate, you will severely miss the deadline.

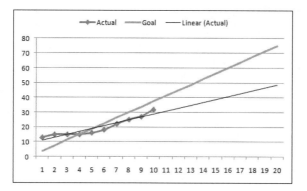

Say that you suddenly do 10 units of production on the 11th day. This brings the project back on track with 42 units complete, when 41.25 are needed to stay headed toward the goal. However, when the trendline looks at your average daily production, it sees that you spend 10 days only averaging 3 units a day. The trendline is not convinced that just because you had one good day, you will make the final goal. In this case, the trendline adjusts the projection from 50 to about 57. This makes the trendline seem like a bit of a cynic. However, in reality, the trendline is just using simple math to analyze your behavior so far when working on this project.

Adding the Trendline Equation to a Chart

To help understand how a trendline is calculated, you can display the equation on the chart.

> **CAUTION**
>
> The More item from most Layout drop-down menus can usually be clicked to format an item. However, this does not work with a trendline. If you click the More button, Excel adds a second trendline to your chart. Instead, you should select Series "Actual" Trendline from the Current Selection drop-down on the left side of the Layout tab and then select Format Selection to access the dialog box.

In the Trendline Options category of the Format Trendline dialog, select Display Equation on the Chart. For a linear trendline, Excel displays a trendline in the form of $y = mx + b$.

Alternatively, you can choose to force the y-intercept to be zero or display the R-squared value on the chart. R-squared is a measure of how closely the trendline fits the existing points. While R-squared can range from 0 to 1, values closer to 1 indicate that the trendline is doing a good job of representing the data points.

In Figure 2.39, the equation predicts that you magically started with 6.8 units done on Day 0 and then have averaged 2.5 units a day thereafter. This is pretty good because in this case, several units were finished in the previous month but did not make up a full case pack, so their totals were added to Day 1 of the current month. The R-squared of 0.85 says that the trendline is a pretty good fit. The bottom line is that you need to focus on production for the next nine days if you want to make the goal.

Figure 2.39
An equation can be added to a chart to see how Excel is fitting the chart to the line.

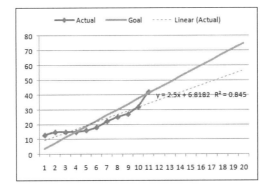

Choosing a Forecast Method

In business, a linear trendline is used most often, which assumes a constant rate of progress throughout the life of the chart. Several other forecast methods are available for trendlines:

- **Exponential trendline**—Used most often in science. Describes a population that is rapidly increasing over successive generations such as the number of fungi in a Petri dish over time.

- **Logarithm trendline**—Results when there is an initial period of rapid growth that levels off over time.

- **Polynomial trendline**—Can describe a line that undulates due to two to six external factors. When you specify a polynomial trendline, you have to specify which order of polynomial. For example, in a third-order polynomial, the line is fit to the equation $y = b + c1x + c2x2 + c3x3$.

- **Power trendline**—Fits the points to a line, where $y = cxb$. This describes a line that increases at a specific exponential rate over time.

- **Moving average trendline**—Used to smooth out data that fluctuates over time. A typical trendline would use a three-month moving average.

Adding Drop Lines to a Line or Area Chart

Area and line charts are great at showing trends, but it is often difficult for the reader to figure out the exact values for data points. Since the line is floating in space, you are counting on the viewer's eye being able to travel from the horizontal axis straight up to the data series line.

A drop line is a vertical line that extends vertically from a line or area chart and extends down to the horizontal axis. As shown in the lower chart in Figure 2.40, the drop lines help you see that the March point is exactly at 300. This would be difficult to discern in the chart shown at the top of Figure 2.40.

To add a drop line, select the chart, and then select Layout, Lines, Drop Lines.

Figure 2.40
Drop lines help you
visualize the exact value
of each point along the
horizontal axis.

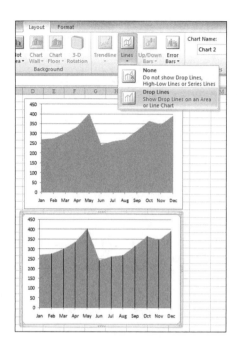

Adding Up/Down Bars to a Line Chart

If you have a line chart with two different data series, you might want to compare the series at each point along the horizontal axis. There are two different options for this comparison that are available in two locations along the Layout tab of the tab.

In the lower chart in Figure 2.41, high-low lines extend from one line to the other line. These are created using Layout, Lines, High-Low Lines.

In the chart at the right in Figure 2.41, up/down bars extend from one line to the other line. These bars appear in contrasting colors, depending on which line is higher at that particular point. To add up/down bars, you select Layout, Up/Down Bars, Up/Down Bars.

Figure 2.41
High-low lines and up/down bars help show the relationship between two series at specific points along the x-axis.

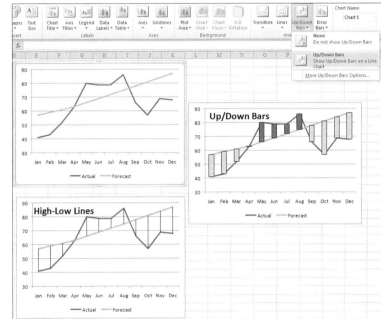

Showing Acceptable Tolerances by Using Error Bars

I used to run monthly sales and operations planning meetings. In these meetings, the leaders of the sales, marketing, engineering, and manufacturing departments would decide on the production plan for each sales model. During the next month's meeting, a chart would compare the previous month's forecast to actual demand. If the demand was more than 20 percent above or below the plan, someone had to present the root causes for that variance. The discussion was often lively: Did the east region really have no clue that Customer XYZ was about to order 1,000 units or was it sandbagging so it could have a lower quota?

To figure out which products required this scrutiny, both the forecast and actual performance were plotted for each product line. Error bars showing the acceptable 20 percent tolerance were added to the forecast line. If the actual line was within the 20 percent tolerance, no discussion was needed.

Excel 2010 makes it easy to add error bars: Select one series in the chart and then select Layout, Error Bars, More Error Bar Options. In the Format Error Bars dialog, choose if the error bars should extend up, down, or both from the line. You can add a cap or have no cap. In the lower section, specify one of five methods for calculating the size of the error bar. Based on the standard deviation, specify that the error bars should extend a fixed number of units. In the sales and operations planning meetings, it was appropriate to add an error bar that was 20 percent of each data point. Therefore, if someone had forecast 200 units of a product, anything from 160 to 240 was an acceptable demand. For the products with a forecast of 8,000, the acceptable tolerance was 6,400 to 9,600.

Figure 2.42 shows a chart with 20 percent error bars.

Figure 2.42
The error bars show an acceptable tolerance or a margin of error around each point.

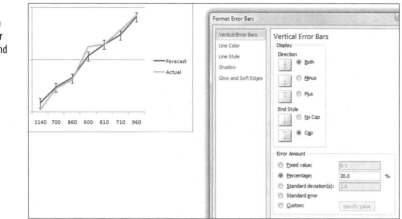

Formatting a Series

It is somewhat strange that there is not a button on the Layout tab for the most popular charting element: the Series element.

To format the series, you can use the Current Selection drop-down on the left side of either the Layout tab or Format tab, and then Choose the appropriate series from the list to select the series. Click the Format Selection button to access the Format Data Series dialog.

> **TIP**
> There are alternative ways to format the data series. If the lines are not too close together, any of these methods will work:
>
> ■ Click an element in the chart to select it. Type Ctrl+1 to access the Format dialog box.
>
> ■ Right-click and element and choose Format from the context menu.
>
> ■ In Excel 2010, you can double-click any element to display the Format dialog box for that element.
>
> However, when you have several data series plotted as lines which are very close together, it is often difficult to click the correct line. In that case, select the series from the Current Selection drop-down on either the Layout or Format tab. Then, choose the Format Selection icon.

The Series Options category allows you to plot a series on a secondary axis. This is useful if one data series contains data that is of a different order of magnitude than the other series. For example, you might chart revenue and gross profit percent. By moving the gross profit percent to the Secondary Axis, you can see detail of revenue in thousands and gross profit percentages in the 50 percent range. When you move one or more series to the secondary axis, you should change the chart type of those series; otherwise, the column markers are drawn on top of each other. Figure 2.43 shows an example where GP% is plotted as a line chart using the secondary axis.

Figure 2.43
GP% is moved to the secondary axis and then changed to a line chart.

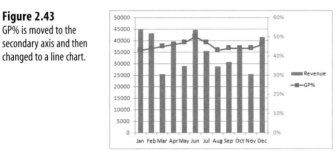

Using the remaining categories, you can edit the Marker style for a series including the marker color, line color, line style, shadow, and 3-D formatting.

Formatting a Single Data Point

The first click on a data series selects the entire series. If you pause for a moment and then perform a second click on a data point, the Current Selection drop-down indicates that you have selected an individual data point. The drop-down might say Series "Profit" Point "2011."

It is interesting that the only way to perform this selection is by performing two single-clicks on the chart. The Current Selection drop-down does not offer a list of all the data points.

After selecting a data point, use the Format Selection button located on the left side of the Layout or Format tab. You can then change the color or marker style of a single point.

Using the Format Tab

When you first install Excel 2010, all the new chart options allow you to create fresh and new-looking charts. If you stay on the Design tab, you can create 21,600 different charts. If you expand to the Layout tab, you can create 601 billion different charts. If you include the 20 themes on the Page Layout tab, you can create 12 trillion different chart types. If this is not enough variability for you or if you get tired of these built-in options, you can head to the Format tab and have microcontrol over the formatting for any element of the chart.

There actually are a few very cool settings on the Format tab. If you venture there, you can create amazing translucent charts to impress your coworkers who have become bored with the standard Excel 2010 charts.

Converting Text to WordArt

The WordArt Styles group on the Format tab is used to apply WordArt styles to any text on a chart. You are not allowed to use the type-twisting options in the Transform menu, but you can add shadow, glow, or reflection to the 20 styles in the WordArt menu.

Using the Shape Styles Gallery

The Shape Styles gallery contains 36 built-in styles that can be applied to any shape. There are really six styles for each of the six accent colors in the current theme. The six styles progress from simple on the first row of the gallery to extreme on the last row of the gallery.

To format a particular element, click that element and choose a new style from the gallery. When using the Shape Styles gallery, keep these tips in mind:

- The colors and effects available in the gallery change if you select a new theme from the Page Layout tab.
- The first time you click a column, select the entire series. A second click selects only one column or data point.
- If you find it difficult to select a particular item on a chart, you can select the item from the Current Selection drop-down at the left edge of the Layout or Format tabs.
- Live Preview works in this gallery. Even though you see the effect after hovering over a tile in the gallery, you actually have to click the tile to apply the style.

Figure 2.44 shows the Shape Styles gallery and six charts that represent the six styles available when the Office theme is active.

Using the Shape Fill and Shape Effects

Some of the best effects are not available in the built-in charts. However, you can access myriad other effects by using the Shape Fill, Shape Outline, and Shape Effects drop-downs on the Format tab. Figure 2.45 shows a chart in which each bar has a different effect from these drop-downs applied.

Figure 2.44
The Shape Styles gallery offers six effects for each of six accent colors.

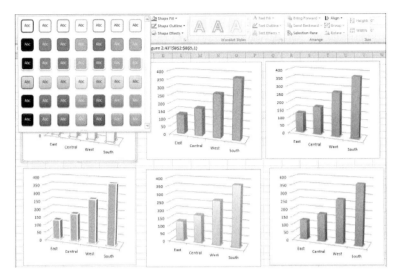

Figure 2.45
These effects are available on the Format tab.

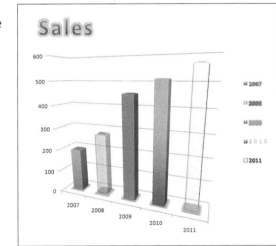

Using Preset Shape Effects

The Preset menu on the Shape Effects drop-down offers 12 built-in combinations of shadow, reflection, glow, soft edges, bevel, and rotation. Figure 2.46 shows the 12 preset thumbnails plus several charts created with the various presets.

For more control of the effects, choose the 3-D Options selection at the bottom of the menu. In the 3-D Format category, the Material drop-down offers 11 textures. The final three textures are translucent textures that give a glass appearance when applied to a bar. In Figure 2.47, the five bars are formatted as wire frame, powder, translucent powder, clear, and plastic.

Figure 2.46
The 12 charts on the sheet match the sequence of built-in presets on the menu.

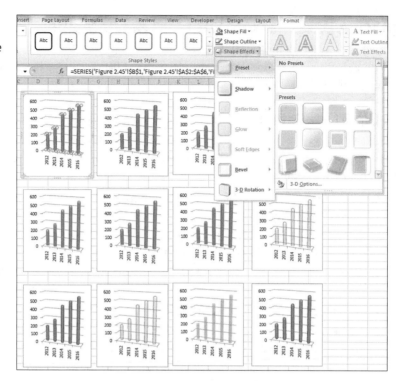

Figure 2.47
These bars were formatted by changing the surface material in the Format Data Point dialog.

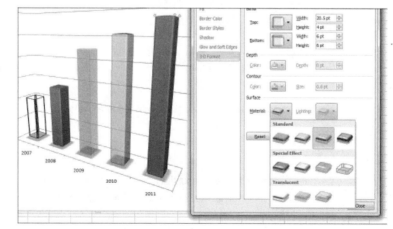

Replacing Data Markers with Clip Art or Shapes

Instead of using columns or cylinders for your data markers, you can replace the column with either some clipart or even a shape from the Shapes gallery. To achieve this effect, change the fill of a data series, and then turn off the border around the data point.

Using Clip Art as a Data Marker

Office Online offers thousands of free clip art images. If you have an Internet connection, you can insert any of these images in a chart to replace the data markers. Follow these steps to create a pictograph:

1. In a 2-D column chart, select a data series. Right-click the data series and select Format Data Series.
2. In the Format Data Series dialog that appears, select the Fill category in the left panel. In the right panel, choose Picture or Texture Fill.
3. Click the Clip Art button. Excel displays a shortened version of the clip art pane, called Select Picture.
4. Select the Include Content from Office Online check box.
5. In the Search Text box, type a keyword to describe the clip art and then click Go.
6. Browse through the returned images. You are looking for something that is cartoonish and narrow. Rather than clip art with a detailed background, look for clip art where only the character appears. When you find an acceptable image, click OK.
7. Click the Border Color category and select No Line.
8. Click Close to close the Format Data Series dialog.

The result is a chart similar to the bottom chart in Figure 2.48. The clip art is stretched to indicate the height of the bar.

> **TIP**
> For best results, do not combine a picture with translucent surfaces.

> **TIP**
> Fans of Edward Tufte may point out that he rails against pictographs in his books. However, what Tufte complained about was both the width and height of the clip art changing in response to increased numbers. Microsoft does not increase the width of the bars, only the height, ensuring that the area of the image stays roughly proportional to the data that it is representing.

Using a Shape in Place of a Data Marker

Replacing a data marker with one of the 175 shapes in the Shape dialog box is slightly more difficult than replacing a data marker with clip art. The fill settings on the Format Data

Figure 2.48
Replace the data markers with shapes or clip art for visual interest.

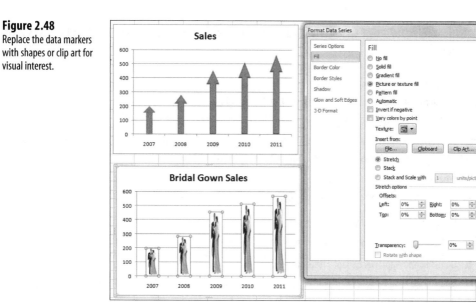

Series dialog do not allow you to specify a shape. However, they allow you to import a shape from the Clipboard.

> **NOTE**
> The AutoShapes from Excel 97 through Excel 2003 have been renamed shapes starting in Excel 2007.

Follow these steps to create the top chart in Figure 2.48:

1. Create a 2-D column chart.
2. Select a cell in the worksheet. From the Insert menu, choose an upward arrow from the Shapes drop-down.
3. Click and drag to draw an arrow on the worksheet.
4. Right-click the shape and then select Copy.
5. Click the data series in the chart. Right-click and select Format Data Series.
6. In the Format Data Series dialog that appears, choose the Fill category in the left panel. In the right panel, choose Picture or Texture Fill.
7. In the Insert From section, click the Clipboard button. Excel replaces the columns with the arrows.
8. Click Close to close the Format Data Series dialog.

This technique works best with 2-D charts. If you attempt to apply a shape to a 3-D column, the shape is pasted to each vertical face of the column.

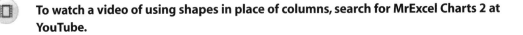 **To watch a video of using shapes in place of columns, search for MrExcel Charts 2 at YouTube.**

Creating a Chart Template

Suppose you need to create a series of charts. You like the look of the translucent glass effect available in Excel 2010. There is not a built-in style for this effect, but you would like to be able to create charts quickly using the glass effect.

The solution is to build one chart and then save that chart as a template. If you indicate that the template is the default chart type, you can quickly create new charts simply by using the Alt+F1 keyboard shortcut.

Follow these steps to create the template:

1. Create a chart. Use a 3-D column chart as the chart type.

2. Using the tools on the Layout tab, remove the legend.

3. Click one of the columns in the chart to select the data series.

4. On the Format tab, select Shape Effects, Bevel, Soft Round.

5. Select Shape Effects, Bevel, 3-D Options. In the Format dialog, in the 3-D Options category, open the Material drop-down and select Clear.

6. On the Design tab, select Save As Template. Give the template a name such as 3DGlass.

7. On the Design tab, select Change Chart Type. Click the Templates category. Click 3DGlass icon in the My Templates window. Select Set as Default Chart.

After completing these steps, you can create a 3-D glass chart by simply selecting the data to be charted and pressing Alt+F1. Excel creates a chart modeled on your glass chart.

> **CAUTION**
>
> If you add multiple chart templates, it becomes annoying to find them again in the Templates folder of the Chart dialog. Microsoft shows all the templates as a thumbnail without displaying the template name. You have to hover over each thumbnail to learn the name of that particular icon.

Next Steps

In Chapter 3, "Creating Charts That Show Trends," you will see examples of charts that show trends such as column and line charts. You will also learn how to use a trendline to project a trend into the future.

Creating Charts That Show Trends

3

Choosing a Chart Type

You have two excellent choices when creating charts that show the progress of some value over time. Because Western cultures are used to seeing time progress from left to right, you are likely to choose a chart where the axis moves from left to right—whether it is a column chart, line chart, or area chart.

> **NOTE**
> The new Sparklines feature is another way to show trends with tiny charts. See Chapter 9, "Using Sparklines, Data Visualizations, and Other Nonchart Methods."

Column Charts for Up to 12 Time Periods

If you have only a few data points, you can use a column chart because they work well for 4 quarters or 12 months. Within the column chart category, you can choose between 2-D and 3-D styles. To highlight one component of a sales trend, you can use a stacked column chart.

> **NOTE**
> This book recommends not using pyramid charts or cone charts because they distort your message. For an example, see the "Lying with Shrinking Charts" section in Chapter 14, "Knowing When Someone Is Lying to You With a Chart."

Line Charts for Time Series Beyond 12 Periods

When you get beyond 12 data points, you should switch to a line chart, which can easily show trends for hundreds of periods. Line charts can be designed to show only the data points as markers or data points can be connected with a straight or smoothed line.

Figure 3.1 shows a chart with only nine data points, which that a column chart is meaningful. Figure 3.2 shows a chart of 100+ data points. With this detail, you should switch to a line chart in order to show the trend.

Figure 3.1
With 12 or fewer data points, column charts are viable and informative.

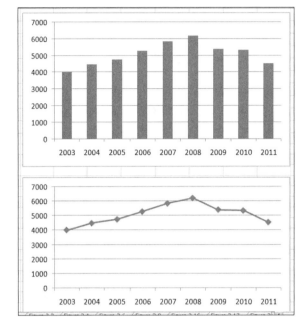

Figure 3.2
When you go beyond 12 data points, it is best to switch to a line chart without individual data points. The middle chart in this figure shows the same dataset as a line chart.

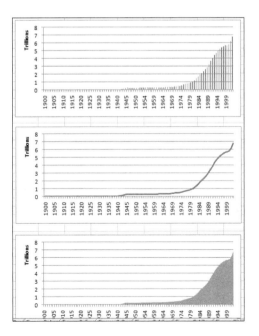

Area Charts to Highlight One Portion of the Line

An *area chart* is a line chart where the area under the line is filled with a shading or color. This can be appropriate if you want to highlight a particular portion of the time series. If you have fewer data points, adding drop lines can help the reader determine the actual value for each time period.

High-Low-Close Charts for Stock Market Data

If you are plotting stock market data, use stock charts to show the trend of stock data over time. You can also use high-low-close charts to show the trend of data that might occur in a range such as when you need to track a range of quality rankings for each day.

Bar Charts for Series with Long Category Labels

Even though bar charts can be used to show time trends, they can be confusing because readers expect time to be represented from left to right. In rare cases, you might use a bar chart to show a time trend. For example, if you have 40 or 50 points that have long category labels that you need to print legibly to show detail for each point, then consider using a bar chart. Another example is illustrated in Figure 3.3, which includes sales for 45 daily dates. This bar chart would not work as a PowerPoint slide. However, if it is printed as a full page on letter-size paper, the reader could analyze sales by weekday. In the chart in Figure 3.3, weekend days are plotted in a different color than weekdays to help delineate the weekly periods.

Figure 3.3
Although time series typically should run across the horizontal axis, this chart allows 45 points to be compared easily.

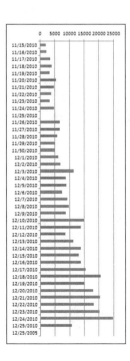

Pie Charts Make Horrible Time Comparisons

A pie chart is ideal for showing how components that add up to 100% are broken out. It is difficult to compare a series of pie charts to detect changes from one pie to the next. As you can see in the charts in Figure 3.4, it is difficult for the reader's eye to compare the pie wedges from year to year. Did market share increase in 2008? Rather than using a series of pie charts to show changes over time, use a 100 percent stacked column chart instead.

Figure 3.4
It is difficult to compare one pie chart to the next.

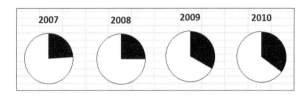

100 Percent Stacked Bar Chart Instead of Pie Charts

In Figure 3.5, the same data from Figure 3.4 is plotted as a 100 percent stacked bar chart. Series lines guide the reader's eye from the market share from each year to the next year. The stacked bar chart is a much easier chart to read than the series of pie charts.

Figure 3.5
The same data presented in Figure 3.4 is easier to read in a 100 percent stacked bar chart.

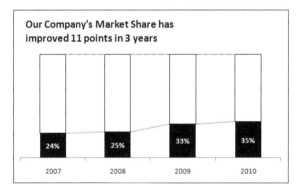

Understanding Date-Based Axis Versus Category-Based Axis in Trend Charts

Excel offers two types of horizontal axes in a trend chart. Having the proper setting can ensure that your message is accurate.

If the spacing of events along the time axis is uniform, it does not matter whether you choose a date-based axis or a text-based axis because the results will be the same. When this occurs, it is fine to allow Excel to choose the type of axis automatically.

However, if the spacing of events along the time axis is haphazard, you definitely want to make sure that Excel uses a date-based axis.

Accurately Representing Data Using a Time-Based Axis

Figure 3.6 shows the spot price for a certain component used in your manufacturing plant. To find this data, you downloaded past purchase orders for that product. Your company doesn't purchase the component on the same day every month; therefore, you have an incomplete dataset. In the middle of the dataset, a strike closed one of the vendors, spiking the prices from the other vendors. Your purchasing department had stocked up before the strike, which allowed your company to slow its purchasing dramatically during the strike.

Figure 3.6
The top chart uses a text-based horizontal axis: Every event is plotted an equal distance from the next event. This leads to the shaded period being underreported.

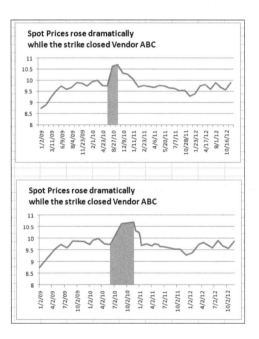

In the top chart in Figure 3.6, the horizontal axis is set to a text-based axis, and every data point is plotted an equal distance apart. Because your purchasing department made only two purchases during the strike, it appears the time affected by the strike is very narrow. The bottom chart uses a date-based axis. In this axis, you can see that the strike actually lasted for half of 2010.

> NOTE
> To learn how to highlight a portion of a chart as shown in Figure 3.6, see "Highlighting a Section of Chart by Adding a Second Series," later in this chapter.

Usually, if your data contains dates, Excel defaults to a date-based axis. However, you should always check to make sure Excel is using the correct type of axis. A number of potential problems force Excel to choose a text-based axis instead of a date-based axis. For example, Excel will choose a text-based axis when dates are stored as text in a spreadsheet and when dates are represented by numeric years. The list following Figure 3.7 summarizes other potential problems.

To explicitly choose an axis type, follow these steps:

1. Right-click the horizontal axis and select Format Axis.

2. In the Format Axis dialog box that appears, select the Axis Options category.

3. As appropriate, choose either Text Axis or Date Axis from the Axis Type section (see Figure 3.7).

Figure 3.7
You can explicitly choose an axis type rather than letting Excel choose the default.

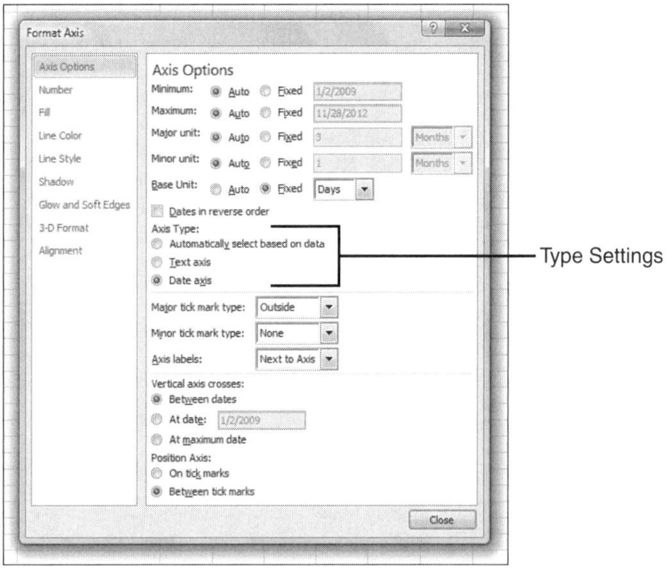

Type Settings

A number of complications that require special handling can occur with date fields. The following are some of the problems you might encounter:

■ **Dates stored as text**—If dates are stored as text dates instead of real dates, a date-based axis will never work. You have to use date functions to convert the text dates to real dates.

■ **Dates represented by numeric years**—Trend charts can have category values of 2008, 2009, 2010, and so on. Excel does not naturally recognize these as dates, but you can trick it into doing so. Read "Plotting Data by Numeric Year" near Figure 3.15 in this chapter.

■ **Dates before 1900**—If your company is old enough to chart historical trends before January 1, 1900, you will have a problem. In Excel's world, there are no dates before 1900. For a workaround, read "Using Dates Before 1900" around Figure 3.16.

■ **Dates that are really time**—It is not difficult to imagine charts in which the horizontal axis contains periodic times throughout a day. For example, you might use a chart like this to show the number of people entering a bank. For such a chart, you need a time-based axis, but Excel will group all of the times from a single day into a single point. See "Using a Workaround to Display a Time-Scale Axis" near Figure 3.19 for the rather complex steps needed to plot data by periods smaller than a day.

Each of these problem situations is discussed in the following sections.

Converting Text Dates to Dates

If your cells contain text that looks like dates, the date-based axis will not work. The data in Figure 3.8 came from a legacy computer system. Each date was imported as text instead of as dates.

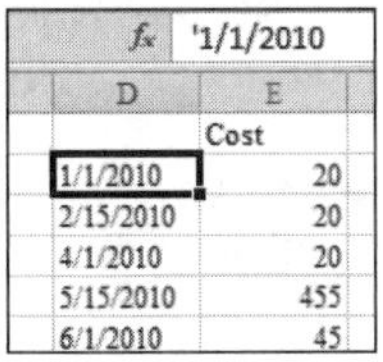

Figure 3.8

These dates are really text, as indicated by the apostrophe before the date in the formula bar.

This is a frustrating problem because text dates look exactly like real dates. You may not notice that they are text dates until you see that changing the axis to a date-based axis has no effect on the axis spacing.

If you select a cell that looks like a date cell, look in the formula bar to see whether there is an apostrophe before the date. If so, you know you have text dates (refer to Figure 3.8). This is Excel's arcane code to indicate that a date or number should be stored as text instead of a number.

Understanding How Excel Stores Dates and Time

On a Windows PC, Excel stores dates as the number of days since January 1, 1900. For a date such as 2/17/2011, Excel actually stores the value 40,591, but it formats the date to show you a value such as 02/17/2011.

On a Mac running Mac OS, Excel stores the dates as the number of days since January 1, 1904. The original designers of the Mac OS were trying to squeeze the OS into 64K of ROM. Because every byte mattered, it seemed unnecessary to add a couple lines of code to handle the fact that 1900 is not a leap year. Excel for the Mac adopted the 1904 convention. On a Mac, 2/17/2011 is stored as 39,129.

3

CAUTION

Selecting a new format from the Format Cells dialog does not fix this problem, but it may prevent you from fixing the problem! If you import data from a .txt file and choose to format that column as text, Excel changes the numeric format for the range to be text. After a range is formatted as text, you can never enter a formula, number, or date in the range. People try to select the range, change the format from text to numeric or date, and hope this will fix the problem—but it doesn't. After you change the format, you still have to use a method described in the "Converting Text Dates to Real Dates" section, later in this chapter, to convert the text dates to numeric dates.

However, it is still worth changing the format from a text format to General, Date, or anything else. If you do not change the format, and then insert a new column to the right of the bad dates, the new column inherits the text setting from the date column. This causes your new formula (the formula to convert text to dates) to fail. Therefore, even though it doesn't solve your current problem, you should select the range, click the Dialog Launcher icon in the lower-right corner of the Number group on the Home tab, and change the format from Text to General. Figure 3.9 shows the Dialog Launcher icon.

Figure 3.9
Many groups on the ribbon have this tiny More icon in the lower-right corner. Clicking this icon leads to the legacy dialog box.

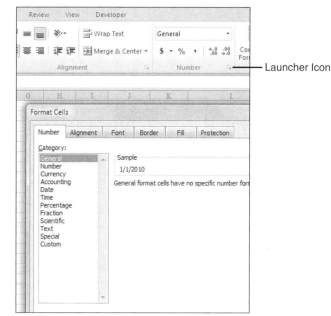

Excel for Windows, which needed to be compatible with Lotus 1-2-3, adopted the 1900 convention. As demonstrated in the next case study, the 1900 convention incorrectly made 1900 a leap year.

Comparing Date Systems

Complete the following case study to see firsthand how important date systems information really is:

1. Enter the number 1 in cell A1.

2. Select cell A1, and then press Ctrl+1 to access the Format Cells dialog.

3. Change the numeric formatting to display the number as a date, using the *Wednesday, March 14, 2001 type. On a PC, you see that the number 1 is January 1, 1900.

4. Type 2 in cell A1. The date changes to January 2, 1900.

> **NOTE**
>
> If you type **60** in cell A1, you see Wednesday, February 29, 1900—a date that did not exist! When Mitch Kapor was having Lotus 1-2-3 programmed in 1982, the programmers missed the fact that there was not to be a leap year in 1900. Lotus was released with the mistake, and every competing spreadsheet had to reproduce exactly the same mistake to make sure that the billions of spreadsheets using dates produced the same results. Although the 1900 date system works fine and reports the right day of the week for the 40,300 days since March 1, 1900, it reports the wrong day of the week for the 59 days from January 1, 1900, through February 28, 1900.

Now try this:

1. Select cell B5. Press Ctrl+; to enter today's date in the cell.

2. Again, select cell B5. Press Ctrl+1 to display the Format Cells dialog.

3. Change the number format from a date to a number. Your date changes to a number in the 40,000 to 42,000 range, assuming you are reading this in the 2010–2013 time period.

This might sound like a hassle, but it is worth it. If you store dates as real dates (that is, numbers formatted to display as a date), Excel can do all kinds of date math. For example, you can figure out how many days exist between a due date and today by subtracting one date from another. You can also use the WORKDAY function to figure out how many workdays have elapsed between a hire date and today.

Excel provides a complete complement of functions to deal with dates including functions that convert data from text to dates and back. Excel stores times as decimal fractions of days. For example, you can enter noon today as =TODAY()+0.5 and 9 a.m. as =TODAY()+0.375. Again, the number format handles converting the decimals to the appropriate display.

Converting Text Dates to Real Dates

The DATEVALUE function converts text that looks like a date into the equivalent serial number. You can then use the Format Cells dialog to display the number as a date.

The text version of a date can take a number of different formats. For example, your international date settings might call for a month/day/year arrangement of the dates. Figure 3.10 shows a number of valid text formats that can be converted with the DATEVALUE function.

Figure 3.11 shows a column of text dates. Follow these steps to convert the text dates to real dates:

1. Insert a blank Column B by selecting cell B1. Select Home, Insert, Insert Sheet Columns. Alternatively, you can use the Excel 2003 shortcut Alt+I+C.
2. In cell B2, enter the formula `=DATEVALUE(A2)`. Excel displays a number in the 40,000 range in cell B2. You are halfway to the result (see Figure 3.11). You still have to format the result as a date.
3. Double-click the fill handle in the lower-right corner of cell B2. Excel copies the formula from cell B2 down to your range of dates.

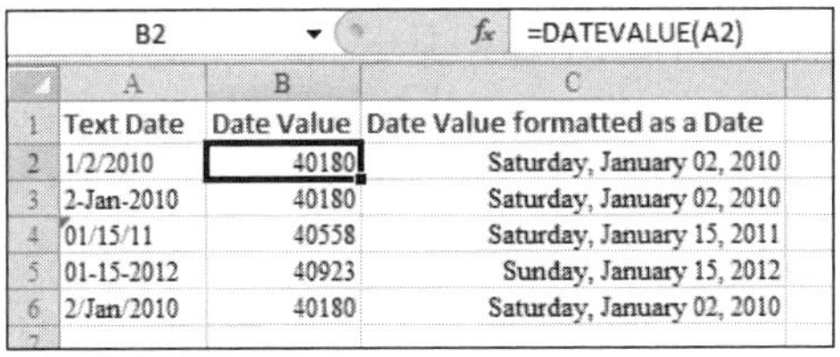

B2 =DATEVALUE(A2)

	A	B	C
1	Text Date	Date Value	Date Value formatted as a Date
2	1/2/2010	40180	Saturday, January 02, 2010
3	2-Jan-2010	40180	Saturday, January 02, 2010
4	01/15/11	40558	Saturday, January 15, 2011
5	01-15-2012	40923	Sunday, January 15, 2012
6	2/Jan/2010	40180	Saturday, January 02, 2010

Figure 3.10
The DATEVALUE function can handle any of the date formats in Column J.

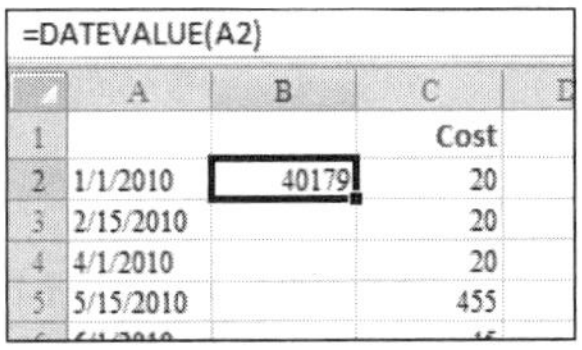

=DATEVALUE(A2)

	A	B	C
1			Cost
2	1/1/2010	40179	20
3	2/15/2010		20
4	4/1/2010		20
5	5/15/2010		455

Figure 3.11
The result of the DATEVALUE function is a serial number.

> **TIP** The fill handle is the square dot in the lower-right corner of the active cell indicator.

4. Select Column B2. On the Home tab, select the drop-down at the top of the Number group and choose either Short Date or Long Date. Excel displays the numbers in Column B as a date (see Figure 3.12). Alternatively, you can press Ctrl+1 and select any date format from the Number tab.
5. To convert the live formulas in Column B to be static values, while the range of dates in Column B is selected, press Ctrl+C to copy. Press Ctrl+V to paste. Press Ctrl to open the Paste Options dialog. Press V to paste as values.
6. Delete the original column A.

> **TIP** If some of the dates appear as #######, you need to make the column wider. To do so, double-click the border between the column B and column C headings.

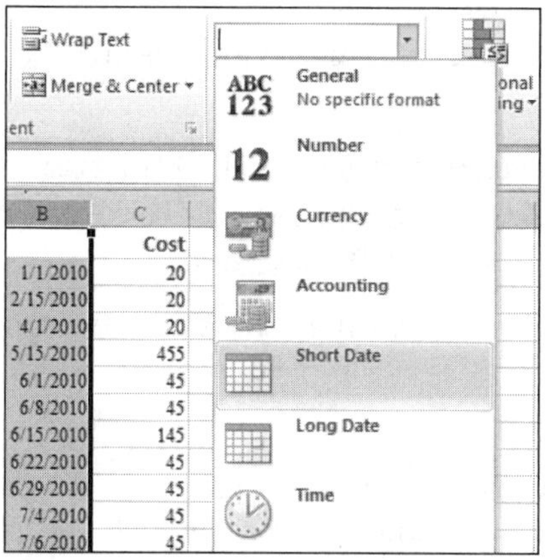

Figure 3.12
Choose a date format
from the Number drop-
down on the Home tab.

After converting the text dates to real dates, insert a line chart with markers. Excel automatically formats the chart with a date-based axis. In Figure 3.13, the top chart reflects cells
that contain text dates. The bottom chart uses cells in which the text dates have been converted to numeric dates.

Figure 3.13
When your original data
contains real dates, Excel
automatically chooses a
more accurate date-based
axis. The bottom chart
reflects a date-based axis.

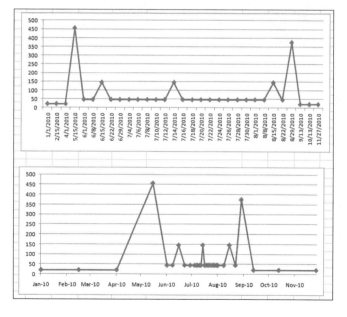

 To watch a video of converting text dates to dates, search for "MrExcel Charts 3"
at YouTube.

There are other methods for converting the data shown in Figure 3.11 to dates. Here are two methods:

Method 1: Select any empty cell. Press Ctrl+C to copy. Select your dates. On the Home tab, select Paste, Paste Special. In the Paste Special dialog, choose Values in the Paste section and Add in the Operation section. Click OK. The text dates will convert to dates.

Method 2: Select the text dates and then, on the Data tab, select Text to Columns, and then click Finish.

Converting Bizarre Text Dates to Real Dates

When you rely on others for source data, you are likely to encounter dates in all sorts of bizarre formats. For example, while gathering data for this book, I found a dataset where each date was listed as a range of dates. Each date was in the format 2/4-6/11. I had to check with the author of the data to find out if they meant February 4th through 6th of 2011 or if they meant February 4th through June 11th. They meant the former.

Used in combination, the functions listed below can be useful when you are converting strange text dates to real dates:

- =DATE(2011,12,31)—Returns the serial number for December 31, 2011.
- =LEFT(A1,2)—Returns the two leftmost characters from cell A1.
- =RIGHT(A1,2)—Returns the two rightmost characters from cell A1.
- =MID(A1,3,2)—Returns the third and fourth characters from cell A2. You read the function as "return the middle characters from A1, starting at character position 3, for a length of 2."
- =FIND("/",A1)—Finds the position number of the first slash within A1.

Follow these steps to convert the text date ranges shown in Figure 3.14 to real dates:

Figure 3.14
A mix of LEFT, RIGHT, MID, and FIND functions parse this text to be used in the DATE function.

	A	B	C	D	E
1	Date	Year	Month	Day	Date
2	2/1-4/10	2010	2	1	2/1/2010
3	2/9-11/10	2010	2	9	2/9/2010
4	2/10-12/10	2010	2	10	2/10/2010
5	12/19-21/10	2010	12	19	12/19/2010
6	B2: =RIGHT(A2,2)+2000				
7	C2: =LEFT(A2,FIND("/",A2)-1)				
8	D2: =MID(A2,FIND("/",A2)+1,FIND("-",A2)-FIND("/",A2)-1)				
9	E2: =DATE(B2,C2,D2)				

1. Because the year is always the two rightmost characters in column A, enter the formula `=RIGHT(A2,2)` in cell B2.

2. Because the month is the leftmost one or two characters in column A, ask Excel to find the first slash and then return the characters to the left of the slash. Enter `=FIND("/",A2)` to indicate that the slash is in second character position. Use `=LEFT(A2,FIND("/",A2))` to get the proper month number.

3. For the day, either choose to extract the first or last date of the range. To extract the first date, ask for the middle characters, starting one position after the slash. The logic to figure out whether you need one or two characters is a bit more complicated. Find the position of the dash, subtract the position of the slash, and then subtract 1. Therefore, use this formula in cell D2:
   `=MID(A2,FIND("/",A2)+1,FIND("-",A2)-FIND("/",A2)-1)`

4. Use the DATE function as follows in cell E2 to produce an actual date:
   `=DATE(B2,C2,D2)`

Plotting Data by Numeric Year

If you are plotting data where the only identifier is a numeric year, Excel does not automatically recognize this field as a date field.

For example, in Figure 3.15 data is plotted once a decade for the past 50 years and then yearly for the past decade. Column A contains four-digit years such as 1960, 1970, and so on. The default chart shown in the top of the figure does not create a date-based axis. You know this to be true because the distance from 1960 to 1970 is the same as the distance from 2000 to 2001.

Listed here are two solutions to this problem:

■ Convert the years in column A to dates by using **=DATE (A2,12,31)**. Format the resulting value with a yyyy custom number format. Excel displays 2005 but actually stores the serial number for December 31, 2005.

■ Convert the horizontal axis to a date-based axis. Excel thinks your chart is plotting daily dates from May 13, 1905, through July 2, 1905. Because no date format has been applied to the cells, they show up as the serial numbers 1955 through 2005. Excel displays the chart properly, even though the settings show that the base units are days.

Using Dates Before 1900

In Excel 2010, dates from January 1, 1900 through December 31, 9999 are recognized as valid dates. However, if your company was founded more than a demisesquicentennial before Microsoft was founded, you will potentially have company history going back before 1900.

Figure 3.16 shows a dataset stretching from 1787 through 1959. The accompanying chart would lead the reader to believe that the number of states in the United States grew

Figure 3.15
Excel does not recognize years as dates.

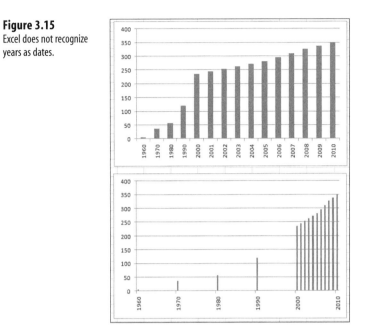

at a constant rate. This inaccurate statement would cause Mr. Kessel, my eighth-grade geography teacher, to give me an F for this book.

Figure 3.16
Dates from before 1900 are not valid Excel dates. A date-based axis is not possible in this case.

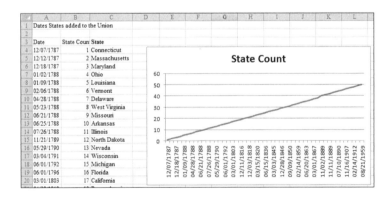

As mentioned previously, formatting the chart to have a date-based axis will not work because Excel does not recognize dates before 1900 as valid dates. Possible workarounds are discussed in the next two subsections.

Using Date-Based Axis with Dates Before 1900 Spanning Less Than 100 Years

In Figure 3.17, the dates in Column A are text dates from the 1800s. Excel cannot automatically deal with dates from the 1800s, but it can deal with dates from the 1900s.

Figure 3.17

Transforming the 1800s dates to 1900s dates and clever formatting allows Excel to plot this data with a date axis.

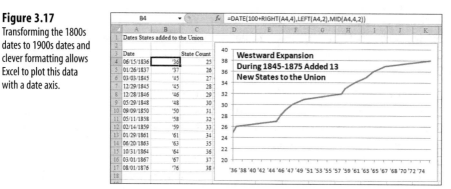

One solution is to transform the dates to dates in the valid range of dates that Excel can recognize. You can use a date format with two years and a good title on the chart to explain that the dates are from the 1800s. However, keep in mind that this solution fails when you are trying to display more than 100 years of data points.

To create the chart in Figure 3.17, follow these steps:

1. Insert a blank Column B to hold the transformed dates.

2. Enter the formula `=DATE(100+RIGHT(A4,4),LEFT(A4,2),MID(A4,4,2))` in cell B4. This formula converts the 1836 date to a 1936 date.

3. Select cell B4. Press Ctrl+1 to open the Format Cells dialog. Select the date format 3/14/01 from the Date category on the Number tab. This formats the 1936 date as 6/15/36. Later, you will add a title to indicate that the dates in this column are from the 1800s.

4. Double-click the fill handle in cell B4 to copy the formula down to all cells.

5. Select the range B3:C17.

6. From the Insert tab, select Charts, Line, 2-D Line, Line.

7. From the Layout tab, select Legend, No Legend.

8. Right-click the vertical axis along the left side of the chart and select Format Axis from the context menu.

9. In the Format Axis dialog that appears, on the Axis Options page, select the Fixed option button next to Minimum and enter a fixed value of 20.

10. Without closing the Format Axis dialog, click the dates in the horizontal axis in the chart. Excel automatically switches to formatting the horizontal axis, and the settings in the Format Axis dialog redraw to show the settings for the horizontal axis. In the Axis Type section, select Date Axis. Click Close to close the dialog box.

11. From the Layout tab, select Chart Title, Centered Overlay Title.

12. Click the State Count title. Type the new title `Westward Expansion<enter>During 1845-1875 Added 13<enter>New States to the Union`. Click outside the title to exit Text Edit mode.

13. Click the title once. You should have a solid selection rectangle around the title. On the Home tab, click the Decrease Font Size button. Click the Left Align button.

14. Carefully click the border of the title. Drag it so the title appears in the top-left corner of the chart.

15. Select the dates in B4:B17. Press Ctrl+1 to access the Format Cells dialog. On the Number tab, click the Custom category. Type the custom number format 'yy. This changes the values shown along the horizontal axis from m/d/yy format to show a two-digit year preceded by an apostrophe.

The result is the chart shown in Figure 3.17. The reader may believe that the chart is showing dates in the 1800s, but Excel is actually showing dates in the 1900s.

Using Date-Based Axis with Dates Before 1900 Spanning More Than 100 Years

Microsoft Excel 2010 doesn't do well with large datasets that span 100+ years. Although I managed to create a date-based axis covering 630 years with 10 data points, a dataset covering 102 years and 40 points cannot display a date-based axis.

However, as Figure 3.18 shows, it is possible to create this chart. To do so, you must transform the date axis into a scale that shows months, hide the axis, and then add your own axis using text boxes. These steps are not for the faint of heart.

First, you need to transform the dates from the 1800s to the 1900s. Next, you will transform the dates spanning 172 years into a range where each month in real time is represented by a single day. This results in a time span of 6 years. You then need to use care to completely hide the labels along the horizontal axis and replace them with text boxes showing the centuries. Lastly, you add a new data series to draw vertical lines at the change of each century.

To create the chart in Figure 3.18, follow these steps:

1. Insert new Columns B and C.

2. In cell B4, enter the formula =DATE(113+RIGHT(A4,4),LEFT(A4,2),MID(A4,4,2)). This transforms the dates from 1787 to a valid Excel date in 1900. Format this cell with a short date format.

3. In cell C4, type the formula =(YEAR(B4)-1899)*12+MONTH(B4) to calculate a number of months. Format this cell as a short date. This formula now reduces 172 years into 172x12 into 2,064 days, where each day represents 1 month of real time.

4. Select cells B4:C4 and double-click the fill handle to copy the formula down to your range of data. The dates in Column B span 1900 to 2072. The dates in Column C span 1900 to 1907. Although the relative position of the data points is correct, you have to hide the axis labels that Excel draws in for the horizontal axis. Therefore, it would be helpful to draw in vertical lines to show where the axis switches from the 1700s to the 1800s. Then draw another line to show where the axis switches from the 1800s to the 1900s.

Figure 3.18
This chart appears to show a date-based axis that spans 200+ years.

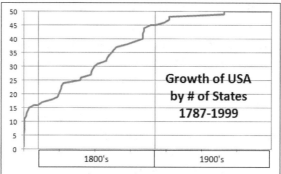

5. Insert a new Column E to hold the data for the second series. This series contains just two nonzero points: one at 1800 and one at 1900. Enter the heading `Divide Line` in cell E3.

6. Look through the dates in Column A. Insert a new row before the first date in the 1800s. In this new row, enter `01/01/1800` in Column A. Copy the formulas in Columns B and C. In Column D, copy the point from the row above. In Column E, enter the value `50`. This draws a single vertical bar from the horizontal axis up to a height of 50.

7. Repeat step 6 to add a new data point for January 1, 1900, and January 1, 2000.

8. Select C4:E55.

9. From the Insert tab, select Charts, Line, Line.

10. On the Layout tab, select Legend, None.

11. Right-click the numbers along the vertical axis and then select Format Axis. Change the Maximum option button to Fixed and enter the value `50`. This changes the vertical axis to show from 0 to 50.

12. On the Layout tab, use the Current Selection drop-down to select Series. Note that there are now only two data points selected in the chart.

13. On the Design tab, select Change Chart Type. Select the first icon in the column section—for a clustered column chart. This draws narrow columns—actually lines—at 1800 and 1900 on the chart. Note that the chart type change affects only the second series because you selected the Divide Line series in step 12.

14. Click the labels along the horizontal axis. These labels show wrong dates such as 1/23/02. On the Home tab, from the Font Color drop-down select a white font. This causes the axis labels to disappear.

15. On the Insert tab, click the Text Box icon. On the chart, draw a text box from the 1800 line to the 1900 line, just below the horizontal axis. The mouse pointer changes into a crosshairs as you draw. Make sure the vertical line in the crosshairs corresponds to the vertical dividing lines. After you create the text box, a flashing cursor appears inside the text box.

16. Type 1800s. Click the edge of the text box to change it from a dashed line to a solid line.

17. While the text box is selected, select Center Align from the Home tab. Select Vertical Center Align. Select Increase Font Size from the Home tab.

18. While the text box is still selected, select Format, Shape Outline, Black on the Layout tab in order to outline the text box.

19. Click the text box and start to drag to the right. After you start to drag, hold down the Shift key to constrain the movement to the right. Hold down the Ctrl key to make an identical copy of the text box. When the left edge of the new text box is aligned with the vertical line at 1900, release the mouse button.

> **TIP**   You must start dragging before you hold down the Ctrl+Shift keys. Microsoft interprets Ctrl-click as the shortcut to select an object's container.

20. Click in the text box and change the text from 1800s to 1900s.

21. On the Layout tab, select Chart Title, Centered Overlay Title. When the title Chart Title appears, it is selected.

22. Click inside the Chart Title text area to enter Text Entry mode. Overwrite the default text in the title by typing Growth of USA, press Enter, type by # of States, press Enter, and type 1787-1999.

23. Click the border of the chart title to exit Text Entry mode.

24. Drag the chart title to a new location in the lower-right corner of the chart.

The result is a chart that appears to show a line chart that spans 217 years. The line is scaled appropriately using a date-based axis.

Using a Workaround to Display a Time-Scale Axis

The developers who create Microsoft Excel are careful in the Format Axis dialog box to call the option a date axis. However, the technical writers who write Excel Help refer to a time-scale axis. The developers get a point here for accuracy because Excel absolutely cannot natively handle an axis that is based on time.

A worksheet in the download files is used to analyze queuing times. In Column A, it logs the time that customers entered a busy bank. Times range from when the bank opened at 10 a.m. until the bank closed at 4 p.m.

After you enter planned staffing levels in Column C, the model calculates when the customer will move from the queue to an open teller window and when he or she will leave the window based on an average of three minutes per transaction.

Data in Columns I:M record the number of people in the bank every time someone enters or leaves. This data is definitely not spaced equally. Only a few customers arrive in the 10:00 hour, while many customers enter the bank during the lunch hour.

The top chart in Figure 3.19 plots the number of customers on a text-based axis. Because each customer arrival or departure merits a new point, the one hour from noon until 1 p.m. takes up 41 percent of the horizontal width of the chart. In reality, this 1-hour period merits only 16 percent of the chart. This sounds like a perfect use for a time-series axis, right? Read on for the answer.

The bottom chart is an identical chart where the axis is converted to show the data on a date-based axis. This is a complete disaster. In a date-based axis, all time information is discarded. The entire set of 300 points is plotted in a single vertical line.

Figure 3.19
Excel cannot show a time-series axis that contains times.

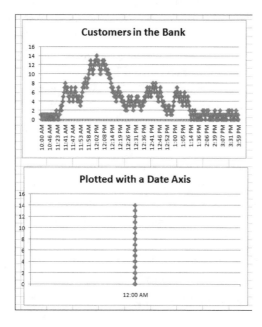

The solution to this problem involves converting the hours to a different time scale (similar to the 1800s date example in the preceding section). For example, perhaps each hour could be represented by a single year. Using numbers from a 24-hour clock, the 10:00 hour could be represented by 2010 and the 3:00 hour could be represented by 2015.

In this example, you manipulate the labels along the vertical axis using a clever custom number format. A few new settings on the Format Axis dialog ensure that an axis label appears every hour.

> **NOTE** In the original chart, a time appeared in Column I, and a formula in Column L simply copied this time so that it would be adjacent to the customer count in Column M. In step 1, the transformation formula is applied to Column L.

Follow these steps to create a chart that appears to have a time-based axis:

1. In cell L2, enter the following formula to translate the time to a date:

   ```
   =ROUND(DATE(HOUR(I2)+2000,1,1)+MINUTE(I2)/60*365,0)
   ```

   Because each hour will represent a single year, the years argument of the DATE function is =HOUR(I2)+2000. This returns values from 2010 through 2013. The other arguments in the date function are 1 and 1 to return January 1 of the year. Outside the date function, the minute of the time cell is scaled up to show a value from 1 to 365, using MINUTE(I2)/60*364. The entire formula is rounded to the nearest integer because Excel would normally ignore any time values.

2. Select cell L2. Double-click the fill handle to copy this formula down to all the data points. The result of this formula ranges from January 1, 2010, which represents the customer who walked in at 10 a.m., to 12/25/2015, which represents the customer who walked in at 3:57 p.m.

3. Select cells L1:M303.

4. From the Insert tab, select Charts, Line, Line with Markers.

5. On the Layout tab, select Legend, None. (After studying Software Quality Metrics (SQM) data for Excel 2007, surely Microsoft realizes that 500 million people instantly turn off the legend in every chart that has a single data series.)

6. Right-click the labels along the horizontal axis and select Format Axis to display the Format Axis dialog box, where you make the following selections:

   In the Axis Type section, select Date Axis.

   For Major Unit, select Fixed, 1 Years.

   For Minor Unit, select Fixed, 1 Days.

   For Base Unit, select Fixed, Days.

   Click Close to close the Format Axis dialog.

7. Return to the transformed dates in Column L. Select L2:L303.

8. Press Ctrl+1 to display the Format Cells dialog. On the Number tab, select the Custom category. A custom number format of yy would display 10 for 2010 and 15 for 2015. Instead, use a custom number format of yy":00". This causes Excel to display 10:00 for 2010 and 15:00 for 2015, which is fairly sneaky, eh?

As you see in Figure 3.20, the chart now allocates one-sixth of the horizontal axis to each hour. This is an improvement in accuracy over either of the charts in Figure 3.19. The additional chart in Figure 3.20 uses a similar methodology to show the wait time for each customer who enters the bank. If my bank offered 12-minute wait times, I would be finding a new bank.

Figure 3.20
These charts show the number of customers in the bank and their expected wait times.

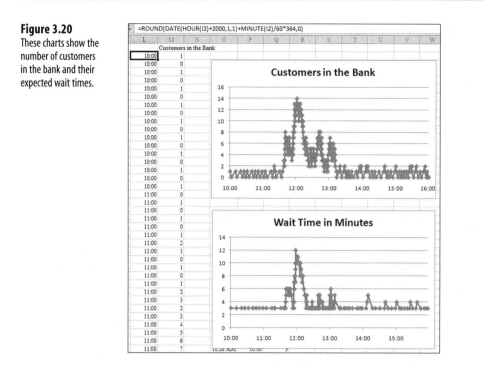

Communicate Effectively with Charts

A long time ago, a McKinsey & Company team investigated opportunities for growth at the company where I was employed. I was chosen to be part of the team because I knew how to get the data out of the mainframe.

The consultants at McKinsey & Company knew how to make great charts. Every sheet of grid paper was turned sideways, and a pencil was used to create a landscape chart that was an awesome communication tool. After drawing the charts by hand, they sent off the charts to someone in the home office who generated the charts on a computer. This was a great technique. Long before touching Excel, someone figured out what the message should be.

You should do the same thing today. Even if you have data in Excel, before you start to create a chart, it's a good idea to analyze the data to see what message you are trying to present.

The McKinsey & Company group used a couple of simple techniques to always get the point across:

- ■ To help the reader interpret a chart, include the message in the title. Instead of using an Excel-generated title such as "Sales," you can actually use a two- or three-line title such as "Sales have grown every quarter except for Q3, when a strike impacted production."

■ If the chart is talking about one particular data point, draw that column in a contrasting color. For example, all the columns might be white, but the Q3 bar could be black. This draws the reader's eye to the bar that you are trying to emphasize. If you are presenting data on screen, use red for negative periods and blue or green for positive periods.

The following sections present some Excel trickery that allows you to highlight a certain section of a line chart or a portion of a column chart. In these examples, you will spend some time up front in Excel adding formulas to get your data series looking correct before creating the chart.

> **TIP**
>
> If you would like a great book about the theory of creating charts that communicate well, check out Gene Zelazny's *Say It with Charts Complete Toolkit*. Gene is the chart guru at McKinsey & Company who trained the consultants who taught me the simple charting rules. While *Say It with Charts* doesn't discuss computer techniques for producing charts, it does challenge you to think about the best way to present data with charts and includes numerous examples of excellent charts at work. Visit www.zelazny.com for more information.

Using a Long, Meaningful Title to Explain Your Point

If you are a data analyst, you are probably more adept at making sense of numbers and trends than the readers of your chart. Rather than hoping the reader discovers your message, why not add the message to the title of the chart?

Figure 3.21 shows a default chart in Excel. Both the legend and title use the "Market Share" heading from cell B71. These words certainly do not need to be used twice on the chart.

Figure 3.21
By default, Excel uses an unimaginative title taken from the heading of the data series.

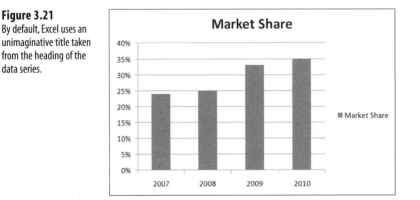

Follow these steps to remove the legend, add data labels, and add a meaningful title:

1. From the Layout tab, select Legend, None, and then select Data Labels, Outside End.
2. Click the title in the chart. Click again to put the title in Edit mode.
3. Backspace to remove the current title. Type `Market share has improved`, press Enter, and type `13 points since 2007`.
4. To format text while in Edit mode, you would have to select all the characters with the mouse. Instead, click the dotted border around the title. When the border becomes solid, you can use the formatting icons on the Home tab to format the title. Alternatively, right-click the title box and use the Mini toolbar to format the title.
5. On the Home tab, select the icon for Align Text Left, and then click the Decrease Font Size button until the title looks right.
6. Click the border of the chart title and drag it so the title is in the upper-left corner of the chart.

The result, shown in Figure 3.22, provides a message to assist the reader of the chart.

Resizing a Chart Title

The first click on a title selects the title object. A solid bounding box appears around the title. At this point, you can use most of the formatting commands on the Home tab to format the title. Click the Increase/Decrease Font Size buttons to change the font of all of the characters. Excel automatically resizes the bounding box around the title. If you do not explicitly have carriage returns in the title where you want the lines to be broken, you are likely to experience frustration at this point.

Figure 3.22
Use the title to tell the reader the point of the chart.

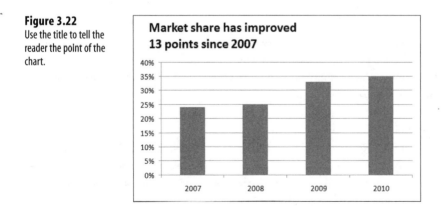

When you have the solid bounding box around the title, carefully right-click the bounding box and select Edit Text. Alternatively, you can left-click a second time inside the bounding

> ┌─ C A U T I O N ──
> │
> │ When you click a chart title to select it, a bounding box with four resizing handles appears. Actually,
> │ they are not resizing handles even though they look like it, which means that you do not have explicit
> │ control to resize the title. It feels like you should be able to stretch the title horizontally or vertically, as
> │ if it was a text box, but you cannot. The only real control you have to make a text box taller is by insert-
> │ ing carriage returns in the title. Keep in mind that you can insert carriage returns only when you are in
> │ Text Edit mode.

box to also put the title in Text Edit mode. Note that the dashed line in the bounding box indicates the title is in Text Edit mode. Using Text Edit mode, you can select specific characters in the title and then move the mouse pointer up and to the right to access the mini toolbar and the available formatting commands. You can edit specific characters within the title to create a larger title and a smaller subtitle, as shown in Figure 3.23.

Figure 3.23
By selecting characters in Text Edit mode, you can create a title/subtitle effect.

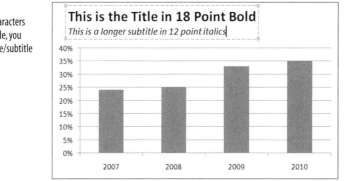

You cannot move the title when you are in Text Edit mode. To exit Text Edit mode, right-click the title and select Exit Edit Text or simply left-click the bounding box around the title. When the bounding box is solid, you can click anywhere on the border except the resizing handles and drag to reposition the title.

Deleting the Title and Using a Text Box

If you are frustrated that the title cannot be resized, you can delete the title and use a text box for the title instead. The title in Figure 3.24 is actually a text box. Note the eight resizing handles on the text box instead of the four resizing handles that appear around a title. Thanks to all these resizing handles, you can actually stretch the bounding box horizontally or vertically.

To create the text box shown in Figure 3.24, follow these steps:

  1. From the Layout tab, delete the original title by choosing Chart Title, None. Excel resizes the plot area to fill the space that the title formerly occupied.

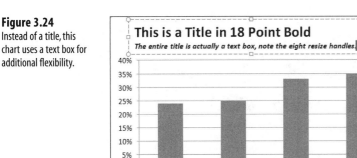

Figure 3.24
Instead of a title, this chart uses a text box for additional flexibility.

2. Select the plot area by clicking some whitespace inside the plot area. Eight resizing handles now surround the plot area. Drag the top resizing handle down to make room for the title.

3. On the Insert tab, click the Text Box icon.

4. Click and drag inside the chart area to create a text box.

5. Click inside the text box and type a title. Press the Enter key to begin a new line. If you do not press the Enter key, Excel word-wraps and begins a new line when text reaches the right end of the text box.

6. Select the characters in the text box that make up the main title and use either the mini toolbar or the tools on the Home tab to make the title 18 point, bold, and Times New Roman.

7. Select the remaining text that makes up the subtitle in the text box and use the tools on the Home tab to make the subtitle be 12 point, italics, Times New Roman.

Microsoft advertises that all text can easily be made into WordArt. However, when you use the WordArt drop-downs in a title, you are not allowed to use the Transform commands found under Text Effects on the Drawing Tools Format tab. When you use the WordArt menus on a text box, however, all the Transform commands are available (see Figure 3.25).

A text box works perfectly because it is resizable and you can use WordArt Transform commands. If you move or resize the chart, the text box moves with the chart and resizes appropriately.

Highlighting One Column

If your chart title is calling out information about a specific data point, you can highlight that point to help focus the reader's attention on it as shown in Figure 3.26. Although the tools on the Design tab do not allow this, you can achieve the effect quickly by using the Format tab.

To create the chart in Figure 3.26, follow these steps:

Figure 3.25
Using a text box instead
of a title allows more
formatting options.

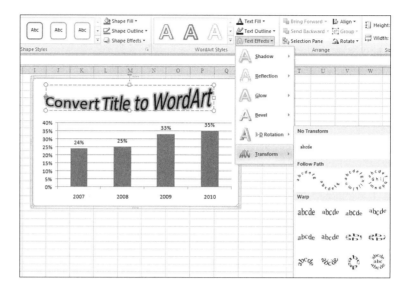

Figure 3.26
The column for Friday is
highlighted in a contrasting color and it is also
identified in the title.

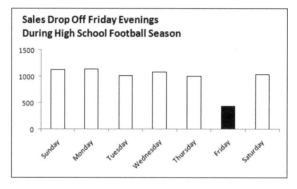

1. Create a column chart by selecting Column, Clustered Column from the Insert tab.

2. Click any of the columns to select the entire series.

3. On the Format tab, select Shape Fill, White. At this point, the columns are invisible. Invisible bars are great for creating waterfall charts, which is discussed in Chapter 4, "Creating Charts That Show Differences." However, in this case, you want to outline the bars.

4. From the Format tab, select Shape Outline, Black. Select Shape Outline, Weight, 1 point. All your columns are now white with black outline.

5. Click the Friday column in the chart. The first click on the series selects the whole series. A second click selects just one data point. If all the columns have handles, click Friday again.

T I P   If you accidentally click outside the series, you might inadvertently deselect the series. Click back on the series to re-select it.

6. From the Format tab, select Shape Fill, Black.

7. On the Layout tab, turn off the legend and the gridlines.

8. Type a title, as shown in Figure 3.26, pressing Enter after the first line of the title. On the Home tab, change the title font size to 14 point, left aligned.

9. Right-click the numbers along the vertical axis and select Format Axis. Change Major Unit to Fixed, 500.

The result is a chart that calls attention to Friday sales.

Replacing Columns with Arrows

Columns shaped like arrows can be used to make a special point. For example, if you have good news to report about consistent growth, you might want to replace the columns in the chart with arrow shapes to further indicate the positive growth.

Follow these steps to convert columns to arrows:

1. Create a column chart showing a single series.

2. In an empty section of the worksheet, insert a new block arrow shape. From the Insert tab, select Shapes, Blck Arrows, Up Arrow. Click and drag in the worksheet to draw the arrow.

3. Select the arrow. Press Ctrl+C to copy the arrow to the Clipboard.

4. Select the chart. Click a column to select all the columns in the data series.

5. Press Ctrl+V to paste the arrow. Excel fills the columns with a picture of the block arrow.

6. If desired, select Format Selection from the Format tab. Reduce the gap setting from 150 percent to 75 percent to make the arrows wider.

The new chart is shown in the bottom half of Figure 3.27. After creating the chart, you can delete the arrow created in step 2 by clicking the arrow and pressing the Delete key.

Highlighting a Section of Chart by Adding a Second Series

The chart in Figure 3.28 shows a sales trend over one year. The business was affected by road construction that diverted traffic flow from the main road in front of the business.

The title calls out the July and August time period, but it would be helpful to actually highlight that section of the chart. Follow these steps to add an area chart series to the chart:

1. Begin a new series in Column C, next to the original data. To highlight July and August, add numbers to Column C for the July and August points, plus the previous point, June. In cell C7, enter the formula of =B7. Copy this formula to July and August.

2. Click on a blank area inside of the chart. A blue bounding box appears around B2:B13 in the worksheet. Drag the lower-right corner of the blue bounding box to the right to

Figure 3.27
Arrows can be used to emphasize the upward growth of sales.

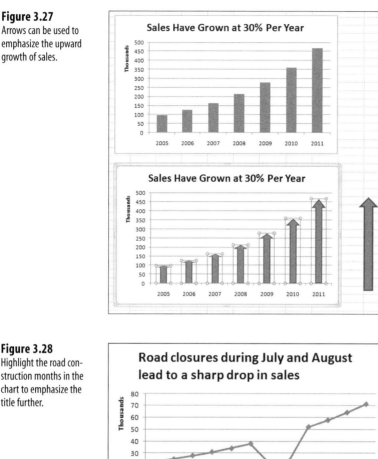

Figure 3.28
Highlight the road construction months in the chart to emphasize the title further.

extend the series to include the three values in Column C. Initially, this line shows up as a red line on top of a portion of the existing blue line.

3. On the Layout tab, use the Current Selection drop-down to select Series 2, which is the series you just added.

4. While Series 2 is selected, select Design, Change Chart Type. Select the first area chart thumbnail. Click OK. Excel draws a red area chart beneath the line segment of June through August.

5. On the Format tab, use the Current Selection drop-down to reselect Series 2. Open the Shape Fill drop down. Choose a grey fill color. The 4th row, 1st column offers a tooltip f White, Background 1, Darker 25% and is suitable.

The top chart in Figure 3.29 shows the gray highlight extending from the horizontal axis up to the data line for the two line segments. Alternatively, you can replace the numbers in Column C with 70,000 to draw a gray rectangle behind the months, as shown in the bottom chart in Figure 3.29.

Figure 3.29
A second series with only three points is used to highlight a section of the chart.

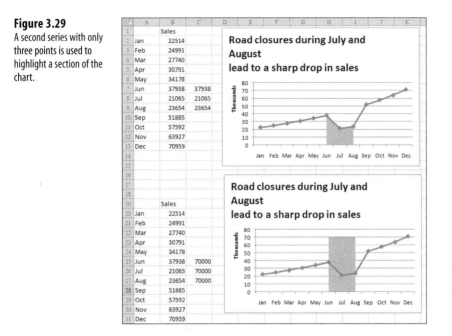

Changing Line Type Midstream

Consider the top chart in Figure 3.30. The title indicates that cash balances improved after a new management team arrived. This chart initially seems to indicate an impressive turnaround. However, if you study the chart axis carefully, you see that the final Q3 and Q4 numbers are labeled Q3F and Q4F to indicate that they are forecast numbers.

It is misleading to represent forecast numbers as part of the actual results line. It would be ideal if you change the line type at that point to indicate that the last two data points are forecasts. To do so, follow these steps:

1. Change the heading above Column B from Cash Balances to Actual.
2. Add the new heading Forecast in Column C.
3. Because the last actual data point is for Q2 of 2011, move the numbers for Q3 and Q4 of 2011 from Column B to Column C.
4. To force Excel to connect the actual and the forecast line, copy the last actual data point (the 7 for Q2) over to the Forecast column. This one data point—the connecting point for the two lines—will be in both the Forecast and Actual columns.

Figure 3.30
It is not clear in the top chart that the last two points are forecasts.

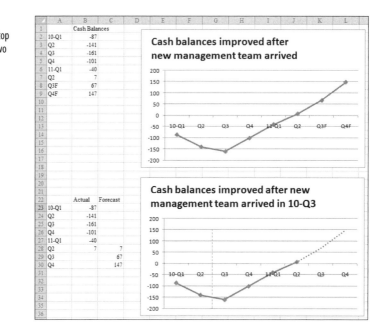

5. Change the last two labels in Column A from Q3F to just Q3 and from Q4F to just Q4.

6. Click the existing chart. A bounding box appears around B2:B9. Grab the lower-right blue handle and drag outward to encompass B2:C9. A second series is added to the chart as a red line.

7. On the Layout tab, select Legend, Legend at Right.

8. Click the red line. In the Format tab, you should see that the Current Selection drop-down indicates Series "Forecast."

9. Select Format, Shape Outline, Dashes and then select the fourth dash option. The red line changes to a dashed line.

10. While the forecast series is selected, select Design, Change Chart Type. Select a chart type that does not have markers.

11. The chart title indicates that a new management team arrived, but it does not indicate when the team arrived. To fix this, change the title to indicate that the team arrived in Q3 of 2010.

12. On the Insert tab, select Shapes, Line. Draw a vertical line between Q2 and Q3 of 2010, holding down the Shift key while drawing to keep the line vertical.

13. While the line is selected, on the Format tab, select Shape Outline, Dashes and then select the fourth dash option to make the vertical line a dashed line. Note that this line is less prominent than the series line because the weight of the line is only 1.25 point.

The final chart is shown at the bottom of Figure 3.30.

Adding an Automatic Trendline to a Chart

In the previous example, an analyst had created a forecast for the next two quarters. However, sometimes you might want to allow Excel to make a prediction based on past results. In these situations, Excel offers a trendline feature in which Excel draws a straight line that fits the existing data points. You can ask Excel to extrapolate the trendline into the future. If your data series contains blank points that represent the future, Excel can automatically add the trendline. I regularly use these charts to track my progress toward a goal or trendline.

The easiest way to add a trendline is to build a data series that includes all the days that the project is scheduled to run. In Figure 3.31, Column A contains the days of the month and Column B contains 125 for each data point. Therefore, Excel draws a straight line across the chart showing the goal at the end of the project. Column C shows the writing progress I should make each day. In this particular month, I am assuming that I will write an equal number of pages six days per week. Column D, which is labeled Actual, is where I record the daily progress toward the goal.

The chart is created as a line chart with the gridlines and legend removed. The trendline is formatted as a lighter gray. The actual line is formatted as a thick line. The top chart in Figure 3.31 shows the chart before the trendline is complete. Notice that the thick line is not quite above the progress line.

Figure 3.31
In the top chart, the actual line is running behind the target line, but it seems close.

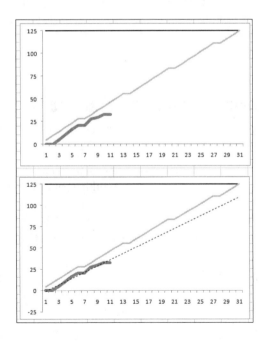

3

To add a trendline, follow these steps:

1. Right-click the series line for the Actual column. Select Add Trendline.

2. The Format Trendline dialog offers to add exponential, linear, logarithmic, polynomial, power, or moving average trendlines. Select a linear trendline.

3. In the Trendline Name section, either leave the name as Linear (Actual) or enter a custom name such as Forecast.

4. When forecasting forward or backward for a certain number of periods, leave both of those settings at 0 because this chart already has data points for the entire month. There are also settings where Excel shows the regression equation on the chart. Add this if you desire.

5. Right-click the trendline to select it. On the Format tab, select Shape Outline, Dashes and then select the fourth dash option. Also, select Shape Outline, Weight, 3/4 point.

The trendline is shown at the bottom of Figure 3.31. In this particular case, the trendline extrapolates that if I continue writing at the normal pace, I will miss the deadline by 15 pages or so.

> **CAUTION**
>
> Excel's trendline is not an intelligent forecasting system. It merely fits past points to a straight line and extrapolates that data. It works great as a motivational tool. For example, the current example shows that it would take a few days of above-average production before the trendline would project that the goal would be met.

Showing a Trend of Monthly Sales and Year-to-Date Sales

In accounting, sales are generally tracked every month. However, in the big picture you are interested in how 12 months add up to produce annual sales.

The top chart in Figure 3.32 is a poor attempt to show both monthly sales and accumulated year-to-date (YTD) sales. The darker bars are the monthly results, while the lighter bars are the accumulated YTD numbers through the current month. To show the large YTD number for November, the scale of the axis needs to extend to $400,000. However, this makes the individual monthly bars far too small for the reader to be able to discern any differences.

The solution is to plot the YTD numbers against a secondary vertical axis. My preference is that after you change the axis for one series, you should also change the chart type for that series. Follow these steps to create the bottom chart in Figure 3.32:

1. Left-click one of the YTD bars to select the YTD series. Right-click the selected series and select Format Data Series. Excel displays the Format Data Series dialog.

Figure 3.32
The size of the YTD bars obscures the detail of the monthly bars.

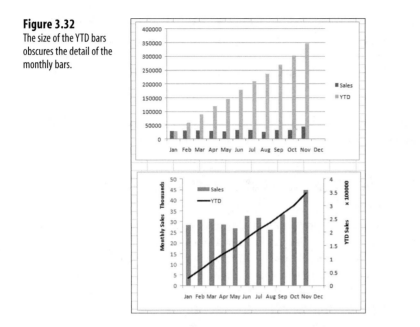

2. In the Format Data Series dialog, select Secondary Axis in the Plot Series On section of the Series Options page. Click Close. Excel creates a confusing chart, where the YTD numbers appear directly on top of the monthly numbers, obscuring any monthly numbers beyond August.

3. Excel deselects the series when you change the chart type. Reselect the YTD series by clicking the YTD line.

4. On the Format dialog, select Shape Outline, Black to change the YTD line to black.

5. From the Layout tab, turn off the gridlines by selecting Gridlines, None.

6. From the Layout tab, select Axes, Primary Vertical Axis, Show Axis in Thousands.

7. From the Layout tab, select Axis Titles, Primary Vertical Axis Title, Rotated Title. Type `Monthly Sales` and press Enter.

8. From the Layout tab, select Axis Titles, Secondary Vertical Axis Title, Rotated Title. Type `YTD` and press Enter.

9. Right-click the numbers on the secondary vertical axis. Select Format Axis. In the Scaling section, select 100,000.

10. Click the legend and drag it to appear in the upper-left corner of the plot area.

11. Click the plot area to select it. Drag one of the resizing handles on the right side of the plot area to drag it right to fill the space that used to be occupied by the title.

12. To present your charts in color, change the color of text in the primary vertical axis to match the color of the monthly bars. To change the color, click the numbers to select them. Use the Font Color drop-down on the Home tab to select a color such as blue. This color cue helps the reader realize that the blue left axis corresponds to the blue bars.

The resulting chart is shown at the bottom of Figure 3.32. The chart illustrates both the monthly trend of each month's sales and the progress toward a final YTD revenue number.

Understanding the Shortcomings of Stacked Column Charts

In a stacked column chart, Series 2 is plotted directly on top of Series 1. Series 3 is plotted on top of Series 2, and so on. The problem with this type of chart is that the reader can't tell whether the total is increasing or decreasing. The reader might not also be able to tell if Series 1 is increasing or decreasing. However, because all the other series have differing start periods, it is nearly impossible to tell whether sales in Series 2, 3, or 4 are increasing or decreasing. For example, in the top chart in Figure 3.33, it is nearly impossible for the reader to tell which regions are responsible for the increase from 2004 to 2009.

Stacked column charts are appropriate when the message of the chart is about the first series. In the lower chart in Figure 3.33, the message is that the acquisition of a new product line saved the company. If this new product line had not grown quickly, the company would have had to rely on aging product lines that were losing money. Because this message is about the sales of the new product line, you can plot this as the first series so the reader of the chart can see the impact from that series.

Using a Stacked Column Chart to Compare Current Sales to Prior-Year Sales

The chart in Figure 3.34 uses a combination of a stacked column chart and a line chart. The stacked column chart shows this year's sales, broken out into same-store sales and new-store sales. In this case, the same-store sales are plotted as the first series in white. The new-store sales are the focus and are plotted in black.

The third series, which is plotted as a dotted line chart, shows the prior-year sales. While the total height of the column is greater than last year's sales, there is some underlying problem in the old stores. In many cases, the height of the white column does not exceed the height of the dotted line, indicating that sales at same store are down.

The process of creating this combination chart involves a few steps during which the chart looks completely wrong. During those steps, overlook the chart and keep progressing through the steps, as follows:

1. Set up your data with months in Column A, old-store sales for this year in Column B, new-store sales for this year in Column C, and last year's sales in Column D.

Figure 3.33
In the top chart, readers are not able to draw conclusions about the growth of the three regions located at the top of the chart.

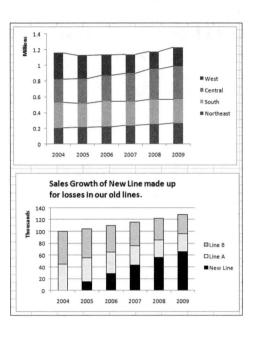

Figure 3.34
Current-year sales are shown as a stacked column chart, with last year's sales as a dotted line.

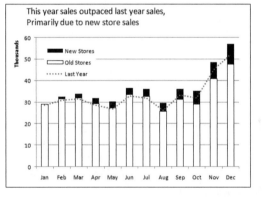

2. Select cells A1:D13 and create a stacked column chart. Initially, Excel stacks prior-year sales on top of the other sales, and you have a chart that is not remotely close to the expected outcome.

3. Click the top bar to select the third series. Select Design, Change Chart Type, Line Chart. An important distinction here is that the first two series are plotted as stacked charts. The third series is plotted as a regular line, not as a stacked line.

4. Use the Format tab to format the third series as a dotted line. Format the colors of the first two series as shown in Figure 3.34.

Shortcomings of Showing Many Trends on a Single Chart

Instead of using a stacked column chart, you might try to show many trendlines on a single line chart, which can be confusing. For example, in the top chart in Figure 3.35, the sales trends of five companies create a very confusing chart.

Figure 3.35
Instead of using a single chart with five confusing lines, compare your company to each other competitor in smaller charts.

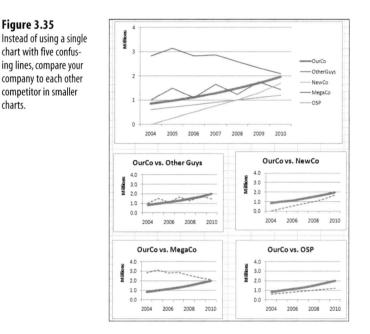

If the goal is to compare the sales results of your company against those of each major competitor, consider using four individual charts instead, as shown at the bottom of Figure 3.35. In these charts, the reader can easily see that your company is about to overtake the longtime industry leader MegaCo, but that quick growth from NewCo might still cause you to stay in the second position next year.

Next Steps

In Chapter 4, you will learn about charts used to make comparisons, including pie, radar, bar, donut, and waterfall charts.

Creating Charts That Show Differences

Comparing Entities

Whereas Chapter 3, "Creating Charts That Show Trends," was concerned with the progression of a trend over time, this chapter focuses on demonstrating the differences between entities. For example, you can use Excel charts to compare each sales region versus the others or your company versus the competitors. In addition, when you want to compare the differences among a handful of entities, a bar chart is the perfect choice because the reader can clearly see the differences between the entities.

The only time you should use a pie chart is when you want to show how components add up to a whole entity. Pie charts are vastly overused, and many guidelines contraindicate their use. You should often instead consider 100 percent stacked column charts, bar of pie charts, or pie of pie charts. These last charts are a bit tricky to master but have some amazing flexibility.

Finally, in this chapter you will learn how to use some more Excel trickery to build a waterfall chart. This type of chart is perfect for telling the story of how a whole entity breaks down into components.

Using Bar Charts to Illustrate Item Comparisons

Bar charts are perfect for comparing items. Bar charts offer a few advantages over column charts for comparing sales of various items:

- People tend to associate column charts—or any other chart in which the data progresses from left to right—as having a time-based component. When you turn the columns on their sides and make them horizontal bars, people tend not to read time into the equation.

■ With a bar chart, the category names can appear in a horizontal orientation, giving plenty of room for longer names. For example, in the chart shown in Figure 4.1, the category names take almost half the chart. However, there is room to get the point across that the "Excel for" series is not selling as well as the general-purpose Excel books.

Figure 4.1
A bar chart allows for lengthy category names and a comparison of different product lines.

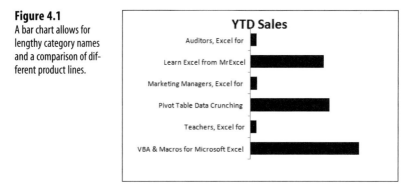

Bar charts are oriented with the first item in the list closest to the bottom of the chart. If you expect people to read a chart from top to bottom, you should sort the categories into descending alphabetical sequence by clicking the ZA button in the Data tab. The bar chart in Figure 4.1 compares sales of six different product lines. It is easy to spot the winners in the chart because the original data set is sorted to have the VBA title at the top of the spreadsheet.

Figure 4.1 uses a clustered bar chart type, although it has only one series to report. Other alternatives are the clustered bar in 3-D, clustered horizontal cylinder, clustered horizontal cone, or clustered horizontal pyramid. As mentioned in Chapter 3, cone and pyramid charts are bad because they misrepresent data; the same advice applies here.

→ For proof, **see** the "Lying with Shrinking Charts" section in Chapter 14, "Knowing When Someone Is Lying to You with a Chart."

For a more powerful arrangement of data, you can sort these categories by sales in ascending sequence. Excel then plots the largest category at the top of the chart. Even more than the chart in Figure 4.1, you can see that the chart in Figure 4.2 depicts a clearer delineation between the winners and losers than the chart in Figure 4.1.

If you think it is silly to sort your data into the reverse order from which you want to present it in the chart, there is a setting in the Format Axis dialog that you can use to correct this logic. Select Layout, Axes, Primary Vertical Axis, Show Right to Left Axis to show the first row in your data set at the top of the chart. Alternatively, you can right-click the category labels, select Format Axis, and select the Categories in Reverse Order check box (see Figure 4.3).

Figure 4.2
Sort the data by ascending sales in order to show the largest bars at the top of the chart.

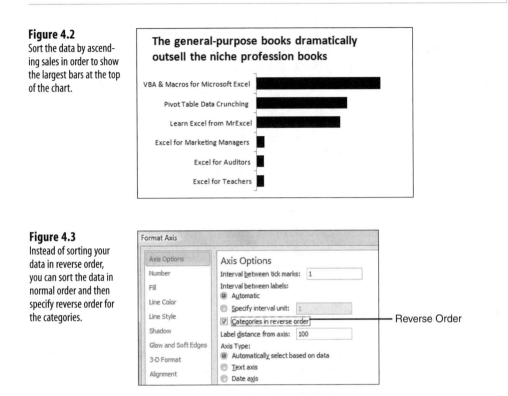

Figure 4.3
Instead of sorting your data in reverse order, you can sort the data in normal order and then specify reverse order for the categories.

Adding a Second Series to Show a Time Comparison

In Figure 4.4, two series are plotted on the bar chart. The original series presents sales data from this year. This data was moved to Series 2 to continue to be plotted as the top bar. The new Series 1 contains sales data from last year, for reference.

Figure 4.4
In this chart, the sales for this year are moved to Series 2. A new Series 1 shows sales from last year; a bit of additional data to show whether sales are increasing or decreasing.

Because the main message is current-year sales, those bars are formatted with a black fill to draw attention to them. The bars for last year are shown with white outlines.

The addition of data from the previous year adds a bit of context to the chart. The reader can tell that Products 2, 3, and 5 are new this year and have no sales history from the previous year. Product 4 was the previous market leader, but its sales have fallen off sharply. Product 1 has experienced good year-to-year growth; it will be interesting to see if the newly emerging products show similar growth in Year 2.

To create the chart in Figure 4.4, follow these steps:

1. Enter product names in Column A.

2. Enter last-year sales in Column B and this-year sales in Column C.

3. Sort the data so that the largest sales from this year are at the bottom of the chart.

4. From the Insert tab, select Bar, 2-D Bar, Clustered Bar.

5. Select Layout, Gridlines, Primary Vertical Gridlines, None.

6. Select Layout, Axes, Primary Horizontal Axis, None.

7. Select Layout, Legend, Show Legend at Top.

8. Select Layout, Chart Title, Above Chart.

9. Click in the title area. Type the first line of the title, press Enter, and type the second line of the title.

10. Click the outline of the title to exit Text Edit mode. On the Home tab, click the Left Align button and the Decrease Font Size button. Drag the title to the left.

11. Click a bar from this year. On the Format tab, select Shape Fill and then select black.

12. Right-click the black bar and select Format Data Series. Change the Series Overlap setting to 25 percent.

13. Click one of the bars for last year. On the Format tab, select Shape Fill, White. On the Format tab, select Shape Outline and then select black.

14. Grab one of the resizing handles in the corner of the chart and drag outward to resize the chart.

Subdividing a Bar to Emphasize One Component

Excel offers a stacked bar chart type that allows you to break a bar such as total sales to show components. In the top chart in Figure 4.5, only one component is called out. The subject of the chart is this one component of product cost, showing how Company A has a significant cost advantage.

You should use this chart type sparingly. The reader of the chart is able to make a judgment about the size of the black bar for the major subcomponent. The reader is also able to make a judgment about the total size of the bar. However, it is difficult to make a judgment about the size of the white component of the bars. Can you tell which company has the lowest other cost? (The answer is Company B.)

The problem becomes worse if you try to show more than two components in the stacked bar chart. For example, the bottom chart in Figure 4.5 is trying to compare the costs of four major components. However, the reader will not be able to learn anything about the additional components.

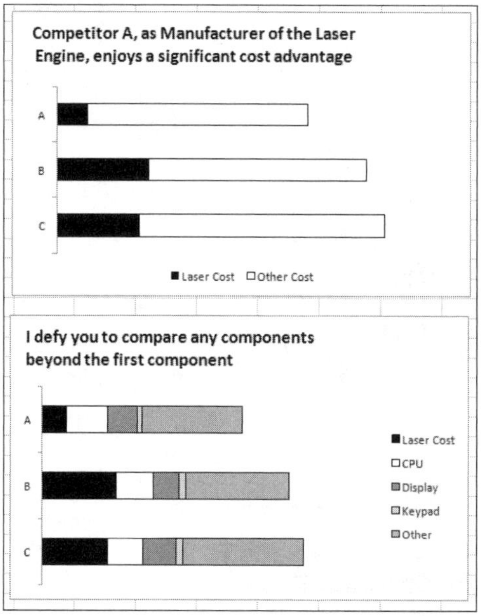

Figure 4.5
A stacked bar chart allows the reader to judge the size of the total bar and the first component bar. Beyond that, it is difficult to make a comparison from one bar to the next.

NOTE The charts in Figure 4.5 were created using Insert, Bar, 2-D Bar, Stacked Bar selection. The individual segments of each bar were formatted using Format, Shape Fill.

Showing Component Comparisons

A component comparison chart is useful when you want to show several parts that add up to a whole. You can use this type of chart to show these concepts:

- The market share of several competitors in a market
- The cost breakdown of a product by subcomponent
- The breakdown of time spent in a day
- The relative size of five major customers and all other customers as a group

These are also all great concepts to show using a pie chart or a 100 percent stacked bar/ column chart. Unfortunately, pie charts are overused in business today. People try to use pie charts to compare items that do not add up to a whole. For example, in Figure 4.6, someone tried to use a pie chart to compare product prices. Without reading the individual prices labeling each pie slice, it is difficult to figure out whether the Hummer H3 or the

Ford Escape hybrid costs more. As discussed in the previous section, using a bar chart is best when you are trying to compare items. The bottom chart in Figure 4.6 shows the same data as the pie chart. However, in this case, it is plotted on a bar chart, which makes it easier to understand.

Figure 4.6
An attempt to use a pie chart to compare prices is misguided. The bar chart in the lower half of the figure is more effective.

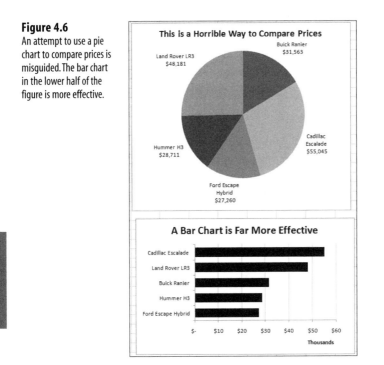

Some of the frustrations with pie charts are humorously summarized by Dick DeBartolo, *Mad*'s Maddest Writer, in the chart in Figure 4.7 that he prepared for this book.

DESIGNING LIKE THE PROS

Dick Debartolo has been writing for *Mad* magazine for more than 40 years. If you are a fan of *Mad*, check out his book, *Good Days and MAD: A Hysterical Tour Behind the Scenes at MAD Magazine*. Dick also hosts the Daily Giz Wiz podcast, which is a review of the latest gadgets and those gadgets that once seemed like a good idea but are now collecting dust in Dick's Gadget Warehouse.

When you are performing component comparisons, the following chart types are effective:

■ A pie chart is appropriate when you are comparing 2 to 5 components.

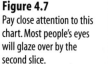

Figure 4.7
Pay close attention to this chart. Most people's eyes will glaze over by the second slice.

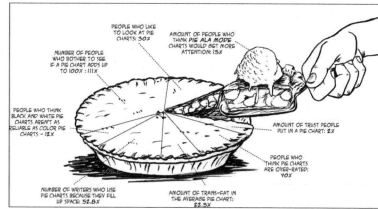

■ A pie of pie chart is appropriate for comparing 6 to 10 components.

■ A bar of pie chart can handle 6 to 15 components.

■ You should use a 100 percent stacked column chart when you want to have two or more pies such as to compare market share from this year to last year. The 100 percent stacked bar, 100 percent stacked line, and 100 percent stacked area are all variations of the 100 percent stacked column chart.

■ A doughnut chart is a strange chart that can occasionally be used to compare two pie charts. However, a 100 percent stacked column chart is usually better for this type of comparison.

Figure 4.8 illustrates when to use which type of chart.

Figure 4.8
Choose the proper type of pie chart based on the number of categories in your data.

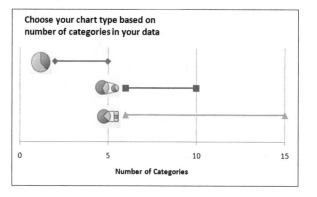

The following sections describe the ins and outs of using pie, 100 percent stacked column, and the other previously mentioned charts.

Using Pie Charts

Pie charts are great for comparing two to five different components. You typically select a range that contains category labels in Column A and values in Column B. Often, the categories are sorted so that the largest value is at the top and the remaining categories are sorted in descending order.

To create a pie chart, from the Insert tab, select the Pie drop-down, as shown in Figure 4.9. The following six icons are located in this drop-down:

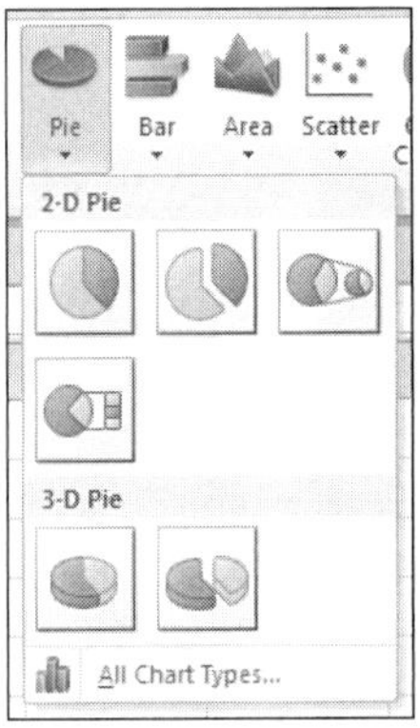

Figure 4.9
You commonly use the first icon to create a 2-D pie chart.

- ■ **2-D Pie**—The pie chart type used most frequently.
- ■ **2-D Exploded Pie**—There is no need to choose this type of pie chart since you can explode a pie or a slice of pie later. This technique is discussed later in this chapter in the "Highlighting One Slice of a Pie by Exploding" section.
- ■ **Pie of Pie or Bar of Pie**—Both of these chart types are effective for dealing with data sets that have too many slices and when you care about the small pie slices.
- ■ **3-D Pie**—This is a regular pie chart tipped on its side so you can see the "edge" of the pie. This is a cool effect when you are trying to decorate a PowerPoint chart. However, it is not as effective if you want someone to read and understand the data.
- ■ **Exploded Pie in 3-D**—This is another option that you probably do not want to choose since you can explode a pie using techniques discussed later in this chapter.

The default pie chart has no labels and includes a legend on the right side to help identify the pie slices. Initially, the first data item appears starting at the 12 o'clock position, and additional wedges appear in a clockwise direction, as shown in Figure 4.10.

In black and white, it is particularly difficult to match the tiny color swatches used in the legend with the pie slices. For this reason, you nearly always want to delete the legend and add data labels, as discussed in the next section.

Excel offers seven built-in layouts for a pie chart. All the layouts that include labels add them inside the pie slices. If you would add a blank font to the pie wedges in Figure 4.10, the font will not be legible on the dark pie slices.

Figure 4.10
The default pie chart uses a legend that is too small and too far from the chart to be effective.

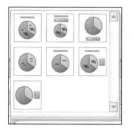

Labeling a Pie Chart

Because a pie chart does not have a lengthy axis running along one edge of the chart, choosing the data labels is an important consideration. Instead of using the built-in Data Label choices on the Layout tab, you can select More Data Label Options from the Data Labels drop-down on the Layout tab. Excel displays the Label Options page of the Format Data Labels dialog, as shown in Figure 4.11.

Figure 4.11
Use the More Data Labels option in the Layout tab to build effective pie chart labels.

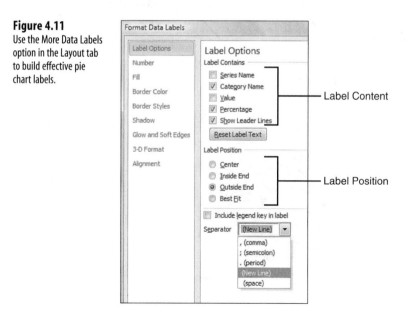

You have options for what the label should contain including the following options:

- **Series Name**—This option does not make sense in a pie chart since every slice has a series name, such as Sales.
- **Category Name**—Choose this option to show the names of items represented by the individual pie slices. When you turn this item on, you can set Legend to None.
- **Value**—Choose this option to show the actual numeric value for this slice from the cells in the spreadsheet. Either the Value or Percentage numeric values are used most often.
- **Percentage**—Choose this option to have Excel calculate the percentage of the pie allocated to each pie slice. This is a number that is not typically in your spreadsheet.
- **Show Leader Lines**—It is recommended that you leave this setting on. If you later reposition a label, Excel draws a line from the label to the pie slice associated with that label.
- **Label Position**—The usual choices for the label position on a pie chart are to either show the label outside the pie slice, indicated by Outside End, or inside the pie slice, indicated by Center.

The final choice in the Label Options page of the Format Data Labels dialog is the Separator drop-down. This option becomes important when you have chosen two items in the Label Contains section. For example, if you have selected Category Name and Percentage, Excel's default choice for a comma as the separator shows the label East, 33 percent. To remove the comma from the pie chart labels, choose either (space) or (New Line) from the Separator drop-down.

Figure 4.12 shows a pie chart with category names and percentages at the outside end of each slice. The data label is separated by a new line character.

Figure 4.12
Displaying the labels at the outside end ensures that the labels can be read.

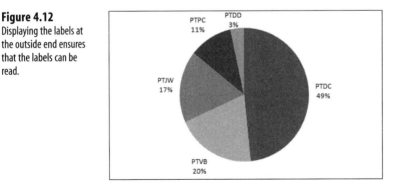

Rotating a Pie Chart

There is an ongoing argument about the rotation of a pie chart. Many people say that the first pie slice should start at the 12 o'clock position, and subsequent pie slices should appear in a clockwise direction. I disagree with this philosophy, from a purely practical point of view. I think that the smallest pie slices should be rotated around so that they appear in the lower-right corner of the pie. This location provides the most room for the labels of the small pie slices to appear without overlapping.

You have control over the rotation of a pie chart. You can right-click a pie chart and select Format Data Series. On the Options dialog that appears, you can change the setting for Angle of First Slice. For example, in Figure 4.13, the bottom pie chart has been rotated 195 degrees, which prevents labels from appearing on top of each other.

Figure 4.13
You can change the angle of first slice to rotate the pie until the data labels have the most room to appear without overlapping each other.

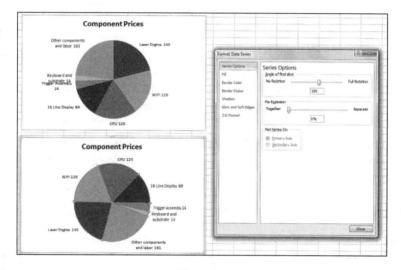

Moving an Individual Pie Slice Label

In a pie chart that has long category names and many slices, you may not be able to find an angle of rotation that enables all the labels to have sufficient room. In this case, you need to move an individual pie slice label.

The first time you click a data label, all the data labels are selected. At this point, you can use icons on the Home tab to change the font or font size.

Clicking a second time on a data label selects only that particular label. You can click the border of the label and drag it to a new position. If the Leader Lines option remains selected (refer to Figure 4.11), Excel automatically connects the label and the pie slice with a leader line. In Figure 4.14, the label for the keyboard has been moved so that it does not crash into the label for the trigger assembly.

Highlighting One Slice of a Pie by Exploding

The first time you click a pie selects the data series, which means it selects all the pie slices. If you then drag outward from the center of the pie, you explode all the slices of the pie.

Figure 4.14
After a second single-click, only one label is selected. You can drag an individual data label into a new position.

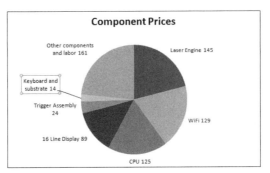

CAUTION

If you want to explode the whole pie, you have to be fairly deliberate about it. If you click once to select all the slices and then click again to drag the slices outward, the second click selects only a single slice. Click outside the pie to select the entire chart, and then click the pie and drag outward. This action selects the pie and explodes it in a single step.

The charts in Figure 4.15 show various levels of explosion. The top-left chart uses a 15 percent explosion factor. Excel allows you to specify up to a 400 percent explosion factor, which really looks pretty silly.

Figure 4.15
Drag outward while a data series is selected to select the entire pie.

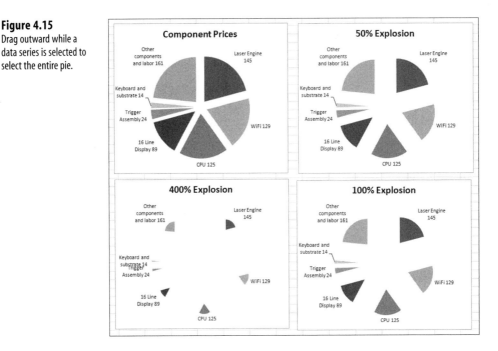

A better technique is to explode just the one slice that is the subject of the pie. For example, in Figure 4.16, a large order cannot ship because of shortages of a tiny assembly. The plant managers had previously decided to cut safety stock on this component. To illustrate that this might have been a poor decision, you can explode just that slice of the pie.

Figure 4.16
You can explode one piece of the pie to call attention to that piece.

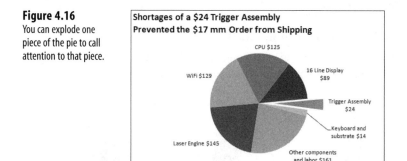

To explode one slice of the pie, click once on the pie to select the entire series. Then click the slice in question one more time to select only that slice. Drag the individual slice outward to explode only that slice, as shown in Figure 4.16.

Highlighting One Slice of a Pie with Color

Instead of exploding a slice of a pie, you can highlight that slice using a contrasting color. A single black pie slice in an otherwise white pie instantly draws the reader's eye, as shown in Figure 4.17.

Figure 4.17
You can plot one slice of the pie in a contrasting color to draw attention to that slice.

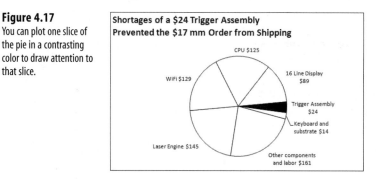

To format the chart as shown in Figure 4.17, follow these steps:

1. Click anywhere on the pie to select the entire pie.
2. On the Format tab, select Shape Fill, White. The entire pie disappears.

3. On the Format tab, select Shape Outline and then select black. The pie is now a white pie outlined in black.

4. Click the one pie slice that you want to highlight.

5. On the Format tab, select Shape Fill and then select black. The single pie slice now stands out from the other slices.

Switching to a 100 Percent Stacked Column Chart

It is difficult for a reader to track the trends from one pie to the next when you are trying to show a trend by using multiple pie charts, as shown in Figure 4.18.

Figure 4.18
It is hard to track trends by looking at multiple pies.

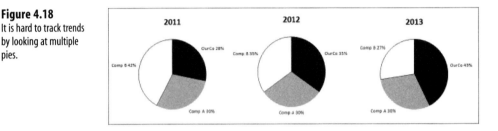

Instead of using pie charts, you can switch to one of Excel's 100 percent charts. For example, in the 100 percent stacked column chart, Excel stacks the values from Series 1, Series 2, Series 3, and so on but scales the column so that each column is exactly the same height. This gives the effect of dividing a column into components, just as in a pie chart.

Excel offers 100 percent versions of column charts, bar charts, area charts, and line charts. To find them, in the Insert Chart dialog, look for charts where both the left and right elements are the same height (see Figure 4.19).

Figure 4.19
These icons all create 100 percent stacked charts.

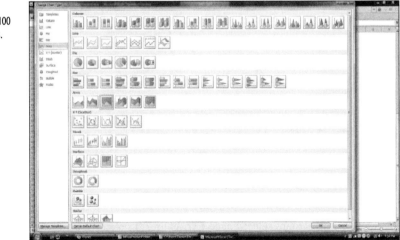

Figure 4.20 shows examples of 100 percent stacked column, area, bar, and line charts. The 100 percent stacked column chart is probably the easiest to interpret. In a 100 percent stacked chart, the reader is able to judge the growth or decline of both the first series and the last series.

Figure 4.20
For year-over-year comparisons, a 100 percent stacked column chart is easier to read than multiple pie charts.

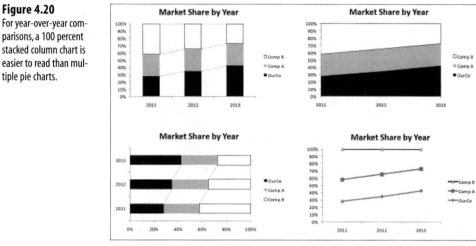

Using a Doughnut Chart to Compare Two Pies

Excel offers another chart type—the doughnut chart—that attempts to compare multiple pies. In a doughnut chart, one pie chart encircles another pie chart.

A reader of the chart in Figure 4.21 can see that the market share for OurCo increased between 2012 and 2013 and that the market share for Comp B decreased between 2012 and 2013. However, it is unlikely that the reader can draw any conclusions about Comp A based on this chart.

In creating the chart in Figure 4.21, you need to go through a number of maddening steps, including the steps listed here:

- Select Layout, Data Labels, More Data Label Options, and then choose to show only the series name as the label. You probably need to leave the legend turned on with this chart because there is not space to legibly fit OurCo 2012 in the thin ring of the doughnut.

- Changing the colors using the Format tab is a tedious process. You cannot format both OurCo sections simultaneously. Instead, click the 2006 ring, and then click 2012 OurCo. Select Format, Shape Fill, and then select black. Repeat these steps for the other five pieces of the doughnut chart.

- To make some data labels white, select the labels for Series 1, then select just one label, and then use the Font Color drop-down on the Home tab. Repeat this step for OurCo for Series 2.

4

Figure 4.21
Doughnut charts are generally difficult to read, although this one does effectively communicate some information.

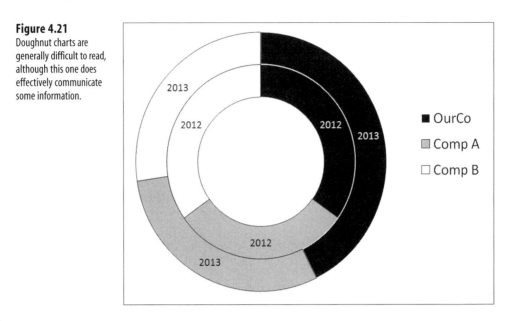

One interesting setting for the doughnut chart is the doughnut hole size. When you right-click the inner series of the doughnut chart and select Format Data Series, the Format dialog box appears. You can use this dialog to change the doughnut hole size—valid values range from 10 percent to 90 percent. The doughnut chart in Figure 4.22 uses a hole size of 10 percent. Reducing the hole size makes the chart more readable in this case.

Figure 4.22
Reduce the doughnut hole size to allow more room for labels on the chart.

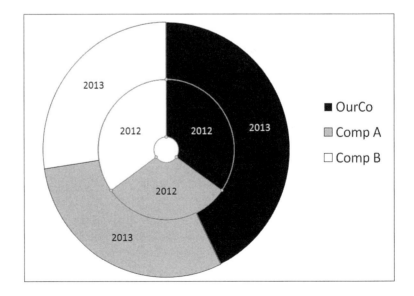

Dealing with Data Representation Problems in a Pie Chart

The 80/20 rule comes into play with pie charts. In many component comparisons, 20 percent of the categories make up 80 percent of the pie. In this case, the tiny pie slices at the end of the pie contain too much detail and are not useful. If you attempt to leave these slices in the pie, the labels needlessly complicate the chart, as shown in Figure 4.23.

As noted in the "Using Pie Charts" section earlier in this chapter, there are several methods that enable you to create the chart shown in Figure 4.23. For example, you can rotate a pie chart and move individual pie labels. However, the process is tedious with this amount of data.

Figure 4.23
The 20 pie slices make this chart difficult to read.

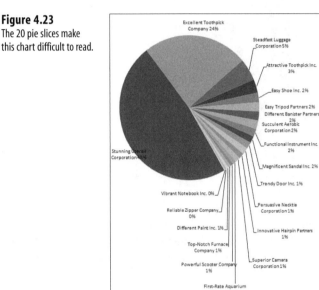

In addition, the data used in Figure 4.23 may not be entirely realistic. Usually, a company has a few major accounts and dozens of minor accounts. If you need a list of all your accounts, you should really show it in a table that lists the customers, sorted in descending sequence.

Usually a pie chart is focused on the top four to five accounts. The message for the reader of the chart in Figure 4.23 is that two major accounts make up 75 percent of the revenue stream. If anything happens to either of those accounts, this company will be in for tough times. To communicate this message, you can replace the last 16 pie slices with a single slice labeled 16 Other Accounts.

Other times you may need to show the detail of the small accounts such as to grow some new mega-customers. In this case, you can switch to a bar of pie or pie of pie chart. These options are discussed in the next sections.

Replacing Smaller Slices with an Other Customer Summary

Replacing smaller slices with an Other Customer summary does not require magic. Instead, you look through your customer list and identify a logical breakpoint between major customers and customers that should be listed as "other."

The example shown in Figure 4.24 includes two customers that are not exactly major to help communicate how quickly sales fall off.

Figure 4.24
The low-tech solution is to add a formula to the worksheet to total all the smaller accounts.

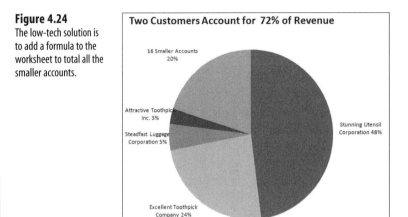

To create this chart, insert a few blank rows to separate the major accounts from the other accounts. In the worksheet, add the label 16 Smaller Accounts. Then enter a SUM function to total all the smaller customers. Finally, change the chart range to include only the major customers and the Other line.

> **TIP**
> You do not have to re-create the chart to specify a new data range. If you click once on the chart, Excel draws a blue rectangle around the data included in the chart. Grab the blue resizing handle at the bottom of the data range and drag upward to include only the major customers and the Other Total row.

In Figure 4.24, the chart is less busy than in Figure 4.23. The title has been improved, and each data label now includes both the category name and percentage.

Using a Pie of Pie Chart

A pie of pie chart shows the smallest pie slices in a new, secondary pie chart. The true volume of the small slices is shown in a slice marked Other in the original pie. Series lines extend from the Other slice to the secondary pie.

This chart type can be used when the focus of your chart is the small slices such as when the focus is on the emerging markets (see Figure 4.25). Together, the five markets in this chart account for a 19 percent share. However, the markets are not doing equally well. The pie of pie chart shows which of the new markets are growing the fastest.

Figure 4.25
A secondary pie shows the detail of the emerging markets.

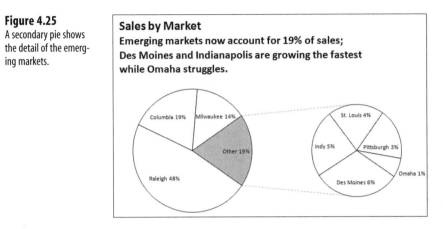

Sales by Market
Emerging markets now account for 19% of sales;
Des Moines and Indianapolis are growing the fastest
while Omaha struggles.

→ Creating the chart in Figure 4.25 requires some tricky steps that are described later in this chapter, in the "Customizing the Split in the 'Of Pie' Charts" section.

Several interesting settings are available in the "of pie" charts. In both the pie of pie and bar of pie charts, you can control the size of the secondary plot compared to the primary pie. You can control the gap between the plots and choose whether the series lines extend from one chart to the next. To access these settings, click inside the chart but outside the pie to deselect the pie. Then right-click the pie and select Format Data Series, and then the Format Data Series dialog appears, as shown in Figure 4.26.

To see a demo of creating pie-of-pie charts, search for MrExcel Charts 4 at YouTube.

In the Format Data Series dialog, you can set the gap between the pies from 0 percent to 500 percent. The gap size is expressed as a percentage of the radius of the main pie. In other words, when you select 100 percent, the gap between the pies is equal to the radius of the main pie, which is 50 percent of the width of the main pie.

You can also set the secondary plot size to be anywhere from 5 percent to 200 percent of the main pie chart. The default setting is 75 percent.

Adjusting either the gap setting or the secondary plot size changes the size of both pies. If you make either the gap or the secondary plot size larger, Excel has to make the main pie smaller in order to fit all three elements into the same plot area. This requires a little bit of high school algebra. For example, if the plot area is 500 pixels wide and the width of the main pie is a variable n, you might encounter these settings:

Figure 4.26
The pie of pie and bar of pie charts offer new settings in the Series Options tab of the Format Data Series dialog.

- With a gap of 100 percent and a secondary plot size of 75 percent, the original pie is n pixels wide, the gap is $0.5n$ pixels wide, and the secondary pie is $0.75n$ pixels wide. This means the total width is $2.25n=500$, so n is 222. This results in a main pie width of 222 pixels, a gap of 111 pixels, and a secondary plot size of 166.50.

- If you increase the secondary plot size to 100 percent and increase the gap to 150 percent, the original pie is n pixels wide, the gap is $0.75n$ pixels wide, and the secondary pie is n pixels wide. This means the total width is $2.75n=500$. The main pie is 181 wide, the gap is 136 wide, and the secondary pie is 181 pixels wide.

Basically, as you increase the size of either setting, the main pie gets smaller. Table 4.1 shows the horizontal size of the main pie, the gap, and the secondary pie for various combinations of gap width and secondary plot size. For example, the main pie can occupy as much as 83 percent of the plot area width if you select a 0 percent gap and a secondary plot size of 20 percent. As you increase the gap and secondary plot size, you might end up with a main pie that occupies as little as 18 percent of the width of the plot area.

Here is an example of how to read the table. The first cell in the table indicates 83%/0%/17%. This means that if you choose a secondary plot size of 20% and a gap size of 0%, then the main pie occupies 83% of the width, the gap is 0%, and the secondary plot occupies 17%. This happens because 17% is 20% of 83%.

For another example, read across row 2. In all of these examples, the secondary plot is to be 50% of the primary pie. In the first column, with a gap size of 0%, the main pie takes 67%, the gap is 0%, and the secondary pie is 33%. Move right to the 100% Gap Size column. Now, the gap is set to be 100% of the second pie. The table shows 50%/25%/25%

meaning that the main pie takes up 50% of the width, the gap takes up 25% of the width, and the second pie takes up 25% of the width.

Table 4.1   Width of Main Pie/Gap/Second Pie

	Gap Size				
Secondary Plot Size	**0%**	**50%**	**100%**	**250%**	**500%**
20%	83%/0%/17%	69%/17%/14%	59%/29%/12%	41%/51%/8%	27%/68%/5%
50%	67%/0%/33%	57%/14%/29%	50%/25%/25%	36%/45%/18%	25%/63%/13%
75%	57%/0%/43%	50%/13%/38%	44%/22%/33%	33%/42%/25%	24%/59%/18%
100%	50%/0%/50%	44%/11%/44%	40%/20%/40%	31%/38%/31%	22%/56%/22%
150%	40%/0%/60%	36%/9%/55%	33%/17%/50%	27%/33%/40%	20%/50%/30%
200%	33%/0%/67%	31%/8%/62%	29%/14%/57%	24%/29%/47%	18%/45%/36%

Figure 4.27 shows the extremes for the gap size and secondary plot size settings.

Figure 4.27
Changing the gap width and secondary plot size can create vastly different looks for the chart.

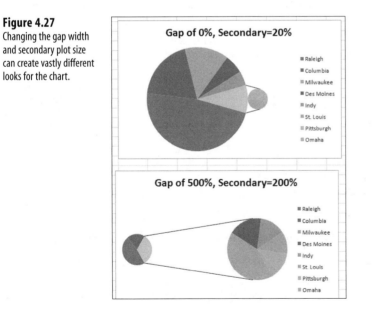

Excel also offers a robust system for choosing which slices should be in the secondary plot. The following section applies to both pie of pie and bar of pie charts.

Customizing the Split in the "Of Pie" Charts

With an "of pie" chart, you have absolute control over which slices appear in the main pie and which slices are sent to the secondary plot. Excel offers a surprising array of ways to control this setting.

When you right-click the pie and select Format Data Series, the Format Data Series dialog appears. The top setting in the dialog is the drop-down Split Series By, which offers the following options:

■ **Split Series by Position**—You can change the spin button to indicate that the last n values should be shown in the secondary pie. Excel then uses the last n values from the original data set in the secondary pie.

■ **Split Series by Value**—When you enter a value in the text box, Excel moves any slices with a value less than the entered value to the secondary pie.

■ **Split Series by Percentage Value**—You can use the spin button to enter a value from 1 percent to 99 percent. Any slices smaller than the entered percentage move to the secondary plot. Note that if there are no slices smaller than that value, the secondary plot appears as an empty black circle.

■ **Split Series by Custom**—This is a flexible setting where you can choose which slices to send to the secondary pie. After choosing Custom from the drop-down, you click an individual slice in the chart. Then, in the Format Data Point dialog, you indicate that the point belongs to the second plot or the first plot. You continue selecting additional slices in the chart and indicating the location for those points.

CASE STUDY: CREATING A PIE OF PIE CHART

At this point, you have enough information to create the chart shown previously in Figure 4.25. Follow these steps to create that chart:

1. Enter markets in Column A and sales in Column B.

2. Sort by sales in descending order.

3. Select the markets and sales cells.

4. From the Insert tab, select Pie, 2-D Pie, Pie of Pie. Excel creates a pie with three items in the secondary plot, a legend, and no labels.

5. From the Layout tab, select Legend, None.

6. Right-click the pie and select Format Data Series. Select Split Series by Position. Select Second Plot Contains the Last 5 Values.

7. With the entire pie still selected, select Shape Outline from the Format tab, and then select black. Select Shape Fill, White to outline all the pie slices but fill them with white.

8. From the Layout tab, select Data Labels, More Data Label Options. Select Category Name and Percentage. Clear the Value check box. Change the separator from a comma to a space.

9. Click the Other slice in the left pie. If the current selection drop-down in the Layout or Format tab does not indicate that you selected Series x, Point n, click the Other slice again.

10. From the Format tab, select Shape Fill, and then select light gray.

11. In the Current Selection drop-down of the Format tab, select Series Lines 1. In the Format tab, select Shape Outline and then select gray. Select Shape Outline, Dashes, and then select the fourth dash choice.

12. Enlarge the chart by clicking one of the resizing handles in the border around the chart. Drag out from the center to enlarge the chart.

13. If a chart title is not visible, on the Layout tab, select Chart Title, Above Chart.

14. Click in the chart title twice. Select the characters and type a new title such as Sales by Market, and then press the Enter key. Type the remaining three lines of the title.

15. Select the characters in the top line of the title. On the Home tab, select 20 Point. Select the remaining lines of the title. On the Home tab, select 18 Point.

16. Click the border of the title. On the Home tab, click Left Align. Drag the title so that it is left-justified above the chart.

Using a Bar of Pie Chart

The bar of pie chart is similar in concept to the pie of pie chart. In the case of bar of pie, the large slices are plotted on a main pie. The smaller slices are moved over to a column chart on the right side of the chart area. All the settings for gap width, series lines, secondary plot size, and which slices move to the second plot area are valid for the bar of pie chart.

Figure 4.28 shows a bar of pie chart. Technically, this should be called a column of pie chart.

Figure 4.28
In a bar of pie chart, the smaller slices are grouped into Other, and the detail is shown in a column chart.

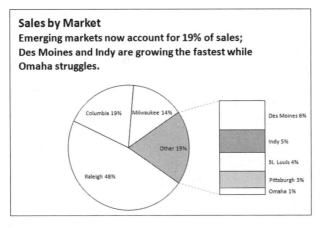

Using a Waterfall Chart to Tell the Story of Component Decomposition

As mentioned in Chapter 3, I spent a few months as a team member of a McKinsey & Company consulting gig when they were brought in to turn around the company where I used to work. McKinsey consultants were experts at creating cool charts including the waterfall chart that is closely associated with that firm.

The waterfall chart is a useful chart because it tells a story. For example, if you are an NPR fan, you might have listened to Ira Glass' "This American Life" weekly radio show. Glass describes the show as a series of stories in which, "this happens, and then this happens, and then this happens, and then this happens...." Similarly, a waterfall chart makes a simple table into a story.

For example, waterfall charts in Figure 4.29 is used to analyze the profitability of a proposal. The chart starts with a tall column on the left side to show the total list price of the products you are selling. The next column appears to float in midair, dropping down from the total list price column to show the total discount that the sales team is proposing. The next column shows net revenue. The rest of the chart is a series of floating columns that show where all the revenue went. A tiny column on the right side shows the profit from the deal.

Figure 4.29
A waterfall chart breaks a single component chart out over several columns.

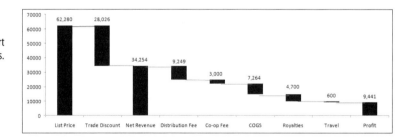

The trick to making the middle columns float is to use a stacked column chart. The second series is the actual columns that appear on the chart. The first series is changed into an invisible color without any lines in order to make the bars in the second series appear to float.

You might start with values such as those shown in Columns A and B of Figure 4.30. The trick to creating a waterfall chart is to move those values into two series. The second series is the height of each column that is actually seen. The first series is an invisible column that makes the other bars appear to float.

Follow these steps to create the chart shown in Figure 4.30:

1. For the three columns in the chart that touch the horizontal axis, set the invisible column to zero and the visible column to the number from Column B.

Figure 4.30
Break the series in
Column B into two series
in E and F.

	A	B	C	D	E	F
1					Invisible	Visible
2	List Price	62,280		List Price	0	62,280
3	Trade Discount	28,026		Trade Discount	34,254	28,026
4	Net Revenue	34,254		Net Revenue	0	34,254
5	Distribution Fee	9,249		Distribution Fee	25,005	9,249
6	Co-op Fee	3,000		Co-op Fee	22,005	3,000
7	COGS	7,264		COGS	14,741	7,264
8	Royalties	4,700		Royalties	10,041	4,700
9	Travel	600		Travel	9,441	600
10	Profit	9,441		Profit	0	9,441

2. The goal for trade discount is to have a floating bar that extends from 62,280 down to 34,254. To have the bar float at this level, you need an invisible bar that is 34,254 tall. Therefore, in cell E3, enter the formula =F4.

3. The height of the floating bar needs to extend from 34,254 to 62,280, so enter the formula =F2-E3 in cell F3.

4. After the Net Revenue bar are all the SG&A expenses. The height of each floating bar should be the amount of the expense. Therefore, in cell F5, enter the formula =B5. Copy this down to cells F6:F9.

5. The formula for the invisible portion of the bars is often difficult to figure out. In this case, starting at the final bar might make this easier. The Travel bar representing $600 needs to float just above the Profit bar of 9,441. Therefore, enter the formula =F10 in cell E9.

6. The Royalties bar of 4,700 needs to float just above the level of the Travel bar. The height of the Travel bar is the height of the invisible bar (9441 in E9) and the height of the visible bar (500 in F9). Therefore, in cell E8 enter =E9+F9. You now have a formula that can be copied.

7. Copy cell E8 to the blank cells in E7:E5.

8. Select the Range D1:F10. From the Insert tab, select Column, Stacked Column.

9. Turn off the legend by selecting Legend, None from the Layout tab.

10. Click the lower Trade Discount bar. On the Format tab, select Shape Fill, White. The lower columns disappear.

11. Select the top column. On the Format tab, select Shape Fill, and then select black.

12. Turn off the gridlines by selecting Gridlines, Primary Horizontal Gridlines, None on the Layout tab.

13. Right-click a top column and select Add Data Labels.

14. Grab each label individually and move it to the top of the column.

> **NOTE**
> Normally, you will choose to put the data labels at the outside end. However, because this is a stacked column chart, the outside end is not an option in the Format Data Labels dialog.

15. To finish the waterfall chart, you need to draw connecting lines from the bottom of one column to the next column. Therefore, on the Insert tab, select Shapes, Line. While holding down the Shift key, draw a line from the top of the first column to the top of the next column. Select Format, Shape Outline, and then select black to darken the line. Repeat this step to connect all the columns.

4

A waterfall chart can be used in many situations to turn a single component column chart into a whole-page chart. These charts present a dramatic picture of all the components in a process.

Creating a Stacked and Clustered Chart

In my seminars, people ask about creating both a stacked and clustered column for each time period, as shown in Figure 4.31. This type of chart can be used to show components of a cost figure compared to a total revenue figure.

Figure 4.31
Cost components stack up against revenue for each quarter.

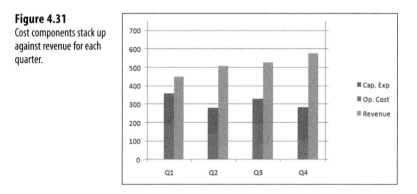

Creating this chart is fairly difficult in Excel because it combines both a stacked column chart and a clustered column chart. Even if you can figure out how to create this chart, Excel has roadblocks to prevent the chart from looking good.

Secret 1: Combining Stacked Columns and Clustered Columns

Say you started out with three series of data and create a stacked revenue chart as shown in Figure 4.32. You need to move the Revenue portion of the column next to stacked cost components.

Figure 4.32
Start with all series stacked.

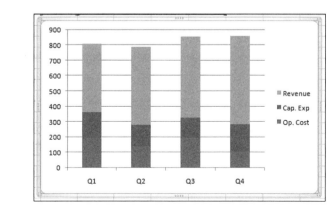

1. Double-click the Revenue portion of one of the columns. Excel displays the Format Data Series dialog.
2. Select Secondary Axis from the Plot Series On and click Close. By moving this series to the secondary axis, you can change the chart type for that one series.
3. With the Revenue series still selected, select Design, Change Chart Type. Select the first column chart, known as a clustered column chart.

The intermediate result shown in Figure 4.33 is horrible. Notice that the Revenue columns are plotted directly on top of the cost columns, making it impossible to see costs in Q2 and Q4.

Figure 4.33
Change Revenue to be a clustered column.

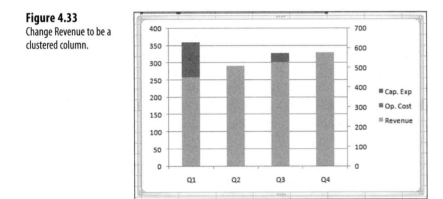

Secret 2: Moving a Series Over by Using Blank Series

To solve the problem in Figure 4.33, you can use another bit of chart magic—inserting some zero series to move the location of the revenue series.

> **NOTE** The following steps, which will solve this problem, assume that you deleted the chart from Figure 4.33 and are starting over.

1. Add two new series to your data table. Call them Blank 1 and Blank 2. Fill in zeros for these series.
2. Create a stacked column chart from the five series. Because you have five series and four quarters, Excel assumes that the Quarters should be category labels instead of series. Click the Switch Row/Column data in the Design tab to correct this.
3. Double-click the Revenue portion of the column and select Secondary Axis.
4. You need to format the blank series, but since they are zero, you cannot format them by double-clicking. Open the first drop-down in the Layout tab and select Series Blank 1. Click Format Selection and select Secondary Axis.

5. Repeat step 4 for the Blank 2 series.

> **NOTE**
> You have now moved Revenue, Blank 1, and Blank 2 to the secondary series. These three series will now be treated as a group. For this reason, if you change the chart type for any one of the series, the chart type will be changed for all three.

6. Series Blank 2 should still be selected. Go to the Design tab and select Change Chart Type. Change the chart type from a stacked column to a clustered column.

You can now see the stacked cost column and the revenue column side-by-side, as shown in Figure 4.34. This is a useful trick.

Figure 4.34
Unlike Figure 4.33, the Revenue column is now shifted to the right.

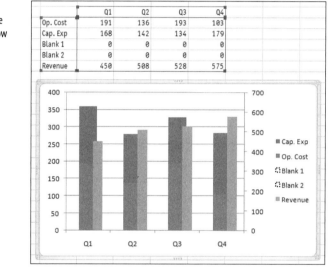

	Q1	Q2	Q3	Q4
Op. Cost	191	136	193	103
Cap. Exp	168	142	134	179
Blank 1	0	0	0	0
Blank 2	0	0	0	0
Revenue	450	508	528	575

> **TIP**
> You may wonder why the revenue chart is shifted to the right. This occurs because the rogue series Blank 1 and Blank 2 are secretly taking up space. Figure 4.35 shows the position of the two blank series. No one sees the blank series since the values are zero, but their presence moves the Revenue column to the right, making the cost column visible.

Although you have overcome the major hurdle in completing the chart, you still have some problems with this chart. The revenue column is narrower than the cost columns. The blank series are showing up in the legend. In addition, the biggest problem is that the revenue column at 450 is showing up shorter than the cost columns that only total 359.

Figure 4.35
The location of the blank series is why the revenue series is shifted to the right.

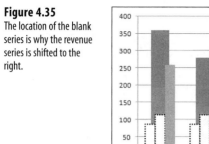

Secret 3: Increasing Gap Width Makes Columns Narrower

Double-click one of the Cost series in the chart. There is a setting in the Format Data Series dialog called Gap Width. As you increase the gap between the series, the net effect is that the column becomes narrower.

There is not a good rule to figure out the correct gap width. You can repeatedly nudge the gap width in Figure 4.36 higher and higher until the size of the cost columns appears to be about the same width as the size of the revenue column. In this case, the setting of 314 percent seems about right.

Figure 4.36
Increase the gap width of the cost series to narrow the width of the cost columns.

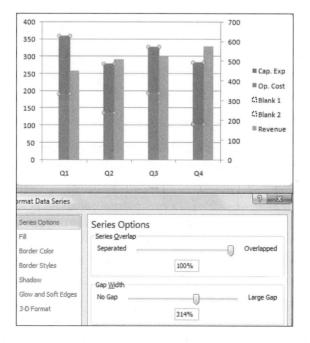

4

Secret 4: Removing Items from the Legend Box

Choices in the Layout tab enable you to hide, show, and reposition the chart legend. You actually have much more control by clicking the legend, but you have to be careful.

Click the legend once to select the entire legend. Next, click one entry to select that single legend entry. With the single legend entry selected, you can change the font size, font color, and font style of that legend entry.

You might initially try something clever like changing the font color to white, but this leaves the marker and also leaves a gap where the legend should be. Instead, press the Delete key to remove that entry from the legend.

Figure 4.37 shows the progression of selecting the entire legend, selecting one blank series, typing delete, selecting the next blank series, and pressing Delete.

Figure 4.37
Select an individual legend entry and press the Delete key.

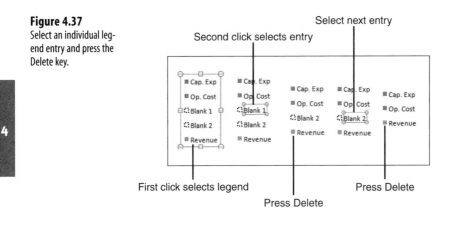

Second click selects entry

Select next entry

First click selects legend

Press Delete

Press Delete

Secret 5: Adjusting Y-Axis Scale When There Are Two Axes

Sometimes you move a series to a secondary axis to show two series that have different orders of magnitude. In this case, you want the revenue and cost series to have the same scale.

You can solve this problem, but there is a cost. Normally, Excel chooses the scale automatically based on the data. If you later plug in new data for this chart and the revenue increased above 700, the upper limit for the chart will grow automatically.

You have to turn off override this behavior for both the left and right axis. This means that if the data later grows larger than the chart, you will have to re-visit the Format Axis dialog to adjust.

1. Double-click the numbers along the left axis. Excel displays the Format Axis dialog. Initially, settings for Minimum, Maximum, Major Unit, and Minor Unit are all set to Auto, as shown in Figure 4.38.

Figure 4.38
Initially the scale is set to automatic.

2. Change the Minimum setting from Auto to Fixed. You can leave the setting at zero.

3. Change the Maximum setting from Auto to Fixed. Type a new upper limit such as 750.

4. Change the Major Unit setting from Auto to Fixed. This setting controls where the gridlines are drawn.

> **TIP**
> I prefer fewer gridlines, so a setting of 250 feels right to me. However, you might prefer a setting of 125 or 100.

At this state, the chart is not yet fixed. You have formatted the left axis to run from 0 to 750. However, the right axis is still running from 0 to 700 (see Figure 4.39).

Figure 4.39
Override settings for left axis.

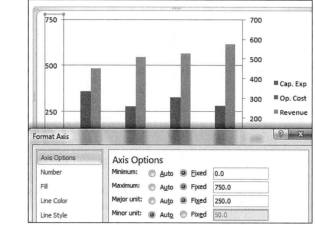

With the dialog box still open, click the Right axis in the chart. Repeat the settings in steps 2 through 4 above. You will briefly see that the right axis is now at the same scale as the left axis, as shown in Figure 4.40.

Once you are sure the axes are set to the same scale, it seems redundant to have the numbers on the right side. Two settings in the current dialog box solve this problem: Change the Major Tick Mark Type to None and Change the Axis Labels to None.

Figure 4.40
Adjust the right axis to be the same as the left.

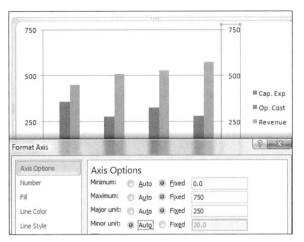

The final chart is shown in Figure 4.41.

Figure 4.41
The final chart makes it look easy.

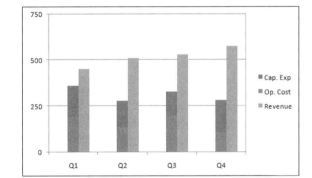

Next Steps

In Chapter 5, "Creating Charts That Show Relationships," you will learn how to create charts that highlight relationships. Scientists often use of scatter charts. However, you will learn how to use scatter charts in a variety of ways in business to demonstrate a correlation, or the lack of a correlation. In addition, you will learn that radar charts can be used to conduct annual performance reviews. Chapter 5 also takes a look at surface charts and frequency distributions.

Creating Charts That Show Relationships

5

Comparing Two Variables on a Chart

The chart types discussed in this chapter are unusual. Scatter, radar, bubble, and surface charts are probably the least understood Excel charts.

Both scatter and bubble charts show the interplay between two or three different variables. They require a bit of care in setting up the data. A scatter chart can help you to figure out whether there is a correlation between two variables. A bubble chart has the unique ability to provide data about a third dimension. The first section in this chapter covers the mechanics of creating scatter charts.

When you are thinking about creating scatter charts to show a relationship, you might need to consider alternative charts such as a paired bar chart, paired chart, or frequency distribution. The second section in this chapter compares the message that you convey with the various chart types. That section describes charts created by charting celebrities such as Gene Zelazny, Kathy Villella, and Alfred E. Neumann.

Radar charts are rarely used, but they are great for providing performance reviews. For example, a radar chart can show how a person scored on 5 to 10 key indicators as spokes emanating from a central point.

Surface charts actually attempt to show a 3-D surface floating above an x,y grid. It is difficult to find a dataset that looks cool with a surface chart, and after you have found an appropriate dataset, it is often difficult to make out the valleys that might occur within the dataset.

The first part of this chapter discusses scatter charts in detail. Although it is easy enough to create a simple scatter chart, many annoying complications can occur when you want to add new data series to the chart or when you want to try to label the chart.

Using XY Scatter Charts to Plot Pairs of Data Points

Figure 5.1 shows a table of average January temperatures for selected U.S. cities. There is no trend or pattern to this data.

City	Jan Temp
Anchorage, AK	13
Austin TX	49.1
Bismark ND	6.7
Charleston WV	32.9
Grand Rapids, MI	22
Honolulu HI	72.6
Los Angeles CA	56
Madison WI	15.6
Minneapolis MN	11.2
Olympia WA	37.2
San Francisco CA	48.5
Tampa FL	59.8

Figure 5.1
When this data is plotted on a column chart, there is no pattern to the data.

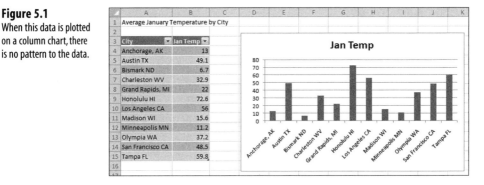

What are the likely causes of variability in January temperature? You might theorize that the most likely cause would be distance from the equator. In Figure 5.2, a new Column B shows the latitude of each city. This dataset is perfect for an XY scatter chart. The latitudes in Column B represent an independent variable. The temperatures in Column C represent a dependent variable. A scatter chart plots one data marker for every pair of latitude and temperature data. In this case, the latitude will be plotted along the x-axis, and the temperature will be plotted along the y-axis.

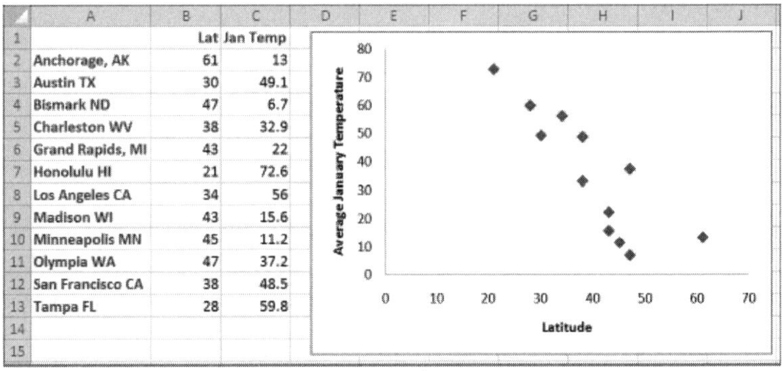

	Lat	Jan Temp
Anchorage, AK	61	13
Austin TX	30	49.1
Bismark ND	47	6.7
Charleston WV	38	32.9
Grand Rapids, MI	43	22
Honolulu HI	21	72.6
Los Angeles CA	34	56
Madison WI	43	15.6
Minneapolis MN	45	11.2
Olympia WA	47	37.2
San Francisco CA	38	48.5
Tampa FL	28	59.8

Figure 5.2
You can plot latitude and temperature on a scatter chart to understand the relationship between the values.

The chart in Figure 5.2 shows a relationship between latitude and temperature: as latitude increases, temperature decreases. You can therefore say that latitude and temperature are inversely related.

> **TIP** If your data is not sorted into numeric sequence, be sure to select Scatter with Only Markers as the chart type. Otherwise, Excel attempts to draw lines from Anchorage to Austin to Bismark, resulting in a line that looks like a scribble. For one such example, turn ahead to Figure 5.9.

Adding a Trendline to a Scatter Chart

To add a tight grid and a trendline to a scatter chart, select Layout 3 from the Chart Layouts gallery on the Design tab. The trendline represents the best-fit line, given the data points. If the trendline is angled diagonally from bottom left to top right, it indicates that the x and y variables appear to be directly related. If the trendline is angled from top left to bottom right, it indicates that the x and y variables appear to be inversely related. In Figure 5.3, the trendline confirms that there is an inverse relationship between temperature and latitude.

Figure 5.3
Add a trendline to confirm the inverse relationship.

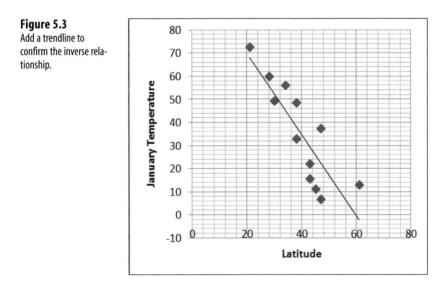

Excel uses a best fit to draw the trendline. Even when there is absolutely no correlation at all between the columns of data, Excel forces a line to fit. In Figure 5.4, the x and y data is random. A horizontal trendline represents the average of all the dots, but it does not indicate any correlation.

In Figure 5.4, Excel has added the equation for the trendline and the R-squared value. An R-squared value close to one indicates a near-perfect correlation. An R-squared value of zero confirms that there is not a correlation between the x and y values. To add this equation to your chart, follow these steps:

1. Select the chart.

2. On the Layout tab, select Trendline, More Trendline Options.

3. In the Format Trendline dialog that appears, select Display Equation on Chart and Display R-squared Value on Chart. Both settings are near the bottom of the dialog, as shown in Figure 5.5. Alternatively, choosing Layout 9 from the Charts Layout gallery on the Design tab will turn on the equation and R-squared.

Figure 5.4
Although a scatter chart of random data might produce a trendline, there is no correlation.

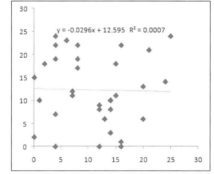

Figure 5.5
Add a trendline formula to the chart by using this dialog.

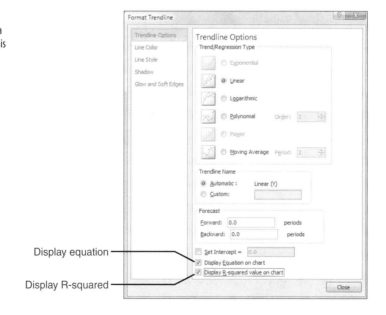

Display equation

Display R-squared

Adding Labels to a Scatter Chart

When you create most other charts in this book, the first column contains labels. In Figure 5.2, there are city names in Column A, but they are not part of the dataset. This is annoying. When you click a data point and choose to display the label, you can see that the data point is at a 47-degree latitude and has an average temperature of 37.2. However, you have to scan through the original dataset to see that the data point in question is from Olympia, Washington (see Figure 5.6).

Figure 5.6
It would be good if you change the label from the x and y values to the label in Column A.

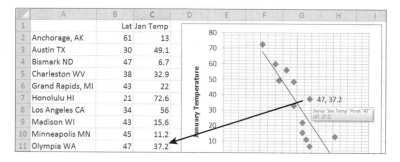

One solution is to write the following VBA macro code:

```
Sub AttachLabelsToPoints()
    Dim Counter As Integer, ChartName As String, xVals As String

    'Store the formula for the first series in "xVals".
    xVals = ActiveChart.SeriesCollection(1).Formula

    'Extract the range for the data from xVals.
    xVals = Mid(xVals, InStr(InStr(xVals, ","), xVals, _
        Mid(Left(xVals, InStr(xVals, "!") - 1), 9)))
    xVals = Left(xVals, InStr(InStr(xVals, "!"), xVals, ",") - 1)
    Do While Left(xVals, 1) = ","
        xVals = Mid(xVals, 2)
    Loop

    'Attach a label to each data point in the chart.
    For Counter = 1 To Range(xVals).Cells.Count
        ActiveChart.SeriesCollection(1).Points(Counter).HasDataLabel = _
            True
        ActiveChart.SeriesCollection(1).Points(Counter).DataLabel.Text = _
            Range(xVals).Cells(Counter, 1).Offset(0, -1).Value
    Next Counter

End Sub
```

If you select the chart and then run this macro, Excel displays the label next to each data point, as shown in Figure 5.7. This is a useful addition to the chart.

T I P If you are not comfortable with VBA, you can download a free add-in, the XY Chart Labeler, from Rob Bovey, at `http://www.appspro.com/Utilities/ChartLabeler.htm`.

Figure 5.7
Relevant labels for XY charts are an asset.

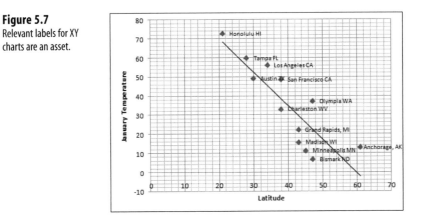

Joining the Points in a Scatter Chart with Lines

Of the five types of scatter chart types in the Change Chart Type dialog shown in Figure 5.8, four are dots joined using lines.

Figure 5.8
Most of the scatter charts are dots joined with lines.

Whereas the dot version of a scatter chart can be sequenced in any order, chaos will result if you try to join the dots with lines. In Figure 5.9, a familiar curve turns to spaghetti when the dots are joined with lines.

In Figure 5.10, using a line to join exactly the same dataset as in Figure 5.9 appears orderly.

T I P If you plan to join points with a line, you need to sort the underlying data into ascending sequence by the x value.

The bottom chart in Figure 5.10 uses Scatter with Smooth Lines and Markers. The top chart in Figure 5.10 uses Scatter with Straight Lines and Markers. The difference is barely perceptible—the line in the bottom chart is just slightly smoother.

Figure 5.9
Chaos results when an unsorted XY chart is joined with lines.

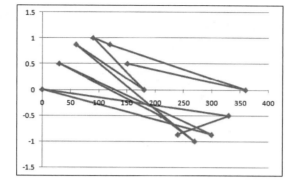

Figure 5.10
If your data is sorted into ascending sequence by the x value, either a straight line or smooth line will work.

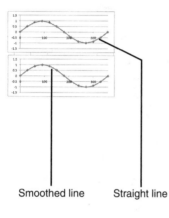

Smoothed line   Straight line

If you use Scatter with Straight Lines and Markers when fewer data points are available, the curve is not as well defined, as shown in the top chart in Figure 5.11. In contrast, you can use Scatter Chart with Curved Lines and Markers to have Excel extrapolate and fill in the curve, as shown in the bottom chart in Figure 5.11

Adding a Second Series to an XY Chart

It is somewhat unintuitive to plot a pair of XY series on a single chart: You create a chart for a single series and then use the Select Data icon to add the second series.

Follow these steps to create an XY chart with two series:

1. Start with an XY series in two columns. For example, on Figure 5.12, the XY series is in Columns B and C.

2. Add the label for this series in the cell above the y points column, such as the No College heading in C1.

Figure 5.11
It is important to use
a smoothed line with
sparse data.

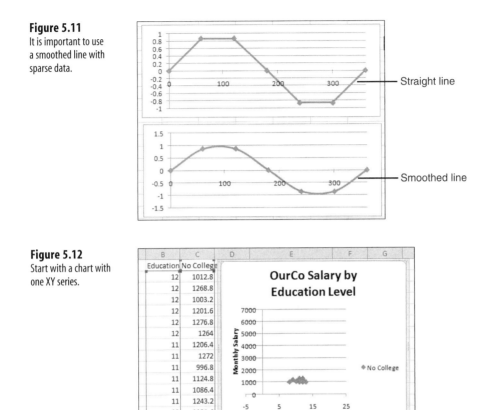

Figure 5.12
Start with a chart with
one XY series.

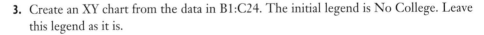

3. Create an XY chart from the data in B1:C24. The initial legend is No College. Leave this legend as it is.

4. Change the title from No College to a title that covers both series.

5. Enter a new series in Columns F:G. Enter the label for the second series in cell G1.

6. Click the chart to select the chart and bring back the Charting Tools tab.

7. From the Design tab, click the Select Data icon. Excel displays the Select Data Source dialog.

8. Click the Add button in the Legend Entries section of the dialog. Excel displays the Edit Series dialog.

9. Click in the Series Name box and select cell G1.

10. Click in the Series X Value box. Highlight cells F2:F15 in the worksheet.

11. Click in the Series Y Values box and backspace to remove the default value of 1. Click the Refers To box and highlight G2:G15. Excel adds sheet names and the dollar signs to make the references absolute, as shown in Figure 5.13.

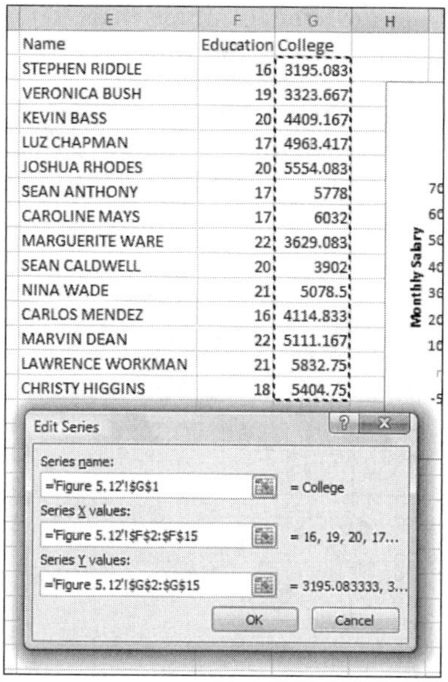

Figure 5.13
The new series is specified in the Edit Series dialog.

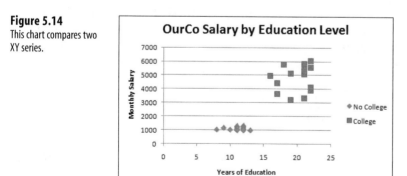

12. Click OK to close the Edit Series dialog. Click OK to return to the worksheet.

The final chart is shown in Figure 5.14.

Figure 5.14
This chart compares two XY series.

Drawing with a Scatter Chart

An unusual use for XY scatter charts with straight lines is to make crude drawings on a chart.

To create a drawing, it helps to trace your drawing onto quadrille graph paper first. You need to choose a point where the left edge and bottom edge cross, which, in this case, will be the (0,0) point. For every point in the drawing, you enter the x and y location. The x location is the number of gridlines from the left edge of the chart to that point. The y location is the distance from the bottom of the chart to the point.

If you need to draw a curve, you can choose as many points as possible around the perimeter of the curve. The more points you can plot, the smoother the curve.

Figure 5.15 shows an x and y dataset.

Figure 5.15
Transfer points from a drawing into columns for x and y.

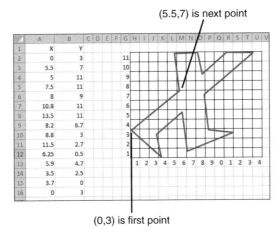

(5.5,7) is next point

(0,3) is first point

Next, select the data from A2:B16. From the Insert tab, you select Insert, Scatter, Scatter with Straight Lines, which is the thumbnail with straight lines and no markers. Excel creates the chart shown in Figure 5.16.

Figure 5.16
Excel connects the x and y points to create a simple drawing.

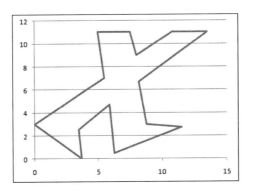

→ See Figure 7.43 in Chapter 7,"Advanced Chart Techniques," for an over-the-top example of this technique.

Using Charts to Show Relationships

You can use several types of charts to illustrate the relationship between two variables, including the following:

- Scatter charts are particularly well suited when comparing two variables that you think are related. Although you can use scatter plots with large datasets, they are limited in that it is difficult to label the points without using some VBA or an add-in. If you have a small dataset, you can use a paired bar chart (turn back to Figure 4.4 for one example or forward to Figure 5.21 for another example) to see the same information. This chart also adds a label so you can see which records are not in line with the others.

- In some cases, a pair of matching charts allows the reader to compare two variables to see whether there is a relationship.

- In the real world, it is rare to find a value that is influenced by only one variable. Usually, a whole host of factors contributes to a result. A bubble chart is a special type of XY scatter chart that attempts to show the interplay between three variables. It is best to use bubble charts for small datasets.

- Radar charts are rarely used charts that allow you to see the relationship between four to six variables.

- In some cases, you might have a population of results and be trying to figure out whether any patterns exist in one variable. In these cases, use of the FREQUENCY function enables you to make sense of the data by grouping members into similar categories and then comparing the categories.

Testing Correlation Using a Scatter Chart

The dataset for a scatter chart is composed of two variables for every row in the dataset. The values in the first column are plotted along the horizontal axis. The values in the second column are plotted along the vertical axis. The heading for the second column becomes the name of that series.

In Figure 5.17, the data in B2:C15 represents a price survey of regional car dealerships for a particular model of vehicle. Each pair of numbers in a row represents the data for a single car. Mileage is in the first column, and price is in the second column. In theory, you would expect that as the miles go up on a car, the price would come down.

If you select the data from B2:C15 and insert a scatter chart, Excel provides the chart shown in the top of Figure 5.17. The chart needs some labels to tell the complete story. Follow these steps to format the chart to look like the bottom chart in Figure 5.17:

Figure 5.17
The default scatter chart at the top requires some formatting before it can be useful.

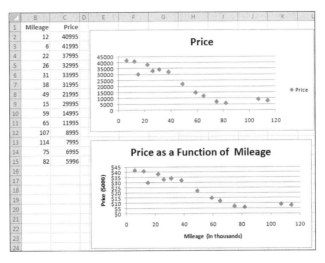

1. From the Layout tab, select Legend, None to remove the legend.

2. From the Layout tab, select Axis Titles, Primary Horizontal Axis Title, Title Below Axis to add the words Axis Title below the horizontal axis.

3. Click Axis Title and type the new axis title `Mileage (in thousands)`.

4. From the Layout tab, select Axis Titles, Primary Vertical Axis Title, Rotated Title to add the words `Axis Title` to the left of the vertical axis.

5. Click the Axis Title and type the new axis title of `Price (in $000)`.

6. Double-click the prices along the y-axis to display the Format Axis dialog. In the middle of the dialog, select Thousands for the Display Units and clear the Show Display Units On Chart check box.

7. While still in the Format Axis dialog, click Number in the left navigation bar. Select Currency with 0 decimal places.

8. Click the title and type a more descriptive title such as `Price as a Function of Mileage`.

In Figure 5.17, it appears that there is a fairly strong relationship between mileage and price. Because the dots slant from top left to bottom right, the variables have an inverse relationship.

You can ask Excel to do a least-squares regression and fit a trendline to the points plotted on the chart. One of the trendline options is to display the regression equation and the R-squared value on the chart.

> **NOTE** Remember that R-squared is a measure of how well a trendline matches the points. R-squared ranges from 0 to 1, with 1 meaning a nearly perfect correlation.

Figure 5.18 shows three different scatter charts. The top chart has a perfect correlation and an R-squared value of 1. The next chart has just a small bit of variation. Individual points appear close to the trendline but are sometimes a bit above or below it. This provides an R-squared value of 0.995. The bottom chart looks like a shotgun blast. There does not appear to be any correlation between those variables, and Excel reports an R-squared value of 0.003. If the dataset is truly random, the trendline is often a straight horizontal line, drawn through the value that marks the average of all of the points.

Figure 5.18
R-squared is a measure of how well a trendline fits the points in a chart.

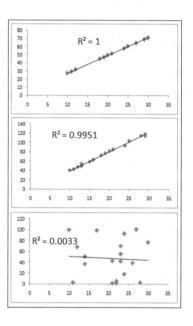

There are a few different ways to add a trendline and the R-squared value to a chart. Follow these steps to see one way:

1. Select the chart.

2. From the Layout tab, select Trendline, More Trendline Options.

3. Select Linear as the trend/regression type.

4. In the bottom of the Format Trendline dialog, choose either Display Equation on Chart or Display R-squared Value on Chart.

5. If you want only the R-squared value on the chart, select the Line Color style and move the Transparency slider to 100 percent.

In Figure 5.19, the R-squared value has been added to both charts. Price and mileage have an R-squared value of 0.849. Price and age have an R-squared value of 0.944. While both sets have correlations, the age of the car seems to have more of an impact on price than does mileage.

Figure 5.19
Based on the R-squared values, age is a better predictor of price than is mileage.

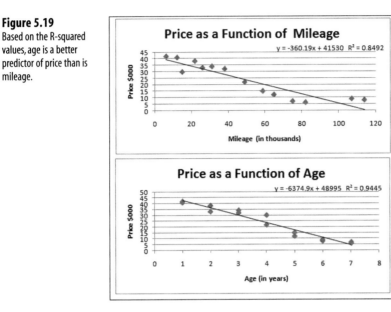

Using Paired Bars to Show Relationships

A scatter chart lacks a straightforward way to label the points with identifying names. If you need to compare two variables and have around a dozen points, a paired bar chart can be more effective than a scatter chart. For example, Figure 5.20 shows a preference for ice cream, based on a survey of two groups: kids and adults.

The chart is sorted by the kids' preference. Any bars toward the bottom of the chart that have a sizable presence on the right are flavors that grow in popularity as the respondents mature.

Figure 5.20
A paired bar chart allows you to compare values for two populations.

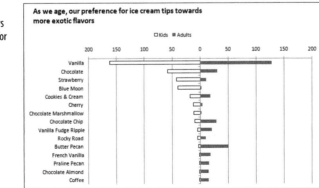

To create this chart in Excel, you need to use a little trickery in several steps. Since this is a stacked bar chart, the values for the left bar have to be in the Excel table as negative to force them to stretch leftward from the axis.

Follow these steps to create the chart in Figure 5.20:

1. Sort your original data by the first series so that it is in descending order.
2. Copy the dataset to the right of the original dataset. In the copy of the dataset, enter the formula -B39 in Cell F39 to create a negative value for the first series (see Figure 5.21).

Figure 5.21
Use a formula to make the first series negative.

	A	B	C	D	E	F	G
36							
37							
38	Flavor	Kids	Adults		Flavor	Kids	Adults
39	Vanilla	162	128		Vanilla	-162	128
40	Chocolate	58	31		Chocolate	-58	31
41	Strawberr	42	11		Strawberr	-42	11
42	Blue Moor	40	2		Blue Moor	-40	2
43	Cookies &	18	18		Cookies &	-18	18
44	Cherry	12	4		Cherry	-12	4
45	Chocolate	11	2		Chocolate	-11	2
46	Chocolate	10	29		Chocolate	-10	29
47	Vanilla Fu	5	21		Vanilla Fu	-5	21
48	Rocky Roa	5	10		Rocky Roa	-5	10
49	Butter Pec	3	50		Butter Pec	-3	50
50	French Va	1	18		French Va	-1	18
51	Praline Pe	1	16		Praline Pe	-1	16
52	Chocolate	1	15		Chocolate	-1	15
53	Coffee	1	15		Coffee	-1	15

3. Select the data for your chart. Press Ctrl+1 to display the Format Cells dialog box. On the Number tab, select the Custom category and type the custom number code 0;0. Click OK. The negative numbers in Column F are displayed without the minus sign.

> **NOTE**
> While you are likely to type only a single format as your custom number format, the field is allowed to have up to four "zones," separated by semicolons. If you have two zones, the first format is for positive numbers, and the second format is for negative numbers. For example, the code 0 ; -0 will display numbers as positive and negative. The code 0 ; (0) will display the negative numbers in parentheses. The code 0 ; will hide the negative numbers. The code 0 ; 0 will force the negative numbers to display without the minus sign and without parentheses. It is difficult to imagine why anyone would want to show negative numbers without the minus sign, until you consider our current example where it certainly comes in handy.

4. From the Insert tab, select Bar, Stacked Bar. Excel creates the chart shown in Figure 5.22.

> **NOTE**
> Note that the custom number format from step 3 carries through to the horizontal axis labels. Even though the kids' numbers are stored as negative, the numbers to the left of the midpoint are shown as positive.

5. From the Layout tab, select Legend, Top to move the legend to the top. Moving the legend changes the legend to a landscape orientation, with the first series on the left and the second series on the right. This arrangement matches the data in the chart.

Figure 5.22
Excel displays the start of a paired bar chart.

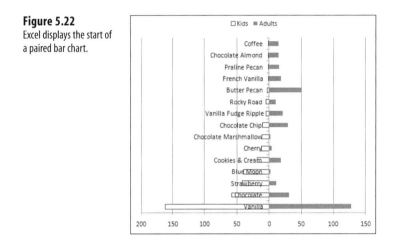

6. Resize the chart vertically to allow enough room for each category name to appear along the axis.

7. Select Vertical (Value) Axis from the Current Selection drop-down on the Layout tab. Then select the Categories in Reverse Order check box, which is the fourth selection in the Axis Options panel.

> **NOTE**
> Steps 8 and 9 are both optional, but they both involve the horizontal axis. If you plan to do either step, select Horizontal (Category) Axis from the Current Selection drop-down and select Format Selection.

8. (Optional) The initial chart is not quite symmetrical, running to 200 on the kids' side and to only 150 on the adults' side. To correct this, specify a fixed minimum of –200 and a fixed maximum of 200.

9. (Optional) Initially the category labels overwrite the left bars. You have to decide how annoyed you are by this. It might be best to keep the labels there. If you want to move them to the left, select Low from the Axis Labels drop-down.

To see a demo of creating this paired bar chart, search for "MrExcel Charts 5" at YouTube.

This example creates a chart that plots a frequency distribution for two populations. While it allows you to compare the preferences of the populations, the case study that follows provides another example of a paired bar chart that lets you examine the correlation between two variables, just as you would do in a scatter chart.

CASE STUDY: COMPARING THE RELATIONSHIP BETWEEN DISCOUNT AND SALES

OurCo employs a staff of 10 sales reps. The sales reps are given a fair amount of discretion in offering sales discounts. A rep is authorized to offer a new customer discount in order to secure a deal. A rep can also offer a large volume discount in order to get the customer to increase the size of an order. Over the years, some of the veteran sales reps have created their own discounts. As long as the order comes in with some reasonable explanation of why the customer was offered a discount, the order is approved. In reality, no one in order processing has ever questioned any discount. There are no checks and balances.

The sales manager defends the discounting practice, asserting that discounting leads to larger sales volumes. Although this could be true, it could also be that less savvy sales reps are using the discount as a crutch when they should be selling on value.

You produce the table in Figure 5.23. If you print this out and take it to the sales manager and, worse, his boss, their eyes will glaze over.

Figure 5.23
This table does not reveal many trends.

	A	B	C	D	E	F	G	H
1	REP	List Price	Revenue		REP	Revenue	Rep	Discount
2	Nathan	117112	111256		Nathan	111256	Nathan	-5%
3	Jessica	90943	84577		Jessica	84577	Jessica	-7%
4	Chad	121842	112095		Chad	112095	Chad	-8%
5	Marlene	85823	74666		Marlene	74666	Marlene	-13%
6	Clara	137095	116531		Clara	116531	Clara	-15%
7	Terry	93104	79138		Terry	79138	Terry	-15%
8	Viola	127573	105886		Viola	105886	Viola	-17%
9	Roy	125019	98765		Roy	98765	Roy	-21%
10	Travis	112962	85851		Travis	85851	Travis	-24%
11	Anita	167835	125876		Anita	125876	Anita	-25%

A better presentation for the same data would be the chart in Figure 5.24. If higher discounts lead to higher sales, then the revenue bars on the right will be sorted from longest to shortest. However, the rep with the lowest discount (Nathan) happens to have one of the highest sales volumes.

Follow these steps to build a paired bar chart to compare discount with revenue:

1. In cell D1, enter the heading Rep. In Cell D2, enter =A2. Select D2. Double-click the fill handle to copy the formula down to D11.

2. In cell E1, enter the heading Revenue. In Cell E2, enter the formula =C2 to copy revenue over to Column E.

5

Figure 5.24
If higher discounts lead to higher sales, the bars on the right would be sorted from longest to shortest.

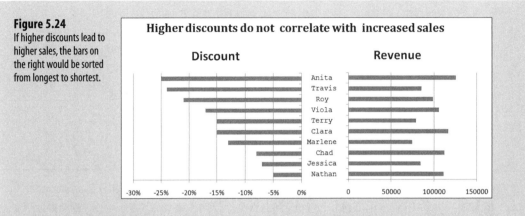

3. Repeat step 1 in column F to build rep names in Column F.

4. Enter the heading Discount in cell G1. Enter the formula =(C2/B2)-1 in cell G2 to calculate discount from a list as a percentage. Select cell G2 and double-click the fill handle to copy the chart down to G11.

5. Select one cell in Column G. Select ZA from the Data tab to sort the data with the smallest discount at the top.

6. Select cells D1:E11. Next, you are going to create the left and right halves of the chart in different steps. The data in cells D1:E11 will be used for the Revenue side of the chart.

7. From the Insert tab, select Bar, 2-D Bar, Clustered Bar. Excel creates a bar chart for revenue. You want to format this chart completely first.

8. From the Layout tab, select Legend, No Legend.

9. Click the border of the chart to select the chart area. From the Format tab, select Shape Outline, None. This allows you to arrange the two charts later without anyone knowing that they are not the same chart.

10. Drag the chart to the lower-right corner of your screen.

11. Click the border of the chart. Start to drag to the left. After you start to drag, press and hold down Ctrl+Shift.

> **NOTE**
> The Ctrl key tells Excel that you want to make a copy of the object. The Shift key constrains the movement in one direction. If you move to the left, the copy will be exactly the same vertical location as the original.

12. Click outside the new chart and then click in the new chart.

13. You do not need the names along the vertical axis. From the Layout tab, select Axes, Primary Vertical Axis, No Axis.

14. You should see a blue box around the revenue cells in Column E. Click the border of the blue outline and drag it to the right so that it surrounds the discounts in Column G. Because those values are negative, the chart flips around, and the bars extend left from an axis on the right side of the chart.

15. Drag the green box around Revenue in E1 over to the Discount heading in G1.

> **NOTE**
>
> It is worth noting that if both of your series were positive, you would need to convert the series for the left chart to be negative. For this, you would use the custom format code 0;0 discussed earlier in this chapter.

16. Click the border of the chart on the left. From the Format tab, select Shape Fill, None to make the area outside the plot area transparent. Doing this allows you to move the chart on the left very close to the axis labels of the chart on the right.

There is one remaining problem: The names along the vertical axis of the right chart are right-aligned. To center-align these labels between the two charts, one approach is to add extra spaces to the right side of the short names in order to move them away from the axis. This trick works best when the labels are in a fixed-width font, such as Courier New. To center the names, follow these steps:

1. Enter this formula in cell D2:

```
=A2&REPT(CHAR(160),ROUNDUP(4-LEN(A2)/2,0))
```
Copy this formula down to the other rows.

2. Click the labels along the vertical axis. On the Home tab, select Courier New from the Font drop-down.

3. If necessary, drag the chart on the left into position. Remember to hold down the Shift key while you drag the chart to constrain the movement in only one direction. This enables you to move the chart sideways without moving it up or down.

Several important steps are necessary to pull off the chart trick. By making one chart and then copying it, you are sure that both charts have the same height and scale. By using No Line on both charts and No Fill on the left chart, you remove many of the clues that this is really two charts.

The title above the chart in Figure 5.24 is a text box. To create the text box, follow these steps:

1. On the Insert tab, select the Text Box icon.

2. Drag in the spreadsheet above the charts and type a title.

3. Click the border of the text box and use the formatting tools on the Home tab to adjust the font size.

The following section describes an example of a paired bar chart.

CASE STUDY: KATHY VILLELLA COMPARES THREE VARIABLES WITH A PAIRED BAR CHART

The paired bar chart discussed in this case study is particularly difficult to emulate in Excel. It is a chart from Kathy Villella, the founder of PowerFrameworks.com. Kathy shows this chart in PowerPoint, but it is created using a custom template.

Kathy emphasizes that you should always have the larger numbers on the left of a chart. The chart in Figure 5.25 compares the revenue of one company to the revenue of an entire industry. The numbers for the entire industry should appear on the left.

5

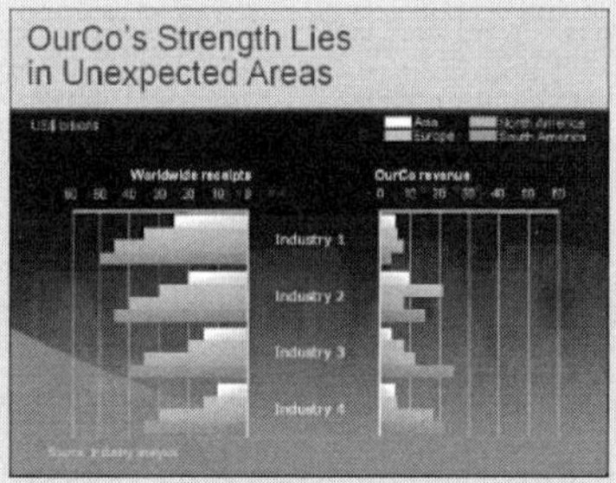

Figure 5.25
This paired bar chart compares one company to the entire industry, providing information for both industry segment and region.

To emulate this chart in Excel, follow these steps:

1. Set up the data in A2:E6 of Figure 5.26 to create the chart shown on the right in Figure 5.25. Put the industry labels across cells B2:B6. Put the regions in cells A3:A6. The title in cell A1 is there for convenience only.

2. Copy cells A1:E6 to A8. Change the second dataset to include data to create the chart on the left in Figure 5.25.

3. Select cells A9:E13. From the Insert tab, select Bar, 2-D Bar, Clustered Bar.

4. In the Design tab, open the Chart Styles gallery. Choose one of the styles that show various shades of blue.

5. Initially, the chart shows a scale from 0 to 30. You need to make this large enough to match the chart on the left side. Right-click the numbers along the horizontal axis and do the following:

   Select Format Axis.

   Select Maximum, Fixed, 60.

   Select Major Unit, Fixed 10.

6. Right-click the labels along the vertical axis and then select Format Axis. Click Categories in Reverse Order.

7. From the Layout tab, select Legend, Show Legend at Top.

8. Click the resizing handle for the chart on the right side and drag to the left to make the chart more like a square than a rectangle.

9. From the Layout tab, select Chart Title, Above Chart. Excel adds a chart, centered above the left chart, above the legend, and a bit too large. Click the Chart Title and type the new title OurCo Revenue. Click the border of the title to select it. From the Home tab, click the Decrease Font Size button until the title is about 12 point. Drag the title so that it appears flush with the left vertical axis. This causes the title to overlay part of the legend.

10. Drag the legend to the upper-right corner of the chart. The legend will be one row tall by four columns wide. Resize the legend, making it about half as wide and more than twice as tall. This action should convince Excel to show the legend in a two-by-two arrangement. If you see only two of the four parts of the legend, click the Decrease Font Size button on the Home tab until the legend appears in a two-by-two arrangement.

11. Click the chart area. From the Format tab, select Shape Outline, No Outline. This removes the line from around the entire chart. Because the final product actually contains two charts, you do not want a border around just one of the charts.

12. Make a copy of the original chart. Click the border of the chart and drag it to the left. After you start to drag, hold down Ctrl+Shift. Drop the new chart just to the left of the original chart. The copy of the chart still points at B2:E7.

13. While the new chart is selected, there is a blue border around B3:E7. Click this border and drag it down so that it encompasses B10:E12. The green border automatically moves to A10:A13. However, the purple border stays around B2:E2. This is okay.

14. Right-click the values along the top of the chart. Select Format Axis. Select Values in Reverse Order and click OK to reverse the direction of the bars so that they run from right to left.

15. Click the Legend in the chart on the left and press the Delete key.

16. Click the labels along the vertical axis in the chart on the left and press the Delete key.

17. Click the plot area. Use the top resizing handle to pull the top of the chart down so that it is even with the top of the chart on the right. As you are dragging, there are two dotted rectangles. You want to focus on the top of the inner rectangle to line it up with the top of the plot area on the right chart.

18. In the chart on the left, change the OurCo Revenue title to Worldwide Receipts. Click the border of the title. Hold down the Shift key while you drag this title so that it is flush with the right side of the axis. After you have deleted the axis labels from the chart, Excel stretches the plot area to fill the entire chart area.

19. Resize the plot area either with VBA or by selecting Shapes, Lines, Line from the Insert tab. Draw a horizontal line below the chart on the right. The line is a measuring tool; draw it from the left baseline to the right plot area. It is important that this line be outside the chart area; you want to draw the line on the spreadsheet.

20. Move the line so that it is under the chart on the left. The right side of the line should line up with the right edge of the plot area. This line provides a guideline in step 21. As you are resizing the chart, keep adjusting until the plot area is the correct size.

21. Click the chart area of the chart on the left. Drag the left resizing handle toward the center of the chart. Release the handle and see if the plot area is about the same size as the line underneath the chart. This is a trial-and-error method. Keep resizing until the plot area and the line are roughly the same size.

22. From the Insert tab, click the Text Box icon. Drag to draw a new text box above the charts. In the text box, type the title `OurCo's Strength Lies`, press Enter, and type in `Unexpected Areas`. Click the border of the text box to select the text box. From the Home tab, change the font to Cambria, change the size to 16 point, and click the Bold button. From the Format tab, select Shape Outline, None. Drag the title into position so that it appears that it is lined up with the left edge of the chart on the left.

The final chart is shown in Figure 5.26.

Figure 5.26
The final Excel chart emulates Kathy Villella's chart.

Using Paired Matching Charts

Since 1950, the "usual gang of idiots" has been satirizing popular culture at *Mad* magazine. Writers Dan Birthcer and George Woodbridge inadvertently came up with an interesting way of comparing two independent variables in the October 1991 panel described in the following case study.

┌─ DESIGNING LIKE THE PROS ─────────────────────────────────
│ Kathy Villella offers templates to help you communicate effectively with PowerPoint and charts at
│ `http://www.PowerFrameworks.com`. Thanks to Kathy for donating this chart.
└──

CASE STUDY: *MAD* MAGAZINE CREATES A PAIRED COMPARISON CHART

A *Mad* magazine article titled "Cause or Coincidence," which was published in October 1991, fictitiously tried to show a relationship between two variables. The writers would hypothesize that the rise in missing person reports happened to coincide with the increase in David Copperfield performances. Of course, not all of the charts were exactly politically correct. Figure 5.27 shows a modern-day version of a *Mad* chart illustrated by Bob D'Amico.

┌──
│   If you are a fan of *Mad*, check out issue 306, pages 30–31, to see all nine of the chart comparisons. A
│   DVD of every *Mad* published from 1950 through 2005 was published in 2006.
└──

Figure 5.27
These chart pairs ponder if there is a causal relationship between two variables.

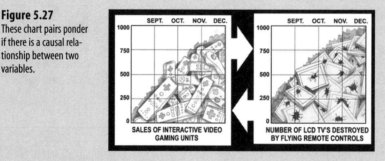

Figure 5.28 shows a similar pair of charts in Excel. To create this illustration, you use two series in each chart. The first series provides a solid background and a line for the area chart. The second series provides the illustration for the area chart.

Follow these steps to create a paired comparison chart in Excel:

1. Set up a dataset in A1:B6 with the information for the left chart. Copy the data in B2:B6 to C2. Add the heading `Football 2` in C1. The data in C1 will become the second series that is used to hold the graphic to fill the area underneath the line.

2. Select A1:C6. From the Insert tab, select Area, 2-D Area, Area.

3. Add vertical gridlines by choosing Gridlines, Primary Vertical Gridlines, Major Gridlines on the Layout tab.

4. Add a title by choosing Chart Title, Above Chart on the Layout tab. Type a title such as `Football Wins`.

Figure 5.28
This Excel chart approximates the *Mad* chart.

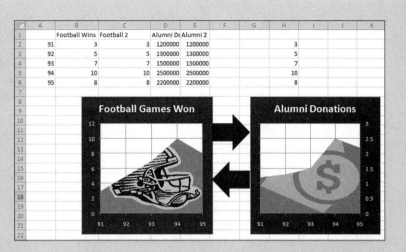

5. Click the area chart. To select the second series, from the Insert tab, select Clip Art to display the Clip Art pane. Search clips for football. When you find a suitable one, click the arrow for the drop-down list to the right of that clip and then select Copy. Press Ctrl+V to paste the clip art into your chart. Most of the Microsoft clips have transparent backgrounds. The Series 1 area, which is the same size and shape as Series 2, will provide a colored background for the transparent clip art.

6. Remove the Legend by choosing Legend, None on the Layout tab.

7. Click the chart area, which is the area inside the chart border but outside the plot area. From the Format tab, select Shape Fill and choose a light blue fill. You will actually use a dark fill later, but the light blue provides the necessary contrast for step 8.

8. Click the title. From the Home tab, choose a white font. Click the vertical axis labels and select white from the font color drop-down. Do the same for the horizontal axis labels.

9. Click the chart area and then select Format, Shape Fill. Choose either a black or dark blue fill.

10. Because the chart is wider than it is tall, shrink the width of the chart so the chart is just slightly taller than it is wide by dragging a resize handle.

11. You can now make a copy of the chart. Click the chart border and drag to the right. After you start to drag, hold down Ctrl+Shift. Drag the chart far enough that you have about a one-column split between the charts.

12. Set up a column for alumni donations in Column D and a column with identical numbers but the heading Alumni2 in Column E.

13. Click the plot area of the second chart, being careful not to select gridlines or the data series. Excel draws a blue border around cells B2:C6. Grab the edge of the blue border and drag to the right so that it surrounds D2:E6. The green outline in B2:B6 is also copied to D1:E1.

14. Change the title of the second chart to `Alumni Donations`.

15. Notice that the plot area on the right side is a bit smaller than the plot area on the left. This is because the numeric labels are longer on the right chart. Choose the labels along the vertical axis. Right-click and select

Format Axis. For Display Units, select Millions. For the Axis Labels drop-down, select High. Click Close. The axis labels move to the right side of the chart.

16. In the Clip Art pane, search for Dollar or Money. Choose one of the clip art icons and then select Copy from the drop-down list on the right. Click the football helmet in the new chart. From the Layout tab, the Current Selection drop-down indicates that Series Alumni 2 is selected. Press Ctrl+V to paste the money clip art into that chart. The final steps are to draw in the arrows.

17. From the Insert tab, select Insert, Shapes, Block Arrow, Right Arrow. From the Format tab, select Shape Fill and then choose a black fill. Select Shape Outline, Black.

18. To add a second arrow, press Ctrl+C when the first arrow is selected. Click a new cell and press Ctrl+V to paste a new arrow. While holding down the Shift key, use the green outline to spin the arrow so that it is pointing left.

19. If necessary, nudge the charts so that the arrows touch each ch art.

Thanks to the usual gang of idiots at *Mad* magazine for providing the concept for this chart.

Adding a Third Dimension with a Bubble Chart

A bubble chart attempts to add a third piece of information to each point in an XY scatter chart. In a bubble chart, the size of the marker varies, based on the third data point for each marker.

The best time to use a bubble chart is when you have a sparse dataset. The size of the bubbles makes it difficult to read the chart when you have too many data points on the chart.

Figure 5.29 shows a bubble chart. The size of each bubble is based on the selling price for a particular model of car. The location of the bubble along the horizontal axis indicates the age of the car. The location of the bubble along the vertical axis shows the mileage of the car.

In theory, cars that are older or have higher mileage should have lower prices. However, you can find some bubbles where the seller of an older car is asking for more money.

Here are some tips for creating bubble charts:

■ You should always leave the heading off the top-left cell in the data range. This rule applies any time you have numbers as the first column of your dataset. It is particularly important with bubble charts.

■ The initial size of the bubbles is always too large since it is initially scaled to 100 percent. If you see too much overlap in the bubbles, you can right-click a bubble and select Format Data Series. In Figure 5.29, the bubbles are scaled down to 30 percent to prevent excessive overlapping.

■ There is an option in the Format Series dialog to have the size data translated into the area of the bubble or the width of the bubble. You should always choose the area of the bubble.

In both charts shown in Figure 5.30, each bubble is two times larger than the previous bubble. The top chart includes the option that the size of data in the third column affects the area of the bubble. This is the default setting, and it is the correct setting. If you instead decide to tie the data in the table to the width of the bubble, you violate the pictograph rule. When you are using pictures for markers, you should increase the marker in only one dimension, not in both dimensions.

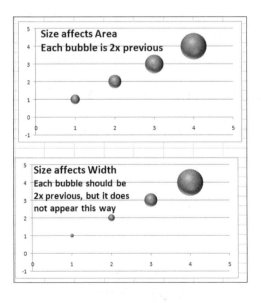

5

> **CAUTION**
>
> The area of a circle is determined with the formula `PI() * Radius^2`. If you have one bubble that is double the size of another and you attempt to demonstrate this by doubling the radius, the actual area of the circle increases geometrically. This is misleading.

To create the chart in Figure 5.29, follow these steps:

1. Set up your data with age in Column A, mileage in Column B, and price in Column C. It is okay to have headings above the data in Columns B and C.

2. Select cells A1:C15.

3. From the Insert tab, select Other Charts, Bubble, Bubble with a 3-D Effect.

4. Right-click one bubble and select Format Series. Change the Scale Bubble Size value from 100 to 30.

5. Right-click the numbers along the vertical axis and select Format Axis. Change Minimum to Fixed, 0.

6. From the Layout tab, select Legend, None.

7. From the Layout tab, select Chart Title, Above Chart. Click the title and type a new title.

8. From the Layout tab, select Axis Titles, Primary Horizontal Axis Title, Title Below Axis. Click the axis title and type the new title `Age (Years)`.

9. From the Layout tab, select Axis Titles, Primary Vertical Axis Title, Rotated Title.

When you need to show the relationship between three variables and you have only a few points to compare, a bubble chart will create an effective presentation of the data.

Using a Frequency Distribution to Categorize Thousands of Points

Suppose your dataset had results of 30,000 trials. Figuring out how to present this data can be difficult. The chart in Figure 5.31 is a first attempt. The data is sorted by the trial number in Column A. A line chart is based on Columns A and B. You cannot tell much of anything from this chart. You can tell that the range is from 20 to 100, but that is about it.

Figure 5.31
This cannot be the best way to plot this data.

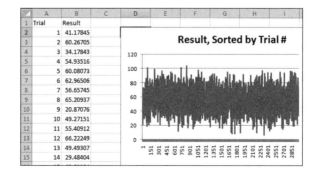

If you sort the data by the result field in Column B, the chart changes into a smooth line, as shown in Figure 5.32. Again, you can tell that the range is from 20 to 100 and that for 60 percent of the chart, the data ranges from 40 to 60.

To create a more useful chart with this data, you need to use a somewhat obscure function. You use the FREQUENCY function to group the data into bins. This function is one of the few functions that returns several different answers all at once. These functions, called array functions, require special care and handling.

Figure 5.32
Some might be able to draw conclusions from this, but this chart is not obvious.

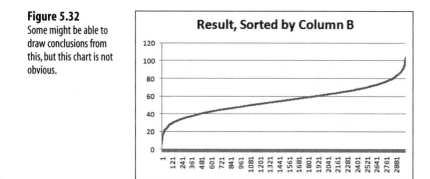

Creating Bins

To make sense of the data in Column B in Figure 5.32, you need to group the results into equal-sized bins. You need to type limits for each bin in a range, going down a column of the worksheet.

If your first bin is the number 0, the FREQUENCY function shows all the trial results less than 0 next to that bin. If the next bin is the number 15, the FREQUENCY function shows all the trial results from the last bin (0) to the current value (15).

To create bins that contain ranges of 15 units each, follow these steps:

1. Type 0, 15, 30, 45, 60, 75, 90, 105, in cells E2:E9. Remember that this range contains eight cells.

2. Because the FREQUENCY function returns one more value than the number of bins that you have, select the empty cells F2:F10, as shown in Figure 5.33. The additional bin is for any results larger than your last bin value.

3. Type =FREQUENCY(.

4. When Excel asks for the data array, enter the trial results from B2:B3001. Type a comma.

5. When Excel asks for the Bins array, enter the values from E2:E9.

6. Type the closing parenthesis, but do not press Enter (see Figure 5.34).

Figure 5.33
It might feel strange, but you are entering one formula in this range.

> **NOTE**
> If you were actually entering nine copies of this formula, you would have to put dollar signs in all those references. However, this is one single formula that will return nine results, which means that you do not need dollar signs.

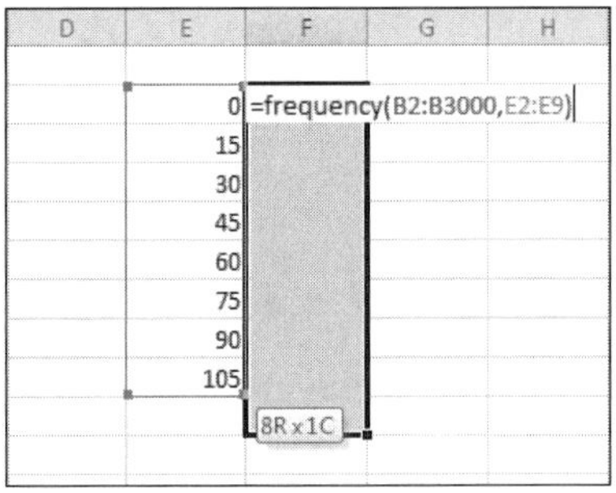

Figure 5.34
It might feel strange, but you are entering one formula in this range.

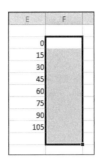

7. Hold down Ctrl+Shift while pressing Enter. Excel returns all nine answers at once. You now have one formula entered in nine cells.

Take a look at the results of the formula shown in Figure 5.35.

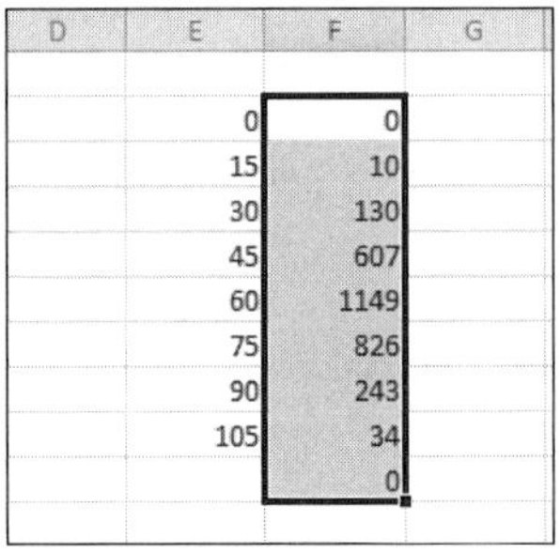

Figure 5.35
These results make sense only if you understand how the bins work.

You have to "know the code" in order to figure out what is going on here. There is a 0 next to the 0, and there is a 10 next to the 15. This means that none of the results was less than 0 and 10 of the results were between 0 and 15. At the other end of the range, there is a 34 next to the 105, and there is a 0 below that. This means that there are 34 results between 90 and 105. The final 0 means that there were no results above 105. When you set up the bin range, you should always bracket the expected results with one bin above and below your expected results. Having a 0 end up as the first and last result means that you have accurately captured all your results.

> **TIP**
>
> If you cannot remember if the 10 means that there were numbers below 15 or above 15, you can always sort the results and count the number that appears in the first range. If the process of creating bins seems extremely confusing, you are not alone. Microsoft hopes to make frequency distribution charts much easier in a future version of Excel.

Creating the Frequency Distribution Chart

The results in Column F in Figure 5.35 are somewhat difficult to decode, but you can improve the appearance of the labels along the axis of the chart.

In Figure 5.36, the formulas in H3:H9 concatenate the bins so that they make more sense. The formula =E2&" - "&E3 concatenates the bin in the previous row, a dash, and the bin in the current row. The formulas in Column I copy the results from the current row of the array formula in F.

Figure 5.36
Use formulas to build a table that makes more sense than the previous results.

	E	F	G	H	I
1					
2	0	0			Frequency
3	15	10		0-15	10
4	30	130		15-30	130
5	45	607		30-45	607
6	60	1149		45-60	1149
7	75	826		60-75	826
8	90	243		75-90	243
9	105	34		90-105	34
10		0			

To create the Frequency Distribution chart, follow these steps:

1. Select cells H3:I9.

2. From the Insert tab, select Column, 2-D, Clustered Column.

3. From the Layout tab, select Legend, None.

4. Normally, there is a fair-sized gap between the columns. If you prefer the columns touch each other, or even that there be less of a gap, you can change the gap width by right-clicking a column, choosing Format Data Series, and then dragging the Gap Width slider to zero percent.

   5. Resize the chart so that it is narrower.

Figure 5.37
Frequency charts typi-
cally eliminate the gap
between columns. This is
strictly your preference.

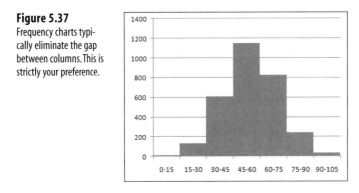

Using Radar Charts to Create Performance Reviews

Radar charts are designed for showing a person's or a company's rating along several performance areas. Here are some typical usages:

■ **Employee performance review**—A manager might rate an employee using a one- to
five-point rating scale in areas such as efficiency, accuracy, timeliness, and so on. While
this data can be presented in a table, a radar chart provides an interesting alternative
presentation.

■ **Customer satisfaction results**—A marketing manager could use a radar chart to summarize the results of a customer satisfaction survey. In this case, one line can be used to
show customer satisfaction along rating areas such as speed, accuracy, and value.

If you want to summarize customer satisfaction results for two companies, you can present
the results as two charts, as shown in Figure 5.38. Alternatively, you can present the results
as two series on a single chart, as shown in Figure 5.39.

You can choose to fill in the chart area or to show the series as a line. You should leave the
chart unfilled when you put two series on one chart.

You can use a radar chart to compare some kind of results from this year versus the same
kind of results from last year. For example, on Figure 5.40, the line for last year is dark
black, and the line for this year is a dashed line in a lighter color.

To create the performance review chart shown in Figure 5.40, follow these steps:

   1. Using the information in Figure 5.40, enter the categories in Column A, starting in
   A2. The category in A2 appears at 12:00 on the chart. The remaining categories are
   arranged in clockwise order.

   2. In cells B1 and C1, enter the headings for last year and this year.

   3. Enter the 1–5 ratings in B2:C6.

Figure 5.38
With only one series, you can choose to fill in the series.

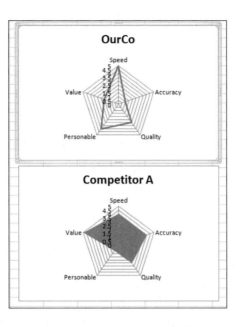

Figure 5.39
When you have two series, you should not fill in the lines so the reader can see the overlap.

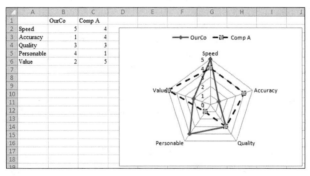

Figure 5.40
Radar charts can compare several values from last year to this year.

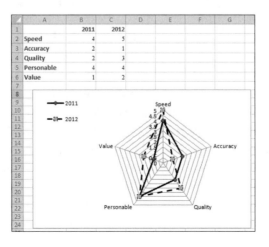

5

4. Select Cell A1:C6. From the Insert tab, select Other Charts, Radar, Radar with Markers.

5. Click the line from this year. From the Format tab, select Shape Outline, Dashes, and then select the fourth choice, called Dash.

All the examples so far show measures that are of similar scale. If you need to show a series that is of a different order of magnitude, you can plot the series on a secondary axis. To do this, select the axis, select Format Axis, and then choose Secondary Axis.

In the celebrity chart described in the following section, the designer used a radar chart for something that is not quite typical. In this case, the designer solves the order-of-magnitude problem by using a logarithmic scale.

CASE STUDY: A CHART FROM GENE ZELAZNY

Gene Zelazny is the director of visual communications for McKinsey & Company. His books on charting and presentations are filled with ideas for effectively communicating information visually.

I asked Gene if he would contribute a chart that does not look like a typical Excel chart. He contributed the chart described in the following section.

A number of retirees were surveyed about their impressions of certain types of companies to provide retirement advice. The resulting data is shown in the table in Figure 5.41. A typical approach to this analysis, a 100 percent stacked bar chart, is shown at the bottom of Figure 5.41.

Figure 5.41
Most people would present this data with a 100 percent stacked bar chart.

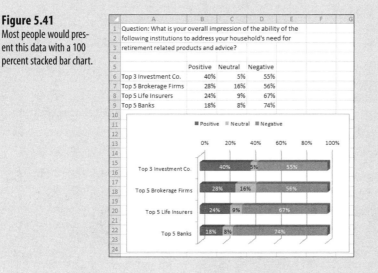

Gene's version of the chart, shown in Figure 5.42, minimizes the neutral answers. All the neutral answers are shown along an imaginary baseline, in equal-size markers. The positive answers are shown as yellow upward-facing arrows. The neutral markers are blue. The negative answers are shown as red downward-facing arrows (see Figure 5.42).

Figure 5.42
Gene's chart will be moderately difficult to re-create in Excel.

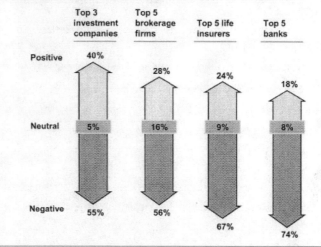

Financial services firms have a credibility gap with consumers on retirement

Question: "What is your overall impression of the ability of the following institutions to address your household's needs for retirement related products and advice?"

To create this chart in Excel, follow these steps:

1. Set up data labels in Column A for the four types of institutions.
2. Type the heading `Negative` in cell B1. Enter negative percentages in B2:B5. For example, the value for investment companies should be entered as `-55%`. This forces the bar to be drawn below the axis.
3. Type the heading `Neutral` in cell C1. Enter 0% in C2:C5.
4. Type the heading `Positive` in cell D1. Enter the positive values from the original table.
5. Make sure that Columns C and D are formatted as percentages with zero decimal places.
6. Format Column B with a custom numeric code of `0%;0%`. This forces negative values to show as positive.
7. Select cells A1:D5. From the Insert tab, select Column, 2-D Column, Stacked Column.
8. Resize the chart using the resize handles so that it is larger—perhaps as large as cells A7:J34.
9. Right-click one of the labels along the axis carefully. Select Format Axis. In the Format Axis dialog, select Axis Labels as High. The titles move so that they are above the chart.

10. Right-click the columns above the axis. Select Add Data Labels. From the Format tab's Shape Fill drop-down, choose a yellow color.

11. Click the data labels. Select a size of 14 point from the Home tab.

12. Click a data label and move it on top of the appropriate column. Repeat for each of the other data labels.

13. Right-click the columns below the axis. Select Add Data Labels. From the Format tab's Shape Fill drop-down, choose a red color.

14. Click the lower data labels. On the Home tab, select 14 point for the font size.

15. Click a data label and move it to below the appropriate bottom column. Repeat for each of the other data labels.

16. From the Format tab's Current Selection drop-down, select Series Neutral. Then select Shape Fill, Green to make the legend entry green.

17. Select the legend by clicking it. On the Home tab, increase the font size to 14.

18. Select the Axis labels. Change the font size to 14.

19. From the Insert tab, select Shapes, Block Arrows, Upward Facing Arrow. Draw an arrow next to the chart.

20. From the Format tab, select Shape Outline, No Outline to remove the border. Then select Shape Fill, Yellow. Choose a yellow to match the upper columns.

21. With the arrow selected, press Ctrl+C to copy the arrow.

22. Click one of the top columns in the chart, and then press Ctrl+V. Excel replaces the columns with a block arrow.

23. Select the arrow. From the Format tab, select Rotate, Flip Vertical and then select Format Shape Fill, Red.

24. Press Ctrl+C to copy the arrow.

25. Click the lower bars in the chart. Press Ctrl+V to paste. The lower bars are replaced by red arrows.

26. Delete the arrow on the worksheet.

27. Right-click any bar and select Format Data Series. Change the gap width to 30 percent.

28. From the Insert tab, select Text Box. Draw a text box for the neutral labels on the first arrow. The text box should be as wide as the arrow. It should extend equally above and below the horizontal axis.

29. With the text box selected, select Shape Fill, Green on the Format tab. Select Shape Outline, No Outline.

30. Press Ctrl+1 to access the Format Shape dialog. Select Text Box from the categories on the left. Change the Internal Margin to 0 inches on the left, right, top, and bottom. Close the Format dialog.

31. From the Home tab, select 14 point, black font, center align, and middle align.

32. Type 5% in the text box.

33. Click the border of the text box. Start to drag right. After you start to drag, hold down Shift+Ctrl to make a copy of the text box and constrain the movement to only horizontal. Drop the text box on the second column and type 16%.

34. Repeat step 33, using 9% for the third column and 8% for the fourth column.

35. Add a title above the chart in the worksheet cells.

The final chart is shown in Figure 5.43.

Figure 5.43
The final Zelazny chart
in Excel.

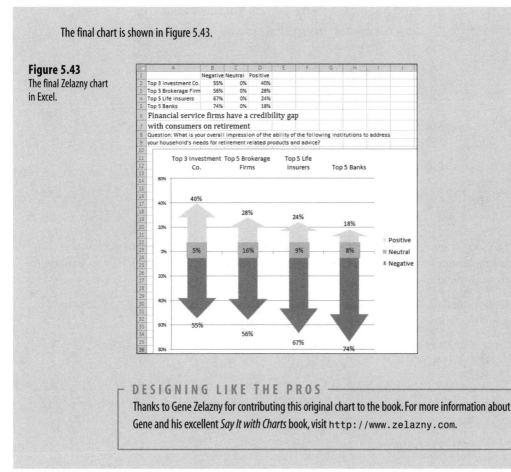

DESIGNING LIKE THE PROS

Thanks to Gene Zelazny for contributing this original chart to the book. For more information about Gene and his excellent *Say It with Charts* book, visit http://www.zelazny.com.

5

Using Surface Charts to Show Contrast

Not many datasets can be plotted as a surface chart, which look like topographic maps. Because you use a surface chart to represent a 3-D surface on a 2-D piece of paper, it is particularly important that your surface be generally sloping toward the front of the chart. Otherwise, you will never see the details hidden by the hill at the front of the chart.

Before you start to build a dataset, you should look at Figure 5.44. The data for the chart is in C3:L12. Each data point requires two headings. Headings for the front axis are in C2:L2. Headings for the side axis are in B3:B12.

Figure 5.44
Study this table and chart to understand how surface charts work.

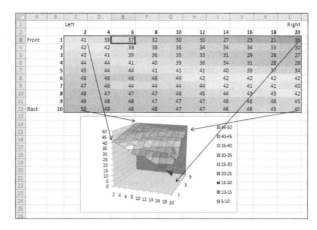

Data at the top of the table appears at the front edge of the chart. Data in the last row of the table appears at the back of the chart. The Front and Back labels in Column A are there to help you keep track of this.

Data in the left column of the table appears in the left side of the chart. The four arrows point out where each corner of the data table ends up in the chart.

To create this chart, you select Cells B2:L12. From the Insert tab, select Other Charts, Surface, 3-D Surface.

Many datasets are not designed to have the smallest numbers at the front of the chart. For example, in Figure 5.45, the top-left chart has the highest numbers along the front wall of the chart.

Figure 5.45
All four charts represent the same data. Each chart provides a different view angle.

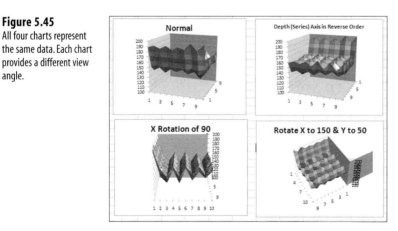

When the front wall of the surface chart is higher than the other points, you can use the techniques that follow to create the other three charts.

Using the Depth Axis

One element unique to surface charts is the depth axis. This is the axis that falls along the right side of the chart in the default orientation.

In the top-right chart in Figure 5.45, the chart has been turned around by having the orientation of the depth axis changed. Follow these steps to create this effect:

1. From the Layout tab, select Current Selection, Depth (Series) Axis.
2. Click Format Selection.
3. Select Series in Reverse Order.

Because the depth axis is treated as a category axis, you do not have control over the minimum or maximum values along the axis. The Format dialog box is limited to settings for the interval between tick marks and labels and where the tick marks and labels appear.

Controlling a Surface Chart through 3-D Rotation

You can spin a surface chart by rotating it. To access the rotation settings, select 3-D Rotation from the Layout tab. This takes you to the 3-D Rotation category of the Format Chart Area dialog, which has the following settings:

- **X Rotation**—This setting ranges from 0 degrees to 359.9 degrees. It rotates the floor of the chart in a clockwise direction, when you are looking down at the chart from above.

- **Y Rotation**—This setting starts at +15 degrees. It is your viewing angle in relation to the baseline of the chart. With an angle of 15 degrees, you are looking slightly down at the chart. With an angle of 0 degrees, many of the 3-D effects disappear. As you increase from 10 to 80 degrees, you have slightly different views of the chart. At 90 degrees, the chart becomes flat, as you are looking directly down from above. You can also enter negative values from 0 to –90. As you move from –10 to –80, you look at the chart from underneath. This might allow you to see better detail. When you reach –90, the chart turns flat again, as you are looking directly up at the chart from below.

Perspective ranges from 0 to 120. A value of 0 creates the least distortion. As you increase to 120, the foreshortening increases, creating distortion similar to what you get with an ultra-wide-angle lens on a camera.

Next Steps

In Chapter 6, "Creating Stock Analysis Charts," you will learn about the process of creating charts to show the performance of stocks and securities. While Excel offers four types of built-in stock charts, they appear dated in light of modern stark charts available on numerous websites. Chapter 6 shows you how to go beyond the four built-in charts to create modern-looking stock charts.

Creating Stock Analysis Charts

Overview of Stock Charts

Excel provides four basic types of stock analysis charts: High-Low-Close, Open-High-Low-Close, Volume-High-Low-Close, and Volume-Open-High-Low-Close. These built-in charts are helpful when you need to display a stock trend for use in an executive dashboard.

Unfortunately, like the old charting in legacy versions of Excel, the stock charts are showing signs of age. If you are familiar with the charts in the *Wall Street Journal* or on http://finance.yahoo.com, you can see that charting technology has definitely left Excel behind.

This chapter guides you on how to coax acceptable results out of the Excel charting engine. However, sometimes it is easier to ditch the Excel stock charts and design your own chart using a line chart.

If you are planning to do dashboard reporting, this chapter provides a few tips to help make your charts smaller than usual, while maintaining readability.

Typically, stock charts in the newspaper or online are represented by one of three chart types: line charts, open-high-low-close (OHLC) charts, or candlestick charts. The following sections discuss each of these chart types.

Line Charts

A line chart shows the closing price of a security every day for a month, quarter, half year, year, or longer. A line chart may show a second series of volume represented as a column chart at the bottom of the chart. For example, in Figure 6.1 a line chart shows the closing price for a security for one year. A volume chart at the bottom shows unusually high activity for the security in February and October.

When creating a line chart in Excel, you do not have to use stock chart types. Instead, you can simply choose a line chart.

One advantage of line charts is that it is easy to add a second security to a line chart to show how the original security is doing compared to an index or a competitor.

Figure 6.1
A line indicates the closing price of the security each day for a year. The column chart at the bottom shows the volume of shares traded each day.

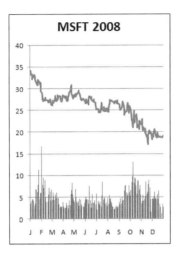

OHLC Charts

An OHLC chart shows a vertical line extending from the low price to the high price for a given period. A dash on the left side of the line indicates the opening price. A dash on the right side of the line indicates the closing price. For example, the chart in Figure 6.2 shows that January opened at 199, the price ranged from 126 to 200, and January closed at 135.

Figure 6.2
This is a true OHLC chart. Excel's built-in types omit the marker for the opening price.

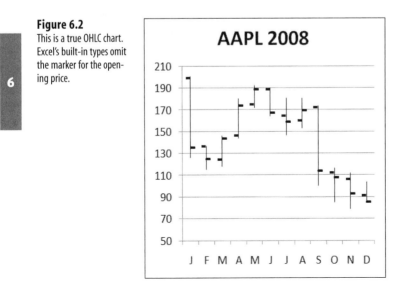

Excel does not have a built-in style for OHLC charts, but it can create a variant of this chart. Excel's high-low-close chart shows the vertical line and the closing line on the right side of the line. However, it is missing the marker for the opening price. Excel's volume-high-low-close chart is a variant of the OHLC chart that is coupled with a volume chart showing trading volume.

→ If you desperately need to show the opening price, see the "Creating OHLC Charts" section later in this chapter.

Candlestick Charts

A candlestick chart has a vertical line that indicates the range of low to high prices for a security. A thicker column indicates the opening and closing prices. If the price of the security closed up, the thicker column appears in white or green. If the price of the security closed down, the thicker column appears in black or red.

This stock chart was named a candlestick chart because each shape appears as a candle with a wick sticking out of the top and the bottom. For example, in Figure 6.3, the security declined in the five months from July through November, before gaining in December.

Excel creates candlestick charts using the Open-High-Low-Close chart type. In another variant, volumes for each period are plotted on a second axis. You can quickly scan this type of chart to see whether the stock has had more winning periods than losing periods.

Figure 6.3
The thicker column indicates the open and closing prices. The thinner line indicates the high-to-low range.

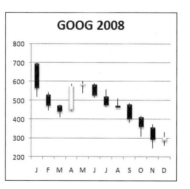

Obtaining Stock Data to Chart

There are plenty of free sources of historical data to chart. To obtain stock data to chart, you can go to http://finance.yahoo.com or another such site and follow these steps:

1. If you do not know the stock ticker symbols for the company of interest, use the Symbol Lookup link that appears next to the Go button in the top navigation bar of the page.

2. Enter a stock ticker symbol in the Get Quotes text box and press the Go button. Yahoo returns a table and a chart showing information about the current day.

3. Click Historical Prices in the left navigation bar. Enter a starting date and an ending date and choose whether you want the data summarized daily, weekly, or monthly. Click Get Prices to generate new results. Yahoo shows columns for date, open, high, low, close, volume, and adjusted close. A minor annoyance is that it shows about 50 dates on a page and then offers a Next link.

4. Instead of copying a page at a time, scroll down and select the Download to Spreadsheet link that appears below the results.

5. In the File Download dialog that appears, click Save. An imaginative name of table.csv is proposed. Save using this name of something, such as MSFTDaily2008.csv.

6. In Excel 2010, select File, Open. In the Open dialog that appears, in the Files of Type drop-down, select Text Files (*.prn, *.txt, *.csv).

7. Browse to the downloaded .csv file and click Open. Excel opens the file. Column A, which contains dates, is typically too narrow, as shown in Figure 6.4. Double-click the border between the Column A and B column headings to make Column A wider.

Figure 6.4

After the CSV file opens in Excel, you need to adjust the column widths.

	A	B	C	D	E	F	G
1	Date	Open	High	Low	Close	Volume	Adj Close
2	########	19.31	19.68	19.27	19.44	46419000	19.08
3	########	19.01	19.49	19	19.34	43224100	18.98
4	########	19.15	19.21	18.64	18.96	58512800	18.61
5	########	19.2	19.33	19.09	19.13	23101000	18.77
6	########	19.26	19.45	19.1	19.17	16880400	18.81
7	########	19.28	19.57	19.01	19.28	47511400	18.92
8	########	19.24	19.29	18.89	19.18	58575400	18.82
9	########	19.42	19.8	19.11	19.12	1.14E+08	18.76
10	########	19.86	20.03	18.99	19.2	80750200	18.94

8. The data is always sorted with the most recent data first. Therefore, click a cell in Column A and select Data, AZ to sort the date into ascending sequence by column.

9. If you have more than one screen of data, from the View tab, select Freeze Panes, Freeze Top Row to ensure that you can always see the headings at the top of the screen.

10. CSV files are not good places to store Excel charts. Before creating any charts, select File, Save As. Select to save as an Excel 2010 macro-enabled workbook.

Rearranging Columns in the Downloaded Data

If you are using one of the Excel built-in stock charts, you should know that Excel is very particular about the sequence of the columns. For example, in a high-low-close chart, the date should be in the first column, followed by a High column, a Low column, and a Close column. This does not match the sequence of the data downloaded from Yahoo.com. You need to be prepared to insert new columns, and then cut and paste data from one column to

another in order to sequence your data as necessary. The following list shows the required sequence of columns for each chart type:

- **Line Chart**—Date in Column A and Close in Column B
- **Line Chart with Volume**—Date in Column A, Close in Column B, and Volume in Column C
- **High-Low-Close**—Date in Column A, High in Column B, Low in Column C, and Close in Column D
- **Volume-High-Low-Close**—Date in Column A, Volume in Column B, High in Column C, Low in Column D, and Close in Column E
- **Open-High-Low-Close as Candlestick**—Date in Column A, Open in Column B, High in Column C, Low in Column D, and Close in Column E
- **Open-High-Low-Close as OHLC**—Date in Column A, High in Column B, Low in Column C, Close in Column D, and Open in Column E
- **Volume-Open-High-Low-Close as Candlestick**—Date in Column A, Volume in Column B, Open in Column C, High in Column D, Low in Column E, and Close in Column F
- **Volume-Open-High-Low-Close as OHLC**—Date in Column A, Volume in Column B, High in Column C, Low in Column D, Close in Column E, and Open in Column F

> **TIP**
> Although you might be tempted to delete the unused columns, it is better to leave them to the right of the data to be charted. This way, if you decide to add a series to the chart later, it is easy to do so.

Dealing with Splits Using the Adjusted Close Column

Before charting data, you should look at the earliest data point and compare the Close column to the Adjusted Close column. If they differ, you know that one of two events happened during the period in question:

- The company declared a dividend. For example, if the company pays out three cents per share, the adjusted price is reduced by three cents for all months that occurred earlier than the dividend.
- If the company declares a stock split, the adjusted close shows the closing price, which pretends the split had occurred previously.

Figure 6.5 shows an example of a stock split. Say that Activision stock began September 2008 at a price of $33.66 and closed the month at $15.43. The stock did not really incur a huge drop during the month.

Activision had declared a two-for-one stock split on September 8, 2008. Every person who had 100 shares on that day watched those shares change into 200 shares. The value of each share was cut in half at the time of the split. In this case, if you start the month with 100

6

Figure 6.5
At first glance, it appears the Activision stock took a nosedive in September.

	A	B	C	D	E	F	G
1	Date	Open	High	Low	Close	Volume	Adj Close
2	1/2/2008	29.65	29.76	25.11	25.87	10705700	12.94
3	2/1/2008	25.95	27.77	25.43	27.22	8311700	13.61
4	3/3/2008	27.11	27.58	26.05	27.31	9247600	13.65
5	4/1/2008	27.34	27.94	26.91	27.05	7279300	13.52
6	5/1/2008	27.1	33.89	27.05	33.75	10148400	16.88
7	6/2/2008	33.66	37.3	33.17	34.07	8922700	17.03
8	7/1/2008	34	38.56	29.58	35.98	14011600	17.99
9	8/1/2008	34.51	36.36	31.79	32.82	9433700	16.41
10	9/2/2008	33.66	34.1	14.04	15.43	12868100	15.43
11	10/1/2008	15.29	15.39	10.26	12.46	12734500	12.46
12	11/3/2008	12.43	12.83	9.22	11.7	11883600	11.7
13	12/1/2008	11.48	11.7	8.28	8.64	12360600	8.64

shares of Activision, valued at $3,366, you will end the month with 200 shares of Activision, valued at $3,086. This is a drop, but not a massive 50 percent drop.

To learn when the split or dividend occurred, you have to look through the table on http://finance.yahoo.com, which shows splits and dividends. This information is not downloaded in the CSV file.

If you are plotting a line chart showing the closing price, you can deal with the split by using the Adjusted Close column. Notice in Figure 6.5 that the Adjusted Close column for January 2008 is $$12.94, half the real closing price of $25.87. Yahoo goes to the trouble of adjusting the closing price to provide a comparable view of the closing price.

If you are plotting a chart showing high, low, and close, you have to add some additional calculations. To do so, follow these steps:

1. Add the new column headings Date, High, Low, Close to H1:K1.

2. Copy the formula =A2 from cell H2 down to all rows. This formula is for the date.

3. Copy the formula =G2 from cell K2 down to all rows. This formula is for the adjusted close.

4. Copy the formula =C2*($G2/$E2) from cell I2 down to all rows.

> **NOTE** This formula in step 4 adjusts the high price from Column C by the same ratio as adjusted close to close. You might change it in some rows. The dollar signs before Columns G and E allow you to copy the formula to Column J for the adjusted low as well.

5. Manually fix any dates where a split occurred.

6. Create your stock charts from the data in Columns H:K, as shown in Figure 6.6.

NOTE The original data showed a high price of $34.10 for September 2008. You can assume that this high happened before the split. In cell I10, divide C10 by 2 to adjust the high to $17.05. If you need the chart to be completely accurate, go back to http://finance.yahoo.com and run a daily report for the month in question. Find the high price after the split and compare it to the calculated high of $17.05. If higher, replace the calculation with the actual high from after the split. The original data showed a low price of $14.04 for September 2008. Compare this low to 50 percent of the pre-split low shown on the daily report and manually adjust in your worksheet if necessary.

Figure 6.6
Most of the adjusted columns are a formula, but you need to use special care in the months in which a stock split occurred.

	A	B	C	D	E	F	G	H	I	J	K
1	Date	Open	High	Low	Close	Volume	Adj Clos	Date	High	Low	Close
2	1/2/2008	29.65	29.76	25.11	25.87	10705700	12.94	1/2/2008	14.8858	12.5599	12.94
3	2/1/2008	25.95	27.77	25.43	27.22	8311700	13.61	2/1/2008	13.885	12.715	13.61
4	3/3/2008	27.11	27.58	26.05	27.31	9247600	13.65	3/3/2008	13.785	13.0202	13.65
5	4/1/2008	27.34	27.94	26.91	27.05	7279300	13.52	4/1/2008	13.9648	13.45	13.52
6	5/1/2008	27.1	33.89	27.05	33.75	10148400	16.88	5/1/2008	16.95	13.529	16.88
7	6/2/2008	33.66	37.3	33.17	34.07	8922700	17.03	6/2/2008	18.6445	16.5801	17.03
8	7/1/2008	34	38.56	29.58	35.98	14011600	17.99	7/1/2008	19.28	14.79	17.99
9	8/1/2008	34.51	36.36	31.79	32.82	9433700	16.41	8/1/2008	18.18	15.895	16.41
10	9/2/2008	33.66	34.1	14.04	15.43	12868100	15.43	9/2/2008	17.86	14.04	15.43
11	10/1/2008	15.29	15.39	10.26	12.46	12734500	12.46	10/1/2008	15.39	10.26	12.46
12	11/3/2008	12.43	12.83	9.22	11.7	11883600	11.7	11/3/2008	12.83	9.22	11.7
13	12/1/2008	11.48	11.7	8.28	8.64	12360600	8.64	12/1/2008	11.7	8.28	8.64

Creating a Line Chart to Show Closing Prices

A line chart is the easiest type of stock chart to create. Instead of using Excel's built-in stock charting types, you will use a line chart. Follow these steps to create a line chart:

1. Download data for the security from http://finance.yahoo.com.

2. Sort the data into ascending sequence by date.

3. Insert a blank Column B after the Date column.

4. Copy the Adjusted Close column from Column H to the new column B.

TIP Whenever your row labels contain dates, the top-left cell of the chart range should be blank.

5. Delete the extra Column H.

6. Clear cell A1.

7. Replace the Adjusted Close heading in B1 with the security symbol and time period such as MSFT 2008.

8. Select your data in Columns A and B.

9. On the Insert tab, select Line, 2-D Line, Line. Excel creates the chart shown in Figure 6.7.

Figure 6.7

Excel creates a line chart showing closing prices.

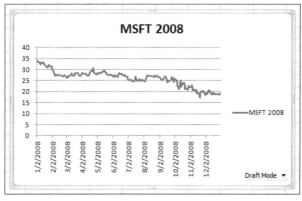

10. Click the legend and press the Delete key. Excel removes the legend from the chart.

11. The value axis currently runs from a low of 0 to a high of 35. During 2008, the security closing prices ran from a low of $17.50 to a high of $35.96.

> **TIP**
>
> If you want to show more detail in the chart, double-click the value axis to open the Format Axis dialog. Change the Minimum setting to Fixed, 15. Change the Maximum setting to Fixed, 35. Keep the dialog box open for step 12.

12. The dates in the horizontal axis are trying to show month, day, and year, as in the original dataset. To display one label for each month, do the following:

   ■ Assuming the Format dialog box is still open, reach behind the dialog with the mouse and click the horizontal axis.

   ■ On the Axis Options dialog, select Major Unit, Fixed, 1, Month.

   ■ Select Axis Type, Date Axis.

   ■ Click the Number category in the left navigation bar.

   ■ Click the Date category.

   ■ Scroll near the bottom of the Type list box and select M. The mmmmm custom type displays a single letter for each month. In the English version of Excel, it displays JFMAMJJASOND, a format regularly seen in the *Wall Street Journal*.

13. Resize the chart so that it is narrower than the default chart. Click the chart border to select the chart. Drag the right resizing handle to the left.

14. If the chart is in Draft mode, open the Draft Mode drop-down and select Turn Off Draft Mode.

The resulting chart is shown in Figure 6.8.

Figure 6.8
When you zoom in on the $20–$30 price range, more details are visible.

Adding Volume as a Column Chart to the Line Chart

A popular option in stock charts is to add a column chart that shows volume of shares traded. This chart usually appears at the bottom of the trend chart.

Continuing with the example from the preceding section, to plot prices in the $15–$35 range with volumes in the 15–300 million range, the volumes have to be plotted on a secondary axis. One trick is to inflate the maximum artificially for the secondary axis by a factor of three or four in order to keep the volume chart in the lower portion, which is the lower quarter to third of the chart.

Follow these steps to create a chart that shows closing prices and volume:

1. Download data from http://finance.yahoo.com.

2. Sort the data into ascending sequence by date.

3. Insert blank Columns B and C after the Date column.

4. Cut the Adjusted Close column from Column I to the new Column B.

5. Cut the Volume column from Column H to the new Column C.

6. Clear the heading from cell A1.

7. Select your data in Columns A:C.

> **TIP**
> If you are seeing the bottom of the worksheet instead of the top of the worksheet, press Ctrl+ twice to move to the top of the dataset.

8. Select Line, 2-D Line, Line from the Insert tab. Excel creates the chart shown in Figure 6.9. Initially, you will only see the line for Volume. The Closing price will appear as a flat line at zero. You will fix this in the following steps.

9. Click the Legend and press the Delete key. Excel removes the legend from the chart.

10. Double-click the Volume series on the chart. Excel displays the Format Series dialog.

6

Figure 6.9
Do not be alarmed that
you can see only volumes.

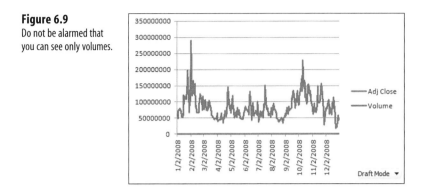

11. Select Secondary Axis. Click OK to close the dialog.

12. While the Volume series is still select, select Design, Change Chart Type. Select the first column chart type. Click OK.

13. On the Layout tab, select Chart Title, Centered Overlay. Type MSFT 2008 and press Enter to change the title.

14. The value axis currently runs from a low of $0 to a high of $35. Although prices of Microsoft (MSFT) stock never dipped below $15 in 2008, you can leave that space to hold the volume portion of the chart. The highest volume was about 300 million shares traded. If you scale the secondary axis to have a maximum value of 600 million shares traded, the volume portion of the chart occupies the lower half of the chart. Right-click the secondary value axis, and then select Format Axis. Change Maximum to Fixed, 6E8 (which is 600,000,000). The tallest column in the volume area of the chart stays below the gridline for $20. Keep the dialog box open for steps 15 and 16.

15. Usually, the analyst does not care how many shares are traded; he or she is interested in the relative scale of the shares being traded. From the chart, you can tell that something remarkable happened when Microsoft traded four times more shares than usual. Thus, you do not need to have any volume numbers along the right side of the chart. Change the Axis Labels drop-down to None.

16. The dates in the horizontal axis are trying to show month, day, and year, as in the original dataset. To display one label for each month, do the following:

   ■ With the Format dialog open, reach behind the dialog and click the dates along the horizontal axis.

   ■ On the Axis Options dialog, select Major Unit, Fixed, 1, Month.

   ■ Select Axis Type, Date Axis.

   ■ Click the Number category in the left navigation bar.

   ■ Click the Date category and select M from near the bottom of the Type list box. This type displays only the first letter of each month name. Therefore, it appears as JFMAMJJASOND.

17. Resize the chart so that it is narrower than the default chart. Click the chart border to select the chart. Drag the right resizing handle to the left.

18. If the Draft mode indicator appears on the chart, open the Draft mode indicator and select Turn Off Draft Mode.

Figure 6.10 shows the resulting chart.

The process of creating line charts is quite straightforward. Although a certain amount of tweaking needs to happen, it is about normal for a chart. In contrast, when creating OHLC charts, you must jump through more hoops, as described in the next section.

Figure 6.10
The final chart shows closing price as a line chart and volumes as columns at the bottom of the chart.

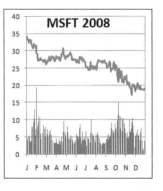

Creating OHLC Charts

Excel offers two built-in chart types that come close to the OHLC chart shown earlier in Figure 6.2. The built-in types both ignore the left-facing dash used to indicate the opening price each day.

Microsoft is not being dense here. Instead, a fundamental flaw exists in the underlying chart engine that makes it difficult to show the left-facing marker. This is why Microsoft does not support the open marker in the built-in charts. As you will see in the sections that follow, you can work around this flaw.

Producing a High-Low-Close Chart

Before progressing to a true OHLC chart, it is best to start with Excel's built-in high-low-close chart. Follow these steps to produce a high-low-close chart in Excel 2010:

1. Download data from `http://finance.yahoo.com`. Because you cannot save a chart in a CSV file, use the Save As command to save the file as a regular Excel file type.

2. Move the Open data from Column B to the blank Column H. Delete the now-empty Column B. This leaves you with dates in Column A, High in Column B, Low in Column C, and Close in Column D.

3. Select your data in Columns A:D.

4. On the Insert tab, select the Other Charts icon. In the Other Charts menu, the first four thumbnails are the four built-in stock charts (see Figure 6.11). Select the first stock icon (High-Low-Close). Excel creates the default chart shown in Figure 6.12.

Figure 6.11
The four built-in stock charts are hidden under the Other Charts icon.

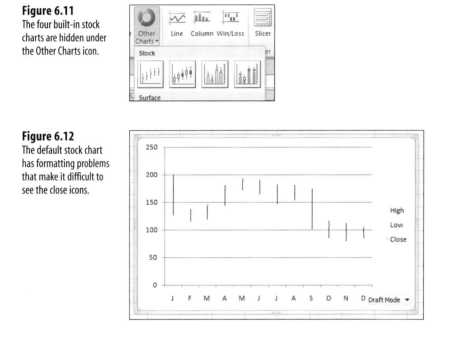

Figure 6.12
The default stock chart has formatting problems that make it difficult to see the close icons.

The default chart leaves a lot to be desired. For example, when looking at the vertical line extending from low to high, notice that it is nearly impossible to see the marker for the close. In addition, the legend on the right side does not add useful information to the chart.

If you turn to the Chart Layouts gallery on the Design tab, you face a perplexing selection. Layouts 1 and 3 appear to be identical. Layout 2 attempts to add data points for high, low, and close, making it impossible to see anything. The gray plot area in Layout 5 is not actually a gray plot area. Instead, it is Microsoft's attempt to draw 100 gridlines. The only interesting layout is Layout 4, in which Excel adds a data table. Layout 4 works for the charts in Figure 6.13 because they have only 12 months.

If you dare to choose any of the layouts from the Chart Styles gallery, the close markers change from being imperceptibly small to being far too large. Because Close is the third series, the markers are automatically upward-pointing triangles. This leads to the mistaken impression that the stock was trending up at the time the market closed (see Figure 6.14).

Figure 6.13
None of the built-in layouts improves the stock chart.

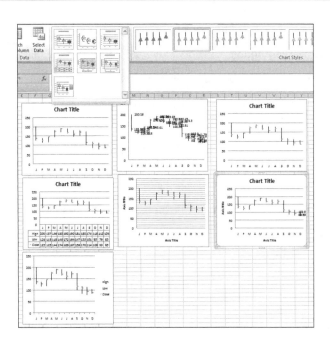

Figure 6.14
If you try to assign a style from the Design tab, you will automatically get triangles, which are the markers traditionally used for the third series.

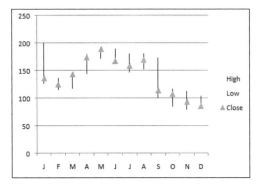

Customizing a High-Low-Close Chart

It is possible to make an acceptable high-low-close chart in Excel 2010. After you delete extraneous chart elements and zoom in, you need to format and change the marker style for the Close series. Here's how you do it:

1. Click the Legend and press the Delete key to remove the legend from the chart.

2. Double-click the Vertical Axis to display the Format Axis dialog box.

3. In the Axis Options category in the Format Axis dialog box, select Minimum, Fixed. Enter a number that is a bit lower than the low value in the chart. In the current example, a low value of 75 is appropriate. Keep the Format dialog box open for steps 4 through 12.

4. On the Layout tab, open the Current Selection drop-down and select Series "Close".

5. Select the Marker Options category along the left side of the dialog.

6. Increase the Size setting to 9 to ensure that the markers are visible.

7. Click the Marker Fill category in the Format Data Series dialog box. Select Solid Fill, and then select the black color.

8. Click the Marker Line Color category in the Format Data Series dialog box. Select Solid Line and then select the black color.

9. Click the horizontal gridlines in the chart.

10. For Line Color, select Solid Line. From the Color drop-down, select gray.

11. Click the Line Style category in the left of the dialog box.

12. Change the width to 0.5 points. Click Close to dismiss the Format dialog box.

13. Select Layout, Chart Title, Center Overlay Title. Type a title of AAPL 2008 and then press Enter.

14. Click the chart border. Drag the right resizing handle to the left to shrink the chart.

Figure 6.15 shows the resulting chart.

Figure 6.15
After formatting the high-low-close chart, you can actually see the close markers.

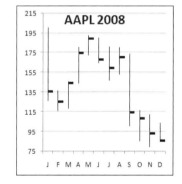

Creating an OHLC Chart

The fundamental barrier to creating a true OHLC chart is that Excel does not offer a left-facing dash as a built-in marker for a chart. However, you can import your own image to use as a marker.

Alternatively, you can use Photoshop to create a new graphic. For example, I created a graphic that was 11 pixels wide and 3 pixels tall. The leftmost five columns of pixels in this graphic are black, and the remaining pixels are transparent. I saved this file as a GIF image named LeftDash.gif. However, if you do not want to go to take the time to create an image like this, you can download this graphics from the web page of examples for this book at http://www.MrExcel.com/chart2010data.html.

The trick to creating an OHLC chart is to start with a high-low-close chart and add the Open series with a custom marker style. Follow these steps to create an OHLC chart in Excel 2010:

1. Start with data that has Date in Column A, High in Column B, Low in Column C, Close in Column D, and Open in Column E. Do not include the Open data in the initial selection. Select the data in A:D.

2. From the Insert tab, select Other Charts, Stock, High-Low-Close. Excel draws a chart. A blue box surrounds the charted data in B2:D13.

3. Click the blue handle in cell D13. Drag to the right to include the Open data on the chart. Excel adds the Open data in a format similar to the Close data.

4. On the Layout tab, select Series Close from the Current Selection drop-down. Click Format Selection.

5. For the Marker Options category, leave the marker as the right-facing dash and change the size to 7.

6. For the Marker Fill category, select Solid Fill. Select black from the color drop-down.

7. For the Marker Line Color category, select Solid Line. Select black from the color drop-down.

8. Without closing the Format dialog box, select Series Open from the Current Selection drop-down on the Layout tab. Once again, select the Marker Options category.

9. Change the Marker Type setting from None to Built-in.

10. In the Type drop-down, select the tenth marker, which is a tiny version of the Picture icon that is prevalent throughout Excel.

11. Click the Marker Fill category in the left navigation bar of the Format Data Series dialog.

12. Select Picture or Texture Fill. Excel updates the chart to show the default brown paper texture. Do not worry how this looks now since you will fix this later.

13. Click Insert from File in the dialog. Navigate to and select LeftDash.gif. Excel automatically adds a line around your marker. Even though the right side of the marker is transparent, Excel outlines the entire marker.

14. For the Marker Line Color category, select No Line. Click Close to close the Format dialog box.

15. On the Layout tab, select Legend, No Legend.

16. Select Chart Title, Above Chart. Type the title `AAPL 2006`.

17. Resize the chart so that it is horizontally smaller.

18. Right-click the numbers along the vertical axis, select Format Axis, and then select Minimum, Fixed, 50.

Figure 6.16 shows the final chart.

> **NOTE** If you are going to add volume to the chart later, you can allow the vertical scale to run from 0 to 100. If you are only showing OHLC on the chart, you can scale the vertical axis from 50 to 100.

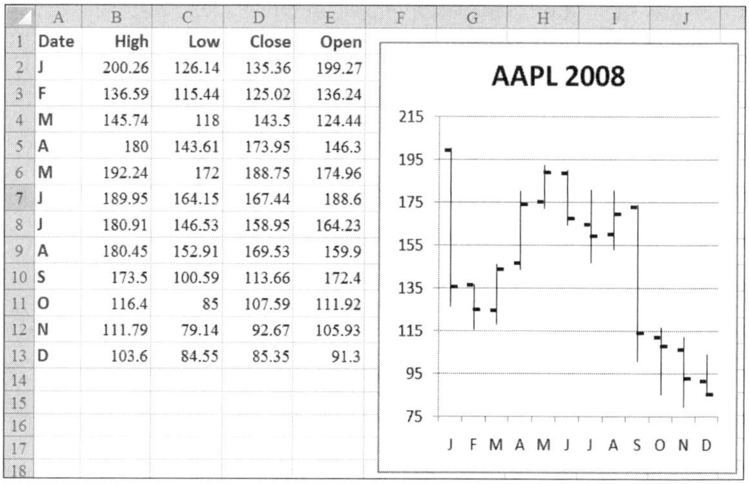

	A	B	C	D	E
1	Date	High	Low	Close	Open
2	J	200.26	126.14	135.36	199.27
3	F	136.59	115.44	125.02	136.24
4	M	145.74	118	143.5	124.44
5	A	180	143.61	173.95	146.3
6	M	192.24	172	188.75	174.96
7	J	189.95	164.15	167.44	188.6
8	J	180.91	146.53	158.95	164.23
9	A	180.45	152.91	169.53	159.9
10	S	173.5	100.59	113.66	172.4
11	O	116.4	85	107.59	111.92
12	N	111.79	79.14	92.67	105.93
13	D	103.6	84.55	85.35	91.3

Figure 6.16
The markers for the Open series are image files created in Photoshop.

The process of adding the open markers adds complexity to creating this chart. However, if you frequently need to create OHLC charts, you can save this chart type as a template to streamline the process in the future. To save a chart as a template, select the chart, and then select Save As Template from the Type group on the Design tab.

Adding Volume to a High-Low-Close Chart

There are two ways to add a volume column chart to a high-low-close chart:

- Microsoft offers a built-in volume-high-low-close chart. However, this built-in chart automatically moves the prices from the left axis to the right axis.
- You can add volumes while keeping the prices along the left axis.

6

Creating a Built-in Volume-High-Low-Close Chart

Follow these steps to create a built-in volume-high-low-close chart:

1. Arrange your data with Date in Column A, Volume in Column B, High in Column C, Low in Column D, and Close in Column E.
2. If you have actual dates in Column A, remove the Date heading from the top-left corner cell.
3. Select the range of data in A:E.
4. On the Insert tab, select Other Charts, Volume-High-Low-Close. Excel creates the chart shown in Figure 6.17.

> **N O T E** Notice that the volume bars in Figure 6.17 are keyed to a different axis than the rest of the chart. However, the scale seems a bit wrong since the volume bars obscure the actual OHLC lines.

Figure 6.17
The volume columns hide the high-low-close markers for most of this chart.

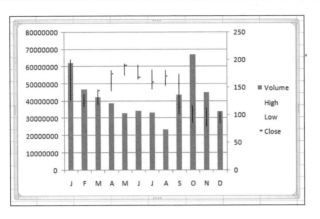

5. Click the Legend and then press the Delete key.

6. Double-click the numbers along the left side of the chart.

7. When the Format Axis dialog appears, click Maximum Fixed and triple the value shown in the box. In this example, you triple the original value of 8.0E7 to 2.4E8.

8. To remove the axis labels for the Volume columns, change the Axis Labels drop-down in the center of the Format Axis dialog to None. Change the Major Tick Mark Type drop-down to None.

9. While keeping the Format dialog open, click the Layout tab and open the Current Selection drop-down. Select Series Close.

10. Click Marker Options in the left navigation bar of the Format Data Series dialog. Increase the size from 5 to 9.

11. The gridlines shown in the chart are for the volume columns. To remove the gridlines and insert gridlines for the prices, on the Layout tab, select Gridlines, Primary Horizontal Gridlines, None. Then select Gridlines, Secondary Horizontal Gridlines, Major Gridlines.

12. From the Current Selection drop-down, select Secondary Vertical (Value) Axis Major Gridlines. The Format dialog box changes to Format Major Gridlines.

13. In the Format Major Gridline dialog, select Solid Line. In the Color drop-down, choose a light gray color to make the gridlines less obtrusive. Click Close to close the dialog box.

14. On the Layout tab, select Chart Title, Centered Overlay Title. Type AAPL 2008 and press Enter.

15. Click the border of the chart to select the chart area. On the Format tab, select Shape Outline, No Outline to remove the extra box around the chart.

16. Reduce the horizontal size of the chart by clicking the right resizing handle and dragging toward the center of the chart.

Figure 6.18 shows the resulting chart. However, it can be a bit disconcerting to have the axis scale appear on the right side of the chart when 99 percent of the charts in the Western world have the axis appear on the left side of the chart. A solution for this problem is provided in the next section.

Figure 6.18
After a number of adjustments, the built-in volume-high-low-close chart does the job, although the axis appears on the wrong side.

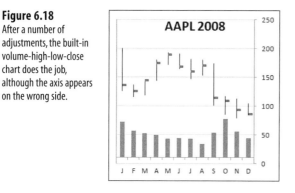

Adding Volume to the Right Axis of a High-Low-Close Chart

Although the method described in this section is a bit more complicated than the method described in the preceding section, it enables you to add the volume to the axis on the right side of the chart. This method abandons the built-in stock chart types and reveals that the stock chart types are really just an interesting mixture of standard settings.

The following steps add volume to the high-low-close chart shown earlier in Figure 6.15. You can expand the concept to add an Open marker as in the chart shown in Figure 6.16.

Follow these steps to create a volume-high-low-close chart:

1. Download data from `http://finance.yahoo.com`. Rearrange the data to show Date in Column A, High in Column B, Low in Column C, Close in Column D, and Volume in Column E.

2. Remove the Date heading from the top-left cell in the range.

3. Although you have data in Columns A:E, select only the data in Columns A:D.

4. On the Insert tab, select Line, 2-D Line, Line. Excel creates the chart shown in Figure 6.19.

5. On the Layout tab, select Series High from the Current Selection drop-down. Click Format Selection and then select Line Color, No Line.

Figure 6.19
This line chart appears to be a long way from the OHLC format you desire.

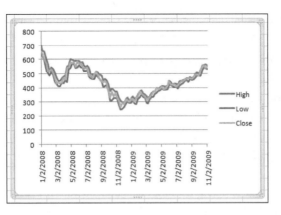

6. Without closing the Format Data Series dialog, select Series Low from the Current Selection drop-down in the Layout tab. In the Format Data Series dialog, select Line Color, No Line. The high and low lines are now invisible, as shown in Figure 6.20.

Figure 6.20
Make the high and low lines invisible.

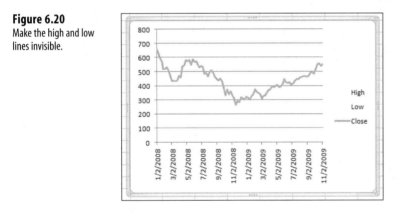

7. Keep the Format dialog open. From the Layout tab, select Lines, High-Low Lines. Excel draws vertical lines between the invisible high and low points, as shown in Figure 6.21.

6

Figure 6.21
Add High-Low lines to draw the vertical lines from the invisible high and low markers.

8. Keep the Format dialog open. Select Series "Close" from the Current Selection drop-down on the Layout tab. In the Format dialog, make the following selections:

- Select Marker Options, Built-In, Type, select the sixth type, which is a right-facing dash.
- Change the Size setting from 5 to 8.
- Select Marker Fill, Solid Fill, and then select black.
- Select Line Color, No Line.
- Select Marker Line Color, Solid Line, and then select black.

9. Click Close to close the dialog box. You have created a high-low-close style chart from the line chart, as shown in Figure 6.22.

Figure 6.22
The line chart is now a high-low-close style chart. Notice the blue resizing handle in the upper-right corner of D2.

	A	B	C	D	E	F	G
1		High	Low	Close	Volume	Adj Close	Open
2	1/2/2008	697.37	655	657	4306400	657	692.87
3	1/7/2008	662.28	622.51	638.25	5958600	638.25	653.94
4	1/14/2008	657.4	598.01	600.25	7466400	600.25	651.14
5	1/22/2008	597.5	519	566.4	1.1E+07	566.4	562.03
6	1/28/2008	573	510	515.9	1.1E+07	515.9	570.97
7	2/4/2008	517.73	488.52	516.69	9350900	516.69	509.07
8	2/11/2008	541.04	513.03	529.64	6165900	529.64	520.52
9	2/19/2008	535.06	497.55	507.8	6051500	507.8	534.94
10	2/25/2008	506.5	446.85	471.18	1.2E+07	471.18	505.95
11	3/3/2008	472.72	426.24	433.35	8830900	433.35	471.51
12	3/10/2008	449.34	413.04	437.92	7553400	437.92	428.83
13	3/17/2008	447.5	412.11	433.55	7804400	433.55	427.99
14	3/24/2008	465.78	434.31	438.08	5605800	438.08	438.43
15	3/31/2008	477.83	432.01	471.09	5842800	471.09	435.64
16	4/7/2008	485.44	455.01	457.45	5156100	457.45	477.03
17	4/14/2008	547.7	441	539.41	9527900	539.41	457.16
18	4/21/2008	560.83	530.29	544.06	5719800	544.06	539.39
19	4/28/2008	602.45	539	581.29	5971800	581.29	545.88
20	5/5/2008	599.49	571.3	573.2	5426200	573.2	598.86
21	5/12/2008	591.19	568.91	580.07	4604000	580.07	574.75
22	5/19/2008	588.88	537.81	544.62	4978800	544.62	578.55
23	5/27/2008	589.92	543.85	585.8	3996500	585.8	544.96
24	6/2/2008	588.04	560.61	567	3998700	567	582.5

10. Grab the blue resizing handle in the upper-right corner of D2. Drag to the right to add Column E to the chart. Do not be concerned that you no longer see the high-low-close markers. You will get them back before the end of the process.

11. From the Current Selection drop-down on the Layout tab, select Series Volume. Click Format Selection. Select Secondary Axis. Click Close. In a bizarre twist, the columns that appeared in step 9 turn into an invisible line chart.

12. On the Design tab, select Change Chart Type. Select the first column chart icon– Clustered Column. The columns reappear.

13. Double-click the numbers along the right axis of the chart.

14. Click Maximum, Fixed. Double the number in the Fixed text box. Select Major Tick Mark Type, None. Select Axis Labels, None.

15. Click the Legend and press the Delete key.

16. Click the labels along the horizontal axis. Select Axis Options, Major Unit, Fixed, 1, Months. For the Number category, select the date type of M. Click Close.

17. Select Layout, Chart Title, Above Chart. Type the chart title `AAPL 2006`.

18. Reduce the horizontal size of the chart.

Figure 6.23 shows the final chart.

Figure 6.23
This volume-high-low-close chart was created from a line chart.

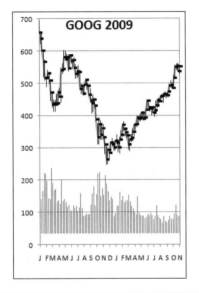

GOOG 2009

NOTE If you try to add volume as a column chart on the secondary axis to one of Excel's built-in stock charts, Excel will indicate that certain types cannot be combined, which will prevent you from producing the chart. If this occurs, you can skip the built-in stock chart type and build the chart as a line chart, as you have seen in this section.

The next section describes candlestick charts, which require the least customization because Excel includes good built-in charts to create candlestick charts.

Creating Candlestick Charts

A basic candlestick chart requires a data range that includes a date in the first column, and open, high, low, and close values in the remaining columns. To create a candlestick chart, follow these steps:

1. Download data from `http://finance.yahoo.com`. Your data will be in the correct sequence, with Date in Column A, Open in Column B, High in Column C, Low in Column D, and Close in Column E.

2. Select your data in Columns A:E.

3. On the Insert tab, select Other Charts, Stock, Open-High-Low-Close. Excel creates the chart in Figure 6.24.

Figure 6.24
The chart shows the default chart created in step 3.

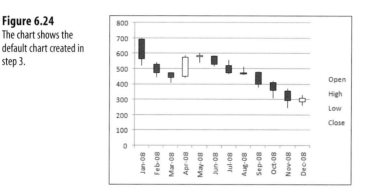

4. Click the legend and press Delete.

5. Double-click the numbers along the vertical axis. Specify a fixed minimum value that is greater than zero but lower than the low value for the range in question.

6. Click the Number section along the left navigation. Select the Date category and then the M type. Click Close to close the dialog box.

7. Select Layout, Chart Title, Above Chart. Type the title GOOG 2008, and then press Enter.

8. Reduce the horizontal size of the chart.

The final chart is shown as the bottom chart in Figure 6.25.

Figure 6.25
After minimal formatting, you have an acceptable chart.

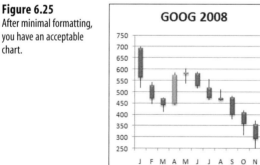

Changing Colors in a Candlestick Chart

By default, Excel makes the candlestick charts monochrome. Stock price increases are shown with white columns. Stock price declines are shown with black columns. If you will be presenting the chart in color, you might prefer another system, such as red for declines and green for increases. If this is the case, it is easy to customize the colors in a chart.

Before adjusting the colors, apply any effects to the chart. For example, open the Chart Styles gallery on the Design tab and choose Style 28 to apply a beveled effect to the up/down bars.

The white up bars and the black down bars are actually two separate objects in the chart. Therefore, first you need to format the up bars and then format the down bars. To change the color of the bars, follow these steps:

1. On the Format tab, select Current Selection, Up Bars 1.
2. Select Format, Shape Fill, and then select green. (In color stock charts, up periods are typically shown in green.)
3. On the Format tab, select Current Selection, Down Bars 1.
4. Select Format, Shape Fill and then select red. (In color stock charts, up periods are typically shown in red.)

Adding Volume to a Candlestick Chart

Excel offers a built-in chart you can use to create a candlestick chart that includes volume bars. However, as with the volume-high-low-close chart, the height of the volume bars is often too large.

Follow these steps to create a chart based on the built-in volume-open-high-low-close chart type:

1. Download data from `http://finance.yahoo.com`. Save the data as an Excel workbook. Insert a new Column B before the Open column. Move the Volume data from Column G to the new Column B. Delete Column G. Your data will be in the correct sequence, with Date in Column A, Volume in Column B, Open in Column C, High in Column D, Low in Column E, and Close in Column F.
2. Remove the Date heading from cell A1.
3. Select your data in Columns A:F.
4. On the Insert tab, select Other Charts, Stock, Volume-Open-High-Low-Close. This is the fourth stock chart thumbnail. Excel creates the top chart in Figure 6.26.
5. Right-click the numbers along the left vertical axis and then select Format Axis. Specify a fixed maximum value that is about double the original amount. Select Major Tick Mark Type, None. Select Axis Labels, None.
6. On the Layout tab, select Legend, None.
7. Select Chart Title, Above Chart. Type the title GOOG 2006 and press Enter.
8. Right-click the labels along the horizontal axis. Select Format Axis. On the Number tab, specify the custom formatting code mmmmm.
9. Reduce the horizontal size of the chart.

6

The final chart is shown as the bottom chart in Figure 6.26.

Figure 6.26
The top chart shows the default chart created in step 4. The bottom chart shows the result of the remaining formatting.

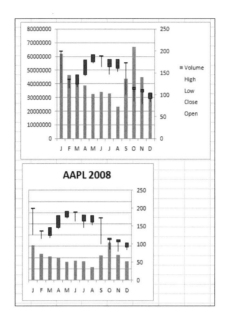

Manually Creating a Candlestick Chart with Volume

The problem with the chart in Figure 6.26 is that the stock prices appear on the right side of the chart. If you prefer to have your stock prices on the left side of the chart, you need to abandon the built-in stock charts. However, before you take this step, you need to have a good understanding of how Excel draws in high-low lines and up/down bars. The following section provides explains the rules for high-low lines and up/down bars.

Figure 6.27 shows four line series on a single chart. The first series is the thick solid line from lower left to upper right. The second series is the dotted line at the top of the chart. The third series starts out as the lowest dashed line but crosses to become the second-lowest line late in the chart.

You can add high-low lines to a chart by selecting Layout, Lines, High-Low Lines. Figure 6.28 shows that the vertical lines extend from the lowest value at each data point to the highest value at each data point. In February, the line extends from the 1 in Series 3 up to the 12 in Series 2. In October, the high-low line extends from the 1 in Series 1 to the 12 in Series 2.

In contrast to high-low lines, up/down bars always extend from the first series line to the last series line. In Figure 6.29, the up/down bars always start at the solid line for Series 1 and extend to the dash-dot line for Series 4. It seems like there would be a setting that you could use to specify that the up/down bars should extend from one series to another series.

Figure 6.27
These four series are used to illustrate the different behavior of high-low lines and up/down bars.

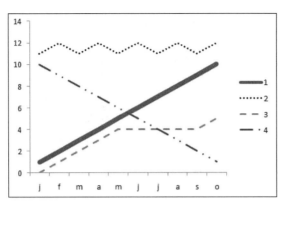

Figure 6.28
High-low lines look at all the line series in the chart and extend from the lowest to the highest at each data point.

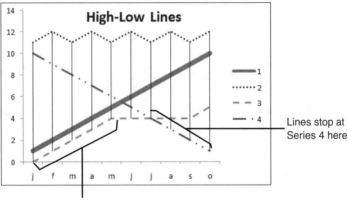

Lines stop at
Series 4 here

Lines stop at Series 3 here

Instead, Excel always draws the up/down bars from the first series to the last series (see Figure 6.29).

> **NOTE**
> Both the high-low lines and up/down bars are valid only for series that are plotted as line charts. If you need to add a series for volume, make sure to plot that series as a column chart so it does not interfere with your high-low or up/down elements. If you need to add a series to show the price of a competing stock, you can add the series as a scatter chart with a smooth line to prevent that series from interfering with the high-low or up/down elements.

To see a demo of high/low lines, search for MrExcel Charts 6 at YouTube.

Figure 6.29
Up/down bars always start at the first series and extend to the last series.

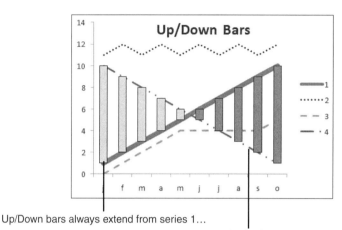

Up/Down bars always extend from series 1…

…to the final series

CASE STUDY: CREATING A CANDLESTICK STOCK CHART SHOWING VOLUME AND A COMPETITOR

Candlestick charts are popular at http://finance.yahoo.com. In addition to a candlestick chart showing the price of one security, a secondary line chart is often added to show the relative price of another security. The chart is designed to show how equal investments in one security or the other will fare over time.

In this case study, the chart you build compares the performance of Apple versus Microsoft from January 2, 2008, through October 30, 2009.

When you download data from the historical tables at http://finance.yahoo.com, make a note of the opening price for both stocks on the starting date. The price for Apple stock was $199.27, while the price for Microsoft stock was $35.79. This means that purchasing one share of Apple would be eqivalent to purchasing about 5.567 shares of Microsoft. To calculate this multiplier, divide the Apple opening price (199.27) by the Microsoft starting price (35.79). To make a successful chart, you want to compare the price for 1 share of Apple to the price of 5.567 shares of Microsoft.

In Figure 6.30, the first few columns show Apple data from http://finance.yahoo.com. Date, Open, High, Low, Close, and Volume occupy Columns A:F. Column G contains the adjusted closing price for Microsoft for each month. Column F shows the start of the calculation of a MSFT index line. This line shows the closing price of Microsoft multiplied by (199.27/35.79). This calculation makes both lines show the value of an initial $199.27 purchase of each security.

Figure 6.30
You can build a column that shows the relative value of Microsoft.

	A	B	C	D	E	F	G	H
1	Date	Open	High	Low	Close	Volume	MSFT Index	MS AdClose
2	Jan-08	199.27	200.26	126.14	135.36	6.2E+07	174.88	31.41
3	Feb-08	136.24	136.59	115.44	125.02	4.7E+07		26.31
4	Mar-08	124.44	145.74	118	143.5	4.2E+07		27.45

To begin building the chart, copy the formula from G2 down to all rows of your dataset. Based on how Excel plots high-low lines and up/down bars illustrated earlier in Figure 6.29, you know that the Open column has to be the first series plotted as a line. The Close column has to be the last series plotted as a line. This means you need to manually change the chart type for the volume series to a column and manually change the chart type for the line series to a scatter chart.

If you started with a stock chart type, you would build the chart with a few series and then add more series later. However, because you are building this chart as a line chart, you can add all six series at once.

To build the chart, do the following:

1. Select the data in A1:G23. On the Insert tab, select Line, 2-D Line, Line. You see a chart with only one visible line. Because the Volume numbers are so large, this is the only line you can initially see (see Figure 6.31).

Figure 6.31
You initially see only one line on the chart.

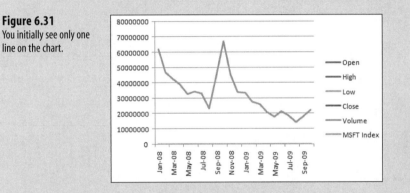

2. Double-click the line chart for Volume. In the Format Data Series dialog, click Secondary Axis. Excel shows six lines on the chart (see Figure 6.32). Close the Format dialog.

Figure 6.32
After you move the volume to a secondary axis, all six lines appear.

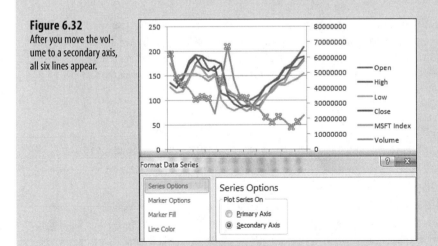

6

3. With the Volume series still selected, select Design, Change Chart Type. Select the first column type. The volume is now plotted as a column.

4. Double-click the numbers along the secondary value axis on the right side of the chart to display the Format Axis dialog box. Select Minimum, Fixed, 0. Select Maximum Fixed. Change the current value for the maximum from 8.0E7 to 2.1E8. This is about 2.6 times the original size to ensure that the volume bars take up only the lower third of the chart.

5. In the same dialog box, change Major Tick Mark Type to None and Axis Labels to None. Close the Format dialog box. You will see that the volume series is now a column chart taking up the lower portion of the plot area, as shown in Figure 6.33.

Figure 6.33
Volume is moved to a small column chart.

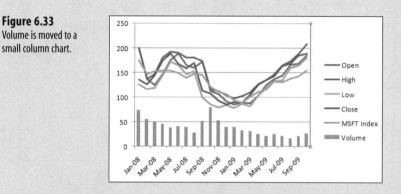

6. Select Series MSFT Index from the Current Selection drop-down on the Layout tab. On the Design tab, select Change Chart Type. Select the final X Y (Scatter) thumbnail:, X Y (Scatter), Scatter with Straight Lines. The line for MSFT goes to practically zero as the MSFT Index is now plotted on the secondary axis. You will correct this in step 7.

7. Select Series MSFT Index from the Current Selection drop-down on the Layout tab. Click Format Selection. Change the Series Options panel to indicate Primary Axis. Change Line Color to Solid Line and then select red. Change Line Style, Dash Type to a dotted line. Close the Format dialog box. Your chart has four series as line charts, one as a column chart, and one as an X Y scatter chart. It is now appropriate to draw in the high-low lines and up/down bars.

8. Select Series Open from the Current Selection drop-down on the Layout tab. Select Layout, Lines, High-Low Lines. Select Layout, Up/Down Bars, Up/Down Bars.

9. Next, to remove the lines from the first four series, on the Format tab, select Series Open. Select Format, Shape Outline, No Outline.

10. Repeat step 9 for High, Low, and Close lines.

11. Add a title by choosing Chart Title, Centered Overlay Title on the Layout tab. Type the title AAPL and press Enter. Drag the title to the top-left corner of the chart. (You need a legend in this chart to indicate that the dotted line is a Microsoft index line. While four of the six legend entries are useless because the line is hidden, the legends for Volume and MSFT Index are worthwhile.)

12. Click the Legend. Click the word Open in the Legend and press the Delete key. The Open item disappears from the legend. To repeat for High, Low, and Close, click the legend, click the word, and then type Delete.

13. Use the Layout tab to select Legend, Show Legend at Bottom. Drag the legend to the lower-left corner. You now have the chart shown in Figure 6.34.

Figure 6.34
Microsoft and Apple were performing in a similar fashion. Apple began to pull ahead in 2009.

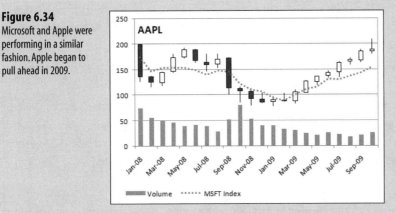

14. Traditionally, http://finance.yahoo.com shows this chart without any prices along the axis. This is because the Microsoft line is a relative index line and not an actual price line. To remove the prices from the axis, double-click the labels on the left axis. Select Axis Labels, None. Alternatively, you can use the Number tab and format them as currency with no decimal places.

The chart in Figure 6.34 presents the interesting concepts listed here:

■ Either the candlestick or the OHLC charts must be created with series that use a line chart type, although you turn off the line in all cases.

■ Any other index lines on the chart must be converted to X Y scatter charts, with a line connecting invisible points. Thus, the only series on the chart that appears as a line really is not a line chart at all.

■ You can add additional index lines to the chart, but each will have to be X Y series.

■ You can squash the volume column chart into the lower third of the chart by fixing the maximum value for the scale at three times the maximum value.

This case study demonstrates that you can duplicate stock charts without using the Microsoft built-in stock chart types. In fact, using a line chart gives you more flexibility to add additional data series to a chart.

6

Creating a Live Chart by Using a Web Connection

In public companies, senior management often spends a lot of time focusing on the current stock price. This might be because they are truly concerned for the individual investors, or it might be that they are interested in the current value of their stock options.

At my employer in the 1980s, an investor relations administrator continually updated a whiteboard showing the stock price of my employer and the two competitors in our industry. Dialing in to a service 24 times a day to update the whiteboard must have been a horrible chore.

Excel offers fabulous tools that automatically queries data from a web page every minute and then refreshes the data in Excel.

> **TIP**
>
> It is best if this process is running in its own instance of Excel. Better yet, this process should be running on a standalone computer. If you have this process running in the same instance of Excel where you are trying to work, you will be interrupted every minute while the web query updates.

> **NOTE**
>
> If you think it is insane to spend $300 on a Netbook computer to update the stock price every minute, consider how insane it was to have a person doing this job manually day after day.

To set up a web query, first you need to move the cell pointer to an out-of-the-way location on the worksheet. The web query returns unformatted data that you nearly always want to reformat. Therefore, the query should be located outside the field of view and you should use formulas or charts to display the data. To build this chart, follow these steps:

1. Select cell A40.

2. From the Data tab, select From Web. A New Web Query dialog box appears that shows the home page selected in your installation of Internet Explorer. For example, you might see Google or Bing or Yahoo in the browser.

3. Use the New Web Query dialog box to navigate to your favorite source of stock quote information such as `http://finance.yahoo.com`. Click in the Get Quotes box, type the ticker symbols MSFT, AAPL, GOOG, and click the Go button. After the web page finishes loading, Excel draws a series of yellow arrows. Each arrow indicates a table on the web page.

> **CAUTION**
>
> Many web pages used tables for the last decade. It used to be that you could find a table that returned only the stock quotes. However, now JavaScript is making some tables obsolete. For this reason, you might need to choose to return the entire web page and use VLOOKUP formulas to locate the data to extract.

4. Scroll down to the table that contains the data you want to import to Excel. While you hover over the yellow arrow, an outline appears that shows the extent of the table. Click the yellow arrow to change it to a green check mark (see Figure 6.35).

Figure 6.35
Select the tables from the web page to be imported.

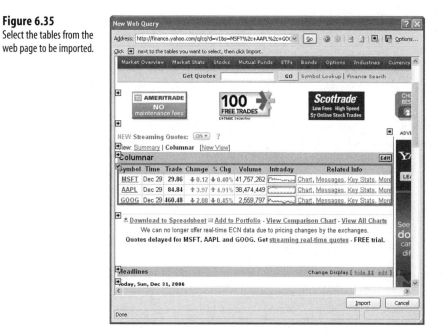

5. Click the Import button. The New Web Query dialog box is dismissed and the Import Data dialog box appears. Confirm the location for the imported data and then click OK. A strange bit of text appears in the active cell. A few seconds later, a text version of the table appears in your spreadsheet. Keep in mind that this is a one-time snapshot of the data. After you build a few formulas and a chart, you can change the properties of the web query to refresh every minute.

> **NOTE**
> You do not want to be working in Excel while the query is set to auto-refresh. It is incredibly annoying to lose focus on the active cell every minute while the Web query refreshes. To alleviate this problem, have the Web query running in one instance of Excel and work in a second instance of Excel.

Creating a Bar Chart with Formulas to Extract Imported Data

Next, you need to build formulas that extract the desired information from the imported data. In this case, a simple bar chart with three points will work fine. The formula in I41 builds some text that is used as both the category value and the label for the bar chart. The formula in I41 is `=A41&" "&C41&" "&E41`. The formula in J41 is more complex, as it has to convert the text value of Down 0.40 percent to a value of -0.4 percent. The formula in J41 is `=IF(LEFT(E41,1)="D",-1*MID(E41,6,4),1*MID(E41,4,4))/100`. Copy these formulas down for the competitor's stock quotes, as shown in Figure 6.36.

Figure 6.36
Build formulas that you
can use to create a chart.

	J41			fx	=IF(LEFT(E41,1)="D",-1*MID(E41,6,4),1*MID(E41,4,4))/100			
	A	B	C	D	E	F	G H	I	J
40	Symbol	Time	Trade	Change	% Chg	Volume	Intr Related Info	
41	MSFT	29-Dec	29.86	Down 0.12	Down 0.40%	41,757,262	Char MSFT 29.86 Down 0.40%	-0.4%
42	AAPL	29-Dec	84.84	Up 3.97	Up 4.91%	38,474,449	Char AAPL 84.84 Up 4.91%	4.9%
43	GOOG	29-Dec	460.48	Down 2.08	Down 0.45%	2,559,797	Char GOOG 460.48 Down 0.45%	-0.5%

Build a chart using the formulas in I41:J43. Format the chart and move it up to occupy a spot in your executive dashboard. In Figure 6.37, a simple bar chart shows the relative increase/decrease of each security.

Figure 6.37
Build a chart that reflects
data from the web query.

	A	B	C	D	E	F	G
1	Today's stock performance as of 12:12 PM						
2							
3			MSFT 29.86				
4			Down 0.40%				
5							
6					AAPL 84.84		
7					Up 4.91%		
8			GOOG				
9			460.48				
10			Down 0.45%				
11							

After the chart is built, change the properties of the web query by right-clicking a cell in the imported data and choosing Data Range Properties.

In the External Data Range Properties dialog box that appears, select the Refresh Every check box. Change the spin button from 60 minutes to 1 minute. In addition, select the check box for Refresh Data When Opening the File (see Figure 6.38). When you click OK, the web query begins to refresh every minute and automatically update your chart in the dashboard.

It is possible to build a dashboard with many different web feeds and charts that update automatically as long as the Internet connection remains live. You can accomplish this without writing any VBA macros.

Making Charts Small for Use in Dashboards

The goal of creating an executive dashboard is to fit a lot of data into a single screen of data.

Figure 6.38
Excel updates the web query every minute.

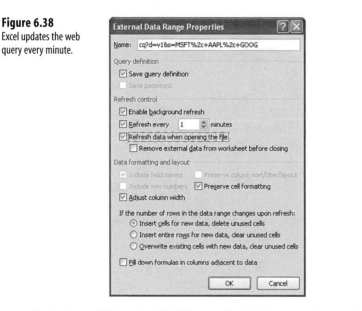

Beginning with Excel 2007, Microsoft added features that makes it easier to scale charts down until they are quite small. In Figure 6.39, the chart at the top is converted to a smaller chart in the lower right by using Layout 11 from the Chart Layouts gallery on the Design tab. The two other charts are not really charts at all, but Sparklines.

→ See Chapter 9, "Using Sparklines, Data Visualizations, and Other Nonchart Methods," for examples of how to create these tiny word-sized charts.

Figure 6.39
Beginning with Excel 2007, it is easier to create small charts for dashboards.

Next Steps

In this chapter, you learned that there are times when you need to think creatively to coax an "impossible" chart out of Excel. In Chapter 7, "Advanced Charting Techniques," you will learn how to use Excel's built-in charting tools to create charts that you do not normally see in Excel.

Advanced Chart Techniques

A Tool Chest of Advanced Charting Techniques

As the host of MrExcel.com, I get to see a lot of wild spreadsheets that people create. I have seen some amazing things come across my desk. This chapter covers some of the usual advanced charting tricks, and some unusual charts that you do not typically see in Excel. At the end of the chapter are a few examples of some charts that impressed me, so that you can see some of the cool things people can coax out of Excel.

The ideas in this section can be useful on most chart types that you work with. They include many techniques that you will come to realize are the basic, why-didn't-I-think-of-doing-that kind of ideas.

Mixing Two Chart Types on a Single Chart

Although the Chart Type dialog does not offer it as a choice anymore, you can represent a chart's series with different chart types. Instead of two lines on a chart, you can show one series as a line and one series as columns. Or you can mix columns and area charts, as shown in Figure 7.1.

To change the chart type for a series, you right-click the series and select Change Series Chart Type from the context menu.

When you change the chart type of a series in a chart, you set up a new chart group. Say that you have a stacked column chart with four series. When you change Series D to be a line chart, then chart group 1 contains the three series in the stacked columns. Chart group 2 contains the line series.

If you then change Series C to be an area chart, that creates a third chart group. The original chart

Figure 7.1
To emphasize one series, you can mix chart types on a single chart.

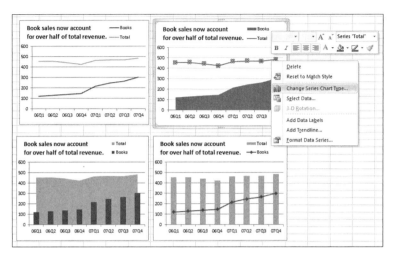

group now contains only the two series that remain in the stacked columns. In Figure 7.2, five series occupy three chart groups.

Figure 7.2
Stacked columns, stacked lines, and an area chart create three chart groups.

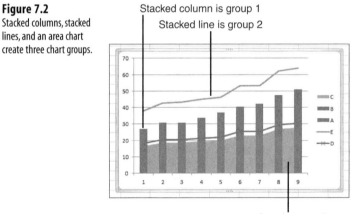

In general, every different chart type in the same chart is in a new group. Moving one or more series to the secondary axis also creates a new chart group. Certain settings such as width of the column markers apply to all of the series in the same group. Some of the examples in this chapter will purposely move a series to the second axis or change the chart type of a series to create a different group, where different settings can apply. If you need to mix clustered and stacked columns, you will have to use this technique.

For best results when mixing chart types, follow these guidelines:

- You should stick with 2-D chart types. Excel does not let you mix 3-D charts.

> **TIP**
> You should mix only certain chart types. Some of the rules are set by Excel. Others are from a good design perspective.

- You can not stack markers from chart group 2 on top of markers from chart group 1. Every chart group starts stacking from the category axis.

- Although Excel will let you do it, you should not mix vertical types with horizontal types. Figure 7.3 shows a chart where one series is moved to a bar chart. Most people will not be able to glean anything from this chart (other than perhaps the fact that you have no sense of design).

Figure 7.3
Although Excel lets you mix column and bar charts, I am not sure why you would.

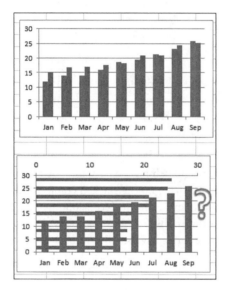

- You can mix circular charts. For example, you can change one series of a doughnut chart to a pie chart.

- Remember that in many cases, a line chart can be changed to an XY scatter with line series. The advantage is that up/down bars and hi-lo lines ignore an XY scatter chart line.

To see a demo of mixing chart types, search for "MrExcel Charts 7" at YouTube.

Mixing Stacked Columns with Clustered Columns

Column charts come in three basic flavors: clustered, stacked and 100 percent stacked. You might think that creating a chart which combines clustered and stacked column, as shown in Figure 7.4 would be easy, but it requires a lot of trickery to create the chart.

Figure 7.4
Compare how sales of components 1A and 1B stack up against a total forecast.

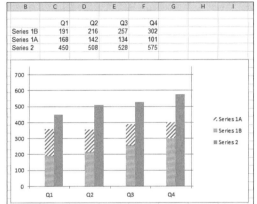

Figure 7.5 will reveal some of the magic behind the curtain. The chart is actually made up of five series. Series 1A and Series 1B make up the stacked column and are tied to the left axis. Series 2 as well as Blank 1 and Blank 2 are clustered columns and are tied to the right axis. In Figure 7.4, the blank series were filled with zeros and were not visible, but were still taking up space. In Figure 7.5, those series have small values so you can see the horizontal space that they are occupying.

Figure 7.5
Two blank series move Series 2 over to the right.

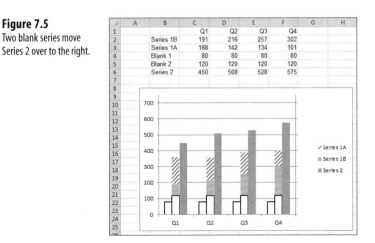

7

There are other tricks along the way of creating the chart. To mix clustered and stacked columns, one chart group has to be moved to the secondary axis. Anytime that you have two values axes, you need to switch to manual scaling to that they stay in sync. To make the stacked column narrower, you will increase the gap width between the columns.

Follow these steps to create the chart in Figure 7.4:

1. Start with data that has Series 1B, Series 1A, Blank 1, Blank 2, Series 2.

2. Create a stacked column chart from that data.

3. Because you have five rows and four columns, Excel assumes that you want the quarters to be stacked. On the Design tab, click Switch Row/Column so that the quarters are running across the horizontal axis. You should have something like the top-left chart in Figure 7.6.

Figure 7.6
Three steps toward the final chart.

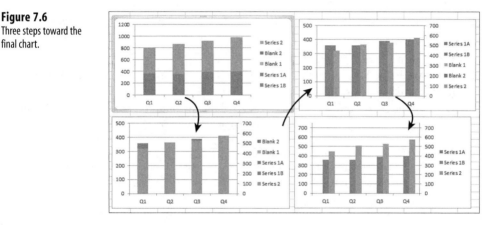

4. Double-click one of the Series 2 columns to open the Format dialog. Select to move Series 2 to the secondary axis. You now actually have Series 1A and Series 1B in one stack and Series 2 in another stack. Unfortunately, because they are on different axis, Microsoft plots those columns directly on top of each other. Series 2 is covering up the detail in Series 1A and Series 1B. You can see this in the bottom-left chart of Figure 7.6.

5. On the Layout tab, select Blank 1 from the first drop-down. Select Format Selection. Move that series to the secondary axis.

6. While the Format dialog is open, select Blank 2 from the drop-down on the Layout tab. Move Blank 2 to the secondary axis. Close the Format dialog.

7. Blank 2 should still be selected. Go to the Design tab and select Change Chart Type. Select a clustered column chart. This changes the chart type of all three series that are on the secondary axis. You now have the top-right chart in Figure 7.6. There are still problems. All the Series 2 columns should be taller than the total of the Series 1

columns. The problem is that the right scale goes from 0 to 700 and the left scale goes from 0 to 500. Also, from an aesthetic point of view, the stacked column is appearing much wider than the clustered column.

8. Double-click the numbers along the right axis to open the Format dialog. Change the Min and Max from Automatic to Fixed. Use 0 as the Min and 700 as the Max. Keep the Format dialog open.

9. Click the left axis on the chart. Change the Min and Max from Automatic to Fixed. Use the same values as in step 8. Keep the format dialog open.

10. Click Series 1A in the chart. The format dialog box now offers a setting called Gap Width. When you increase the gap between columns, you automatically make the columns narrower. Increase the gap width from 150 to about 350. You can tweak this setting until the stacked column and the clustered column look to be about the same width.

11. The rogue blank series are still in the legend. The first click on the word *Blank 1* in the legend selects the whole legend. The second click on Blank 1 selects just Blank 1. Press Delete. Repeat the two clicks to select Blank 2 in the legend. Press Delete.

12. As shown in the bottom-right chart of Figure 7.6, you now have numbers along both the left and right axis. While this might serve as a reminder that you have two axis, you can hide the right numbers. One easy way: Click the numbers to select them. Go to the font color drop-down on the Home tab. Select a white font.

> NOTE For this monochrome book, the patterns of the stacked columns were changed to a pattern fill. Double-click the series. In the left navigation of the Format dialog, select Fill, then pattern fill.

Moving Charts from One Worksheet to Another

You can combine charts from many worksheets into a single dashboard by moving the charts from their original locations.

For example, if your sales data is on a sales worksheet, you can build the chart on the sales worksheet. When the chart is selected, you select Move Chart from the Design tab. You can then choose to move the chart to a different worksheet (see Figure 7.7).

The chart continues to point to data on the original worksheet, but you end up with an uncluttered screen of just charts. Even though the charts are on a new worksheet, they still respond to data changes on the source worksheets.

Using Shapes to Annotate a Chart

Excel offers 165 shapes on the Insert tab. Any of these shapes can contain text and can be added to a chart to call attention to certain aspects of the chart. As an example, in the chart in Figure 7.8, a block arrow shape points out reduced revenue levels in July through September. A callout below the chart points to the reduced June profits.

Figure 7.7
You use the Move Chart dialog to build a dashboard of charts on a single sheet.

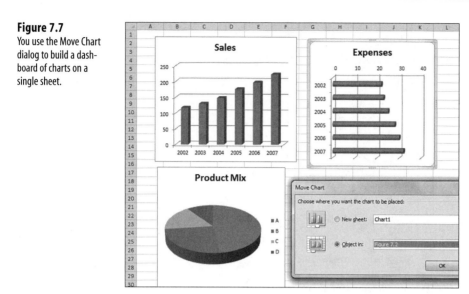

Figure 7.8
Shapes with added text annotate key points in this chart.

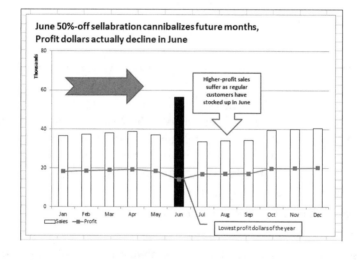

> **TIP**
> There is one trick to using shapes on your chart: Make sure your chart is active before you click a shape in the Insert tab. If the chart is not active and you draw a shape over the chart, the shape is actually anchored to a particular cell in the worksheet.

To add a shape to a chart, you follow these steps:

1. Click the chart.
2. On the Insert tab, open the Shapes drop-down. This drop-down offers 165 shapes in 8 categories, as shown in Figure 7.9.
3. Click a shape. Your mouse pointer changes to a small plus sign.

7

Figure 7.9
You can choose from
these 165 shapes.

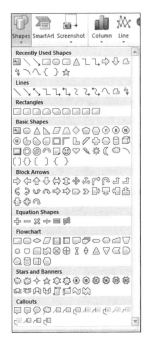

4. Click and drag on the chart to draw a shape. The initial shape is filled with a solid color.

5. Use the white resizing handles to adjust the size of the shape. Use the yellow diamond handles to change the inflection points of the shape. Use the green rotation handle to rotate the shape. All the shapes in Figure 7.10 are right arrow callout shapes that have been modified by dragging the yellow inflection handles.

6. From the Format tab, select Shape Fill, White, and then Shape Outline, Black to remove the fill color from the shape.

7. Right-click the shape and select Edit Text.

8. Type your text in the shape.

9. Use the formatting icons on the Home tab to change the alignment and font size of the text in the shape.

> **NOTE**
> Because you are planning on adding text to these shapes, you should not plan on rotating the shapes unless you want the text to be rotated, too.

When working with shapes, you will note that the Shapes drop-down includes a number of lines and arrows. While adding an arrow to a chart, you can hover over an existing shape to reveal four red connector dots. If you start or end an arrow on a connector dot, the arrow automatically moves when the connected shapes move.

Figure 7.10
You can use the handles to resize, reshape, and rotate a shape.

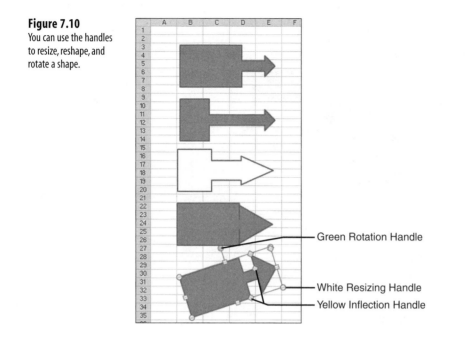

Green Rotation Handle

White Resizing Handle
Yellow Inflection Handle

Making Columns or Bars Float

In Figure 7.11, the black bars appear to float in midair. This type of chart is good for showing the components of a whole.

The secret is that you plot the floating bars as Series 2. Series 1 is a dummy series that you fill using No Fill and No Outline in Excel.

There are some interesting settings involved in creating the charts shown in Figure 7.11. You follow these steps to create the chart in the figure:

1. Set up a data table to split the single series into two series. In Figure 7.12, Column B shows the sales for each category. The formulas in Column C:E are the data used to create the chart. The formulas in Column C copy the values from Column A. The formulas in Column E copy Column B.

2. Enter 0 in Cell D2. This is the "height" of the invisible column. For the first series, the height is therefore zero.

3. In Cell D3, enter =D2+E2. This formula adds the starting height of the last column (D2) and the height of the previous column (E2).

4. Double-click the fill handle in Cell D3 to copy the formula down to the rest of the series. Your data should now look like the data shown in Figure 7.12.

5. Select Cells C1:E6. From the Insert tab, select Column, Stacked Column. Excel creates the chart shown in Figure 7.13.

7

Figure 7.11

The floating columns or bars demonstrate how components make up a whole.

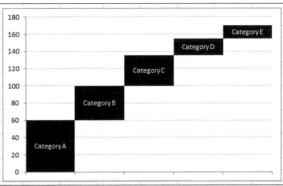

Figure 7.12

Formulas in Column C show the starting point for each column. That series will later become invisible.

	A	B	C	D	E
1		Sales		Invisible	Sales
2	Category A	60	Category A	0	60
3	Category B	40	Category B	60	40
4	Category C	35	Category C	100	35
5	Category D	20	Category D	135	20
6	Category E	15	Category E	155	15

6. From the Layout tab, select Legend, None.

7. Click any of the lower columns to select the first series. From the Format tab, select Shape Fill, No Fill. You might think that Excel is still outlining the first series, but those lines are the selection border. Click away from the series to make the selection disappear completely.

Figure 7.13

You can see the Invisible series before it disappears.

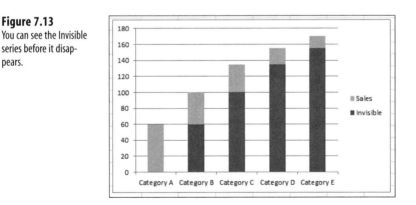

8. Right-click the visible series and select Format Data Series. In the Series Options category, set Gap Width to No Gap.

9. The second series is whichever color happens to be the second accent color in the current theme. While the series is selected, select Shape Fill and select a desired color.

10. Right-click the second series and select Add Data Labels. If your series fill color is dark, you cannot see the labels at all. Right-click in the center of one column and if you are lucky, you actually select the label. If you are not lucky, use the Current Selection drop-down in the Layout tab to select Series Sales Data Labels.

11. With the data labels selected, select Font Color on the Home tab, and then select a font color that contrasts with the column. You can now see that Microsoft has labeled the columns with the sales value. Click the Bold button on the Home tab. After changing the label in step 13, you might come back to the Home tab to change the font size so that the labels completely fit in the column.

12. From the Layout tab, select Format Selection. Excel displays the Format Data Labels dialog.

13. In the Format Data Labels dialog, change Label Contains from Value to Category Name. Note that in Label Position, you do not have a choice for Outside End, and that is really the choice you want. Turn toward Redmond and grumble that Microsoft disabled this choice in stacked charts. Click Close to close the dialog. Your chart now has the categories shown as labels on the columns and along the horizontal axis. This is a redundant use of ink.

14. Right-click the labels along the baseline and select Format Axis. Change the Axis Labels drop-down to None. Change Major Tick Mark Type to None, and then click Close.

The preceding steps create the column chart shown in Figure 7.11.

Using a Rogue XY Series to Label the Vertical Axis

The chart in Figure 7.14 shows annual scores against a government performance index. The actual index number is not as relevant as the ranges shown in A11:B15. These ratings decide whether a company can continue to do business in a particular segment. The top chart has default Excel gridlines at levels of 2, 4, 6, and so on. It would be better to create gridlines at the specific category levels of 7, 12, 18, 23, and 28.

The goal is to draw gridlines at unevenly spaced locations of 3, 8, 13, 18, 23, and 27. There is not a good way to adjust the gridlines to show horizontal lines for each category. The main problem is that Excel treats the collection of horizontal gridlines as a single object. When you format one major gridline, all major gridlines change. If each gridline could be formatted individually, you could draw a gridline every one unit and make most of the gridlines invisible.

The gridlines in the bottom chart of Figure 7.14 are actually error bars that are attached to an invisible XY series added to the chart. This solution may seem bizarre. It is not one of those obvious, do-two-steps-and-you-are-done solutions.

7

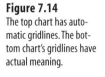

Figure 7.14
The top chart has automatic gridlines. The bottom chart's gridlines have actual meaning.

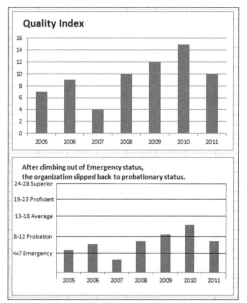

CASE STUDY: CONVERTING A SERIES TO GRIDLINES

This is a fairly complex set of steps, but the results are worth the work. If you actually try it a few times, you will realize how perfectly it works and appreciate the flexibility to both replace the gridlines with new gridlines and to replace the vertical axis labels with new labels. This example includes more figures than usual so you can easily see how it works.

You follow these steps to create arbitrary gridlines and labels:

1. Somewhere on the worksheet, build a table of the locations for each arbitrary gridline. In this case, you want the gridlines to be drawn between 7 and 8, so use numbers such as 7.5, 12.5, and so on in a column. Tip: Make sure that those values are not in the same column as the original dataset. With the data in N18:N22, step 3 works as expected. If the values were in B18:B22, step 3 adds the new points to the end of the existing Series 1.

2. To the left of those labels, fill an identical column with zeros.

3. Select the one-column range that contains the new gridline locations. Press Ctrl+C to copy. Click the chart and press Ctrl+V to paste. Excel adds the data as a new series, as shown in Figure 7.15. Even though this new series has a different number of points than the first series, Excel takes a guess and draws the new series as a clustered column series.

4. Click one of the new columns to select the second series. From the Design tab, select Chart Type, XY (Scatter), Scatter with Only Markers. Because you have mixed a traditional chart with a scatter chart, Excel adds a second horizontal axis at the top of the chart and a second vertical axis at the right of the chart. Out of desperation, Excel applies Series 2 to the secondary axis on both the horizontal and vertical axes.

In step 5, you will edit the SERIES function to show Excel where the x values are stored for the second series. If you are not familiar with the SERIES function, read the sidebar that follows before moving to step 5.

Figure 7.15
When you paste the points to the chart, Excel adds them as a clustered column series.

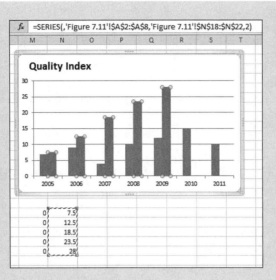

Figure 7.16
You might be thinking that this series has nothing to do with arbitrary gridlines.

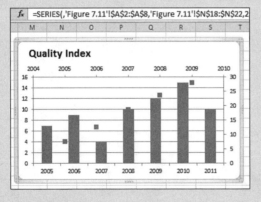

Understanding the SERIES Function

Before proceeding to step 5, you need to understand the SERIES function. If you select a series in a column, line, or bar chart, Excel displays a function in the formula bar. The function has four arguments:

```
=SERIES(Series Name, Labels for Series, Values for Series, Series Sequence)
```

The series formula for the first series looks like this:

```
=SERIES($B$1, $A$2:$A$8, $B$2:$B$8,1)
```

This means that the series will be known as the score series, based on Cell B1. The labels for the horizontal axis are the years in Cells A2:A8. The values for each point are in Cells B2:B8. The final 1 indicates that this is the first series in the chart.

When you paste new data into the chart, Excel has to guess what you mean. The SERIES function for series 2 is:

```
=SERIES(,Indicators!$A$2:$A$8,Indicators!$N$18:$N$22,2)
```

7

This means that the second series has no name. Excel guessed that the axis labels should be in Cells A2:A8. Excel knows that the marker values are in Cells N18:N22. The final 2 indicates that this is the second series.

When faced with a problem, computer programmers tend to try to shoehorn a new feature into an old paradigm, and this certainly seems to be the case with the XY charts. In an XY chart, every marker has two locations. You have to specify an x location and a y location. Rather than create a new function to handle XY charts, however, the spreadsheet architects decided that they could replace the labels as the second argument of the SERIES formula and store the x values there. I am sure it made sense at the time, but that is why it is so difficult to label XY charts!

5. Click one of the markers for the second series. Wait a few seconds until Excel displays the SERIES function in the formula bar. Then click in the formula bar and change the second argument of the SERIES formula to point to the zeros in cells M18:M22:

   =SERIES(,Indicators!$M$18:$M$22,Indicators!$N$18:$N$22,2)

6. Press Enter to accept this formula. As shown in Figure 7.17, Excel moves the five markers to the left vertical axis, which is the default x location for 0. The secondary horizontal axis at the top of the chart now runs from 0 to 1, in 0.2-unit increments. You will clean all this up later, but it is important to see that the top marker is at that location because it has an x value of 0 and a y value of 28.

Figure 7.17
The second series markers are now glued to the left axis.

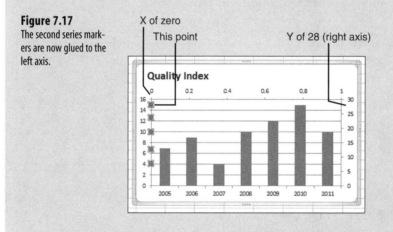

7. To explicitly make sure the scale for the left and right axes match, double-click the labels along the left axis to format the primary vertical axis. Make sure the axis shows a fixed minimum of 0 and a fixed maximum of 28. Do not close the Format dialog box.

8. With the Format dialog open, click the numbers along the right horizontal axis. Set the scale as fixed with a minimum of 0 and a maximum of 28. While in this panel of the dialog box, change Axis Labels to none. Change Major Tick Mark type to None. Keep the Format dialog box open.

9. Click the numbers above the chart. In the Format dialog, set a fixed minimum of 0 and a fixed maximum of 1. In Figure 7.18, note that the top marker along the left axis has moved to the top of the chart. This is because you changed the secondary axis maximum from 30 to 28, as shown in Figure 7.18. Set the Major Tick Mark type to None and the Axis Labels to None. Keep the Format dialog box open.

10. Click the numbers along the left axis. Change the Major Tick Mark Type to None. Change the Axis Labels to None.

11. From the Layout tab, select Gridlines, Primary Horizontal Gridlines, None.

Figure 7.18
Make sure that all the axes have fixed upper and lower bounds.

12. Click the border surrounding the plot area. In the Format dialog, select Border Color from the left navigation panel. Select No Line.

13. Right-click one of the markers along the left vertical axis. Select Add Data Labels. Excel adds the wrong labels, in the wrong place, as shown in Figure 7.19.

Figure 7.19
You will have to replace those axis labels and move them to a new location.

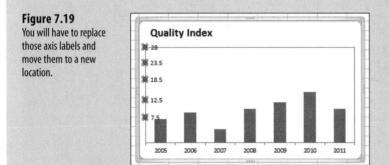

14. Click the top data label (the 28). Initially, all five data labels are selected. Click the data label again, and just that label is selected. Type a new data label, such as 24-28 Superior. Repeat this step for each marker in Series 2.

> **TIP**
> Chapter 13, "Using Excel VBA to Create Charts," includes a macro that labels all the points in an XY chart. You can use that macro instead of repeating step 13 once for each data label.

15. Click the plot area to deselect the data labels. Again click the data label to select all the Series 2 data labels. Right-click the labels and select Format Data Labels.

16. Select Left for Label Position. Excel moves the data labels a few millimeters to the left, until they hit the left edge of the chart area.

17. Click the plot area. Grab one of the left resizing handles. Resize the plot area so it is smaller by dragging a left resizing handle to the right. When you have made enough room for the long Series 2 labels, let go of the mouse.

18. From the Layout tab, select Series 2 from the Current Selection drop-down. Also from the Layout tab, select Error Bars, More Error Bars Options. Excel seems to erroneously take you to the Format dialog box for vertical error bars. In reality, though, Excel has added both x and y error bars. It chooses to show you the Format dialog box for the vertical error bars. Close the dialog box.

19. In the Current Selection drop-down, select Series 2 X Error Bars. Click Format Selection. Change Direction to Plus. Change End Style to No Cap. Set Error Amount to Fixed, with a value of 1.0. From the Line Style category, select a width of 1.5 to make the error bars a bit more substantial. Click Close to close the dialog box.

20. In the Current Selection drop-down, select Series 2 Y Error Bars. When those error bars are selected, press Delete to delete the y error bars.

21. Select Series 2 from the Current Selection drop-down. Click Format Selection. In the Marker Options category, select None. Excel erases the markers from the y-axis.

22. Type a more descriptive title for the chart.

The final chart is shown in Figure 7.20. This technique is particularly interesting because for many steps, it appears as if you are heading in the wrong direction.

Figure 7.20
The labels along the y-axis look so simple to add, but a casual Excel user would have a difficult time discovering how to put them there.

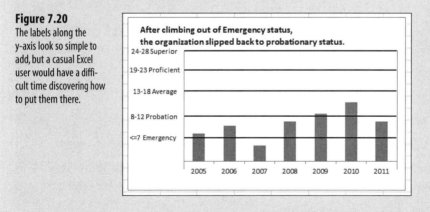

If you try the steps a few times, this workaround starts to seem natural and almost poetic. The rogue XY series comes into play in the next example, which involves stacking many charts on a single chart.

Showing Several Charts on One Chart by Using a Rogue XY Series

Figure 7.21 shows a single chart that appears to stack up four different charts. This chart is especially useful because one of the middle series, which is the subject of the chart, has a particularly low Q3 value. If you used a series of overlaid area charts, you would never be able to see the Q3 value in question. Note that it is important that all four charts in the stack have the same scale. Even with the current arrangement, it is difficult to compare one year to another. Which Q1 is largest? Without looking at the data, you cannot really tell.

Figure 7.21
This stacked arrangement of charts allows you to compare one year to the next.

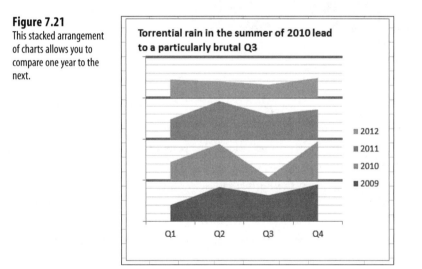

The chart is actually a stack of seven area charts. The second, fourth, and sixth charts are invisible charts that are the complements to the first, third, and fifth charts. For example, if you have decided that the range for each chart should be 0 to 250, then the formula for each point in the second series will be 250 minus the corresponding point in the first series.

You follow these steps to set up the data for this chart stack:

1. Insert blank columns before years 2, 3, and 4.
2. The formula in the blank column should be 250 minus the column to the left. Copy to all three blank columns. Your data should like the data shown in Figure 7.22.

7

Figure 7.22
You can add a series between each year to force the next year to start at an even increment of 250.

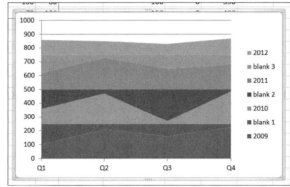

	A	B	C	D	E	F	G	H
8		2009	blank 1	2010	blank 2	2011	blank 3	2012
9	Q1	100	150	110	140	120	130	110
10	Q2	210	40	220	30	230	20	100
11	Q3	160	90	20	230	150	100	80
12	Q4	225	25	235	15	180	70	120
13								

Figure 7.23
The chart initially shows seven areas.

3. Select the range of data. From the Insert tab, select Area, Stacked Area. Because there are four rows and seven columns, Excel creates the chart with the data reversed: four series with seven points each.

4. From the Design tab, select Switch Row/Column to create the chart as seven series with four points each. The chart appears as shown in Figure 7.23.

5. In the chart, click Series 2. From the Format tab, select Shape Fill, No Fill. There is a fast way to repeat for Series 4 and Series 6; click Series 4. Press F4. Click Series 6. Press F4.

6. Double-click the numbers along the vertical axis to open the Format dialog. Then do the following:

   ■ Select Maximum, Fixed, 1000.

   ■ Select Major Unit, Fixed, 250.

   ■ Select Minor Unit, Fixed, 50.

   ■ Select Axis Labels, None.

   ■ Select Major Tick Mark Type, None.

7. Type three columns of data. The first column is the new data labels that you want to appear along the y-axis. This could be four sets of 0, 50, 100, 150, and 200. In the next column, fill zeros down the column for the x location of the XY points. In the next column, type values from 0 to 1,000, in 50-unit increments for the y locations of the XY points.

8. Although the second column contains x locations, you initially add only the y locations to the chart. Select the third column, containing y locations and the heading above the data.

9. Press Ctrl+C to copy the data. Select the chart. Press Ctrl+V to paste the new series to the chart. You now have a complete mess, as shown in Figure 7.24.

Figure 7.24
The new series initially ruins the chart.

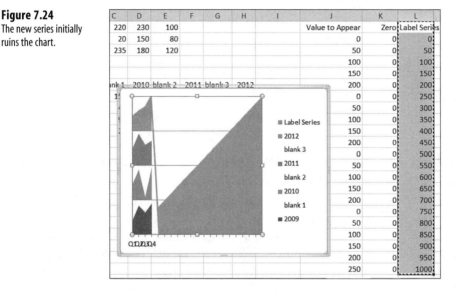

10. Click the new Label series. From the Design tab, select Change Chart Type, XY (Scatter), Scatter with Only Markers.

11. Select Series Label Series from the Current Selection drop-down in either the Layout or Format tab.

12. Wait until the formula bar shows the SERIES function. Edit the third argument to point to the column of zeros. Do not include the label for the zero heading:

    `=SERIES(Stacked!$L$3,Stacked!$K$4:$K$24,Stacked!$L$4:$L$24,8)`

    Markers will appear along the vertical axis as shown in Figure 7.25.

13. Double-click the numbers along the right vertical axis to display the Format dialog box. Then do the following:
    - Select Maximum, Fixed, 1000.
    - Select Major Tick Mark Type, None.
    - Select Axis Labels, None.
    - While the Format Axis dialog remains open, click the axis labels along the top of the chart and select Major Tick Mark Type, None. Then select Axis Labels, None.

Figure 7.25
After you add the x values as the second argument in the SERIES function, the markers move to the left vertical axis.

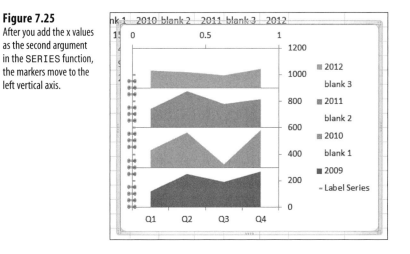

14. Right-click the markers along the left vertical axis. Select Add Data Labels. Right-click the data labels and then select Format Data Labels. Select Label Position, Left.

15. Click the plot area. Grab the bottom-left resizing handle and drag toward the center of the chart until there is enough room for the new labels.

16. From the Layout tab, select Primary Horizontal Gridlines, Display Major & Minor Gridlines. Format the major gridlines to have a thicker line weight by selecting Vertical (Value) Axis Major Gridlines from the Current Selection drop-down. Then, from the Format tab, select Shape Outline, Weight, and select 21/2 point.

17. Select Series Label Series from the Current Selection drop-down on the Format tab. Click Format Series, Marker Options, Marker Type to None. In Figure 7.26, you can see that three issues remain. The legend contains entries for the blank series. The Q1 and Q4 points do not extend to the left and right axes. The labels along the left side of the chart run from 0 to 1,000 instead of 0 to 250 repeatedly.

Figure 7.26
You still have to fix the legend and the labels along the left axis.

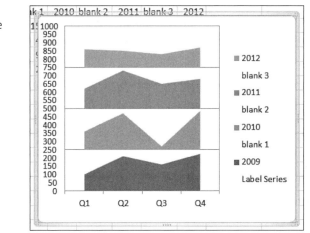

18. Click the Legend to select the whole legend. Click again on the Blank 3 legend entry to select only that entry and press Delete. Excel removes that entry from the legend. Repeat with Blank 2, Blank 1, and Label Series to delete them from the legend. To fix the labels along the y-axis, you have three choices:

- Write some VBA (see Chapter 13).
- Download Rob Bovey's XY Chart Labeler utility from `http://www.appspro.com/Utilities/ChartLabeler.htm`.
- Repeat step 19 several times.

19. To fix the labels manually, click the data labels on the left side of the chart to select all the labels. Click just the 250 label. Type 0 and press Enter. Repeat to change the 300 label to 50, the 350 label to 100, and so on.

20. Add a title, if desired.

21. Notice that there is a gap between the left vertical axis and the Q1 label. To remove this gap, right-click the Q1 label and select Format Axis. The bottom setting on the Axis Options category is the Position Axis option button. Change from Between Tick Marks to On Tick Marks. In Figure 7.27, the right chart is set to On Tick Marks. The left chart is set to Between Tick Marks.

Figure 7.27
You choose where to position the axis.

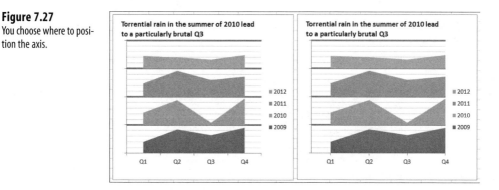

When you distribute this chart to others, they will be wondering how you managed to make Excel put four charts on a single chart. Actually, your manager will not even know this is difficult, but other people who use Excel might be impressed.

Creating Dynamic Charts

In this section, dynamic refers to a chart that expands, contracts, changes, or moves in response to changes in the underlying worksheet.

In many cases, you need to change the SERIES function attached to a data series to calculate a series on-the-fly. However, the examples in this section rely on four worksheet functions:

VLOOKUP, MATCH, INDEX, and OFFSET. In case you are new to these functions, coverage of each of them follows.

Using the OFFSET Function to Specify a Range

The OFFSET function allows you to specify a rectangular range of data. You have to provide five arguments to specify the range:

- **Any starting cell**—An example is Sheet1!A1.

- **A number of rows to move down from the starting cell to the first cell in the range**—If you specify a positive number, the range starts below the starting cell. If you specify 0, the range starts in the same row as the starting cell. If you specify a negative number, the range starts above the starting cell.

- **A number of columns to move right from the starting cell to arrive at the first cell in the range**—You can specify a positive number to move right, 0 to stay in the same column as the starting cell, or a negative number to move to the left.

- **The number of rows in the range**—If you specify 1, you describe a range that is one row tall.

- **The number of columns in the range**—If you specify 1, you describe a range that is one column wide.

To understand the various types of ranges that the OFFSET function can return, consider the shapes in Figure 7.28.

Figure 7.28
Examples of the OFFSET function.

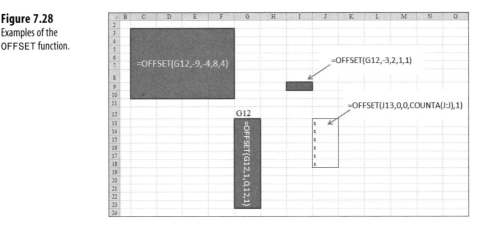

The top-left shape in Figure 7.28 highlights a range that is eight rows tall by four columns wide. If the starting cell is G12, you would have to move nine rows up from the starting cell and four columns left from the starting cell to arrive at the top-left corner cell of the range. The function to refer to this range is =OFFSET(G12,-9,-4,8,4).

The box underneath Cell G12 is 12 rows tall by one column wide. It starts one row from the starting cell of G12 and zero columns to the right. The function to refer to this range is =OFFSET(G12,1,0,12,1).

The single cell in I9 is three rows above the starting cell, two columns to the right, one row tall, and one column wide. The formula is =OFFSET(G12,-3,2,1,1).

Of course, it is silly to write any of these formulas. If you knew that your chart range was always going to be in Cells G13:G23, you would just refer to Sheet1!G13:G23. The power of the OFFSET function is that you can use other functions for some of the arguments. For example, you could count the category labels in your dataset today by using the formula COUNTA($J:$J). The formula =OFFSET(J13,0,0,COUNTA(J:J),1) starts in Column J and extends down to include the number of cells with data in Column J. This formula counts on the data in Column J to not include any blank cells.

Using VLOOKUP or MATCH to Find a Value in a Table

The VLOOKUP function does a vertical lookup. It looks for a particular value in the first column of a lookup table. When the first exact match is found, Excel returns a particular column from that row of the table.

VLOOKUP usually has four arguments: VLOOKUP(lookup_value, table_array, col_index_num, [range_lookup]).

- **Lookup value**—This is the name or value you are trying to find. In Figure 7.29, it is the name in Cell A1.

Figure 7.29
Examples of the VLOOKUP and MATCH functions.

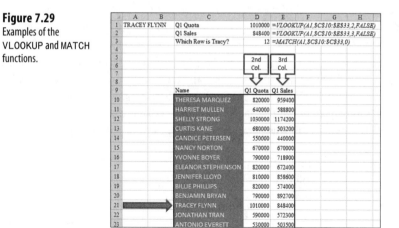

- **Table array**—This is a rectangular range of cells. Excel searches the first column of the table array in an effort to find a cell that has the same value as the lookup value. In Figure 7.29, this is the range C10:E33. If you plan on copying the VLOOKUP formula in either direction to find additional customers or columns, you should use the F4 key to make the table array absolute.

While editing a formula, pressing the F4 key will toggle a cell reference through the four possible relative/absolute/mixed reference states. The first press of F4 changes A1 to $A$1. The next press of F4 freezes only the row number, A$1. The next press of F4 freezes only the column, $A1. The next press of F4 returns to a relative reference of A1.

How does Excel know which reference to change? If the cursor is inside a reference or immediately to the right of a reference, Excel will change that reference. While entering the previous formula, if you use the mouse to select C10:E33 and then press F4 before typing the comma, Excel will add dollar signs to both C10 and E33 at the same time. If you need to add dollar signs to only C10 or only E33, select the characters in the formula bar before pressing F4.

- **Column index number**—This specifies the column Excel should return as the result of the formula. The columns are numbered 1, 2, 3, and so on, starting with the column that contains the lookup value. In Figure 7.29, specifying 2 would give you the Q1 quota for the person. Specifying 3 would give you the Q1 sales. Note that specifying 1 would give you the person's name again. Although this might seem silly, because you already have the person's name as the lookup value, you can sometimes use VLOOKUP to test to see whether the lookup value is a valid name in the table array. In this case, it is fine to specify 1 as the column index. Note that if you need to copy this function across several columns to return the second, third, fourth, and fifth columns from table array, you can use COLUMN(B1) instead of using 2 as the third argument. As the formula is copied to the right, Excel automatically returns COLUMN(C1), COLUMN(D1), COLUMN(E1), and so on, which then ask for the third, fourth, and fifth columns from the table array.

- **Range lookup**—This is either TRUE or FALSE. You specify FALSE to indicate that you are looking for an exact match. In the FALSE version, the table array can be in any order. If you instead specify TRUE, Excel returns the value of the closest match that is equal to or lower than the lookup value. In the TRUE version, the table array must be sorted in ascending order. If you leave off this parameter, it is the same as specifying TRUE.

VLOOKUP is a workhorse function in Excel. If you have ever dabbled in Access, you might have joined tables to bring new columns from a lookup table into a query. The VLOOKUP function allows you to simulate joining tables in Excel.

In Figure 7.29, a VLOOKUP function in Cell D1 asks for the second column of the table array and finds the Q1 quota for the sales rep listed in Cell A1. A second VLOOKUP in Cell D2 asks for the third column of the table array and finds the Q1 sales. The HLOOKUP can do a horizontal lookup, in case your table array has the key values across one row.

There is a curious variant of VLOOKUP called the MATCH function, which looks for a lookup value in a one-column-wide lookup array. When a corresponding value is found in the

lookup array, Excel tells you the relative row number within the lookup array where the match is found. MATCH can also find a value in a one-row-tall lookup array, similar to the HLOOKUP function.

This seems completely useless. Has your manager ever called you to ask, "By the way, can you tell me in what relative row number within a range that customer is located?" This is a bit of trivia that rarely comes up in conversation. However, bear with me because the MATCH function can be useful when combined with the INDEX function, which is discussed in the next section.

The MATCH function requires arguments that are similar to the first, second, and fourth arguments of the VLOOKUP function:

- **Lookup value**—This is the value that you are trying to find.
- **Lookup array**—This is the first column of the table array range from VLOOKUP. This is the column where Excel looks to find a match for the lookup value.
- **Match type**—This is conceptually similar to using TRUE or FALSE as the fourth argument in the VLOOKUP function. A FALSE in VLOOKUP requires an exact match. In the MATCH function, a 0 requires an exact match. A TRUE in VLOOKUP returns the next-smallest value from a sorted table array. Similarly, a 1 in MATCH returns the next-smallest value. (Remember that spreadsheets store TRUE as a 1.) MATCH offers one more option for match type. If you specify -1, Excel finds the next-largest value from the descending sorted lookup array.

> **TIP**
>
> Did you know that FALSE is equivalent to 0? You can actually specify FALSE as the third argument in MATCH, and it works like a 0.

In Figure 7.29, a MATCH function in Cell D3 looks for the sales rep from Cell A1 in the range C10:C33. Note that although the match is actually on Row 21, this row is the 12th row in the table array. Thus, the MATCH function returns 12.

Both the VLOOKUP and MATCH functions are CPU intensive, particularly when the lookup table contains thousands of records. The lengthy part of the function is finding the matching record from the first column of the lookup table. After Excel locates that value, moving right to grab the second or third column is relatively quick.

Combining INDEX and MATCH

Initially, the INDEX function does not seem that useful. Its syntax, which is used in a later chart example, is as follows:

```
=INDEX(Rectangular Range, Which Row in the Range, Which Column in the Range)
```

=INDEX(A1:Z26,5,10) returns the value at the 5th row and 10th column of the range A1:Z26. There are certainly easier ways to refer to Cell J5 such as =J5.

> **TIP**
>
> If the range specified as the first argument contains only one column, you can leave the third argument out of the function. By default, Excel assumes that you are talking about the first column.

The INDEX function becomes powerful when you use a MATCH function as the second argument to specify which range to return.

In Figure 7.30, a processor-intensive MATCH function in Cell D1 finds the row number where the sales rep can be found. Relatively fast INDEX functions in Cells D2 and D3 then return the value from that row in the quota or sales column.

The next three charting examples make use of the OFFSET, VLOOKUP, INDEX, and/or MATCH functions to change a chart in response to changes in the underlying worksheet.

Figure 7.30
Examples of the MATCH and INDEX functions.

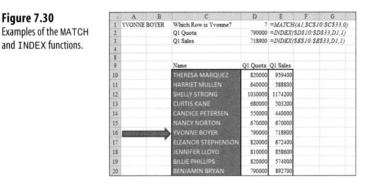

Using Validation Drop-Downs to Create a Dynamic Chart

This example creates a chart that is a bit like a pivot chart, except it uses a drop-down on the worksheet to choose which data to chart.

Figure 7.31 shows a simple chart that compares sales to quota by quarter for a particular sales rep.

Figure 7.31
This simple chart could be part of an executive information system for a vice president of sales.

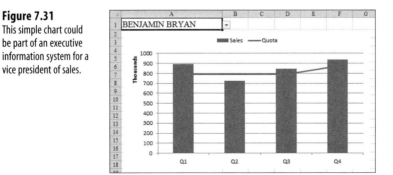

When you click in Cell A1 of this chart, a drop-down appears. When you open the drop-down and select a new sales rep, the chart instantly updates to show that particular sales rep's figures (see Figure 7.32).

This chart is not that amazing; it uses just some basic Excel tools that are hiding on the worksheet.

First, hidden out of sight in Row 63 is all the data needed to create the chart for any particular sales rep. Sales reps are in A64:A87. Their individual quota and sales figures are in Columns B:K (see Figure 7.33).

Figure 7.32
If you choose a new rep from the drop-down in A1, the chart updates.

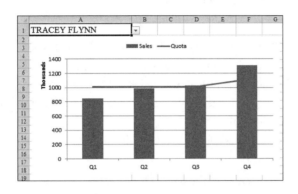

Figure 7.33
The source data for all charts is hidden.

	A	B	C	D	E
63	Name	Q1 Quota	Q1 Sales	Q2 Quota	Q2 Sales
64	THERESA MARQUEZ	820000	959400	820000	1066000
65	HARRIET MULLEN	640000	588800	640000	614400
66	SHELLY STRONG	1030000	1174200	1030000	1153600
67	CURTIS KANE	680000	503200	680000	537200
68	CANDICE PETERSEN	550000	440000	550000	528000
69	NANCY NORTON	670000	670000	670000	730300
70	YVONNE BOYER	790000	718900	790000	758400
71	ELEANOR STEPHENSON	820000	672400	820000	680600
72	JENNIFER LLOYD	810000	858600	810000	955800
73	BILLIE PHILLIPS	820000	574000	820000	623200
74	BENJAMIN BRYAN	790000	892700	790000	726800
75	TRACEY FLYNN	1010000	848400	1010000	989800
76	JONATHAN TRAN	590000	572300	590000	525100
77	ANTONIO EVERETT	530000	503500	530000	482300
78	PHILIP FRAZIER	600000	426000	600000	408000
79	CAROLYN CASH	1050000	787500	1050000	945000
80	BRANDY SNIDER	1000000	890000	1000000	1090000
81	DANIEL HERMAN	580000	440800	580000	522000
82	BERTHA FAULKNER	510000	438600	510000	423300
83	VERA GOODMAN	850000	748000	850000	799000
84	BRADLEY LEBLANC	560000	487200	560000	621600
85	JACOB SHANNON	500000	355000	500000	365000
86	BRANDY GIBBS	880000	466400	880000	660000
87	JEAN PACE	550000	330000	550000	335500
88					

Hidden behind the chart are a number of formulas:

- In Cell A2, the formula =MATCH(A1,A64:A87,0) indicates the location of the sales rep selected in Cell A1.

■ In C4:F5, formulas similar to =INDEX($A$64:$K$87,$A$2,2) pull the information for the selected sales rep and format it into two data series. The structure of the original dataset is typical of how accounting keeps track of such data. If the original dataset were in a different format, a simpler formula could be written. As it is, the third argument of this formula had to be edited in each of the other seven cells after being copied to C4:F5. To avoid editing each formula, you could replace the 2 with COLUMN(B1). You could also abandon the MATCH formula in Cell A2 and build eight VLOOKUP formulas here, and that would be fine; it is a matter of personal preference.

To create the drop-down in Cell A1, you follow these steps:

1. Select Cell A1.

2. From the Data tab, click the top half of the Data Validation icon.

3. In the Data Validation dialog that appears, change the Allow drop-down from Any Value to List. New fields appear in the dialog, including a Source field.

4. Click the Reference box at the right side of the Source field and select the A64:A87 range, which contains names.

5. By default, the In-cell Drop down check box is selected. Leave it selected. Click OK to close the dialog.

Figure 7.34 shows the structure of the data hidden behind the chart as well as the completed Data Validation dialog box.

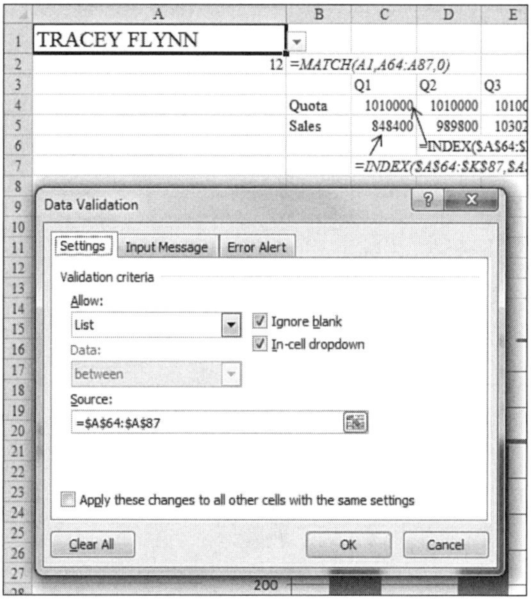

Figure 7.34
Formulas convert the name in Cell A1 into a chartable dataset. The drop-down in Cell A1 appears because of the Data Validation settings.

After you set up the formulas, you create a chart from B3:F5. You follow these steps to create the chart:

1. Select the Range B3:F5. From the Insert tab, select Column, Clustered Column.
2. Click any column marker in the chart for quota. From the Design tab, select Change Chart Type, Line, Line.
3. From the Layout tab, select Legend, Show Legend at Top.
4. From the Layout tab, select Axes, Primary Vertical Axis, Show Axis in Thousands.
5. Click outside the plot area but inside the chart border to select the chart area. From the Format tab, select Shape Outline, No Outline.
6. Drag the selection border of the chart to move it to Cell A2, and then resize the chart so that it covers any of the formulas behind the chart.

As mentioned earlier, this chart is not really dynamic. The worksheet is dynamic and responds using formulas. The chart is always plotting a static range of data. The chart in the next example is truly dynamic, expanding or contracting as data is added or removed from the spreadsheet.

Using Dynamic Ranges in a Chart

A chart based on a dynamic range expands or contracts as new data points are added to a specific range.

The chart in this example requires an understanding of the SERIES function and the OFFSET function.

> **NOTE** If you are not reading straight through this chapter, you should review the SERIES function discussion in the "Using a Rogue XY Series to Label the Vertical Axis" section, earlier in this chapter. You should also read the OFFSET discussion in the "Using the OFFSET Function to Specify a Range" section, earlier in this chapter.

As shown in Figure 7.35, the data for the chart is initially located in A5:B16. There are headings in Cell A4 and Cell B5. The COUNTA() function, described later, counts all the entries in Column A and subtracts 1 to factor out the heading. This approach requires two assumptions, which you have to work to control:

- There should be no other data anywhere in the million other rows of Column A. You should not build new tables down below, and you should not add a title in Cell A1. If you are doing either of these things, you will have to adjust the COUNTA() function to subtract more than just the first heading cell.

- Customers should always start in Cell A5 and extend in a contiguous range. You should not leave a blank cell in Cell A17 and type a new customer in Cell A18. This will not work. If you want to delete a customer from the chart, you need to delete the entire row containing the customer. You should not delete the values in Row 8, leaving a blank row.

> **NOTE** In the example that follows, the sheet name in the sample file is called Dynamic Chart. The workbook name is 7-Dynamic1.xlsm. Sheet names with spaces are more difficult to deal with than sheet names without spaces. The SERIES formula requires you to fully qualify the named ranges. For this example, substitute the appropriate workbook or worksheet range names.

To build this chart, you first build and format a static chart. You then make the chart a chart that will dynamically resize. Here's how you create this chart:

1. Select the data in Cells A4:B16. From the Insert tab, select Bar, 2D Bar, Clustered Bar.

2. From the Layout tab, select Legend, None.

3. Right-click the customer names along the left side of the chart and select Format Axis to open the Format dialog box.

4. Select Categories in Reverse Order.

5. Select Specify Interval Unit and make sure the unit is 1. Close the Format dialog box.

6. Resize the chart so that it is taller.

7. Click outside the chart. You now need to define a couple of range names that point to a dynamic range of data.

8. From the Formulas tab, select the Name Manager.

9. Click the New button. Excel displays the New Name dialog.

10. Type a name such as Customers.

11. Leave Workbook as the scope.

12. Adding a comment, which was new in Excel 2007, helps when you want to document how a complicated name works.

13. Set Refers to Box to the following:
    ```
    =OFFSET('Dynamic Chart'!$A$5,0,0,COUNTA('Dynamic Chart'!$A:$A)-1,1)
    ```
    This basically says to start in Cell A5, move zero rows down, and zero columns over but to include as many entries as are found in Column A, except for the heading.

14. Click OK to return to the Name Manager dialog. You then see the new name added in the box.

15. Repeat steps 9 through 14 to assign a name to a formula for the sales values. Use the name Sales, and use the following formula in step 13:
    ```
    =OFFSET('Dynamic Chart'!$B$5,0,0,COUNTA('Dynamic Chart'!$A:$A)-1,1)
    ```
    Note that the fourth argument is still counting the number of customer names in Column A. This allows a new customer to appear but have a blank in Column B to

indicate zero sales. People should never leave a cell blank to indicate a zero, but this would handle it in case they did.

> **NOTE** After you have set up the relatively complicated Customers named range, you could base the Sales range as being 1 column offset from the first range. A formula of =OFFSET(Customers,,1) would achieve the same result as the formula in step 15.

16. Close the Name Manager dialog box.
17. Test whether your range names are working. Click in the Name Box drop-down just to the left of the Formula bar. Type Customers and press Enter. Excel highlights the range of customers. Repeat for sales. Type a new test customer in A17. Type Customers in the name box again and press Enter. Excel should now highlight a range that has been extended to include the new customer. If this is not working, go back and check the formulas you entered in steps 13 and 15.
18. Click the chart to activate it.
19. Click the data bars in the chart. Wait for Excel to display the SERIES formula in the formula bar, which should initially look like this:
```
=SERIES('Dynamic Chart'!$B$4,'Dynamic Chart'!$A$5:$A$16,
    'Dynamic Chart'!$B$5:$B$16,1)
```

> **NOTE** The SERIES formula is too long for the physical constraints of this book. You will not see the continuation arrow at the beginning of the second line in your formula.

The first argument in this formula means that the series name comes from Cell B4. The labels along the vertical axis come from Cells A5:A16. The values for each bar are located in B5:B16. This is the first (and only) series in the chart.
20. On the Design tab, click the Select Data button. Excel displays the Select Data Source dialog.
21. In the left side of the Select Data Source dialog, select Series1 and click Edit. Excel displays the Edit Series dialog.
22. Assuming that Sales is a workbook-level name, you have to specify the workbook name in apostrophes, an exclamation point, and then the range name as the series values. In my workbook, this is ='7-Dynamic1.xlsm'!Sales. Click OK.
23. On the right side of the Select Data Source dialog, select Edit for Axis Labels. Excel displays the Axis Labels dialog.
24. In the Axis Labels dialog, type a similar reference that points to Customer. In my case, this is ='7-Dynamic1.xlsm'!Customers. Click OK to close the Axis Labels dialog.

7

25. Click OK to close the Edit Series dialog. In the formula bar, you should see the following new SERIES formula:

```
=SERIES('Dynamic Chart'!$B$4,'7-Dynamic1.xlsm'!Customers,
    '7-Dynamic1.xlsm'!Sales,1)
```

Figure 7.35 shows the final chart.

Figure 7.35
As new customers are added to the bottom of the data range, the series formula automatically expands. Customers and Sales are names that are defined using the OFFSET function.

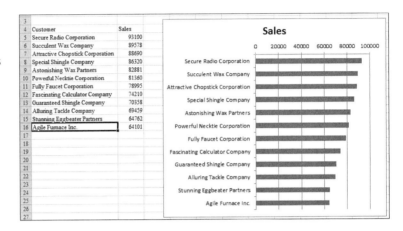

> ┌ **C A U T I O N** ──
> If you are a careful typist, you can edit the SERIES formula in the formula bar in Excel. However, there is no error checking, so if you mistype something, you lose the data for your chart.

This example uses the OFFSET function to automatically expand a chart. The next example uses the OFFSET function to chart a rolling 12 months of data.

Creating a Scrolling Chart

An interesting dynamic chart is a chart that shows a scrolling 12 months of data. In Figure 7.36, 36 months of data are available and are shown in the bottom chart. However, you can show a scrolling 12 months in the top chart. As you move the scrollbar, the top chart shows a closer view of a 12-month segment of the longer chart.

In Figure 7.36, a gray box shades the portion of the bottom chart that is shown in the top chart.

In Figure 7.37, the scrollbar is moved left to show a different portion of the detail.

You follow these steps to create a scrolling chart:

1. Format your dates with a MMMMMYY custom format. The five M's are the code to force the month to be displayed with only the first letter of the month. This allows more dates to fit across the bottom of the chart.

Figure 7.36
When the scrollbar in
Row 2 is scrolled toward
the right, you see recent
months.

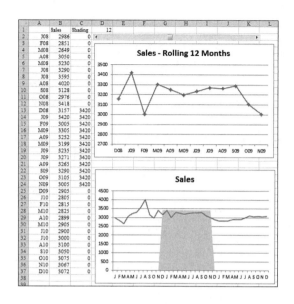

2. Select the data in Cells A1:B37. From the Insert tab, select Line, Line. Delete the legend. Excel creates a basic line chart with all 36 months of data.

3. Move the chart so that it starts in Row 22. Make a copy of the chart that starts in CellD3 by Ctrl+dragging the chart border to D3.

4. Deselect the chart. Enter a number between 1 and 25 in Cell D1.

Figure 7.37
Note the number 17 in
Cell D1. This cell changes
in response to the scrollbar changes.

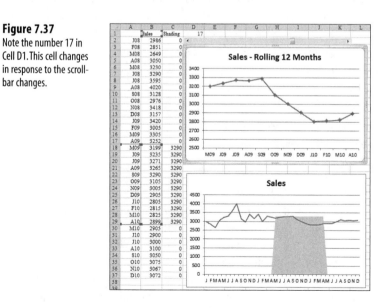

5. From the Formulas tab, select Name Manager. Click the New button.

6. Type Months in the Name field. In the Refers To field, enter the following:

   ```
   =OFFSET(Scroll!$A$1,Scroll!$D$1,0,12,1)
   ```

   This says to start from Cell A1 of the Scroll worksheet, move down the number of rows in Cell D1, and then take a range that is 12 rows by 1 column. Click OK to accept the name.

7. Add another name. Type the name SalesByMonth. In the Refers To box, use: =OFFSET(Scroll!$A$1,Scroll!$D$1,1,12,1) The only change is that in the third argument, you move right one column to grab data from Column B.

8. Click the line series in the first chart. Wait for the SERIES formula to appear in the formula bar. Edit the formula so that it looks like this:

   ```
   =SERIES(Scroll!$B$1,'7-Dynamic.xlsm'!Months,
       '7-Dynamic.xlsm'!SalesByMonth,1)
   ```

9. Test the chart. Enter a new number between 1 and 25 in Cell D1. The top chart should change. You now need to provide an easy way for the reader to change the number in Cell D1. This can be accomplished through a scrollbar. The icon for adding a scrollbar is located on the Developer tab. Open the Insert drop-down and find the Scrollbar icon in the center of the second row of Form Controls. Since many people do not have the Developer tab available in the Ribbon, you can use step 10 to add the scrollbar control to the Quick Access toolbar.

10. From the Office icon menu, select Options. Select Quick Access Toolbar. In the top-left drop-down, select Commands Not in the Ribbon. Browse through the list box on the left for Scroll Bar (Form Control). Select this item and click the Add button to add the control to the Quick Access toolbar. Click OK to close the Excel Options dialog.

11. Click the newly added scrollbar control in the Quick Access toolbar. After clicking the scrollbar icon, drag to draw a scrollbar control on the worksheet. Drag from the top left of Cell D2 to the bottom right of Cell K2.

> **TIP** Depending on your computer, the Quick Access toolbar mentioned in step 11 is the row of icons either immediately below or immediately above the Ribbon.

12. Right-click the scrollbar and select Format Control.

13. Change Minimum Value to 1 and Maximum Value to 25. Set Incremental Change to 1. For Cell Link, click the Refers To button and select Cell D1. Click OK. Click outside the scrollbar to deselect it. To test the scrollbar, drag the slider. The value in Cell D1 should change. The top chart should also change.

14. Change the chart title of the top chart to indicate that it is a rolling 12 months. The top chart is now complete. If you want to draw the shaded box on the bottom chart, continue with the following steps.

15. Enter the heading Shading in Cell C1.

16. Enter the following formula in Cell C2:

```
=IF(AND(ROW(A1)>=$D$1,ROW(A1)-$D$1<12),MAX(SalesByMonth),0)
```

Copy this formula down to the other 35 months.

17. Select the Range C1:C37. Press Ctrl+C to copy the range. Select the bottom chart. Press Ctrl+V to paste a new series to the chart.

18. Click the line for the second series. From the Design tab, select Change Chart Type, Area Chart.

19. Click the area chart to select the second series. From the Format tab, select Shape Fill and select light gray to make the box less obtrusive.

The scrollbar makes this chart fun to use. People will be encouraged to interact with the chart, which will mean they spend more time with the chart. Perhaps it is a bit gimmicky. Perhaps it makes sense when you have 20 years of monthly data. I can certainly understand the argument that the 12-month chart is less informative than the 36-month chart. However, the scrolling chart is here in this book because it is unusual.

Modifying the Scrollbar Example to Show the Last 12 Months

In the previous section, a scrollbar was used to determine which 12-month range was plotted on a chart. You can use similar concepts without the scrollbar. Say that you always want to display the latest 12 months of data. After you add a new month to the end of the range, and you want the chart to automatically shift to show the last 12 months. This would be the start of the OFFSET formula:

```
=OFFSET(A1,Some Number of Rows,0,12,1)
```

This formula always grabs 12 rows by 1 column. The trick is figuring out where to start the selection to get the last 12 months.

You can figure out how many months are present in Column A by using =COUNTA(A:A). When there are 36 months, you want to use the data A26:A37. This means you need to move 25 rows down from a starting position of Cell A1. Thus, the Some Number of Rows argument would be =COUNTA(A:A)-11.

To create a chart that shows the latest 12 months, you follow the steps in the previous example except that in step 6, the formula for months should be =OFFSET(Scroll!$A$1, COUNTA(Scroll!$A:$A)-11,0,12,1) and in step 7, the formula for SalesByMonth should be =OFFSET(Scroll!$A$1,COUNTA(Scroll!$A:$A)-11,1,12,1).

Creating Advanced Charts

The last few examples in this chapter are unconventional charts that you can create. Each chart requires a few tricks to coax the result out of Excel.

7

Thermometer Chart

A thermometer chart is a big way to display a single number. It is great for use on a dashboard display where you want everyone to see progress toward a goal.

To create a thermometer chart like the one shown in Figure 7.38, you follow these steps:

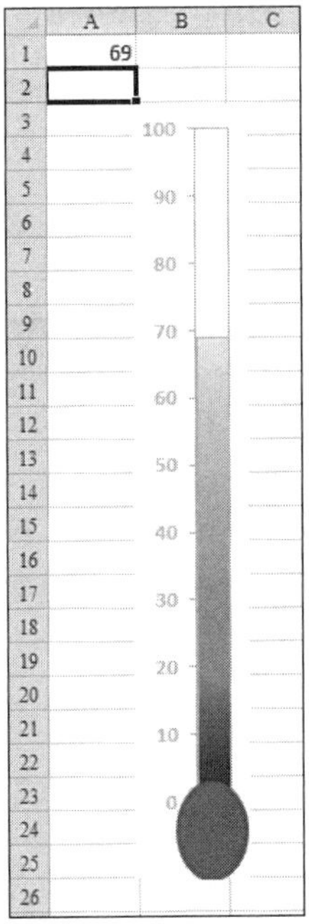

Figure 7.38
This chart is a single column based on the number in Cell A1.

1. Enter a number between 0 and 100 in Cell A1.
2. Select Cell A1. From the Insert tab, select Column, 2-D Column, Clustered Column.
3. From the Layout tab, select Legend, None.
4. From the Layout tab, select Axes, Primary Horizontal Axis, None.
5. From the Layout tab, select Gridlines, Primary Horizontal Gridlines, None.
6. Right-click the single column and select Format Data Series. Change Gap Width to 0 percent. For the Fill category, select Gradient Fill. In the Preset Colors drop-down, select the ninth thumbnail, a blend from red to orange. For Border Color, select Solid Line and then choose an orange color from the drop-down. You can leave the Format dialog open while you do steps 7 and 8.
7. Select Plot Area from the Current Selection drop-down. Format the border color as a solid line and choose an orange color.
8. Select the chart area and format the border as No Line. Close the Format dialog box.
9. Resize the chart area so that it is narrow and long.

10. Right-click the numbers along the vertical axis. Select Format Axis. Then do the following:

   - Select Minimum, Fixed, 0.
   - Select Maximum, Fixed, 100.
   - Select Major Unit, Fixed, 10.
   - For the Line Color category, select Solid Line and then select orange.
   - Click OK to close the Format dialog box.

11. With the axis labels still selected, select Font Color and then select orange on the Home tab.

12. Select the plot area. Drag the bottom resizing handles up so that there is space between the bottom of the plot area and the bottom of the chart area.

13. From the Insert tab, select Shapes, Basic Shapes and then select an oval. Hold down the Shift key while you draw a circle at the bottom of the chart. Note that the Shift key forces the oval shape to be drawn as a circle.

14. From the Format tab, select Shape Fill, and then select a dark orange, and then select Shape Outline and select a dark orange color for the ball at the bottom of the thermometer.

Benchmark Chart

A benchmark chart shows sales for each period as a column chart. The quota, goal, or benchmark for the period is shown as a cap. If the sales exactly meet the quota, the sales column fits perfectly into the cap. If sales fell short of the quota, you see some whitespace between the cap and the column.

You follow these steps to create a benchmark chart like the one in Figure 7.39:

1. Enter Months in Column A, Sales in Column B, and Quota in Column C.

2. Create a clustered 2-D column chart from the data. Delete the legend.

3. Click the Quota series in the chart. From the Design tab, select Change Chart Type and then select Scatter (XY). Excel automatically moves the series to a secondary axis.

4. Select one of the quota data markers. Right-click and select Format Data Series. Select Primary Axis.

5. Make sure the quota series is still selected. From the Layout tab, select Error Bars, More Error Bar Options. Close the Error Bar Format dialog and open the Current Selection drop-down from the left side of the Ribbon. If you see Series Quota Y Error Bars, select that and press the Delete key. Select Series Quota X Error Bars and click Format Selection. Change Fixed Value from 1.0 to 0.2. For the Line Style category, select a 3-point width.

6. Select Series Quota from the Current Selection drop-down. Click Format Selection. For the Marker Options category, select None.

Figure 7.39
The horizontal markers on each column indicate where the quota had been for that month.

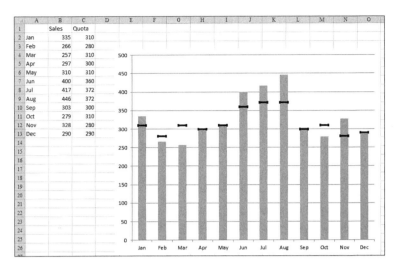

The horizontal lines in this chart are actually error bars that show the goal or quota for each month.

Delta Chart

You can use a delta chart to plot revenue and a quota as line charts. A special data marker appears halfway between the two lines to show the percentage of quota (see Figure 7.40). The hard part of creating a delta chart is getting the labels to float halfway in between the two lines.

Figure 7.40
The labels automatically float halfway between the two lines.

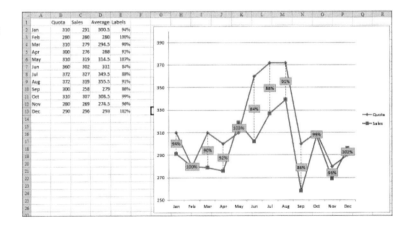

You follow these steps to create a delta chart:

1. Set up a dataset with months in Column A, quota in Column B, and revenue in Column C.

2. In Column D, enter the following formula to average revenue and quota:

   `=AVERAGE(B2:C2)`

   This will be the location point for the data label. Copy the formula down the column.

3. In column E, enter the formula `=C2/B2` to hold the label. This formula will show the percentage to quota. Format the results as a percentage with zero decimal places and copy the formula down the column.

4. Create a chart from Cells A1:D13. From the Insert tab, select Line, Line with Markers.

5. Select Value Axis from the Current Selection drop-down on the Layout tab. Click Format Selection. Choose a fixed minimum and a fixed maximum that are appropriate to zoom in on the data in the chart.

6. Select Series Average from the Current Selection drop-down on the Layout tab. Click Format Selection. Select to move the series to the secondary axis. This allows the labels to be adjusted for just this series.

7. Select Secondary Vertical (Value) Axis from the Current Selection drop-down on the Layout tab. Choose the same minimum and maximum as in step 5.

8. Close the Format dialog box.

9. Click the Average series to select it. From the Design tab, choose Select Data.

10. Click the Average series on the left side of the Select Data Source dialog. On the right side of the dialog, click the Edit button. Excel displays the Axis Labels dialog, where you can select new Horizontal Category Axis Labels. Point to the percentages in Column E. Click OK to close the Axis Labels dialog. Click OK to close the Select Data Source dialog.

11. Make sure Average Series is still selected. From the Layout tab, select Data Labels, More Data Label Options. In the Format Data Labels dialog, select Category Name, and deselect Value. Then do the following:

    - For Label Position, select Center.

    - For Fill, select Solid Fill and choose a light color.

    - For Border Color, select Solid Line and choose a dark color.

12. Click the Average series to select it. From the Format ribbon tab, select Shape Fill, No Fill. Select Format, Shape Outline, and then select No Outline. Close the Format dialog box.

13. From the Layout tab, select Lines, High-Low Lines. Select High Low Lines 1 from the Current Selection drop-down. From the Format tab, select Shape Outline, Dashes, and then select the fourth dash selection.

14. From the Layout tab, select Axes, Secondary Value Axis and set it to None.

15. Click the Average entry in the legend. The first click selects the whole legend. The second click selects just the Average entry. Press Delete to remove that entry.

Because the average series was converted to an XY chart, you could have a separate set of category labels for the series. This allows the markers to be at one height while displaying the label from a different value.

Amazing Things People Do with Excel Charts

The last few examples are not charts that you are likely to create. They are just a few displays that you will not believe are created in Excel. In each case, the author created the display using VBA.

Earl Takasaki submitted the Civil War chart shown in Figure 7.41 as an entry to a MrExcel.com Challenge of the Month as the most innovative use of graphics in Excel. With this chart, you can enter a cannon trajectory in an attempt to hit a target. The trajectory of the shot is graphed at the bottom of the figure.

Earl's workbook and many other entries from this contest are available for download at `http://www.mrexcel.com/pc11.shtml`.

Mala Singh of XLSoft Consulting created the chart in Figure 7.42. Mala used a shape to create a cross-section of a river at the proposed location for a bridge.

Figure 7.41
The graph at the bottom teaches students about physics.

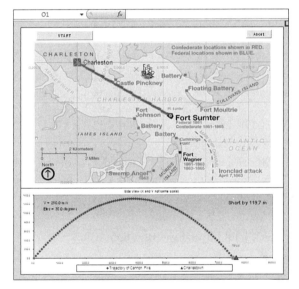

In Figure 7.43, Mala drew the bridge abutment using an XY chart in Excel.

Brett Bernardo sent in the chart shown in Figure 7.44 for his entry in the innovative charts contest at MrExcel.com. The VBA macro in this proprietary system starts with a manifest and actually draws the 3-D bundles in the Excel workbook.

You can read more about innovative chart entries at `http://www.mrexcel.com/pc15.php`.

Figure 7.42
Blue shapes create the profile of the river at the bridge location.

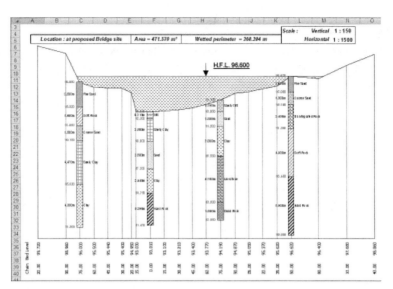

Figure 7.43
If you do not have AutoCAD, this blueprint is actually an XY chart.

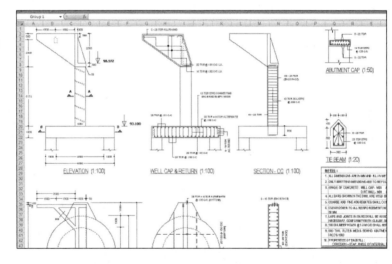

Figure 7.44
VBA macros draw bundles to scale as they should be loaded on a truck.

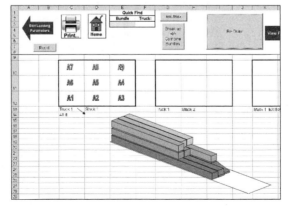

7

Next Steps

In Chapter 8, "Creating and Using Pivot Charts," you will learn how to summarize thousands of rows of detailed data into a summary chart. Pivot tables are Excel's most powerful feature. The pivot chart feature was vastly improved beginning with Excel 2007.

7

Creating and Using Pivot Charts

8

Creating Your First Pivot Chart

Pivot tables are the most powerful feature in Excel. A pivot table allows you to summarize a million records of transactional data in Excel with a few mouse clicks. A pivot chart is an extension of the pivot table concept. While building a summary of your data using a pivot table, you can specify that the results be presented in a chart. With the resulting chart, you can quickly filter to see a summary of records that match current criteria. You can also replicate a pivot chart so that you have one chart for each region, product, customer, and so on.

New in Excel 2010 Pivot Tables

There have been a number of changes around pivot tables in the last two versions of Excel. Excel 2010 adds a new graphical filter known as *slicers*. The paradigm for creating pivot tables changed in Excel 2007. Instead of dragging fields to the actual chart, you now drag the fields to drop zones in the PivotTable Field List.

> **NOTE**
> This is true unless you are using an old Excel 2003 XLS file and you are in compatibility mode. In this case, you still drag fields to the report as before.

Excel 2007 also introduced a series of new conceptual filters such as Last Month, Next Week, and This Year.

The controls that made pivot charts so ugly were removed in Excel 2007 but are back in Excel 2010. You can still turn them off if you actually liked the clean look of 2007 pivot tables. In Excel 2007, the PivotChart Filter Pane held the controls that were removed from the chart. Since those controls returned to the chart, the PivotChart Filter Pane has been banished and will spend the rest of its days living in a cave in South Carolina.

The drop zones have been renamed starting with Excel 2007. The old Page fields are now named Report Filter fields. The old Data Fields are now named Σ Values fields. When you are creating a pivot chart, Excel further renames the row fields as Axis fields and renames column fields as Legend fields.

By default, a pivot chart is now created on the same worksheet as the underlying pivot table. This is a welcome improvement: You can now easily see the relationship between the pivot table and the pivot chart. If you want to print only the pivot chart, you can either set the print range to include just the chart, select the chart before printing, or you can select the Charting Tools Layout tab and then select the Move icon to move the pivot chart to a new worksheet.

CAUTION

The new features from Excel 2007 and Excel 2010 are not compatible with Excel 2003 pivot tables. If you have a pivot table that was originally created in Excel 2003, Excel assumes that you might want to be able to save the file with backward compatibility, so it turns off the new features for that pivot table. To overcome this problem, you should use File, Convert to save the file as an Excel 2007-2010 workbook and then re-create the pivot table from your dataset.

Deciding Which Comes First: The Table or the Chart

The examples in this chapter assume that you have set out to create a pivot chart. However, if you have an existing pivot table, you can add a pivot chart by selecting one cell in the pivot table and pressing Alt+F1. Either way, you should follow these simple rules:

- Any fields in the column area such as those going across the columns at the top of the pivot table will be converted to series. You should have either one or zero fields in this area.

- Any fields in the row area such as those going down the left column of the report will become categories along the horizontal axis.

Rules for Preparing Underlying Pivot Data

Pivot tables work best when they are created from transactional data. Every row in a dataset should represent a detailed transaction. You do not want any sort of a summary in your dataset. If you have months going across the columns, this dataset is not ideal for creating pivot charts. A report with months going across the columns is a cross-tab summary of the detailed records in your dataset. You should go back to the person who provided that dataset and see if you can get the original underlying data that person used to produce the summary.

Your data should have no blank columns or blank rows. An occasional blank cell is not fatal but really compromises the pivot table engine's internal logic. If you have 99,999 cells with numbers and 1 blank cell, Excel assumes that the column contains text and chooses to count the records instead of summing them. If you can, you should fill any blank cells with zeros before you begin.

> **TIP**
>
> To find and fill any blank cells with zeros, you select the cells in your dataset and then select Home, Find & Select, Go to Special. In the GoTo Special dialog, select Blanks, and then click OK. All the blank cells in your selection are then selected. Next, you type a zero and then press Ctrl+Enter to put the zero in all the cells in the selection.

Every column should have a unique one-cell heading. These headings will appear in the PivotTable Field List box, so they should be relatively short but meaningful.

It is not necessary, but you might want to convert your dataset to a table before creating a pivot table. The advantage is that if you later add new records to the table, you can easily refresh your pivot chart without re-specifying the range of data to be used. To create a table, you select a cell in the dataset and press Ctrl+T.

Creating Your First Pivot Chart

You follow these steps to create your first pivot chart:

1. Select one cell in your dataset and then select Insert, PivotTable, PivotChart, as shown in Figure 8.1.

> **NOTE**
>
> The leftmost icon on the Insert tab is a PivotTable icon, which has a top half and a bottom half. Instead of clicking the top half of the icon, you need to click the bottom half, where you can access the PivotChart menu item.

Figure 8.1
You use the drop-down at the bottom of the PivotTable icon to access the PivotChart menu item.

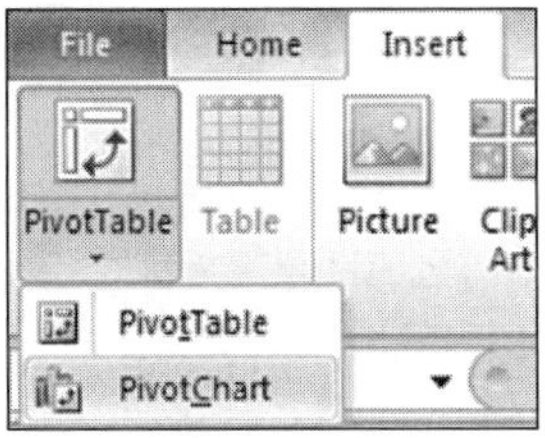

2. In the Create PivotTable with PivotChart dialog, Excel guesses about the extent of your dataset. If your dataset is either a table or follows the rules given earlier, Excel

guesses correctly. In this dialog, you can choose to create the pivot table on the current worksheet or on a new worksheet. The default is to use a new worksheet. Click OK.

You now have the makings of a blank pivot table and pivot chart. There are four elements visible on the worksheet shown in Figure 8.2:

- Columns A:C contain a blank area where the pivot table will be built.
- Columns E:M contain the area where the chart will be built.
- The PivotTable Field List box contains a list of fields at the top of the dialog and four drop zones at the bottom of the dialog.

> **NOTE** If your field list looks different from the one in Figure 8.2, you can select the drop-down at the top of the list and select Fields Section and Areas Section Stacked.

Four new PivotChart Tools tabs appear on the Ribbon. The first three tabs—Design, Layout, and Format—are identical to the charting tabs you have been using throughout this book. You can use the Analyze tab to toggle on or off the PivotTable Field List box or PivotChart Filter Pane box or to refresh the pivot chart (see Figure 8.2).

Figure 8.2
You are ready to start building a pivot chart by adding fields to the report.

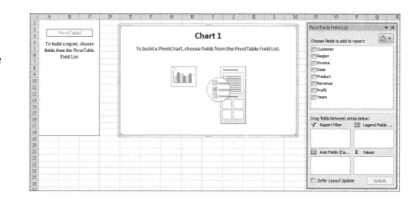

Suppose you want to create a chart that summarizes revenue by product. To do so, you follow these steps:

1. Select the check box next to the Product field in the top of the PivotTable Field List box. Excel shows a unique list of products in Column A of the pivot table. The Product field heading appears in the Axis Fields section of the PivotTable Field List box. You do not see a chart yet; you need to specify at least one field in the Σ Values area of the PivotTable Field List box.

2. Click the Profit field in the top of the PivotTable Field List box. If your data contains no blank cells, the Profit field appears in the Σ Values area of the field list, and your

chart appears as shown in Figure 8.3. If the Profit field instead moves to the Axis Fields area, you have one or more blank or text cells in your data. In an ideal world, you would fix these. Instead, you can drag the field from the Axis Fields drop zone to the Σ Values drop zone. Select Field Settings and change the calculation from Count to Sum.

Figure 8.3
Excel starts with the default chart, as defined in your copy of Excel.

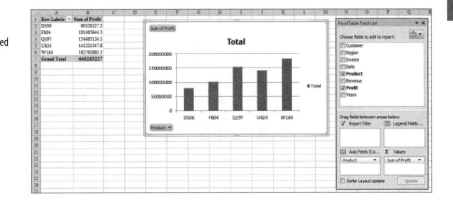

The summary in Figure 8.3 is remarkable. Even if you count clicking the PivotTable icon as two clicks, you need only five mouse clicks to summarize the 100,000+ records of data from Figure 8.1 into the summary chart in Figure 8.3.

Changing the Chart Type and Formatting the Chart

You can use the tools on the Design tab to change from a default chart type to almost any other chart type. To change the chart type, you select Design, Change Chart Type and select a chart type from the gallery.

> **TIP**
> Keep in mind that you cannot use scatter, XY, or bubble charts as pivot charts.

You can use the tools on the Layout tab to change elements such as data labels, titles, or the 3-D rotation. Figure 8.4 shows the data from Figure 8.3 recast as a 3-D pie chart. To create this chart, you use the familiar tools on the Design and Layout tabs:

1. On the Design tab, select Change Chart Type, and then select a 3-D pie chart.
2. Click the title that says Total. Type a meaningful title, such as Profit by Product.

> **TIP**
> Do not be concerned that the title in step 2 does not change as you are typing. The words are appearing in the formula bar and will appear in the title when you press Enter.

3. Select Layout, Legend, None.

4. Select Data Labels, More Data Label Options, Category Name, Percentage, Outside End. Clear the Value check box.

5. Select PivotChart Tools Analyze, Field Buttons, Hide All.

Figure 8.4
With just a few clicks, you can change the default pivot chart to any other available chart type.

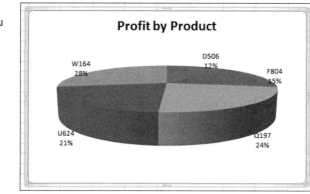

Adding Additional Series to a Pivot Chart

The first pivot chart in this chapter plotted a single series. You can specify values in another text field that can be used to differentiate the single series into multiple series.

To specify a field as the legend, you need to drag the field from the top of the PivotTable Field List box to the Legend Fields drop zone. To create the chart in Figure 8.5, you follow these steps:

Figure 8.5
You can add a field to the Legend drop zone in order to break the total into multiple series.

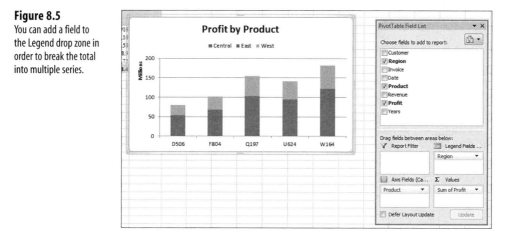

1. Select Design, Change Chart Type, Stacked Column.
2. Drag the Region field to the Legend Fields drop zone. Excel breaks the total revenue into three series.
3. Select Layout, Legend, Show Legend at Top.
4. Select Layout, Axes, Primary Vertical Axis, Show Axis in Millions.

Returning to a Pivot Table for Advanced Operations

Pivot tables are very powerful. A subset of pivot table operations are available in the pivot chart interface. Sometimes, however, you need to return to the pivot table in order to carry out an advanced operation. After you have made the change to the pivot table, you can then click the pivot chart in order to return to the pivot chart interface.

One example of an advanced operation is grouping daily dates up to months and years. Because the underlying data is transactional, it is reported at the daily level.

> **TIP**
>
> Do not try to add the five years of daily dates to a pivot chart. It will take forever for the chart to render. Instead, delete the pivot chart, make the change to the pivot table, and then bring the chart back.

To build a chart comparing year over year sales, follow these steps:

1. Click the pivot chart. Press the Delete key. You will still have the pivot table and the pivot table field list.
2. Remove Product from the Column Labels field.
3. Remove Region from the Row Labels field.
4. Drag Date to the Row Labels field. You now have the pivot table shown in Figure 8.6.

Figure 8.6
There are too many daily dates to create a readable pivot chart.

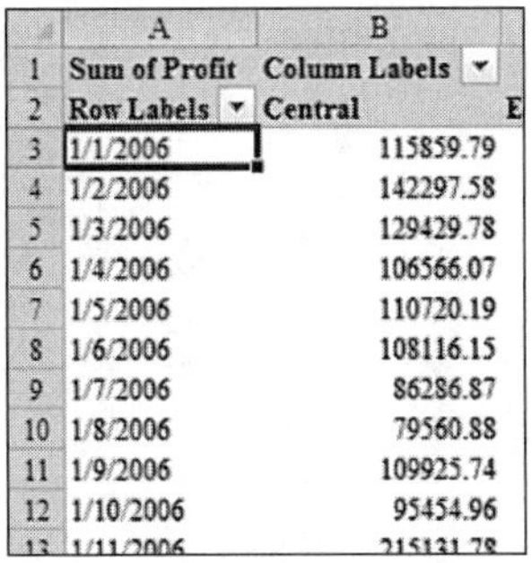

	A	B
1	Sum of Profit	Column Labels
2	Row Labels	Central
3	1/1/2006	115859.79
4	1/2/2006	142297.58
5	1/3/2006	129429.78
6	1/4/2006	106566.07
7	1/5/2006	110720.19
8	1/6/2006	108116.15
9	1/7/2006	86286.87
10	1/8/2006	79560.88
11	1/9/2006	109925.74
12	1/10/2006	95454.96
13	1/11/2006	215131.78

To group the data in the Date field, you follow these steps:

1. Select any date cell, such as cell A3.

2. From the Options tab, select Group Field.

3. In the Grouping dialog, Excel defaults to grouping by months. You need to add Years in the Grouping dialog box. Otherwise, Excel will add January of this year and January of last year into a single value called January (see Figure 8.7).

Figure 8.7
You select Months and Years from the Grouping dialog.

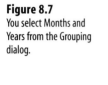

4. Click OK. Excel adds a new virtual field called Years to your field list and adds this field to the Row Labels field. The original field called Date is recast to include months.

5. Move Date to the Column Labels field. Leave Year in the Row Field.

6. Click the PivotChart icon in the PivotTable Tools Options tab. Excel puts away the PivotTable Tools tabs and brings back the PivotChart Tools tabs.

7. You lost any existing chart formatting when you deleted the chart in step 1. Format the chart as desired. In Figure 8.8, the field buttons have been hidden and the vertical axis shown in millions.

After grouping, you can see details by month and year, as shown in Figure 8.8.

Figure 8.8
Excel presents a year-over-over year comparison.

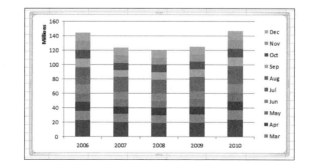

Filtering a Pivot Table

The following sections discuss the three ways to filter a pivot chart report:

1. Slicers, which were introduced in Excel 2010, provide intuitive control when filtering a dataset.

2. If you have used pivot tables before, you will find that the Report Filter field works similarly to Page Fields in legacy versions of Excel. You can add a field to the Report Filter field and choose to limit the report to one or more values from the filter.

3. Beginning in Excel 2007, you can also apply logical filters to fields in either the Axis or Legend fields. These filters allow you to specify various ranges. For example, you can select dates that occur in this year or customers that fall alphabetically between A and E.

Filtering Using Slicers

Slicers are the new visual way to filter pivot tables and pivot charts in Excel 2010. Figure 8.9 shows a pivot chart with five slicers. The chart is currently showing Central region sales for 2009 for three products. Eight customers happened to have a purchase for that combination of fields.

Figure 8.9
Slicers provide a way to visually filter a pivot chart.

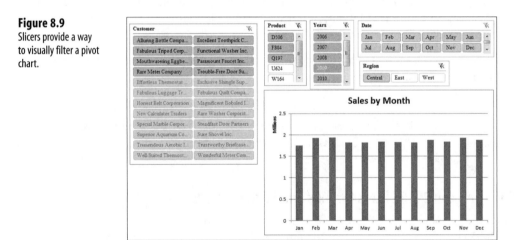

By choosing different items from the various slicers, you can quickly run any type of ad hoc report.

To set up slicers, follow these steps:

1. Before you define slicers, create a pivot chart.

2. Click the chart. Use the Cut command. Page down and paste the chart in a blank section of the worksheet. You will want plenty of room above and to the left of the chart to hold the slicer.

3. While the chart is selected, go to the Analyze tab and select Insert Slicer.

4. Choose as many fields as you wish from the Insert Slicers dialog and click OK. All of the slicers appear in the center of the screen in an overlapping fashion. You will want to rearrange the slicers.

5. Drag the resize handles in the corner of the slicer to resize. While a slicer is active, use the Columns setting on the Slicer Tools Options tab. Slicers with many short values such as the month abbreviations do well with many columns. Items with long values such as customer name do better with fewer columns and a vertical orientation.

6. You can choose a different color for each slicer from the Slicer Styles gallery on the Slicer Tools Options tab (see Figure 8.10).

Figure 8.10
Adjust the color and number of columns using Slicer Tools Options tab.

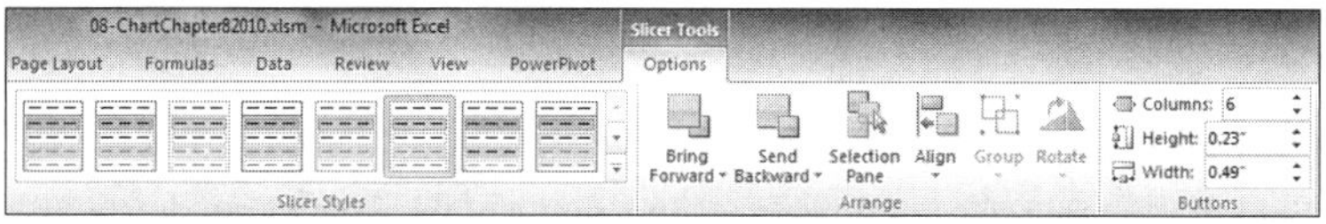

If you are providing the pivot chart and slicers as a sort of dashboard, hide the gridlines unchecking Gridlines in the View tab. You can also hide the horizontal and vertical scrollbars by using File, Options, Advanced, Display Options For This Workbook, Show Horizontal Scrollbar.

When you click an item in the slicer, you select that one item. To select multiple items, hold down the Ctrl key while selection items.

CAUTION

Slicers work only in Excel 2010. If you choose filters from a slicer and then open the workbook in Excel 2007, there will be no visual indication that the fields have been filtered.

Using the Excel 2010 Filters for Axis and Legend Fields

If your pivot chart was created in a new Excel 2007 worksheet and never existed as an Excel 2003 pivot table, you can try out the filters available for the Legend and Axis fields.

You can filter a pivot table using hidden filter buttons in the Field List portion of the Pivot Table Field List. If you hover over a field in the top of the Field List, a secret drop-down arrow appears. Open this drop-down to access filters for that field.

Depending on the field type, you might have value filters, date filters, or text filters.

The Date Filters list, shown in Figure 8.11, allows you to select transactions that fall into a number of virtual date periods. These periods recalculate when you open the file in a later month. So, if you select records from last month, the report updates after you refresh the report in a new month.

Figure 8.11
Date filters allow you to select records from a certain quarter, month, or period.

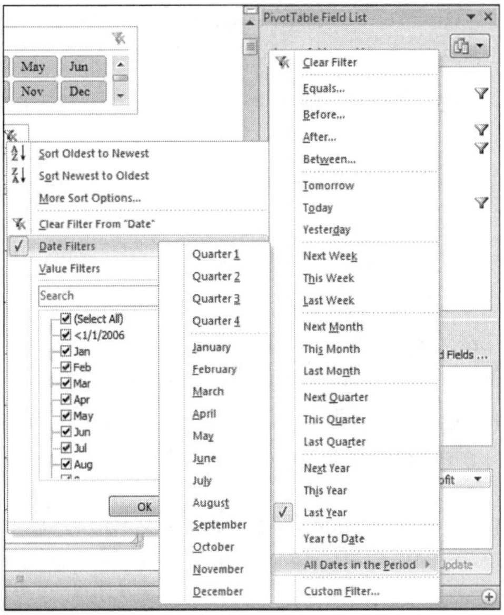

Value filters are more powerful than the other types of filters discussed so far. While label and date filters allow you to filter the items in the list based on the items themselves, value filters allow you to filter the items in the list based on values in other fields. For example, you can choose all customers where the sum of revenue is over $1 million. Or you can use the Top 10 Filter to limit the pivot chart to the top five customers.

Every Axis and Legend field features a value filter. You will also see either label or date filters based on the type of data that Excel finds in the original column.

> **NOTE** To see the date filters, all the values in the original column must be formatted as dates when you create the pivot table. One single cell with a text value in a column of one million dates will cause Excel to show a label filter instead of a date filter.

Creating a Chart for Every Customer

The Show Report Filters Pages functionality allows you to copy a pivot table for every value in a Report Filter field. This would be a fantastic bit of functionality to have available for pivot charts. However, when you use this feature, Excel copies the pivot table but not the pivot chart.

You have a couple of choices in solving this problem. First, you could set up a simple looping macro in VBA to print the chart for each value in the report filter. Or, you could follow these basic steps:

1. Set up a pivot chart that has the proper formatting. Make sure the Customer field is in the Report Filter area.

2. Select the pivot chart. Select Design, Save as Template. Define that template as the default chart type.

3. Select a cell in your pivot table. The PivotTable Tools tabs appear.

4. Look for the Options button on the far left of the Options tab. Do not click the Options button. Instead, click the drop-down at the right side of this button.

5. Select Show Report Filter Pages.

6. In the Show Report Filter Pages dialog that appears, select Customer and then click OK. Excel copies the current worksheet once for each customer.

7. Select the worksheet for the first customer. Select a cell in the pivot table. Press Alt+F1. Excel creates a pivot chart on the worksheet.

Repeat step 7 for each additional customer. Every time you press Alt+F1, you can wonder why the fine folks at Microsoft could not have allowed pivot charts to work with the Show Report Filter Pages feature.

 For an demo of creating charts for every customer, search for "MrExcel Charts 8" at YouTube.

CASE STUDY: STRATIFYING INVOICE AMOUNTS

You cannot create a scatter chart based on a pivot table. Although scatter charts are best for stratifying data, you can still achieve the same effect by using a pivot chart.

During the process of building a pivot chart, there are two steps during which you might temporarily have thousands of data points along the axis field. Rather than ask Excel to attempt to render a chart with thousands of data points, it would make more sense to build the analysis as a pivot table first, group the fields, and then convert it to a pivot table.

You follow these steps to analyze invoice sizes for the five largest customers in your dataset:

1. Select one cell in your data.

2. From the Insert tab, select the top half of the PivotTable icon.

3. Click OK to confirm the information in the Create PivotTable dialog.

4. Drag the Revenue field to the Σ Values drop zone.

5. Drag a second copy of the Revenue field to the Row Labels drop zone.

6. Right-click one value in Column A of your pivot table and select Group from the context menu.

7. As shown in Figure 8.12, Excel suggests grouping the data into strange groups, starting at 8002.40. Change those figures to round numbers, perhaps 5000 to 130000, in increments of 5000. Click OK.

8. Add Customer as the first Row Labels field. Then move Customer before Revenue by dropping the field slightly above the Revenue button in the Row Labels drop zone.

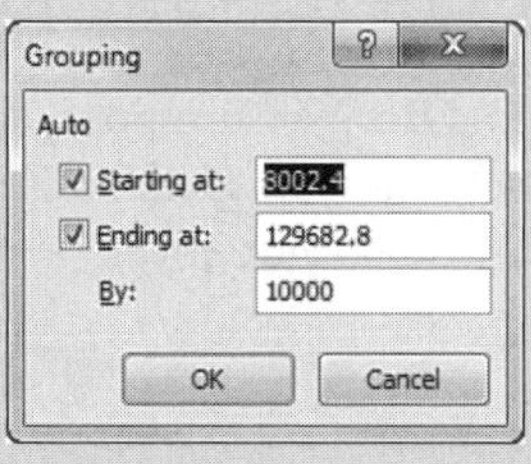

Figure 8.12
When grouping numeric values, Excel suggests strange starting points. You should round them to even ranges.

9. Hover the mouse above the Customer field at the top of the PivotTable Field List. A new drop-down appears. Click this drop-down. Select Value Filters, Top 10. Select Top 5 Items by Sum of Revenue. Click OK.
10. Hover the mouse over the Revenue field in the Σ Values area of the PivotTable Field List box. Click the drop-down and Select Value Field Settings.
11. In the Value Field Settings dialog that appears, change Sum to Count. Click OK.
12. In the Options tab, click the PivotChart icon. Select a Stacked Columns chart. Click OK.
13. In the Layout tab, select Lines, Series Lines.
14. Also in the Layout tab, select Legend, No Legend.

The result is the chart shown in Figure 8.13. For each customer, you can expect the invoices to be grouped around a central value. If you see any invoices that fall far outside the normal range, they might be worthy of audit. In Figure 8.13, for example, you can see that Fabulous Tripod tends to order in the $10,000 to $30,000 range, yet they had at least one invoice in the $125,000 range. This might be the result of a keying error because it is so far outside the norm.

	A	B
1		
2	Region	(All)
3	Date	(All)
4		
5	Row Labels	Count of Revenue
6	Fabulous Tripod Corporation	5590
7	5000-10000	233
8	10000-15000	1357
9	15000-20000	1432
10	20000-25000	1396
11	25000-30000	853
12	30000-35000	318
13	125000-130000	1
14	Honest Belt Corporation	5608
15	5000-10000	240
16	10000-15000	1344
17	15000-20000	1442
18	20000-25000	1348
19	25000-30000	897
20	30000-35000	337
21	Paramount Faucet Inc.	5606
22	5000-10000	216
23	10000-15000	1327

Figure 8.13
Grouping created a stratification of invoice amounts.

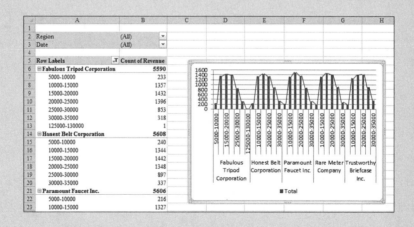

TIP

To find the invoice(s) outside the $10,000 to $30,000 range for Fabulous Tripod, you can go back to the original pivot table and double-click the value next to the 125000-130000 range for Fabulous Tripod. Excel then extracts all the records that make up that data and presents them on a new worksheet for you.

Next Steps

Pivot charts are about as high-tech as you can get. In some cases, you do not need a chart to present your data. Chapter 9, "Using Sparklines, Data Visualizations, and Other Nonchart Methods," goes low-tech, showing you how to use the new sparkline feature or various formula tricks to build graphic displays of information right in your spreadsheet cells.

Using Sparklines, Data Visualizations, and Other Nonchart Methods

Edward Tufte wrote about small, intense, simple data words in his 2006 book, *Beautiful Evidence*. Tufte called them sparklines and produced several examples where you could fit dozens of points of data in the space of a word. Six months later, the Excel team began planning for Excel 2010 and Tufte's concepts made it into Excel 2010.

Sparklines join other Excel 2007 additions such as:

- **Data bars**—This tool offers a tiny, in-cell bar chart for each number in a range. The reader's eye is drawn to the largest numbers because of the size of the bars.

- **Color scales**—Color scales, also called heat maps, color cells in a range of colors. You can use one of six built-in schemes where red is high and blue is low, or green is high and red is low, or you can define your own color scheme.

- **Icon sets**—You can now add a tiny icon next to each number in a range. Icons can use a traffic light metaphor, power bar metaphor, or arrow metaphors to show which data points are the best performers in a dataset.

With each of these new data visualizations, Excel requires only three clicks to get a result. However, each visualization offers advanced settings that give you finer control.

This chapter starts by discussing the new sparklines, then data visualizations and finally some of the legacy data visualizations, such as using the REPT function to build bar charts in cells.

Fitting a Chart Into the Size of a Cell with Sparklines

Excel's implementation of sparklines offer line charts, column charts, and a win/loss chart. See Figure 9.1 for an example of each.

■ **Win/Loss**—The 1951 Pennant Race in Rows 7 and 8 show two examples of a Win/ Loss chart. In this case, each event in a baseball game is represented by either an upward facing marker to indicate a win, or a downward facing marker to indicate a loss. This type of chart shows winning streaks. The final three games were the playoff between the Dodgers and the Giants, with the Giants winning 2 games to 1.

■ **Sparkline**—The sparkline in Row 12 shows 120 monthly points of the Dow Jones Industrial Index showing the closing price for each month in one decade.

■ **Sparkcolumns**—Rows 16 through 21 compare monthly high temperatures for various cities. The minimum and maximum values for each city are marked in a contrasting color. Curitiba, in the southern hemisphere has its warmest month in February.

Figure 9.1
Excel 2010 offers three
types of sparklines.

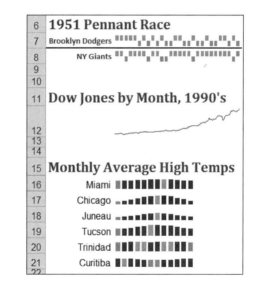

Sparklines can exist as a single cell such as the Dow Jones example or as a group of sparklines such as the temperature example. When sparklines are created as a group, you can specify that all of the sparklines should have the same scale or that they should be independent. There are times where each is appropriate.

The sparkline feature offers the ability to mark the high point, the low point, the first point, the last point, and/or all negative points.

There is no built-in way to label sparklines. However, sparklines are drawn on a special drawing layer that was added to Excel 2007 to accommodate the data visualizations discussed later in this chapter. This layer is transparent, so with some clever formatting, you can add some label information in the cell behind the sparkline.

Creating a Group of SparkLines

The worksheet in Figure 9.2 includes a decade of leading economic indicators. You want to add sparklines to the table.

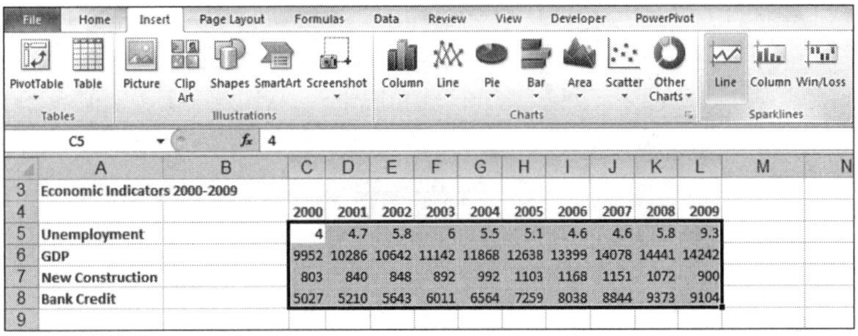

Figure 9.2

Add space in your table for the sparklines.

1. Insert a blank column between Columns A and B. This will provide room for the sparklines to appear next to the labels in Column A. You might find that you do not need to print the table of numbers, just the labels and sparklines will suffice.
2. Select the data in C5:L8. Note that you do not include any headings in this selection.
3. On the Insert tab, select Column from the Sparkline Group. Excel displays the Create Sparklines dialog.

> **NOTE**
> This dialog is the same for all three types of sparklines. You have to specify the location of the data and the location where you want the sparklines. Because your data is 4 rows by 10 columns, the Location Range must be a 4-cell vector. You can either specify one-row by four-columns or four rows x 1 column.

4. Select B5:B8 as the location range, as shown in Figure 9.3.
5. Click OK to create the default sparklines.

As shown in Figure 9.4, the sparklines have no markers. They are scaled independently of each other. The unemployment max of 9.3 reaches nearly to the top of Cell B5, indicating the maximum for Unemployment is probably about 10. By contrast, the maximum for GDP in B6 is closer to 14,500.

The Show group of the Sparkline toolbar allows you to mark certain points on the line. In Figure 9.5, the high point is marked with a dot. This one change adds a lot of information to the sparklines. New Construction peaked in 2006. GDP and Bank Credit peaked in 2008. Unemployment peaked in 2009. Did the drop in new construction in 2007 foretell the other items?

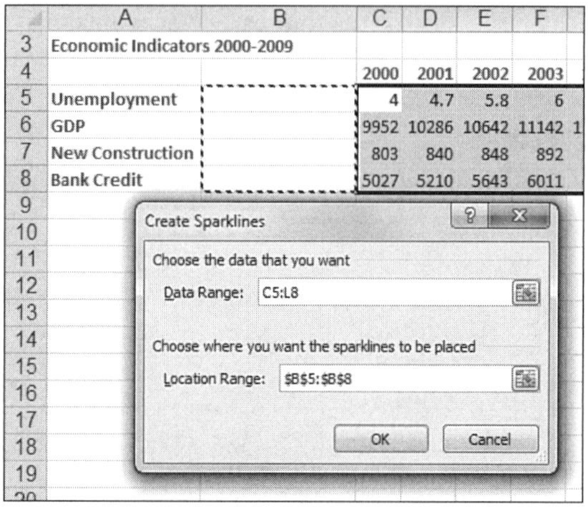

Figure 9.3
Preselect the data range, and then specify the location range.

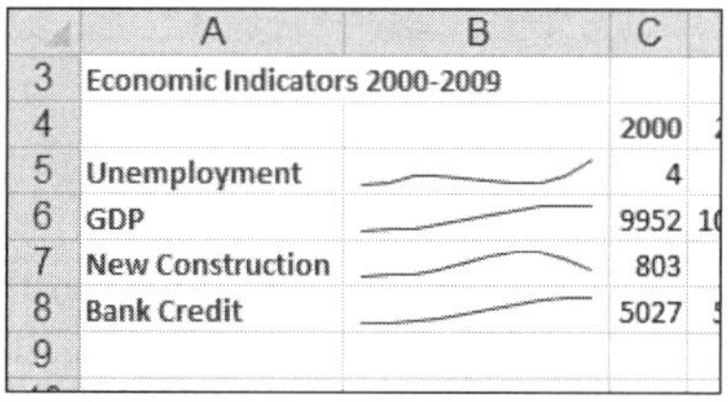

Figure 9.4
Default sparklines have no markers and are auto-scaled to fit the cell.

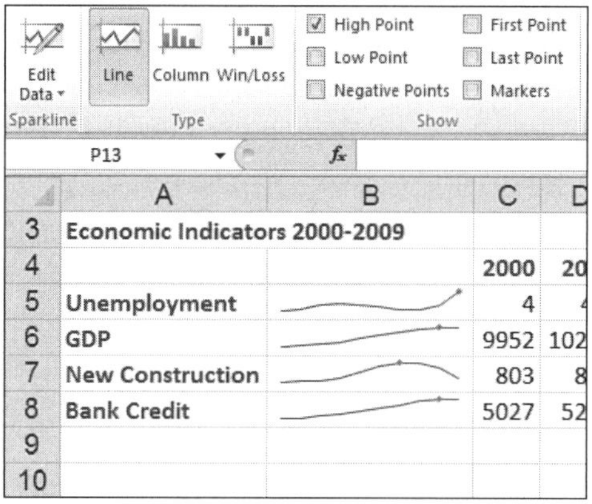

Figure 9.5
Adding a marker at the high point adds key information to the sparkline.

Built-In Choices for Customizing Sparklines

The Sparkline Tools Design tab offers several built-in choices for customizing sparklines:

- The **Edit Data** drop-down allows you to re-specify the data range for the source data and the location. If you have to add new data to existing sparklines, you can do so here. Generally, you would edit the location for the whole group, but the drop-down menu allows you to edit data for a single sparkline.

- The **Type** group allows you to switch between Line, Column, and Win/Loss charts.
- The **Show** group offers the second-most useful settings in the tab. Here, you can choose to highlight the High Point, Low Point, First Point, Last Points. Note that if there is a tie for High or Low point, both points in the tie will be marked. You can also choose to highlight all points and/or the negative points.
- For sparklines, any item that you choose in the Show group is drawn as a marker on the line. You can control the color for each of the six options using the Marker Color drop-down, discussed in the following section.
- For sparkcolumns, the markers are always shown. Choosing any of the five other choices will cause those particular columns to be drawn in a different color.
- For Win/Loss, you will generally always select Markers and Negative. This is how the losses show in a contrasting color from the wins.

Figure 9.6 shows examples of the various options:

- In Cell B3, the high, low, first, and last points are shown.
- In Cell B5, all markers are shown in the same color.
- When you select Markers and Negative, all points appear, but you can change the negative points to another color, as shown in Cell B7.
- In Cells B11 and B13, the chosen markers are shown in a contrasting color.
- Cell B9 and B15 show examples where the horizontal axis is shown. This helps to differentiate positive from negative. Note that the axis always appears at a zero location.

The Style gallery seems to be a huge waste of real estate. In the Office theme, it offers 36 ugly alternatives for sparkline color. This group also offers the Sparkline Color drop-down, which is the standard Excel 2010 color chooser. The color chosen here controls the line in a sparkline. The Marker Color drop-down is where you can control the color of the High, Low, First, Last, Negative points, as well as the default color for regular markers. Figure 9.7 shows the Marker Color drop-down.

The Group group is where you logically unlink a set of sparklines.

Any changes that you make on the Design tab apply to all of the sparklines in the group. This is usually a desired outcome. However, if you needed to mark the High point in one line and the Low Point in another line, you would want to ungroup the sparklines. You can also group sparklines or clear sparklines using icons in the Group group. The Axis drop-down appears in this group and contains the most important settings for sparklines. You will learn how to use the Axis drop-down in the next example.

Controlling Axis Values for Sparklines

Figure 9.8 shows a group of sparkcolumns showing the average high temperature for several cities. These cities are a mix of tropical and frigid cities.

Figure 9.6
Use the Show Group to highlight certain points.

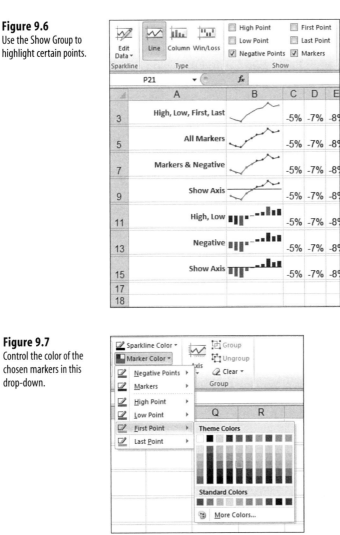

Figure 9.7
Control the color of the chosen markers in this drop-down.

The default behavior of sparklines is that each sparkline in the group gets its own scale. This worked for the varying economic indicators shown previously in Figure 9.1. However, it does not work here.

When the vertical axis scale is set to Automatic, you can never really know the high and low of the scale in use. If you study the data and the sparkline for Trinidad, it appears as if Excel has chosen a min point of 84.8 and a max point of 89. Without any scale, you might thin that Trinidad in January is as cold as Chicago in January.

Figure 9.9 shows the options available in the Axis drop-down on the right end of the Sparkline Tools Design tab. The important settings here are the choices for the Minimum value and Maximum value.

Figure 9.8
The automatic vertical scale assigned to each sparkline does not work in this example.

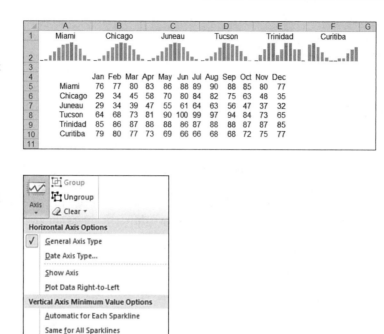

Figure 9.9
Control the vertical axis using this drop-down.

	Group
	Ungroup
Axis	Clear ▾

Horizontal Axis Options

✓ General Axis Type

Date Axis Type...

Show Axis

Plot Data Right-to-Left

Vertical Axis Minimum Value Options

Automatic for Each Sparkline

Same for All Sparklines

✓ Custom Value...

Vertical Axis Maximum Value Options

Automatic for Each Sparkline

Same for All Sparklines

✓ Custom Value...

If you change the min and max to the setting of Same For All Sparklines, then all six sparklines in this group will have the same min and max scale. The sparklines in Figure 9.10 initially look better. Juneau is never as warm as Tucson. However, you still do not know what the max and min values are. Take a close look at Chicago. It appears that the January high temperature is about zero, but the data table shows that the average high temperature in January is 29. You can estimate that these columns run from a min of 28 to a max of 101, based on looking through the data.

Figure 9.10
Force all sparklines to have the same vertical scale.

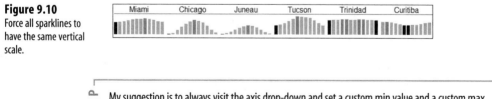

TIP
My suggestion is to always visit the axis drop-down and set a custom min value and a custom max value. In Figure 9.11, the minimum is 0 and the maximum is 100.

Figure 9.11
For absolute control, define a custom min and max value.

Setting Up Win/Loss Sparklines

The data for a Win/Loss sparkline is simple: Put a 1 (or any positive number) for a win. Put a -1 (or any negative number) for a loss. Put a zero to have no marker.

In Figure 9.12, you can see the data for a pair of Win/Loss sparklines. The 2 in Cell F3 does not cause the marker to appear any taller than any of the 1s in the other cells. It does cause the marker to appear as a different color if you choose to mark the high point. Maybe you can think of a use where you need to show two different colors among the wins or losses.

Figure 9.12
Datasets for wins and losses consist of 1s and -1s.

Showing Detail by Enlarging the Sparkline

Professor Tufte's definition of sparklines included the word *small*. If you are going to be showing the sparklines on a computer screen, there is no reason that the sparklines have to stay small.

When you increase the height and width of the cell, the sparkline automatically grows to fill the cell. If you merge cells, the sparkline will fill the complete range of merged cells.

In Figure 9.13, the 279-game season of the Harlem Globetrotters seemed as if it needed more than just one cell, so Cells B2 and C2 were merged. In Cell B4, the row height was increased to 30 to show more detail.

Figure 9.13
Increase cell size or merge cells to increase the detail in the sparkline.

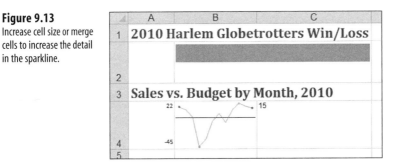

Labeling a Sparkline

The examples of sparklines created by Tufte in *Beautiful Evidence* almost always labeled the final point. Some examples included min and max values or a gray box to indicate the normal range of values.

Figure 9.13 shows labels for Min and Max to the left of the sparkline and a label for the final point to the right of the sparkline. Those labels are simply cell values. To create the label on the left, follow these steps:

1. Type the high value. Press Alt+Enter four times to move to the fifth line of text in the cell. Type the low value. Press Ctrl+Enter.

2. Format the cell as 8 point or smaller.

3. Use the Right Align and Top Align icons on the Home tab to position the labels at the right edge of the cell.

To label the final point, you can precede the value with the appropriate number of Alt+Enter keystrokes to vertically position the label close to the correct place.

If you set a row height equal to 110, you can fit ten lines of text in the cell using Alt+Enter. Even with a height of 55, you can fit five lines of text. This will allow the label for the final point to get near to the final point.

In Figure 9.14, the city labels are simply values typed in the same cell as the sparkcolumns. The max scale was set to 120 to make sure that there was room for the city name to appear. The Month abbreviations below the charts are "J F M A M J J A S O N D" in 6.5 point Courier New font. After trying both 6 point and 7 point and not having the labels line up with the columns, I ended up using 6.5 point and adjusted the column widths until the columns lined up with the labels.

Figure 9.14

Labels are created by typing in a small font in the cell.

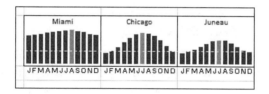

In Figure 9.15, a semitransparent gray box indicates the acceptable limits for a measurement. In this case, anything outside of 95 percent to 105 percent is sent for review. Those gray boxes are simply Shapes from the Insert tab.

Some tips when setting up the box:

1. Temporarily change the first two points in the first cell to be at the min and max for the box.

2. Increase the zoom to 400 percent.

3. Draw a rectangle in the cell.

4. Use the Drawing Tools Format tab to set the outline to None.

5. Under Shape Fill, select More Fill Colors. Select a grey. Because shapes are drawn on top of the sparkline layer, drag the transparency slider up to about 70 percent transparent.

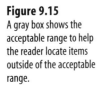

Figure 9.15
A gray box shows the acceptable range to help the reader locate items outside of the acceptable range.

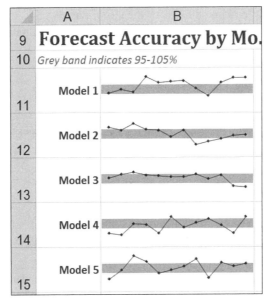

6. Use the resize handles to make sure the top and bottom of the box go through the first and second points of the line.

7. After getting the box sized appropriately, reset the first two data points back to their original values.

8. Copy the cell that contains the first box. Paste onto the other sparkline cells. Because the sparklines are not copied, only the box will be pasted.

> **TIP**
> It is possible to copy sparklines. You have to copy both the sparkline and the data source in a single copy. If your copy range includes both elements, then the sparkline will get pasted.

Using Data Bars to Create In-Cell Bar Charts

A data bar is a swath of color that starts at the side of a cell and extends into the cell based on the value of the cell. Small numbers get less color. The largest numbers might be 100 percent filled with color. This creates a visual effect that enables you to visually pick out the larger and smaller values. Figure 9.16 shows many examples of data bars.

Many new options are available in Excel 2010 data bars:

- Data bars can be solid or a gradient. In Excel 2010, the default gradient bar has a border. Tufte and others complained that the gradient in E14:E20 were misleading. The gradient is useful for helping to see the numbers behind the data bar. Contrast the solid bar in B2 and the gradient in B8. By adding the border around the gradient, Microsoft leaves no doubt where the data bar ends, but allows the numbers to show through.

Figure 9.16
The data bars illustrate many of the new properties in Excel 2010 data bars.

	A	B	C	D	E
1	A	12			
2	B	22	Female	Age	Male
3	C	9	9	20	5
4	D	2	12	30	14
5	F	1	16	40	20
6			21	50	24
7	A	12	10	60	10
8	B	22	9	70	7
9	C	9	6	80	5
10	D	2	5	90	0
11	F	1			
12					
13	Store	Over/Under Budget	Over/Under Budget		Over/Under Budget
14	Akron	0.8%	0.8%		Akron
15	Alliance	4.5%	4.5%		Alliance
16	Canton	3.6%	3.6%		Canton
17	Dover	-3.3%	-3.3%		Dover
18	Louisville	-1.9%	-1.9%		Louisville
19	Medina	-1.3%	-1.3%		Medina
20	Salem	3.3%	3.3%		Salem
21					

■ Values of zero now actually get no data bar as shown in Cell E10. Previously, the smallest value would get 4 pixels of color.

■ Data bars can now be negative. Negative bars are shown in a different color and usually extend to the left of a central axis. You have three choices in where to place the zero axis. In Cells B14:B20, the setting is Automatic. Because the largest positive number is further from zero than the smallest negative number, the axis appears slightly to the left of center. This allows the bar for 4.5 percent in B15 to appear larger than the bar for -3.3 percent in B17. You can also force the axis to appear in the center as in Cells C14:C20. Alternatively, in a bizarre setting, you can force the negative bars to extend in the same direction as the positive values, but with a different color.

There are two philosophical ways to show the negative bars. You can assign -3.3 percent the most color since it is farthest from zero, or you can assign -1.3 percent the most color since it is the mathematically the largest of the negative numbers (-1.3 percent > -3.3 percent).

NOTE

Excel 2010 uses the latter method in Cells E14:E20. I am lobbying for the former method.

■ You can control the color of the positive bar, positive bar border, negative bar, negative bar border, and axis color.

■ With Excel 2010, bars can now extend right-to-left, as shown in Cells C3:C10. This allows comparative histograms as in C2:E10.

The following options are not new in Excel 2010, but still remain from Excel 2007:

- You can specify the scale of the data bars. While the scale is initially set to automatic, you can specify that the min/max are set to a certain number or to the lowest value, a percentage, a percentile, or a formula.

- You can choose to show only the data bar and to hide the number in the cell. This is how words were included in Cells E14:E20. The numbers are hidden by the conditional formatting dialog, and then a linked picture of the words is pasted over the cells. Since the data bars are on a drawing layer above the regular drawing layer, this works.

- You can format the number in the cell with a custom number format of specific text. For example, a custom number format of "Akron" in cell E14 will always show the word Akron in the cell, no matter what number is typed in the cell.

- All data bars in a group have the same scale. This is unlike sparklines where the scale is allowed to change from graphic to graphic.

Creating Data Bars

Creating data bars requires just a few clicks. You follow these steps:

1. Select a range of numeric data. Do not include the total in this selection. If the data is in noncontiguous ranges, hold down the Ctrl key while selecting additional areas. This range should be numbers of similar scale. For example, you can select a column of sales data or a column of profit data. If you attempt to select a range that contains both units sold and revenue dollars, the size of the revenue numbers will overpower the units sold numbers, and no color will appear in the units sold cells.

2. From the Home tab, select Conditional Formatting, Data Bars. You see six built-in colors for the data bars: blue, green, red, orange, bright blue, and pink. The colors appear both in solid and gradient forms. Select one of them.

> **NOTE** If you do not like the six basic colors Excel offers for data bars, you can choose any other color, as described in the next section.

The result is a swath of color in each cell in the selection, as shown in Figure 9.17.

Customizing Data Bars

By default, Excel assigns the largest data bar to the cell with the largest value and the smallest data bar to the cell with the smallest value. You can customize this behavior by following these steps:

1. From the Conditional Formatting drop-down on the Home tab, select Manage Rules.

2. From the Show Formatting Rules drop-down, select This Worksheet. You now see a list of all rules applied to the sheet.

3. Click the Data Bar rule.

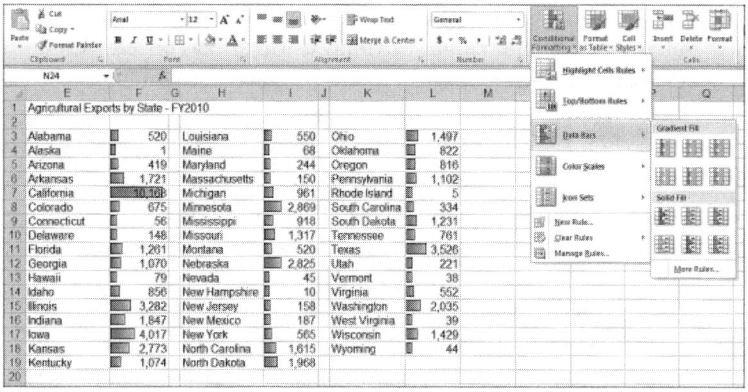

Figure 9.17
After applying a data bar, you can see that California is a leading exporter of agriculture products.

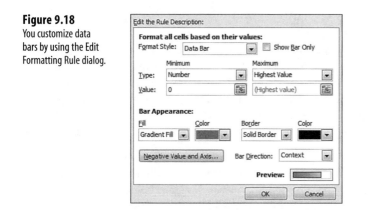

4. Click the Edit Rule button. You see the Edit Formatting Rule dialog, as shown in Figure 9.18.

Figure 9.18
You customize data bars by using the Edit Formatting Rule dialog.

There are a number of customizations available in this dialog:

■ Select the Show Bar Only setting to hide the numbers in the cells and to show only the data bar.

■ For the Minimum and Maximum values, you have choices of Automatic, Number, Percent, Percentile, Formula, or Smallest/Largest Number. If you choose Automatic, Excel will choose a minimum and maximum value. You can override this by setting one value to a specific number.

■ In the Bar Appearance section, you can specify gradient or solid fill for the bar. You can specify a solid border or no border. Two color chooser drop-downs allow you to change the color of the bar and the border.

- The Bar Direction drop-down allows you to choose Context, Left to Right or Right to Left. The default choice of Context will always be left to right, unless you are in an international edition of Excel where the language reading order is right to left.

When you choose Negative Values and Axis, you have new settings to adjust the color of the bar and the border for negative bars. You can also control if the zero axis is shown at the cell midpoint, or at an automatic location based on the relative size of the negative and positive numbers. If the axis is shown, you can adjust the color, too.

> **CAUTION**
>
> One frustrating feature with data bars is that you cannot reverse their size, using the smallest bar for the highest number and vice versa. Although in some scenarios, such as top 100 rankings, the lowest score might deserve the largest bar, there is no way to make this happen with data bars. If you need to do this, you could consider using color scales or formulas to reverse the values.

Showing Data Bars for a Subset of Cells

In the data bars examples given in the previous sections, every cell in the range receives a data bar. However, what if you just want some of the values such as the top 20 percent or the top 10 to have data bars? The process for making this happen is not intuitive, but it is possible. Basically, you apply the data bar to the entire range. Then you add a new conditional format (a very boring format) to all the cells that you do not want to have data bars. For example, you might tell Excel to use a white background on all cells with values outside of the top 10.

The final important step is to manage the rules and tell Excel to stop processing more rules if the white background rule is met. This requires clever thinking. If you want to apply data bars to cells in the top 10, you first tell Excel to make all the cells in the bottom 40 look like every other cell in Excel. Turning on Stop If True in the Conditional Formatting Rules Manager dialog is the key to getting Excel to not apply the data bar to cells with values outside of the top 10.

Figure 9.19 shows data bars applied to only the top 10 states.

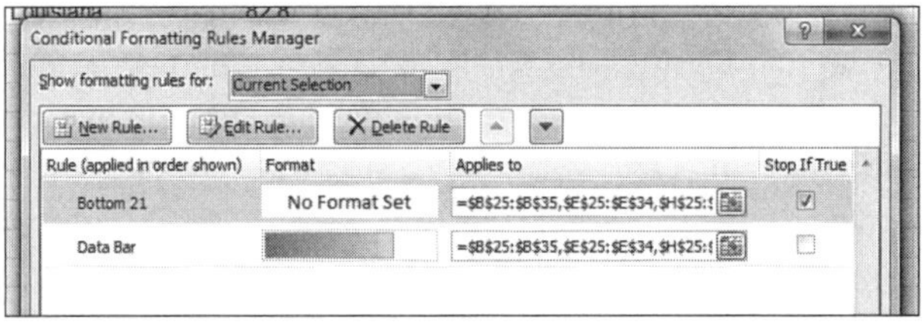

Figure 9.19
Using Stop If True after formatting the lower 21 with no special formatting allows the data bars to appear only on the top states.

Using Color Scales to Highlight Extremes

Color scales are similar to data bars. However, instead of having a variable-size bar in each cell, color scales use gradients of two or three different colors to communicate the relative size of each cell. Here's how you apply color scales:

1. Select a range that contains numbers. Be sure not to include headings or total cells in the selection.

2. Select Conditional Formatting, Color Scales from the Home tab.

3. From the Color Scales fly-out menu, select one of the 12 styles to apply the color scale to the range.

> **NOTE**
> Note that the fly-out menu in step 3 offers subtle differences to which you should pay attention. For example, the first six options are scales that use three colors. These are great onscreen or with color printers. The last six options are scales that use two colors. These are better with monochrome printers.

In a two-color red-white color scale, the largest number is formatted with a dark red fill. The smallest number has a white fill. All of the numbers in between receive a lighter or darker shade of pink based on their position within the range (see Figure 9.20).

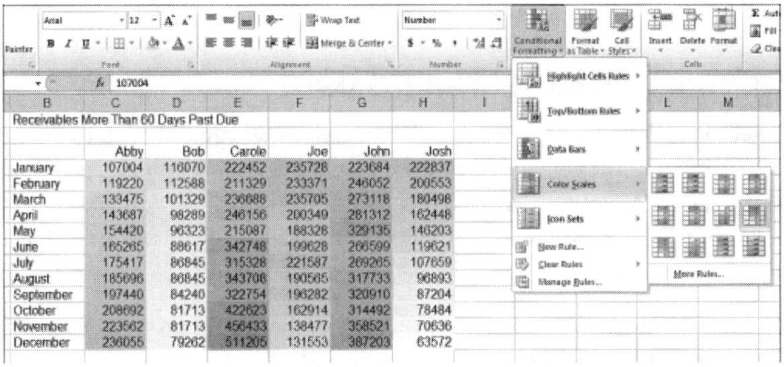

Figure 9.20
Excel provides a range of shading, depending on the value. You can see that Carole and John's receivables have been increasing throughout the year.

Customizing Color Scales

You are not limited to the color scales shown in the fly-out menu. If you select Home, Conditional Formatting, Manage Rules, Edit Rule, you can choose any two or three colors for the color scale.

You also have choices of where to assign the smallest, largest, and midpoint values (see Figure 9.21).

You should be aware of one strange situation. Normally, Excel will let you mix conditional formatting in the same range. You might apply both a color scale and an icon set.

Figure 9.21
You can choose any colors to use in the color scale.

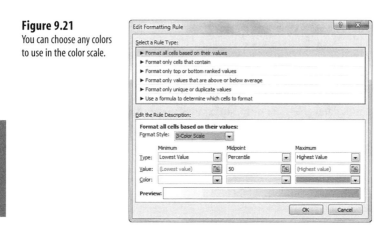

If you have a three-color scale applied to some cells and choose a different three-color scale from the fly-out menu, the latter choice will overwrite the first choice.

However, Excel treats two-color scales as a different visualization than three-color scales. If you have a three-color scale applied and you then try to switch it to a two-color scale using the fly-out menu, Excel will create two rules for those cells. The latter two-color scale will be the only one to appear in Excel 2010, but you might be confused when you go to the Manage Rules dialog to see two different rules applied to the cells.

Using Icon Sets to Segregate Data

Icon sets, which were popular with expensive management reporting software in the late 1990s, have now been added to Excel. An icon set might include green, yellow, and red traffic lights or another set of icons to show positive, neutral, and negative meanings. With icon sets, Excel automatically applies an icon to a cell, based on the relative size of the value in the cell compared to other values in the range.

Excel 2010 ships with 20 different icon sets that contain three, four, or five different icons. The icons are always left-justified in the cell. Excel applies rules to add an icon to every cell in the range:

- **Three-icon sets**—For the three-icon sets, you have a choice between arrows, flags, two varieties of traffic lights, signs, stars, triangles, and two varieties of what Excel calls *3 Symbols*. This last group consists of a green check mark for the good cells, a yellow exclamation point for the middle cells, and a red X for the bad cells. You can either get the symbols in a circle (that is, 3 Symbols(Circled)) or alone on a white background (that is, 3 Symbols). One version of the arrows is available in gray. All the other icon sets use red, yellow, and green.

- **Four-icon sets**—For the four-icon sets, there are two varieties of arrows: a black-to-red circle set, a set of cell phone power bars, and a set of four traffic lights. In the traffic light option, a black light indicates an option that is even worse than the red light.

The power bars icons seem to work well on both color displays and monochromatic printouts.

■ **Five-icon sets**—For the five-icon sets, there are two varieties of arrows, boxes, a five-power bar set, and an interesting set called *5 Quarters*. This last set is a monochromatic circle that is completely empty for the lowest values, 25 percent filled, 50 percent filled, 75 percent filled, and completely filled for the highest values.

> **CAUTION**
>
> Three of these sets are new in Excel 2010. If you choose Three Triangles, Three Stars, or Five Boxes, those icon sets will not appear if the workbook is opened in Excel 2007.

Setting Up an Icon Set

Icon sets require a bit more thought than the other data visualization offerings. Before you use icon sets, you should consider whether they will be printed in monochrome or displayed in color. Several of the 20 icon sets rely on color for differentiation and look horrible in a black-and-white report.

> **TIP**
>
> After creating several reports with icon sets, I have started to favor the cell phone power bars, which look good in both color and black and white.

To set up an icon set, you follow these steps:

1. Select a range of numeric data of a similar scale. Do not include the headers or total rows in this selection.

2. From the Home tab, select Conditional Formatting, Icon Sets. Select 1 of the 20 icon sets. Figure 9.22 shows the 3 Stars choice selected.

Moving Numbers Closer to Icons

In the top rows of Figure 9.23, the icon set has been applied to a rectangular range of data. The icons are always left-justified. Numbers are typically right-justified. This can be problematic. Someone might think that the icon at the left side of Cell G3 is really referring to the right-aligned number in F3.

You might try centering the numbers to get the numbers closer to the icons in Rows 7-9. This will drive purists crazy, because the final digit of the 100 in Cell H8 does not line up with the final digits of Cells H7 and H9.

A better solution is to use the Alignment tab of the Format Cells dialog. Select Right (Indent) for the horizontal alignment. Bump the indent figure up to move the numbers closer to the icon. In Rows 12-14, the indent is set at four characters.

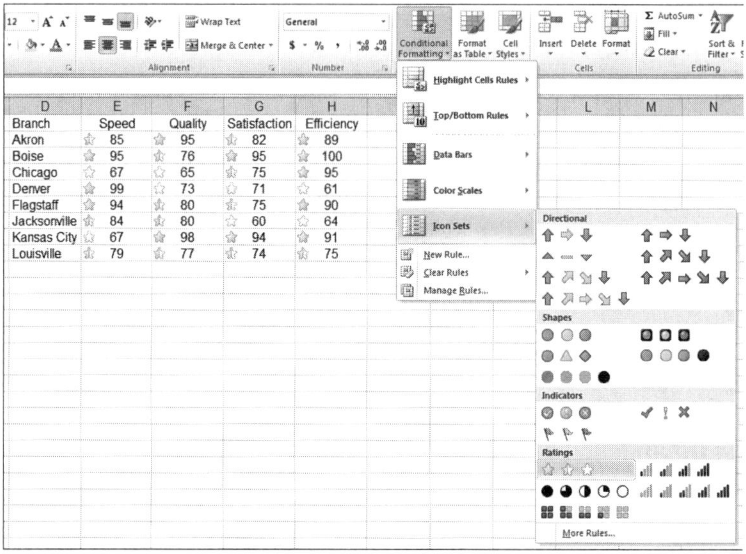

Figure 9.22
You can choose from the
20 icon sets.

If you do not want to show numbers at all, you can edit the conditional formatting rule and select Show Icon Only. Rows 17 through 19 show this solution. Ironically, when the numbers are no longer displayed, you can position the icons by using the Left Align, Center Align, and Right Align icons.

The over-the-top solution in Rows 22-24 involve using Show Icon Only and then pasting a linked picture of the numbers from other cells.

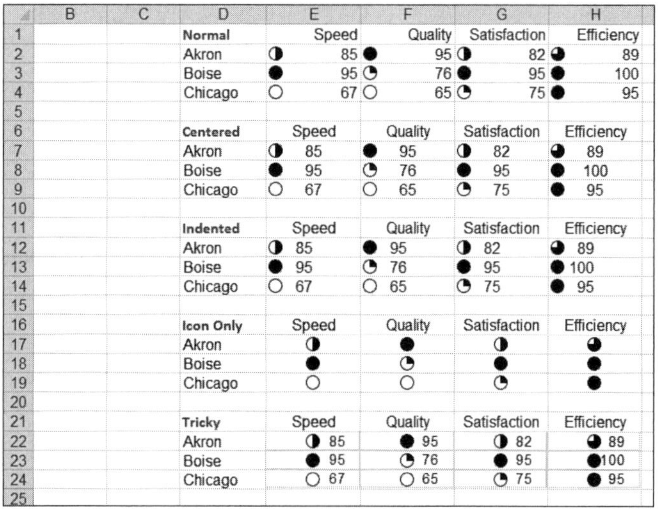

Figure 9.23
Changing the alignment
of the numbers moves
them closer to the icon.

	B	C	D	E	F	G	H
1			Normal	Speed	Quality	Satisfaction	Efficiency
2			Akron	◑ 85 ●	95 ◐	82 ◐	89
3			Boise	● 95 ◓	76 ●	95 ●	100
4			Chicago	○ 67 ○	65 ◓	75 ●	95
5							
6			Centered	Speed	Quality	Satisfaction	Efficiency
7			Akron	◑ 85	● 82	◑ 82	◑ 89
8			Boise	● 95	◓ 76	95	100
9			Chicago	○ 67	○ 65	◓ 75	● 95
10							
11			Indented	Speed	Quality	Satisfaction	Efficiency
12			Akron	◑ 85	● 95	◑ 82	◑ 89
13			Boise	● 95	◓ 76	● 95	● 100
14			Chicago	○ 67	○ 65	◓ 75	● 95
15							
16			Icon Only	Speed	Quality	Satisfaction	Efficiency
17			Akron	◑	●	◑	●
18			Boise	●	◓	●	●
19			Chicago	○	○	◓	●
20							
21			Tricky	Speed	Quality	Satisfaction	Efficiency
22			Akron	◑ 85	● 95	◑ 82	◑ 89
23			Boise	● 95	◓ 76	● 95	●100
24			Chicago	○ 67	○ 65	◓ 75	● 95
25							

Here are the steps to create Rows 22 through 24:

1. Select one of the cells with the icon set formatting.
2. From the Home tab, select Conditional Formatting, Manage Rules.
3. In the Conditional Formatting Rules Manager dialog, click the Icon Set rule, and then click Edit Rule.
4. In the middle of the Edit Formatting Rule dialog, select Show Icon Only. Click OK twice to close the two dialog boxes.
5. Select all the cells that contain icons and click the Align Center button on the Home tab.
6. Page down so that you are outside of the printed range. Stay in the same column. Set up a formula to point to the number in the top left corner of the icon set range. Copy this formula down and over to be the same size as your icon set range. This gives you a range of just the numbers.
7. Format this range of numbers to be right-aligned with an indent of 1. Choose the range and press Ctrl+1 to display Format Cells. On the Alignment tab, open the Horizontal dropdown and choose Right (Indent). Increase the Indent spin button to 1.
8. Copy this range of numbers.
9. Go back to the original set of icons and Paste, Picture Link. A picture of the original numbers will appear, behind the icons.

CASE STUDY: REVERSING THE SEQUENCE OF ICONS

Say that you have data to track reject rates for several manufacturing lines. You apply an icon set that offers green check marks, yellow exclamation points, and red X icons.

In the default view of the data, Excel always assumes that higher numbers are better. However, that is not the case in this situation, where higher reject rates are bad.

Unlike with color scales or data bars, with icon sets, you can reverse the order. To do so, you follow these steps:

1. Select one cell in your data.
2. From the Conditional Formatting drop-down on the Home tab, select Manage Rules.
3. Click Icon Set to select this rule. The rule color changes from gray to blue.
4. Click the Edit Rule button. The Edit Formatting Rule dialog appears.
5. In the Edit Formatting Rule dialog, select the Reverse Icon Order button. Click OK twice to close both open dialog boxes.

Creating a Chart Using Conditional Formatting in Worksheet Cells

In the old days, charts were drawn by hand, using a sheet of graph paper and a pencil. Think about the Excel worksheets on your computer. Basically, an Excel worksheet is a very large sheet of graph paper, with 17 billion tiny little boxes.

You can create plenty of charts right on a worksheet, without ever invoking the Excel charting engine. Figure 9.24 shows such a chart. The gray bars in D2:R6 are drawn based on conditional formatting rules in response to data entered in B2:C6. Note how the bars have expanded or contracted in the bottom image when starting or ending years are adjusted.

I created this worksheet for a friend who was trying to visualize the years of production for various models of Mullins Steel Boats. The years stretch from Cell D1 and would extend as far right as necessary. To make the chart narrow, you can select Vertical Text from the Orientation drop-down in the Home tab. You can then resize the columns to a column width of 2.

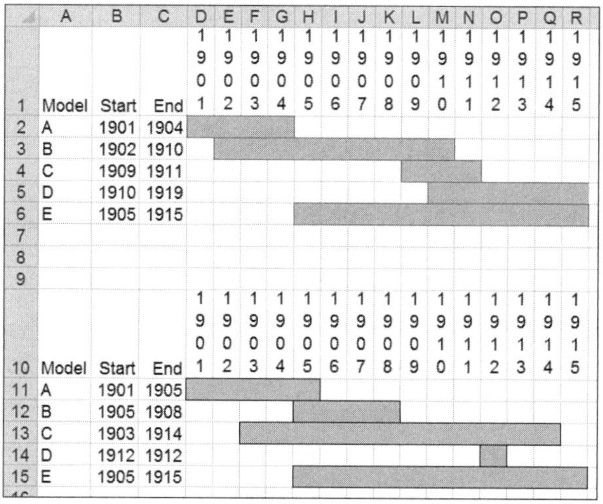

Figure 9.24
The gray bars are created through a series of conditional formatting rules.

The logic for creating the bars is as follows:

- If the start and end year are equal and they match the year in Row 1, color the cell gray, with borders on all four sides.

- If the start year in Column B matches the year in Row 1, color the cell gray. Include left, top, and bottom borders.

- If the end year in Column C matches the year in Row 1, color the cell gray. Include right, top, and bottom borders.

■ If the year in Row 1 is greater than the start year and less than the end year, color the cell gray, with top and bottom borders but no side borders.

You follow these steps to create the conditional formatting rules for this logic:

1. Select the range D2:R6.

TIP

Although you have selected many cells, you write the conditional formatting rules as if they applied to the top-left cell, which is D2.

2. From the Home tab, select Conditional Formatting, Manage Rules. Excel displays the Conditional Formatting Rules Manager dialog.

3. Click the New Rule button. Excel displays the New Formatting Rule dialog.

4. In the top half of the dialog, select Use a Formula to Determine Which Cells to Format. The bottom half of the dialog box redraws to show Format Values Where This Formula Is True.

5. Enter the formula =$B2=D$1 for the first condition. This formula checks whether the start year in Column B of the current row is equal to Row 1 of the current column. It is crucial that you enter dollar signs before the B and 1 but not before the 2 and D.

6. Click the Format button in the dialog. On the Fill tab, choose a fill color for the cell. On the Border tab, click None and then click the Top, Bottom, and Left. Click OK to close the Format Cells dialog. Click OK to close the New Formatting Rule dialog. If you click the Apply button, you should see that the first cell for each bar is drawn in the worksheet.

7. Repeat steps 3 and 4 and then enter the formula =$C2=D$1 for the second rule; this is the formula to format the last cell of the bar. The Format selection is the same color fill as in step 6. On the Border tab, select None, Top, Bottom, and Right.

8. Repeat step 7 and then enter the formula =AND($B2<D$1,$C2>D$1) for the third rule; this is the formula to format center cells in the bar. The Format selection is the same fill as in step 6. On the Border tab, select None, Top, and Bottom.

9. Repeat step 7 and then enter the formula =AND($B2=$C2,$B2=D$1) for the last rule; this is the formula to find where the model was only available for a single year. The Format selection is the same fill color as in step 6. On the Border tab, select Outline. Rules are added to the beginning of the rule list. By entering this rule last, you ensure that it is evaluated first.

At this point, your Conditional Formatting Rules Manager dialog should look similar to the one in Figure 9.25.

This example is complicated by the fact that you draw borders on the appropriate edges of each cell. If you instead used a solid black fill, you could create the effect with a single rule, using the formula =AND($B2<=D$1,$C2>=D$1).

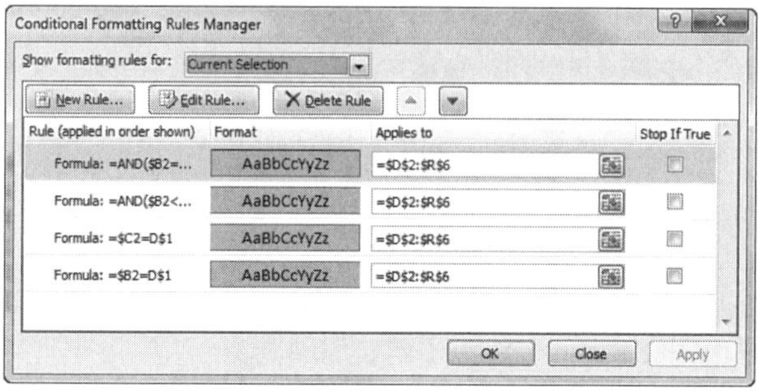

Figure 9.25
Four rules create the chart.

9

Creating a Chart Using the REPT Function

The REPT function, which has been around since Excel 5, takes two arguments. The first argument is the text to repeat. The second argument is the number of times to repeat the text.

In Figure 9.26, Column B shows cotton exports. The numbers range from 1,337 down to 13. You create the bar charts in Column C by repeating the | character numerous times. However, instead of showing a line of 1,337 pipe characters in Cell C4, the repeat argument in Cell B4 is 1,337 divided by 10. Therefore, Cell C4 contains 133 vertical bars. Cell C20 contains one vertical bar.

> **TIP**
>
> Keep in mind that even though 13.7 divided by 10 is 1.3 bars, Excel shows only complete bars.

The result of the REPT function can be left- or right-justified. In Figure 9.27, the results in Column E are right-justified, and the results in Column G are left-justified to create a comparative histogram. The formulas on the right side of the chart use a REPT function concatenated with a space and then the value. The formulas on the left side of the chart concatenate the value, a space, and the REPT function.

To see a demo of using the REPT function for charting, search for "MrExcel Charts 9" at YouTube.

Next Steps

In Chapter 10, "Presenting Excel Data on a Map Using Microsoft MapPoint," you will learn how to combine Microsoft Excel with Microsoft MapPoint to visually show geographic data. Several of the examples included in this chapter show tables of data by state. Think how these examples would take on a whole new meaning if they were plotted on a map. Microsoft MapPoint adds this functionality to Excel.

Figure 9.26
Using the REPT function is a quick way to produce a bar chart right in a worksheet. The trick is to use the proper scaling factor.

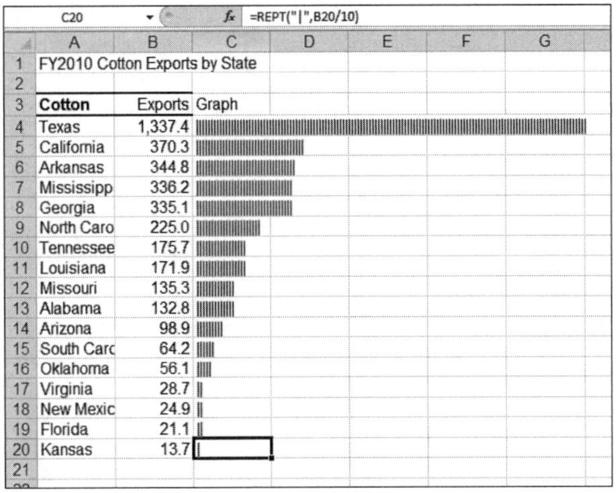

Figure 9.27
Here, pairs of REPT functions create a comparative histogram.

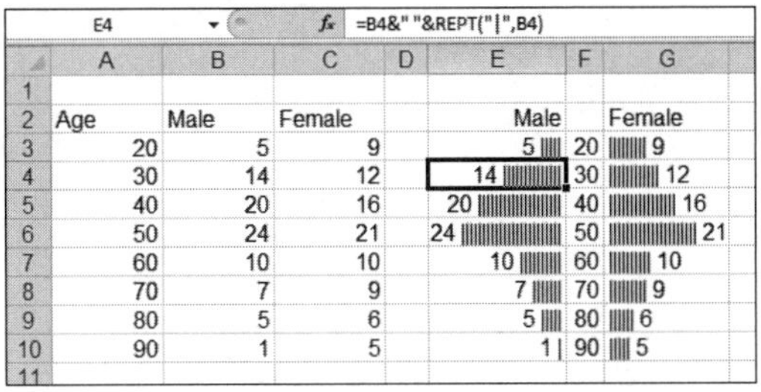

Presenting Excel Data on a Map Using Microsoft MapPoint

10

Plotting Data Geographically

In many cases, the best way to present data is to plot it on a geographic map. Mapping software used to cost thousands of dollars. However, Microsoft offers a product called Microsoft MapPoint 2010. MapPoint is available in editions for North America and Europe.

Figure 10.1 shows a Starbucks database plotted on a map. Note how the stores are concentrated in the heart of the city, but appear in any semi-populated region. Any dataset with a geographic component such as street addresses, zip codes, postal codes, latitude and longitude, states, or provinces are suitable for mapping.

With MapPoint, you can zoom in to get a view of locations by street in a neighborhood (see Figure 10.2) or zoom out to see trends over the whole country (see Figure 10.3).

When you install MapPoint, new icons appear on the Add-Ins tab that allows you to plot your data on a map within Excel. For a bit more functionality, you can save your Excel data as an Excel workbook and import it into MapPoint.

> **TIP**
>
> MapPoint 2010 has a list price of $299 and regularly sells at Amazon.com for $269. However, Microsoft seems to regularly give MapPoint to CIOs as an incentive for attending conferences. Consequently, you can often find brand-new, factory-sealed versions of MapPoint for sale on eBay for less than $100.

Figure 10.1
Stores plotted on a map.

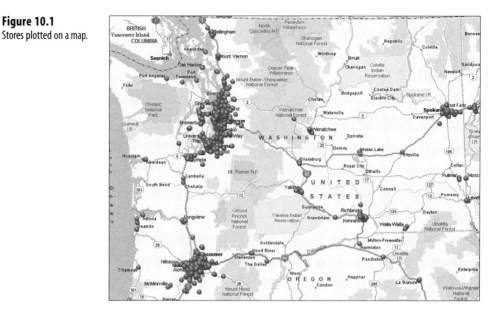

Figure 10.2
You can zoom in to a neighborhood view.

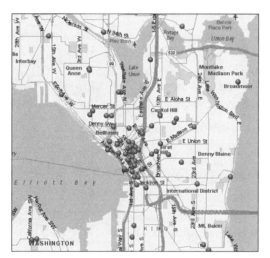

Building a Map in Excel

Figure 10.4 shows a database of locations for a chain of stores in the United States. You hope to sell products to those stores and need to analyze their geographic locations.

To create a map for this data in Excel 2010, you follow these steps:

1. Make sure that MapPoint is installed on your computer. You should have an extra Add-Ins tab available on the ribbon, with one or more MapPoint Map icons.

Figure 10.3
You can also zoom out to a country view.

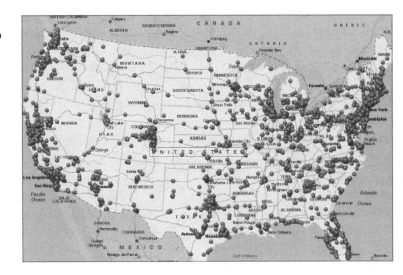

Figure 10.4
This data lends itself to geographic analysis.

	A	B
1	City	State
2	Scottsboro	AL
3	Grand Bay	AL
4	Robertsdale	AL
5	Livingston	AL
6	Boligee	AL
7	Eutaw	AL
8	Tuscaloosa	AL
9	Cottondale	AL
10	Eastaboga	AL
11	Oxford	AL
12	Eutaw	AL
13	Cottondale	AL
14	Gadsden	AL
15	Fort Payne	AL
16	Brewton	AL
17	Hope Hull	AL

2. Select your data in Excel, including headings. MapPoint recognizes headings such as Latitude, Longitude, City, State, and Zip Code.

3. Click the MapPoint Map icon on the Add-Ins tab.

> **TIP**
> At this point, you might encounter an annoying bug. MapPoint 2010 can finally import data from XLSX and XSLM files. However, the add-in for MapPoint 2010 will insist that your file has not been saved and offer to save it for you. The resulting Save As dialog box indicates a file extension such as XLSX, but the file is actually saved as an XLS file. Therefore, as you go along with saving the file, you might be presented with a list of file compatibility issues. If you need your file to stay as an Excel 2007-2010 file type, consider saving the relevant data to an Excel 2003 file.

10

4. Excel displays the Link Data Wizard dialog. For each column in your selection, Excel shows the column heading and then a drop-down that identifies the data type for that column (see Figure 10.5). Valid data types are Name, Address, City, County, State, Country, Zip Code, Census Tract, Latitude, and Longitude. If you have columns in your data that are not in the list, select <Other Data> for that column. For example, if you had sales figures for each store, you would select <Other Data>.

Figure 10.5
For each column in your data set, either identify it as a geographic column or select <Other Data>.

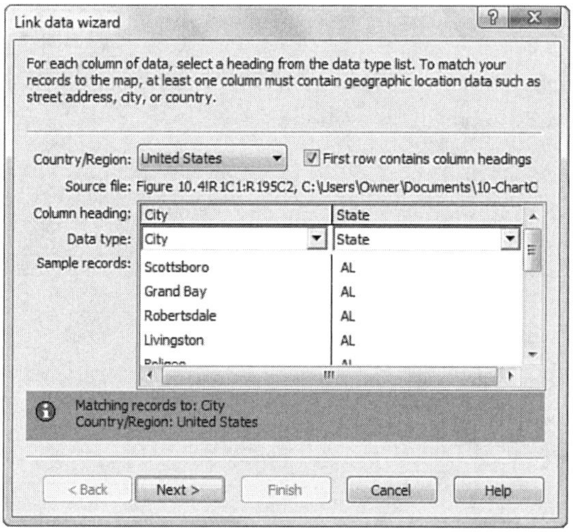

5. Click Next, and then click Finish. Excel attempts to find a matching location for each record in your database.

6. After Excel finds all the exact matches, it reports any items that were not matched. For example, in Figure 10.6 the spelling of Assaria Kansas appears to be wrong in the dataset. For each unmatched record, choose a location and click OK or simply click Skip Record if you do not know the location.

Figure 10.6
You usually have to manually match a few records from a dataset.

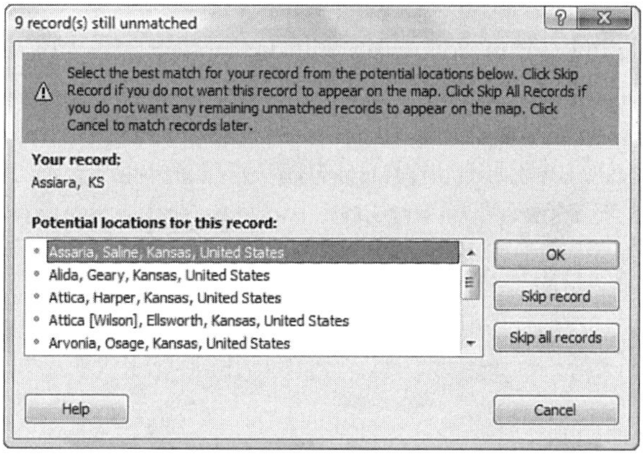

7. Repeat step 6 for each unmatched record. After you match the last record, Excel plots each record as a thumbtack on a map and zooms in to show the complete set of data points.

8. While the map is active, the Excel ribbon is replaced with a MapPoint menu and toolbar. From the toolbar, select the Legend and Overview icon, as shown in Figure 10.7. Excel adds a sidebar showing the Pushpins set.

Figure 10.7
Toggle on the legend so you can change the properties for the pushpin set.

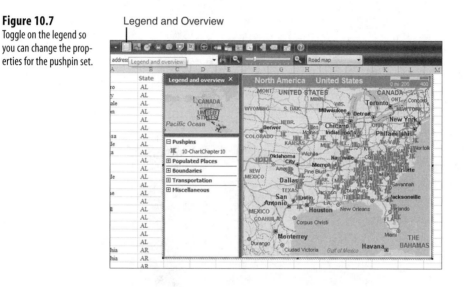

9. Right-click the pushpin in the legend and select Properties

10. In the Properties dialog, change the symbol from a thumbtack to a small circle, as shown in Figure 10.8.

11. Click OK to close the Properties dialog box.

12. Click the Legend and Overview icon in the toolbar to remove the legend.

> **NOTE** Excel always tightly crops the map to include all the pushpins in the dataset. Use the Zoom Out icon in the toolbar to see a 50,000-foot view of the data. In Figure 10.9, you can see that the stores are concentrated in the southeastern part of the United States.

Navigation in MapPoint 2010 has changed since previous versions. The Select icon is gone from the toolbar. If you click the map and drag, you can move the map to re-center the portion of the map in the visible window.

Two magnifying glass icons surround a zoom slider in the toolbar. Avoid the temptation to use those magnifying glasses to zoom in and zoom out. You have much more control by nudging the zoom slider in the MapPoint toolbar.

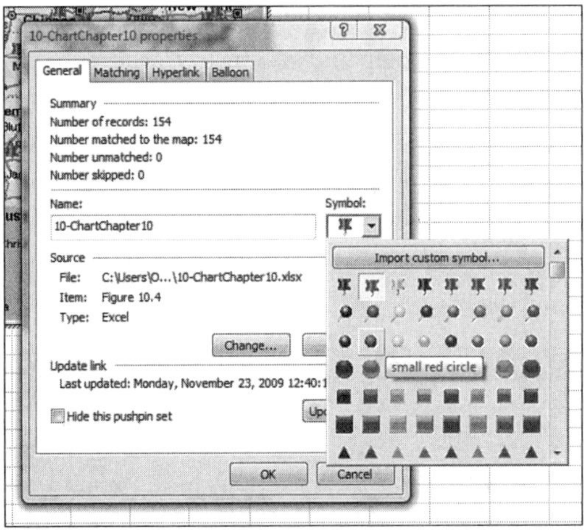

Figure 10.8
The small circle icons work better than thumbtacks on a map with hundreds of mapped points.

Figure 10.9
You can zoom out to see the entire country.

While the map is active, you can use the menu commands View, Zoom Map, To Data to zoom in to all of the data points. If you inadvertently zoom to far out using the Zoom Out magnifying icon, you can use the Zoom To Data to get back to a view that covers all of your data points.

A drop-down appears at the bottom right of the MapPoint toolbar. If your map is too cluttered, open this and change from a Road Map to a Data Map.

Showing Numeric Data on a Map

If your dataset includes some numeric data, you can represent that data on a map. MapPoint offers many options for representing numeric data:

■ Shaded Area, Shaded Circle are like the Excel 2010 icon sets. You can use from two to eight colors to represent different levels of sales or units or population.

- Sized Circle is somewhat like the data bar concept. Each point on the map will be marked with a circle. Larger circles represent larger sales.

- Multiple Symbol is similar to a Shaded Circle, except you can use different shaped symbols for different levels of sales. If you would prefer a triangle for large sales and a square for small sales, the Multiple Symbol

- Pie Chart and Column Chart are useful for showing component sales for each point. You might want to compare hardware and software sales by state.

- Sized Pie Chart combines the Sized Circle concept with the Pie Chart concept. The size of the circle indicates overall sales. The components will be shown as wedges within the pie chart.

- Series Column Chart is great for showing a small time series chart for each point. If you want to show sales by year for the last 3 to 5 years for each state, this chart will work.

In Figure 10.10, you have sales by state over four consecutive years. This data is ideal for using a Series Column Chart in MapPoint.

Figure 10.10
Create a time-series chart for each state.

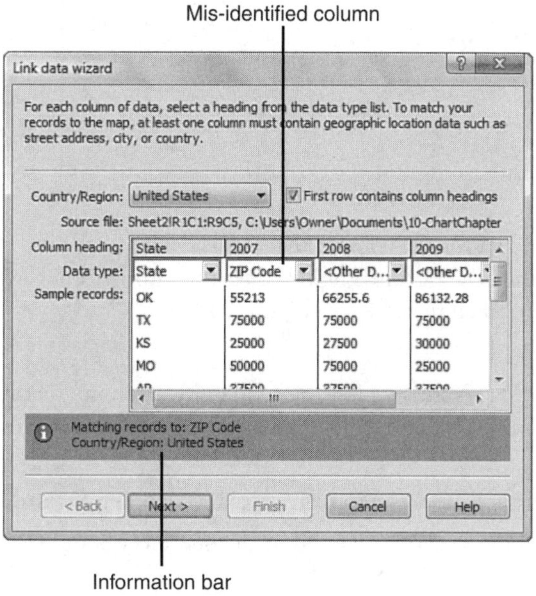

Mis-identified column

Information bar

To create a time-series chart, follow these steps:

1. Select your data including the headings.

2. From the Add-Ins tab, select MapPoint Map.

> **NOTE** Pay close attention to the Link Data Wizard dialog box. This box is overly anxious to find some column that looks like zip code information. In Figure 10.11, the dialog initially guesses that the 2007 sales column is zip code. After testing with various datasets, the erroneous Zip Code field can happen in any column that happens to start with five integer values less than 99,999. You will notice that because one field is identified as a zip code, the information bar at the bottom of the dialog says that it is going to match the data fields to zip codes instead of states.

Figure 10.11
Excel tries to find a column that might contain zip codes.

```
Link data wizard                                              ? ☒

For each column of data, select a heading from the data type list. To match your
records to the map, at least one column must contain geographic location data such as
street address, city, or country.

Country/Region:  United States        ▼    ☑ First row contains column headings
     Source file:  Sheet2!R1C1:R9C5, C:\Users\Owner\Documents\10-ChartChapter

 Column heading: | State   | 2007     | 2008        | 2009
      Data type: | State ▼ | ZIP Code ▼| <Other D... ▼| <Other D... ▼
 Sample records: | OK      | 55213    | 66255.6     | 86132.28
                 | TX      | 75000    | 75000       | 75000
                 | KS      | 25000    | 27500       | 30000
                 | MO      | 50000    | 75000       | 25000
                 | AR      | 37500    | 37500       | 37500

 ⓘ  Matching records to: ZIP Code
     Country/Region: United States

        < Back      Next >       Finish       Cancel       Help
```

3. Open the drop-down for the column that is misidentified as a zip code. Change the data type to <Other Data>. This should cause the information bar to indicate that records will be matched to State (see Figure 10.12).

4. Click Next.

5. In the next step, MapPoint asks for you to identify a column that will be the primary key. In this example, use State. Click Finish. The map appears with a single pushpin in each state.

6. In the MapPoint toolbar, click the icon for Data Mapping Wizard.

7. In the Data Mapping Wizard – Map Type dialog, select Series Column Chart, as shown in Figure 10.13. Click Next.

8. In the Data Mapping Wizard – Dataset dialog, leave the default setting of Edit an Existing Data Map. Click Next.

9. Choose each of your yearly sales fields in the Data Mapping Wizard – Data Fields dialog. Choose to show the data by State (see Figure 10.14).

10. In the Data Mapping Wizard – Legend dialog, choose if your data should be plotted as a Continuous Range or a Logarithmic Range. Click Next and then click Finish.

Figure 10.12
After correcting field type drop-downs, the information bar corrects itself automatically.

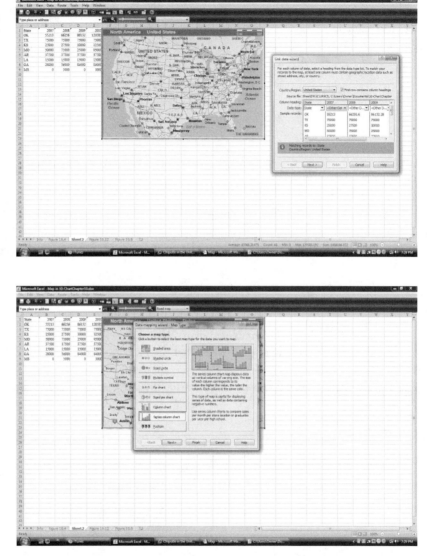

Figure 10.13
Select Data Mapping Wizard.

TIP

The logarithmic option mentioned in step 10 is good if you have series with dramatically different orders of magnitude.

11. Change the Map Style drop-down from Road Map to Data Map. This clears the road data from the map, making it easier to see the column charts.

12. Nudge the MapInfo zoom slider at the top of your screen slightly to the left. This will zoom out a bit.

Figure 10.14
Choose the numeric columns for the column chart.

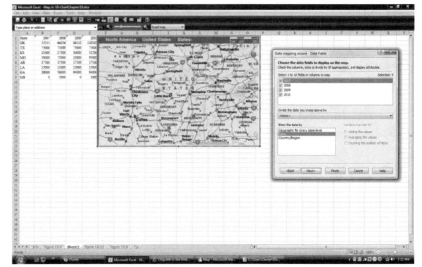

13. Click outside of the map to embed the map in the worksheet. To later edit the map, double-click the map.

Figure 10.15 shows the completed map. Note that the legend identifies the maximum value of the vertical axis and also identifies that the years run from 2007 to 2010.

Figure 10.15
The completed map shows column charts for eight states.

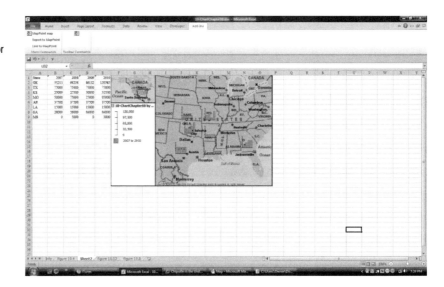

Using Other Map Styles to Illustrate Data

The shaded area map style is great if you have data that can be aggregated by zip code, census tract, county, or state. For example, Figure 10.16 shows an earthquake index that is plotted by county.

You can use the dozens of datasets that ship with MapPoint. To do this, after inserting a map, select Data, Data Mapping Wizard, and then select to use Demographic Data. Using this data, you can shade your map by income, percentage of owner-occupied housing, even earthquake index as shown in Figure 10.16.

Figure 10.16
This shaded area map shows an earthquake index by zip code.

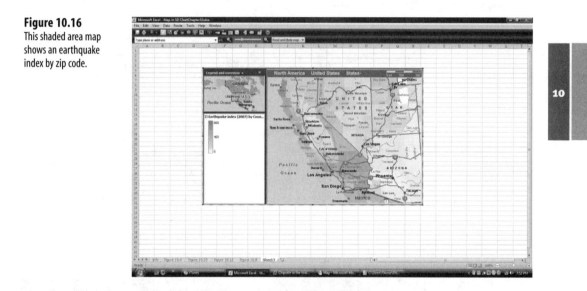

10

Almost every business has a mailing list of its customers. If you have this data in Excel and you have MapPoint, you can plot up to 10,000 customers on a map.

Seeing your customers on a map helps you to plan advertising and helps you understand how far your customers travel to reach your location. To plot your company's customers on a map, follow these steps:

1. Import your customer list into Excel. Be sure to add headings such as Name, Address, City, State, and Zip Code. Save the data as an Excel 2003 workbook.

2. Start MapPoint. Select Data, Import Data Wizard.

3. Browse to and select your Excel file.

4. Confirm the field mapping. Click Next and then click Finish. MapPoint matches your fields up with known addresses.

5. If there are unmatched records, MapPoint shows you any close guesses. When you are matching at the address level, you are likely to have a high rate of unmatched addresses. If you are in a hurry, click Skip All Records to map the records that do match.

6. Select a pushpin map. Click Next.

7. Change the symbol from a thumbtack to a small circle. Click Finish.

Typically, you might have a few stray customers who visited your business while they were traveling. These distant customers cause MapPoint to zoom out to show all the customers.

Click the map and drag to put your business in the center of the map. Use the zoom slider to zoom in to the area around your business. You now have a map of the densest concentration of customers, as shown in Figure 10.17. This enables you to determine which newspapers or radio stations might be effective for reaching other customers who live in the same area as your current customers.

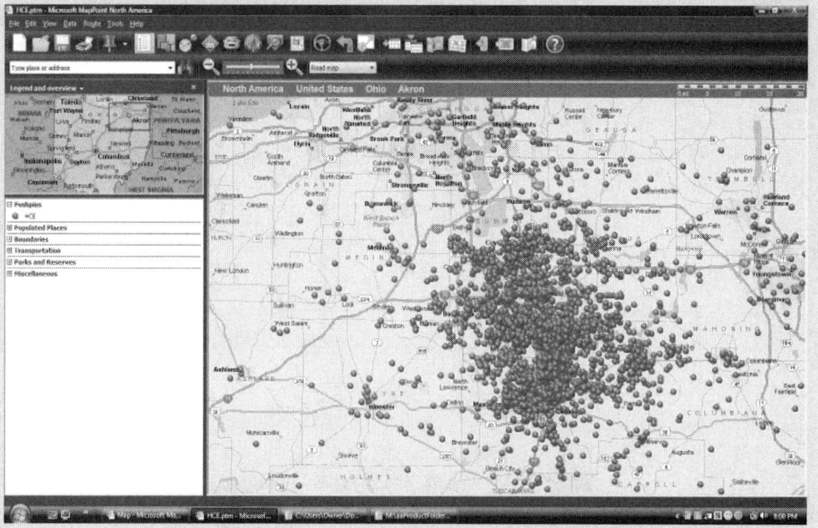

Figure 10.17
This is a powerful type of map for a business owner. It helps you see where your customers are from and think about ways to reach other customers in that area.

To see a demo of mapping customers, search for "MrExcel Charts 10" at YouTube.

Next Steps

In Chapter 11, "Using SmartArt Graphics and Shapes," you will learn how to use Excel's new business diagramming tools to communicate relationships and organization charts.

Using SmartArt Graphics and Shapes

11

Images and artwork provide an interesting visual break from tables of numbers. Excel 2007 introduced a new array of business diagrams called SmartArt. While Excel 2003 offered six types of business diagrams, SmartArt in Excel 2010 offers 129 types. These diagrams communicate messages about your organization and processes.

The Office team envisioned that SmartArt would be most popular in PowerPoint presentations, so SmartArt is designed for static messages. Later in this chapter, you will learn how to convert SmartArt to shapes, allowing the words in the diagram to come from calculations in the cells.

This chapter covers the following:

- **SmartArt**—SmartArt is a collection of similar shapes, arranged to imply a process, groups, or a hierarchy. In legacy versions of Excel, SmartArt was known as diagrams. As in legacy versions, with Excel 2010 it is easy to add new shapes, reverse the order of shapes, and change the color of shapes. Office 2010 includes a text editor that allows for Level 1 and Level 2 text for each shape in a diagram. Many styles of SmartArt include the capability to add a small picture or logo to each shape.

- **Shapes**—You can add interesting shapes to a document. A shape can contain words; it is the only art object in which the words can come from a cell on the worksheet. You can add glow, bevel, and 3-D effects to shapes. In legacy versions of Excel, shapes were known as AutoShapes. Microsoft added some new shapes starting in Excel 2007 and several formatting properties.

- **WordArt**—You use WordArt to present ordinary text in a stylized manner. You can use it to bend, rotate, and twist the characters in text. In Excel 2010, you can add glow, bevel, and material effects. WordArt has been completely redesigned from legacy versions of Excel. A limited version of WordArt is available for formatting titles and labels in Excel charts.

Using SmartArt

You use SmartArt to show a series of similar shapes, where each shape represents a related step, concept, idea, or grouping. SmartArt in Excel 2010 is an enhanced version of business diagrams from legacy versions of Excel. In Excel 2010, Microsoft has addressed many of the shortcomings of business diagrams, including the following:

- Each shape has an associated text editor.
- Shapes can contain Level 1 text for headlines and Level 2 text for body copy.
- Thirty styles now allow shapes to include an image.
- Automatic settings in SmartArt can automatically resize the text in all shapes to allow the longest text to fit.
- SmartArt styles allow you to apply glow and bevels to an entire SmartArt diagram.

The goal of SmartArt is to allow you to create a great-looking graphic with minimal effort. After you define a SmartArt image for your text, you can quickly change to any of the other 129 styles by clicking the desired style in the gallery. Figure 11.1 shows four different SmartArt layouts:

- **Basic Process**—In this style, all text is typed as Level 1.
- **Accent Process**—This style puts the Level 1 text in the background and highlights the Level 2 text in the foreground boxes.
- **Picture Accent Process**—This style gives equal weight to the Level 1 and Level 2 text. Pictures are added behind each shape.
- **Picture Accent List**—Unlike the process charts, a list chart does not include arrows to indicate a process.

> **TIP**
> If you want to fine-tune the text in a particular shape, you can use the Format tab to micromanage any element in the SmartArt.

Elements Common Across Most SmartArt

A SmartArt style is a collection of two or more related shapes. In most styles, you can add additional shapes to illustrate a longer process. A few styles are limited to only n items. Each shape can contain a headline (Level 1 text), body copy (Level 2 text), and a graphic. Some of the 129 styles show only Level 1 text. If you switch to a style that does not display

Figure 11.1
Subtle differences in four of the 129 possible SmartArt styles give more weight to either Level 1 or Level 2 text. Notice that the Level 1 text is prominent (top), in the background (second), small (third), or vertical (bottom).

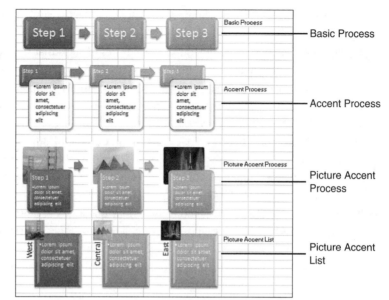

Level 2 text and then switch back before closing the workbook, the shape remembers the Level 2 text it originally had. New in Excel 2010, any text that is not visible in the SmartArt diagram is discarded when the file is saved and closed. This prevents you from accidentally sending out text that you forgot to delete.

> **NOTE** Thirty of the 129 SmartArt layouts can include pictures. A limitation in Excel 2007 required you to add pictures as the last step; changing from one picture layout to another would cause the pictures to be lost. Microsoft improved SmartArt in Excel 2010 to allow the pictures to remain as you change to different layouts.

While you're editing SmartArt, a text pane that is slightly reminiscent of PowerPoint appears. You can type some bullet points in the text pane. If you demote a bullet point, the text changes from Level 1 text to Level 2 text. If you add a new Level 1 bullet point, Excel adds a new shape to the SmartArt.

A Tour of the SmartArt Categories

The SmartArt gallery groups the 129 SmartArt layouts into seven broad categories:

- **List**—This category is designed to show a nonsequential list of information. Variations include horizontal, vertical, and bending lists. Some lists include chevrons, and some include pictures. In general, these styles do not include arrows between shapes.
- **Process**—This category is designed to show a sequential list of steps. Variations include horizontal, vertical, bending, equations, funnels, gears, and several varieties of

arrows. Some process charts allow the inclusion of images. Most styles include arrows or other connectors to convey a sequence.

- **Cycle**—This category is designed to show a series of steps that repeat. It includes cycle charts, radial charts, a gear chart, and a pie chart.

- **Hierarchy**—This category is designed to show organization charts, decision trees, and other hierarchical relationships. Variations include horizontal and vertical charts and charts with and without connecting lines.

- **Relationship**—This category is designed to show a relationship between items. Many of the layouts in this category are duplicated from the other seven categories. This category includes examples of arrow, chart, cycle, equation, funnel, gear, hierarchy, list, process, pyramid, radial, target, and Venn chart layouts.

- **Matrix**—This category is designed to show four quadrants of a list. The Titled Matrix layout offers a fifth block for an overall title. The new Cycle Matrix allows for Level 2 text outside the main blocks.

- **Pyramid**—This category is designed to show containment, overlapping, proportional, or interconnected relationships.

- **Picture**—All the layouts that contain pictures are repeated in this category. Microsoft added 16 new picture layouts that appear only in this category in Excel 2010. Some of these picture layouts are appropriate for only pictures with little or no text.

Figure 11.2 shows one version of each of the eight categories.

Figure 11.2
SmartArt diagrams exist
in eight broad categories.

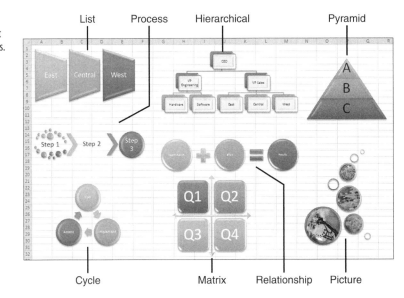

Inserting SmartArt

Although there are 129 different layouts of SmartArt, you follow the same basic steps to insert any SmartArt layout:

1. Select a cell in a blank section of the workbook.

2. From the Insert tab, select SmartArt from the Illustrations group. The Choose a SmartArt Graphic dialog appears.

3. From the left side of the Choose a SmartArt Graphic dialog, choose a category.

4. Click a SmartArt type in the center of the Choose a SmartArt Graphic dialog.

5. Read the description on the right side. This description tells you whether the layout is good for Level 1 text, Level 2 text, or both. In Figure 11.3, you can see that the Vertical Chevron List layout is good for large amounts of Level 2 text.

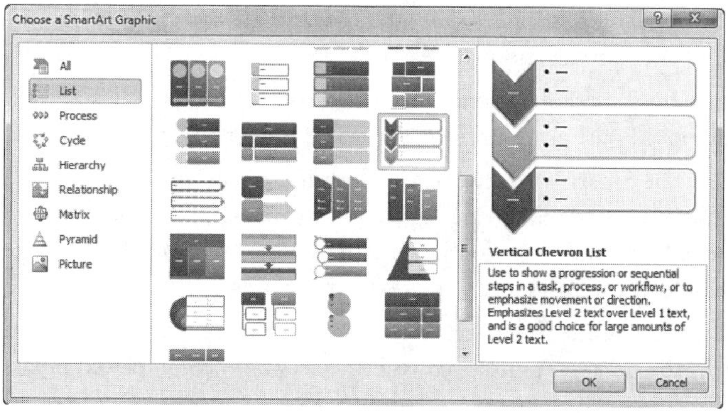

Figure 11.3
The information for each style provides information about if a particular style is appropriate for more Level 1 or Level 2 text.

6. Repeat steps 4 and 5 until you find a style suitable for your content. Then click OK. As shown in Figure 11.4, an outline of the SmartArt is drawn on the worksheet. The flashing insertion cursor is in the first item of the text pane. One element of the SmartArt is selected. When you type text at the flashing insertion point, it is added to the selected shape.

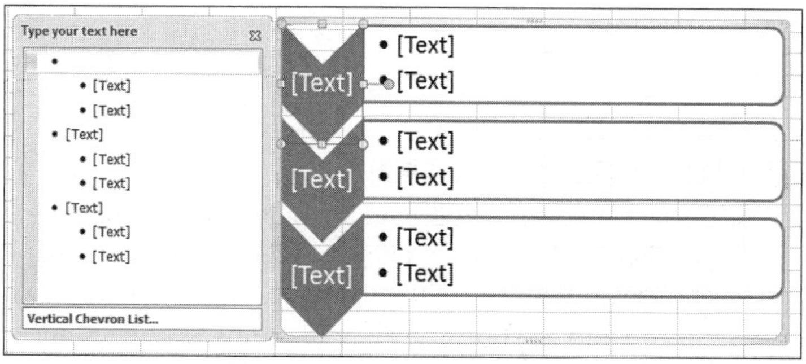

Figure 11.4
When you type in the text pane, the text is added to the selected element of the SmartArt.

7. Fill in the text pane with text for your SmartArt. You can add, delete, promote, or demote items by using icons in the SmartArt Tools, Design, Create Graphic group. The SmartArt updates as you type more text.

> **NOTE** In many cases, adding a new Level 1 item adds a new shape element to the SmartArt. If you add longer text to the SmartArt, Excel shrinks all the elements to make the text fit.

8. Make the entire SmartArt graphic larger, if needed, by grabbing the resizing handles in the corners of the SmartArt and dragging to a new size. After you resize the graphic, Excel resizes the text to make it fit in the SmartArt at the largest size possible.

9. If you like, change the color scheme of the SmartArt, which initially appears in one color. To do so, from the SmartArt Tools Design tab, select Change Colors from the SmartArt Styles group. Excel offers several versions of monochromatic styles and five styles of color variations for each shape.

10. Choose a 2-D or 3-D style from the SmartArt Styles gallery on the Design tab. The Inset and Polished styles have a suitable mix of effects but are readable.

11. Move the SmartArt to the proper location. Position the mouse over the border of the SmartArt, avoiding the eight resizing areas. The cursor changes to a four-headed arrow. Click and drag the SmartArt to a new location. If you drag the SmartArt to the left side of the worksheet, the text pane moves to the right of the SmartArt.

12. Click outside the SmartArt. Excel embeds the SmartArt graphic in the worksheet and hides the SmartArt tabs. Figure 11.5 shows some completed SmartArt.

Figure 11.5
You click outside the SmartArt boundary to embed the completed SmartArt.

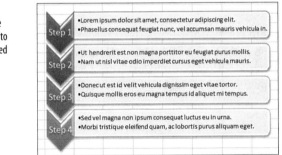

Changing the Color of SmartArt Graphics

The Design tab's Change Colors drop-down offers 38 different color schemes for each theme. Five options in the Colorful category offer to mix up the colors used for each shape. Thirty other options offer five varying shades of each of six accent colors.

Changing the Theme colors on the Page Layout tab affects the colors offered in the Change Colors drop-down.

Applying a SmartArt Style

The Design tab offers a large gallery of 14 different SmartArt styles. There are five 2-D styles in a section labeled Best Fit for Document. There are also nine 3-D styles.

Choosing a style from the gallery applies a different mix of bevel, shadow, transparency, gradient, reflection, and glow to all shapes. The built-in styles range from subtle to outlandish. Some of the later 3-D styles, such as Bird's Eye Scene and Brick Scene, are very hard to read. If you are trying to present bad news that no one can read, you might want to choose the later 3-D styles. Otherwise, the second and third 3-D styles, known as Inset and Cartoon, seem to offer a great mix of effects and readability. Figure 11.6 shows a Continuous Arrow Process graphic with the 14 different styles applied.

Figure 11.6
The SmartArt styles range from simple to over-the-top. The Inset and Polished styles offer a mix of style and readability.

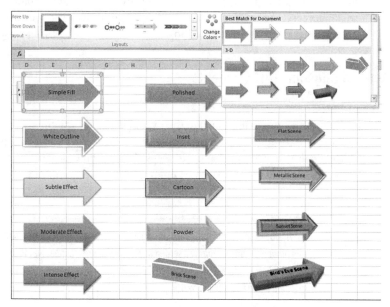

Changing Existing SmartArt to a New Style

There are a couple of ways to change SmartArt to a new style:

■ You can left-click the SmartArt, and then select the SmartArt Tools, Layouts from the Design tab to choose a new layout. As shown in Figure 11.7, the Layouts drop-down initially shows only the styles that Excel thinks are a close fit to the current style. If you want to access the complete list of styles, you have to select More Layouts. The advantage of this method is that Live Preview shows you the changes before you commit to a style.

Figure 11.7
Browse other layouts.

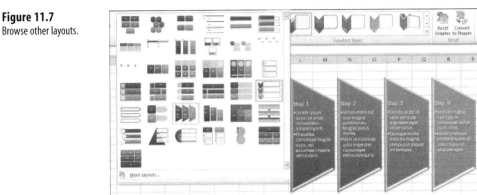

■ A faster way to access the complete list of styles is to right-click between two shapes in the SmartArt and select Change Layout from the context menu. This step is a little tricky because you cannot click an existing shape; you must click inside the SmartArt border—but on a section of the SmartArt that contains nothing.

Micromanaging SmartArt Elements

There are two tabs on the Ribbon for SmartArt tools: the Design and Format tabs.

The Design tab allows you to change the overall design of the SmartArt. If you stay on the Design tab, Microsoft makes sure that your SmartArt looks good. It keeps the font for all Level 2 text consistent for all shapes. It keeps all the shapes proportional. If you have a particular need to override some aspect of one shape, however, you can do so on the Format tab.

> **CAUTION**
>
> When you change any setting on the Format tab, Microsoft turns off the automatic formatting for the other elements. Changing a setting on the Format tab is a great way to make horrible-looking SmartArt. If you absolutely have to use the Format tab, you should first get your SmartArt as close as possible to the final version by using the Design tab.

Changing Text Formatting in One Element

In Automatic mode, Excel chooses a font size that is small enough to show the longest text completely. This can cause problems if you have one shape with long text and short text everywhere else. In this case, Excel chooses a small font size for the long text and then forces all the other items to have the same tiny text, too. In such a situation, you might want to override the text size for the shape that has the longest text. Excel then automatically resizes the font size in the remaining automatic shapes to be larger.

The mini toolbar is useful for making these types of changes. You select the text either directly in the shape or in the text pane. Immediately after you complete the selection, you should watch for an almost-transparent formatting box to appear. Then you immediately move the mouse to the box to prevent it from disappearing. You can then change the font size by using the drop-down in the mini toolbar. If you allow the mini toolbar to disappear, you can use the formatting tools on the Home tab to change the font size.

In Figure 11.8, the long Level 2 text in step 4 was resized. Excel then calculated the proper text size for steps 1 through 3, resulting in the text in the top three shapes automatically growing to a larger font size.

Figure 11.8
When you manually override the font size in the fourth shape, the text in the remaining three shapes automatically becomes larger.

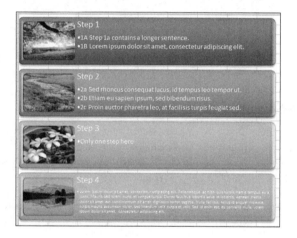

Changing One Shape

There are many items you can edit for a SmartArt shape. To see how this works, you can click any shape in the SmartArt and then try the following:

- Use the green handle to rotate the shape.
- Use the resize handles to resize the shape.
- Use the move handle to nudge the shape.
- Select Change Shape from the Format tab to change the outline to a different shape.
- Select settings from the Shape Styles group to change fill, outline, and effects for the shape.
- Select settings from the WordArt Styles group to change the text inside the shape.
- Right-click the shape and select Format Shape to have complete control over the shape.

In general, SmartArt created on the Design tab looks uniform and neat. When you move to the Format tab, the possibility for chaos arises. For example, the SmartArt in Figure 11.9 contains mixed effects, font sizes, and rotation; it was created in the Format tab.

Figure 11.9
After experimenting with the Format tab, you can select Reset Graphic on the Design tab to turn the SmartArt back into something more uniform.

Controlling SmartArt Shapes from the Text Pane

The text pane represents a fantastic improvement over business diagrams in Excel 2003. By using only the keyboard, you can add or delete shapes and promote or demote items. Further, the text pane includes proofing tools such as spell check. Using the text pane is similar to creating bullet points in a PowerPoint slide.

Figure 11.10 shows a newly inserted pyramid SmartArt in Excel. By default, most new SmartArt diagrams have three shapes, but you can change that number by using the text pane.

Figure 11.10
A default SmartArt includes three shapes. You can edit the number of shapes by using the text pane.

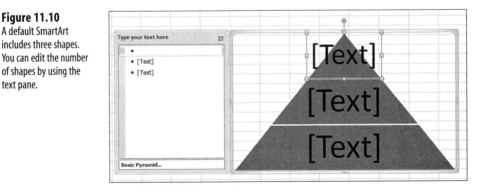

The following rules apply to the text pane for SmartArt:

- Press the up-arrow and down-arrow keys to move from one line to another.
- Press the Enter key to insert a new line below the current line. The new line will be at the same level as the current line. Adding a new Level 1 line inserts a new shape in the SmartArt.

- Press the Tab key to demote Level 1 text to Level 2 text.
- Press Shift+Tab to promote Level 2 text to Level 1 text.
- Press the Backspace key on an empty line to delete the line.
- Press Delete at the end of any line to combine text from the next line with this line.
- Press End to move to the end of the current line.
- Press Home to move to the beginning of the current line.

As you add shapes, Excel continues to attempt to squeeze them into the default size. You can resize an entire piece of SmartArt by using the resizing handles around the SmartArt.

As an example of how the text pane works, you can use the following steps to customize the inverted pyramid graphic shown in Figure 11.10 into the one shown in Figure 11.11. This example illustrates how quickly and simply you can change from the default SmartArt with three shapes to any number of shapes:

1. Type **Shape 1**, and then press Enter.
2. Type **Subtext**, and then press Tab to demote the item. Then press the down-arrow key to move to text 2.
3. Type **Shape 2**, and then press Enter.
4. Type **Point 1**, and then press Tab and Enter.
5. Type **Point 2**, and then the Down Arrow key.
6. Type **Shape 3**, and then press Enter.
7. Type **Point 3**, and then press Tab and Enter.
8. Excel wants the next item to be Level 2 text, so press Shift+Tab to promote this item.
9. Type **Shape 4** and then press Enter, type **Shape 5** and then press Enter, type **Shape 6** and then press Enter.
10. Type **Point 4**, and then press Tab.
11. Using the mouse, resize the SmartArt so that it is larger.
12. From the SmartArt Styles gallery on the Design ribbon tab, choose a color scheme.

The result is shown in Figure 11.11. As this example shows, by using only the keyboard and the text pane, you can quickly expand SmartArt and add Level 2 subpoints.

Adding Images to SmartArt

Thirty SmartArt layouts in the Picture category are designed to hold small images in addition to text. In some of these styles, the picture is emphasized; in others, the focus is on the text, and the picture is an accent.

When you select one of these styles, you add text with the text pane and then specify pictures by clicking on the picture icon inside each Level 1 shape. The SmartArt shows a picture icon next to bullet points in the text pane and also in each shape (see Figure 11.12).

11

Figure 11.11
You can add additional shapes and subpoints simply by using the text pane.

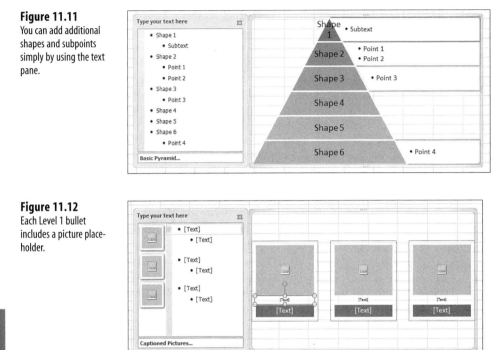

Figure 11.12
Each Level 1 bullet includes a picture placeholder.

You can click a picture icon to display the Insert Picture dialog. You can then choose a picture and click Insert. You repeat this process to add each additional picture. The pictures are automatically cropped to fit the allotted area, as shown in Figure 11.13.

Figure 11.13
Pictures have been added to each shape.

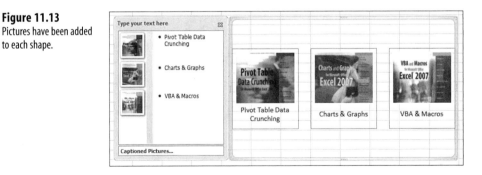

Special Considerations for Organization Charts

Hierarchical SmartArt can contain more than two text levels. As you add more levels to the SmartArt, Excel continues to intelligently add boxes and resize them to fit.

Figure 11.14 shows a diagram created in the Hierarchy style. In this style, each level is assigned a different color.

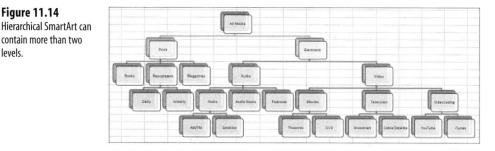

Using Assistant Shapes in Organization Charts

The first style available in the Hierarchy category is the Organization Chart style. You use this style to describe reporting relationships in an organization. There are a few extra options in the Ribbon for organization charts. For example, select one manager shape in your organizational chart diagram. The Add Shape drop-down on the Design tab includes the option Add Assistant, as shown in Figure 11.15. You can select this option to add an extra shape immediately below the selected level.

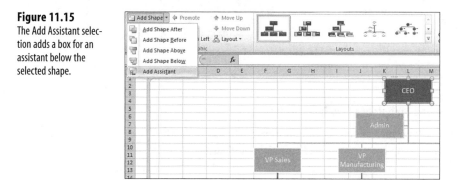

Arranging Subordinates on an Organization Chart

In the Create Graphic group of the Design tab, the Layout drop-down offers four options for showing the boxes within a group. First, you select the manager for the group. Then you select the appropriate type from the drop-down to affect all direct reports for the manager. Figure 11.16 illustrates the four options for the Layout drop-down:

- **VP of Sales**—This option shows a standard organization chart. The regions are arranged side by side.

- ■ **VP of Manufacturing**—This option has a right-hanging group. The departments are arranged vertically to the right of the line.

- ■ **VP of Engineering**—This option has a left hanging group. The departments are arranged vertically to the left of the line.

- ■ **CFO**—This option has a Both group. The direct reports are listed in two columns under the manager, on both sides of the vertical line.

In each group, the assistant box is arranged to the left of the vertical line.

Figure 11.16
Organization charts include options to control the arrangement of direct reports.

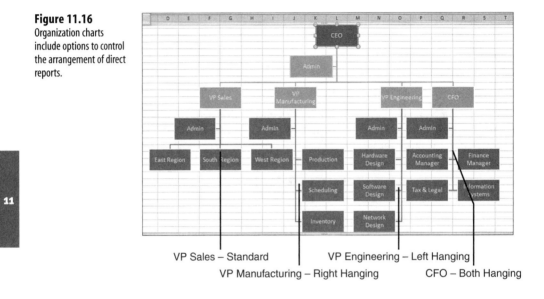

VP Sales – Standard

VP Engineering – Left Hanging

VP Manufacturing – Right Hanging

CFO – Both Hanging

Showing Dotted-Line Reporting Relationships

The SmartArt graphics engine cannot automatically create dotted-line reporting relationships. However, you can manually add a line to a diagram.

> **NOTE**   You should get your graphic as close to being done as possible before adding manual shapes. Any subsequent changes to the text pane require manual repositioning of the lines.

To add a dotted line, follow these steps:

1. Prepare the organization chart, using the SmartArt tools.

2. From the Insert tab, select the Shapes drop-down.

3. Click the elbow connector.

4. Draw a line that connects the appropriate two boxes on the organization chart. Grab the yellow diamond handle to lower the horizontal portion of the line to be at the same height as the lower box. Don't worry that the line is the wrong weight and style.

5. Click the line to select it.

6. In the Drawing Tools, Format tab, select the Shape Outline drop-down. From the Weight fly-out menu, choose a thicker line style, such as 3 pt.

7. Access the Shape Outline drop-down again. From the Dashes fly-out menu, choose one of the dotted-line styles.

Figure 11.17
Add the shape, drag the yellow diamond into position, then format the line as dotted.

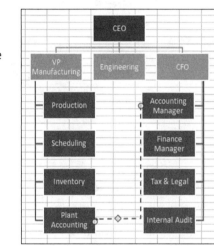

Using Limited SmartArt

Most of the SmartArt examples described so far are expandable: As you add Level 1 text, new shapes are added to the SmartArt. However, the SmartArt styles listed below cannot be expanded (see Figure 11.18).

- Both gear and funnel charts are limited to three items. If you add additional items to the text pane, each appears with a red X. These items do not display in the SmartArt, but they are stored until the file is saved and closed in case you later change to another SmartArt layout. For privacy reasons, the extra text is discarded when you save and close the file.

- Many of the arrow layouts in the Relationship category are limited to two shapes.

- The Matrix layouts are limited to four quadrants. Grid Matrix offers four quadrants plus a title, as shown in the center of Figure 11.18.

- The Segmented Pyramid style can be expanded, but it must contain 1, 4, 9, or 16 shapes. As soon as you add a fifth style to the SmartArt in the upper-left corner of the display, an entire row is added to the bottom of the pyramid, resulting in the SmartArt shown in the lower right of Figure 11.18.

■ The Equation style can be expanded, but the answer is always the last Level 1 item in the text pane.

Figure 11.18
Arrows, gears, funnels, and matrix shapes have certain limitations on the number of shapes they can contain.

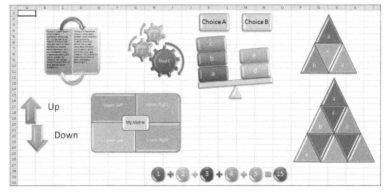

Choosing the Right Layout for Your Message

With 129 built-in layouts of SmartArt graphics, choosing the right layout can be daunting.

The following questions are designed to help you narrow down your choices, assuming that you do not want to further customize the look of a graphic:

■ Do you need accent images in the shape? If so, select Bending Picture Accent List, Picture Caption List, Horizontal Picture List, Picture Accent List, Continuous Picture List, Vertical Picture Accent List, Vertical Picture List, Picture Accent Process, or Radial List.

■ Do you have extremely long sentences of Level 2 text? If so, choose Vertical Box List or Vertical Bullet List.

■ Do you need to show a continuous process? If so, choose one of the cycle charts: Text Cycle, Basic Cycle, Continuous Cycle, Block Cycle, or Segmented Cycle.

■ Do you need to show a circular process that can travel both ways? If so, select Multidirectional Cycle.

■ Do you need to show a process that progresses from left to right? If so, choose Basic Process, Accent Process, Continuous Arrow Process, Alternating Flow, Process Arrows, Detailed Process, Continuous Block Process, Picture Accent Process, Basic Chevron Process, or Closed Chevron Process.

■ Do you need to show many processes that progress from left to right? If so, select Chevron List.

- Do you need to show a process that progresses from top to bottom? If so, choose Vertical Process, Segmented Process, Vertical Chevron List, or Staggered Process.

- Do you need to show a one-way process and need to fit many shapes into a small area? If so, choose Basic Bending Process, Circular Bending Process, Repeating Bending Process, or Vertical Bending Process.

- Do you need to show an organization? If so, select Organization Chart.

- Do you need to show a hierarchy? If so, choose one of the pyramid, radial, matrix, target, or hierarchy layouts.

- Do you need to make a decision between two choices? If so, select Balance.

- Do you need to show how parts add together to create an output? If so, choose an Equation or a Funnel layout.

- Do you need to illustrate two opposing forces? If so, choose Diverging Arrows, Counterbalance Arrows, Opposing Arrows, Converging Arrows, or Arrow Ribbon.

- Do you need to illustrate a containment chart? If so, choose Nested Target or Stacked Venn.

Exploring Business Charts That Use SmartArt Graphics

The examples in this section show off a few of the 129 different SmartArt graphics that might be suitable for your business presentations.

> NOTE To see more examples of SmartArt, take a look at *Leveraging SmartArt Graphics in the 2007 Microsoft Office System*, an e-book published by Que (ISBN 0-7686-6833-6).

In particular, a few of the examples in this section show layouts that are a bit more difficult than average to utilize.

Illustrating a Pro/Con Decision by Using a Balance Chart

The Balance layout is used to illustrate weighing two alternatives, as shown in Figure 11.19.

The layout requires two Level 1 text entries to represent the boxes at the top of the graphic. You can then have up to three Level 2 entries for each Level 1 entry. The scale tips in the direction of the side that has more boxes.

Illustrating Growth by Using an Upward Arrow

Microsoft had to create a new shape, called a swoosh arrow, to add the Upward Arrow layout. This layout holds up to five bullets of Level 1 text. Any Level 2 text is shown below the Level 1 text. This makes it very difficult to fit any Level 2 text beneath the first bullet point of Level 1 text.

Figure 11.19
This graphic leans either left or right, depending on which side has more Level 2 text entries.

In Figure 11.20, a few bullet points of Level 2 text are placed beneath the final Level 1 text entry to provide a caption for the whole chart.

Figure 11.20
The swoosh arrow shows up to five bullets of Level 1 text.

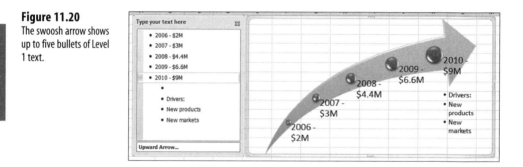

Showing an Iterative Process by Using a Basic Cycle Layout

Several cycle process charts are available in the SmartArt gallery. In some layouts, the arrows are too small to be seen. The Basic Cycle layout offers a good balance between text-holding shapes and arrows (see Figure 11.21).

Figure 11.21
The Basic Cycle layout offers a balance between text and arrows.

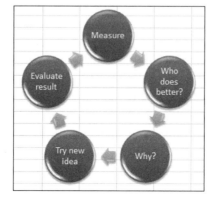

Showing a Company's Relationship to External Entities by Using a Diverging Radial Diagram

The radial layouts show the relationship of one center entity to several entities around the perimeter of the diagram, as shown in Figure 11.22. Whereas many layouts offer a hub-and-spokes arrangement, the Diverging Radial layout adds arrows that point outward from the central diagram to each external shape.

The text for the central circle should be entered as a single bullet of Level 1 text. You build the remaining shapes around the perimeter by adding Level 2 bullets.

Scouts
Food Bank
Red Cross
Community Chest
Meals on Wheels
Crisis Services

Figure 11.22
The Diverging Radial layout shows how a central organization supports many other organizations.

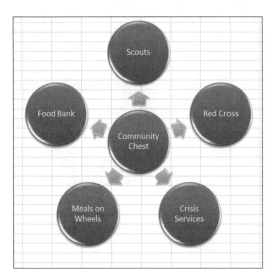

Illustrating Departments Within a Company by Using a Table List Diagram

The Table List layout holds a single entry of Level 1 text as a title across the top of the diagram. Each Level 2 entry causes the diagram to be vertically split. You could show additional bullets in each box by adding Level 3 text (see Figure 11.23).

Accounting
Auditing
• Certifies effectiveness of internal controls
Credit
• Collection of receivables from customers
Finance
• Raise, allocate, and use monetary resources
Payables
• Ensure vendors are paid in a timely manner
Tax
• Manages and pays the corporations payments to government entities

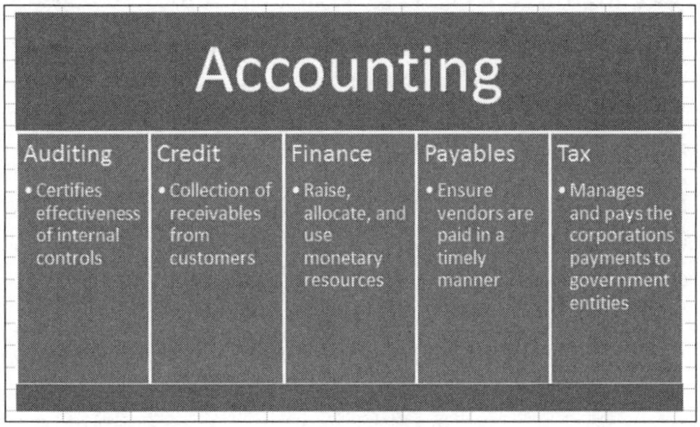

Figure 11.23
You can illustrate groups within a whole by using the Table List layout.

11

Adjusting Venn Diagrams to Show Relationships

The Basic Venn layout illustrates two to seven overlapping circles. Unfortunately, all the Venn diagrams created by the SmartArt engine show circles that are perfectly overlapping, as shown on the left side of Figure 11.24. This is not how relationships usually happen.

To create Venn diagrams that actually represent relationships, you can usually adjust the size of each circle and the percentage of overlap in the circles. For example, on the right side of Figure 11.24, the diagram indicates that while 80 percent of the bowling team is made up of people from the accounting department, fewer than one-fifth of the accountants are on the bowling team. To create this chart, you follow these steps:

Figure 11.24
Venn diagrams require adjustment to show the real size and proportion of overlap.

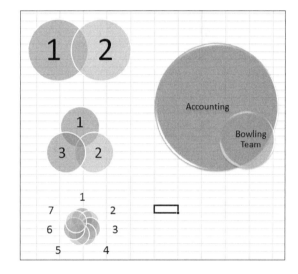

1. Add a SmartArt diagram with a Basic Venn layout.

2. Enter two Level 1 text entries and name them `Accounting` and `Bowling Team`.

3. Click the Accounting circle. Excel displays resizing handles. Drag a resizing handle out from the center of the circle to make the circle larger.

4. Click the Bowling circle. Drag a resizing handle inward to make the circle smaller.

5. While the resizing handles are displayed, drag the Bowling circle so that about 80 percent of that circle is inside the larger circle.

Understanding Labeled Hierarchy Charts

To figure out two of Excel 2010's hierarchy charts—Labeled Hierarchy and Horizontal Labeled Hierarchy—you almost need a Ph.D. However, when you figure out the bizarre layouts required in the text pane, these are handy hierarchy charts.

The Horizontal Labeled Hierarchy (see Figure 11.25) offers a horizontal hierarchy chart that progresses from left to right. Each level of the chart lies in a colored band with a title. To create this chart, follow these steps:

Figure 11.25
Getting the titles at the top of each band requires Level 1 shapes at the end of the text pane.

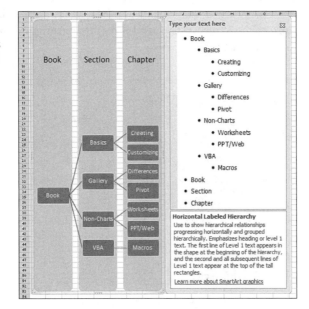

1. Create a single Level 1 item.

2. Beneath the first Level 1 item, build the complete hierarchy of Level 2, Level 3, and so on.

3. Count the number of levels in the hierarchy, including the first level. The chart in Figure 11.25 includes three levels. Remember this number for step 4.

4. At the bottom of the text pane, add new Level 1 entries. The first new Level 1 entry should include the title for the leftmost level of the hierarchy. The second new Level 1 entry should include the title for the second level of the hierarchy. Do not add any Level 2 text to these Level 1 entries.

When the number of bottom Level 1 entries exactly matches the number of levels in the hierarchy, the diagram snaps into place, with the titles lining up in the colored bands.

Using Other SmartArt Layouts

With Excel's 129 built-in layouts, you can use SmartArt graphics in a wide variety of ways. During Power Excel seminars that I conduct, I often show a slide with a few of the new graphics such as the funnel or gear charts. A clever accountant in one of my audiences wryly pointed out that the funnel chart would be perfect for illustrating the ingredients in a martini (see Figure 11.26).

Although Microsoft does not currently allow SmartArt to be created using VBA, it does allow someone with an understanding of XML to create brand-new SmartArt layouts. *Leveraging SmartArt Graphics in the 2007 Microsoft Office System*, an e-book published by Que (ISBN 0-7686-6833-6), includes several examples written by Suat Ozgur. It is easy to create new layouts that use different shapes such as pentagons instead of circles or change the default proportions of the SmartArt layouts. I expect that many third-party vendors will begin offering custom SmartArt types for sale.

Figure 11.26
Your use of SmartArt diagrams for illustrating business concepts is limited only by your imagination.

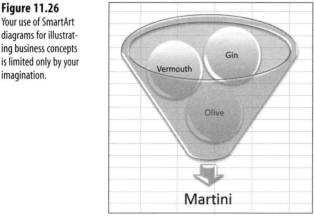

Overall, SmartArt is a great addition to the Office family. The one real drawback related to SmartArt in Excel 2010 is the inability to link cell content to the text in SmartArt. To do that, you have to use shapes, as described in the following section.

Using Shapes to Display Cell Contents

Shapes were known in legacy versions of Excel as AutoShapes. Microsoft has added new shapes to the already long list of shapes available in AutoShapes. In addition, Excel 2010 shapes have some new formatting options, such as shadow, glow, and bevel.

Perhaps the best part of shapes is that you can tie the text on a shape to a worksheet cell. In Figure 11.27, for example, the shape is set to display the current value of Cell B26. Every time the worksheet is calculated, the text on the shape is updated.

Figure 11.27
Shapes can be set to display the current value of a cell.

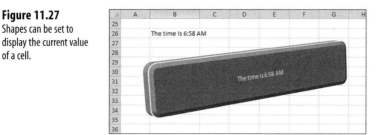

You follow these steps to insert a shape into a worksheet:

1. Select a blank area of the worksheet.
2. From the Insert tab, open the Shapes drop-down.
3. Select 1 of the 159 basic shapes, as shown in Figure 11.28.

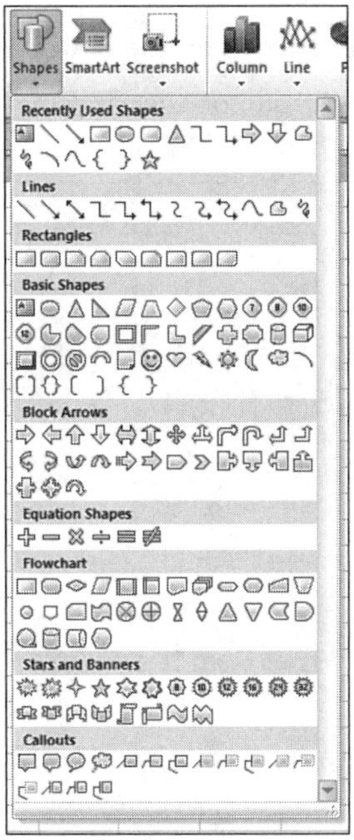

Figure 11.28
Choose from these shapes.

4. When the mouse pointer changes to a small crosshair, click and drag in the worksheet to draw the shape.
5. Choose a color scheme from the Shapes Styles drop-down.
6. Select Shape Effects, Preset and select an effect.
7. Look for a yellow diamond on the shape. Change the inflection point for the shape, if necessary. On the rounded rectangle, for example, sliding the yellow diamond controls how wide the rounded corners are.
8. Look for a green circle on the outside of the shape. Drag this circle to rotate the shape, if necessary.
9. To include static text in the shape, click in the middle of the shape and type the text. You can control the style by using the WordArt Styles drop-down. You can control text size and color by using the formatting buttons on the Home tab. The shape can include text from any cell, but it cannot perform a calculation. If you want the shape to include a calculated value, skip this step and follow steps 10 through 12.

10. If desired, add a new cell that will format a message for the Shape. As shown in Figure 11.29, you can add the formula `="We are at "&TEXT(B13,"0%")&" of our goal!"` to an empty cell to convert the calculation in Cell B13 to a suitable message.

11. Click the middle of the text box as if you were about to type some text.

12. Click in the formula bar and type `=B14` and then press Enter. As shown in Figure 11.29, the shape displays the results from the selected cell.

13. To increase the size of the text, use the Font group on the Home tab.

14. To add effects to the text, use the WordArt group on the Drawing Tools Format tab.

Figure 11.29
This shape picks up the formula from Cell B14 to show a message that changes with the worksheet.

	Rounded Rectangle 1		f_x	=B14								
	A	B	C	D	E	F	G	H	I	J	K	L	M
1												
2												
3												
4												
5			**WE ARE AT 55% OF OUR GOAL WITH**								
6												
7			**$82,123 COLLECTED TO DATE!**								
8												
9												
10												
11	Goal	250000										
12	Actual	82123										
13	Progress	55%										
14		We are at 55% of our goal with $82,123 collected to date!										

To see a demo of assigning a formula to a shape, search for "MrExcel Charts 11" at YouTube.

Working with Shapes

The Drawing Tools Format tab contains options to change the shape style, fill, outline, effects, and WordArt effects.

In the Insert Shapes group of the Format tab, choose Edit Shape and then Change Shape to change from one shape to another shape.

If you right-click a shape and select Format Shape, Excel displays the Format Shape dialog, with the fine-tuning settings Fill, Line, Line Style, Shadow, 3-D Format, 3-D Rotation, and Text Placement.

Using the Freeform Shape to Create a Custom Shape

Despite my friendly relationship with Microsoft, I have not convinced them to add the MrExcel logo to the Shapes gallery (yet). However, you can build any shape by using the Freeform line tools in the Shapes gallery.

After you create a shape, you can add 3-D effects, glow, and so on to make a cool-looking version of your company logo, as shown in Figure 11.30.

To create a custom shape, follow these steps:

1. Insert a picture of the shape that you can use as a guide to trace.

Figure 11.30
This shape was created with the Freeform shape tool and then enhanced using the Drawing Tools section of the Format tab.

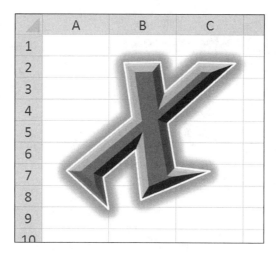

2. From the Insert tab, select the Shapes drop-down. In the Lines section, the last two shapes are Freeform and Scribble. Select the Freeform shape.

3. Click one corner of your logo.

4. Move the mouse to the adjacent corner of the logo and click again.

5. Repeat step 4 for each corner. If your logo has a curve, click several times around the perimeter of the curve. The more often you click, the better the curve will be.

6. When you arrive back at the original corner, click one final time to close the shape and complete the drawing.

7. Use the effect and fill settings to color and stylize the logo.

Using WordArt for Interesting Titles and Headlines

WordArt was been rewritten for Excel 2007. As in legacy versions, WordArt is best used sparingly—possibly for a headline or title at the top of a page. It is best used for impressive display fonts to add interest to a report. You would probably not want to create an entire 20-page document in WordArt.

To use WordArt, follow these steps:

1. Select a blank section of a worksheet.

2. From the Insert tab, select the WordArt drop-down.

3. As shown in Figure 11.31, select from the 30 WordArt presets in the drop-down. Don't worry that these presets seem less exciting than the WordArt in prior versions of Excel. You will be able to customize the WordArt later.

4. Excel adds the generic text Your Text Here in the preset WordArt you chose. Select this default text and then type your own text.

5. Select the text. Choose a new font style by using either the mini toolbar that appears or the Home tab.

Figure 11.31
Excel offers 30 WordArt presets.

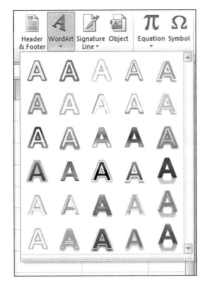

6. Use the WordArt Styles group on the Drawing Tools Format tab to color the WordArt. To the right of the Styles drop-down are icons for text color and line color and a drop-down for effects. The Effects drop-down includes the fly-out menus Shadow, Reflection, Glow, Bevel, and 3-D Rotation.

7. To achieve the old-style WordArt effects, from the Format tab, select Drawing Tools, WordArt Styles, Text Effects, Transform, and then select a shape for the text. Figure 11.32 shows the WordArt with a Wave 1 transformation.

Figure 11.32
WordArt includes the Transform menu to bend and twist type.

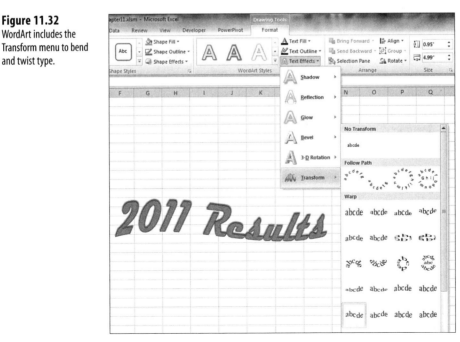

CASE STUDY: CONVERTING SMARTART TO SHAPES TO ALLOW DYNAMIC DIAGRAMS

Microsoft's official position is that you cannot use formulas to populate the text pane in SmartArt diagrams. However, using the steps in this section, you can simulate this effect.

The diagram in Figure 11.33 looks like a SmartArt Table Hierarchy layout, yet the values in all the shapes are fed from formulas on the Excel worksheet.

Figure 11.33
This looks like a SmartArt diagram, but the values come from formulas on the worksheet. Although using formulas this way sounds simple, the feature is not hooked up in Excel 2010.

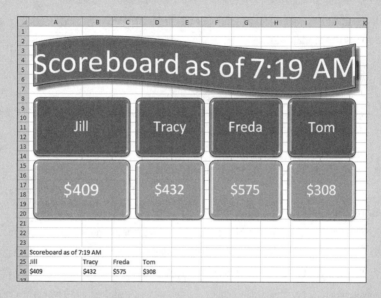

You achieve the live formulas in the SmartArt diagram by cheating slightly. In the steps that follow, you first use the SmartArt diagram engine and then convert the SmartArt diagram to a collection of shapes.

> **CAUTION**
>
> This solution does not work when the number of shapes needs to change in response to the values in the Excel worksheet. The number of shapes has to remain the same. Only the text in the shapes is based on live formulas.

To build the workbook shown in Figure 11.33, follow these steps:

1. Select Insert, SmartArt and choose a Table Hierarchy from the relationship group.

2. Build a static SmartArt diagram with a single Level 1 item, four Level 2 items, and a Level 3 item for each Level 2 item. Type sample values in the text pane. The sample values should be about the same size as the real values that you expect to have in the final diagram.

3. On the Page Layout tab, change the Theme to Opulent.

4. On the SmartArt Tools Design tab, change the SmartArt Styles to Cartoon.

5. Use the Change Colors tab to select Colorful, Accent Colors.

6. Click the Level 1 shape. On the Format tab, use the Change Shape drop-down to select a wave shape.

7. Also on the Format tab, select Shape Styles, Shape Effects, Shadow, Offset Diagonal Bottom Right.

8. Select Shape Styles, Shape Effects, Shadow, Shadow Options.

9. In the Format Shape dialog box, change the distance from 4 points to 9 points.

10. Select the text within the Level 1 shape. On the Format tab, select WordArt Styles, Text Effects, Transform, Wave1.

11. On the SmartArt Tools Design ribbon tab, click Convert to Shapes. This converts the SmartArt diagram to a collection of shapes. You no longer have access to the SmartArt tools or the text pane. You should do this step only after you have the diagram in its final appearance.

12. Create an external query in row 30 to retrieve TicketID, Associate, and SaleTotal from a point-of-sale system. Set up the query properties to refresh every minute.

13. In cell A24, enter the formula `="Scoreboard as of "&TEXT(NOW(),"H:MM AM/PM")`.

14. In cells A25:D25, type the names of the four associates working in the store today.

15. In cell A26, enter the formula `=TEXT(SUMIF($B$31:$B$300,A25,$C$31:$C$300),"$#,##0")`.

16. Copy the formula from Cell A26 to B26:D26.

17. Select the text in one shape. Click in the formula bar and type a formula such as `=A24`.

18. Use the mini toolbar to center the text and select the same size as used for similar shapes in the diagram.

19. Repeat steps 21 and 22 for the other eight shapes.

Throughout the day, the external query brings new data into the worksheet, and it is presented in the scoreboard diagram (refer to Figure 11.33).

Although this is a tedious process, it is a way to use the SmartArt engine to create a great-looking scoreboard in Excel. It is unfortunate that Microsoft did not have time to hook up the decade-old Shapes formula functionality for SmartArt graphics. Although I had hoped this would come in Excel 2010, the one addition in Excel 2010 was the Convert To Shapes command, which shortened this case study by four steps.

Next Steps

In Chapter 12, "Exporting Charts for Use Outside of Excel," you will learn how to share your charts and graphics with others through either PowerPoint or by publishing to the Web. While the charting functionality between Excel and PowerPoint left much to be desired in Excel 2003, you should be able to flawlessly share charts and SmartArt graphics between Excel 2010 and PowerPoint 2010.

Exporting Charts for Use Outside of Excel

Presenting Excel Charts in PowerPoint or Word

Although Excel is a great place for you to create charts, you might need to share charts with others, either in PowerPoint, as Word documents, as web pages, as PDF documents, or simply as graphic files.

Excel 2010, Word 2010, and PowerPoint 2010 share the same charting engines. This makes it possible to copy and paste charts from one application to the other without the unpredictability that often happened when moving charts from Excel 2003 to PowerPoint 2003.

There is a dizzying array of options for how to paste the chart in PowerPoint or Word. Each option offers different advantages and potential disadvantages.

The new Paste Options menu works appears in PowerPoint 2010 and Word 2010 offering five paste alternatives in addition to the regular paste. Paste Special offers nine more choices bringing the total paste choices to fifteen. Further, some of those 15 choices behave differently if you are saving to a document that will be saved in compatibility mode.

When you are trying to decide which paste method to use, consider some of the questions listed below.

Do you want the PowerPoint or Word chart to respond to data changes in the Excel file?

If this is important to you, then use Paste, Paste Special, Paste Link, Microsoft Excel Chart Object. Every time that you open the PowerPoint presentation, you will be given the opportunity to update the charts with data from the source Excel file.

If you want to have the ability to refresh the chart to get new data, then select the default Paste option.

The chart will keep the data at the time of the paste, but you have the ability to use Chart Tools Design, Refresh to retrieve the current data from Excel.

If you absolutely do not want the chart in PowerPoint to change when the underlying data changes, you can use one of the Embed options from the Paste Options menu or Paste as Picture.

Do you love the formatting in Excel or do you want the chart to take on the look and feel of the Word or PowerPoint document?

A default paste will allow your chart to change in response to theme changes in the PowerPoint or Word document. This is probably the best choice, as the chart will look like it is part of the other document.

However, you might really want to keep those custom colors that you lovingly created in Excel. In those cases, you will want to use the K or F choices in the Paste Options menu. K will Keep Source Formatting and Embed Workbook. F will keep Source Formatting and Link Workbook.

If you really want the PowerPoint chart to keep up with formatting changes in the Excel chart, the only option is to select Paste, Paste Special, Paste Link, Microsoft Excel Chart Object. With this option, you will not have the ability to edit the chart in PowerPoint or Word. Your only choice is to update the link. This is the only option that will bring formatting changes from Excel to the Word or PowerPoint document.

Will the PowerPoint file and the Excel file stay in the same locations?

Say that you are creating a PowerPoint presentation. When you are making the presentation, will PowerPoint still have access to your Excel file? Alternatively, are you sending the PowerPoint presentation to your boss who will be presenting from another computer?

If the PowerPoint presentation has access to the original Excel file, all of your options are available and can be used.

But, if the PowerPoint file will be used on a different computer, you might want to consider choosing the K or H options from the Paste Options menu. These choices will embed the entire workbook in the PowerPoint presentation.

As you can imagine, there are disadvantages to this, including the following:

- The PowerPoint file size increases by the size of the Excel file.
- There are privacy concerns. Even if your chart is based on one tiny 40-cell range on Sheet1, your boss can double-click the chart and access all of the data anywhere in the workbook.
- When you embed the workbook, any changes made to the original workbook will not update the chart.

If you are concerned about privacy and the workbook contains sensitive data, then you should paste the chart as a picture or as a screen clipping. This will get a snapshot of the current chart but the person using the PowerPoint or Word document will not be able to see any other data in the workbook.

In addition, if you are concerned about privacy and you want the chart to keep the formatting of the target PowerPoint document, you should consider re-creating the chart in PowerPoint.

Do you want to have access to the Office 2010 charting tools in the target document?

When you use Paste as Picture or Paste as Link, you will lose the ability to edit and format the chart in Word or PowerPoint. Well, if you paste as picture, you do have access to the Picture Tools Format tab, so you can add a fancy border. You will not have access to the Charting Tools Format, Layout, and Design tabs.

The following sections compare the various methods for getting a chart from Excel to PowerPoint.

Copying a Document from Excel and Pasting to PowerPoint Sets Up an As-Needed Link

Copying a chart as a live chart linked to the original workbook is the easiest method of getting a chart from Excel to PowerPoint. You basically just copy the chart from Excel and paste it to PowerPoint.

With this method, you have full access to all the Charting Tools tabs in PowerPoint. You can customize the chart to match the theme of the PowerPoint presentation, and you can choose new layouts, styles, and so on.

The data remains linked to the original workbook. If you change the workbook and later open the PowerPoint presentation, the chart reflects the new numbers from the Excel workbook.

> NOTE
> This feature works only if the PowerPoint presentation still has access to the original Excel file. Otherwise, PowerPoint shows a static version of the last-known numbers in the chart.

The simplest method is to copy the chart from Excel and Paste the chart into PowerPoint. Excel then sets up what I will call a weak link between the presentation and the Excel workbook.

This method has the following pros and cons:

Pro: If you want to change the formatting of the chart in PowerPoint, you have full access to the charting tabs.

Pro: By default, the chart will respond to changes in the theme of the PowerPoint presentation. You will have a chart that has the same look and feel of the rest of the presentation.

Con: By default, you will lose your original colors from the Excel chart. To overcome this, use the F option from the Paste Options menu – Keep Source Formatting and Link Data.

Con: Any subsequent changes to the formatting of the Excel chart will never appear in the PowerPoint chart. You can force PowerPoint to get data changes, but you will never get the formatting changes. To overcome this problem, see Setting up a Link, below.

Con: This method does not work perfectly with documents stored in compatibility mode. Changes to the theme will not affect the linked chart.

Pro: The PowerPoint file size remains small. Excel does not embed the entire workbook in the PowerPoint file.

Pro: You have icons on the Charting Tools Design tab to either refresh the data or edit the data. Provided that the original Excel file is still available in the original folder, the workbook is opened and current data is used to redraw the chart. If the Excel workbook has been moved or renamed, you can use the File, Information, Related Files to change the linked location.

Con: If the original workbook is not available, you cannot refresh data in the chart. However, this only becomes an issue if someone clicks on the Refresh icon in the Charting Tools Design tab. If you are doing a presentation and stay away from that icon, you will successfully present using a cached version of the Excel chart.

Pro: Although there is a link between the PowerPoint document and the Excel workbook, you will not be nagged with Information Bar warnings that there are links in the document.

Neutral: If data in the underlying Excel workbook changes, the new data will not automatically appear in the PowerPoint presentation. You have to explicitly click Charting Tools Design, Refresh Data.

To copy the chart, you follow these steps:

1. Open both PowerPoint and Excel.
2. In Excel, select the chart.
3. Press Ctrl+C or click the Copy icon on the Home tab.
4. Switch to PowerPoint by pressing Alt+Tab.
5. Paste by pressing Ctrl+V or clicking the Paste icon on the Home tab to perform a default paste.

The chart fills the text area of the slide. The data stays the same, but the theme colors and effects are changed to reflect the active theme in the destination slide show. The Chart Tools ribbon icons are available, as shown in Figure 12.1.

By using the default paste, you have set up a weak link between the Excel workbook and the PowerPoint slide. With this link, you have the best of both worlds; you can keep the original data in the PowerPoint chart, or you can get new data from Excel.

Figure 12.1
Copying and pasting is
the simplest method for
getting a chart from Excel
to PowerPoint.

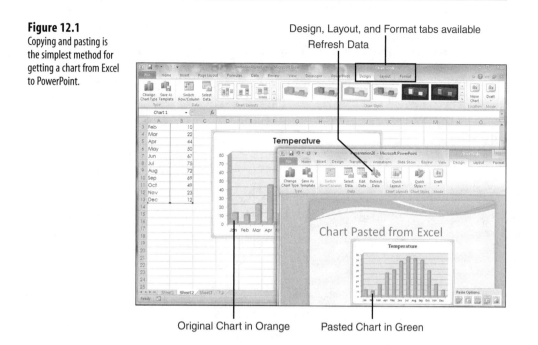

Design, Layout, and Format tabs available

Refresh Data

Original Chart in Orange   Pasted Chart in Green

To illustrate, consider this example:

1. Close the PowerPoint presentation.

2. In the Excel workbook, change the data in the chart. In Figure 12.2, the temperature for July has been adjusted to 55 degrees.

3. In the Excel workbook, use Page Layout, Theme to choose a new theme.

4. In the Excel workbook, change some other aspect of the chart, such as varying the colors by point (see Figure 12.2).

5. Save the Excel workbook.

Figure 12.2
Change the chart in Excel.

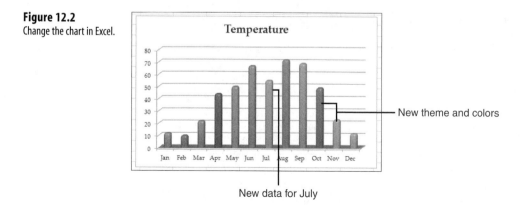

New theme and colors

New data for July

6. Close the Excel workbook.

7. Open the PowerPoint presentation. No warning appears in the information bar that a link is present. You are not asked to update the links. The original chart is presented with the original data (see Figure 12.3). Even though a link appears, you can run the slide show without ever needing the original Excel file.

Figure 12.3
The chart appears with the original data.

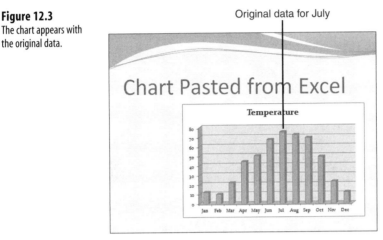
Original data for July

8. Click the chart in PowerPoint. The Chart Tools tabs appear.

9. On the Chart Tools Design tab, select Refresh Data. As shown in Figure 12.4, the chart is updated to show the lower temperature for July. While the data is updated, none of the other formatting changes appear in the chart. The chart is still green and the colors of the columns do not vary by point.

12

Figure 12.4
Use Refresh Data to bring in new data from Excel without changing the formatting.

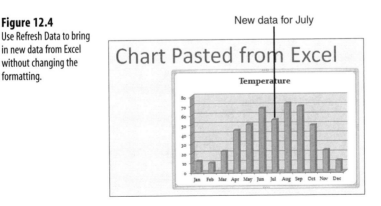
New data for July

10. In PowerPoint, choose a new theme from the Design tab. The colors, fonts, and effects used in the chart are updated to match the theme in PowerPoint (see Figure 12.5).

Figure 12.5
The chart has data from Excel but matches the theme from PowerPoint.

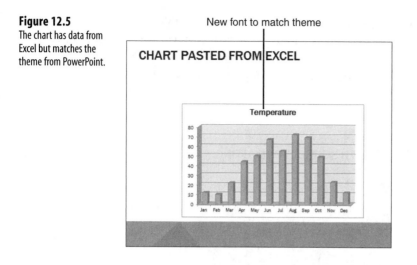

As you can see, the default is pretty cool: You have the ability to get new data from Excel, but the formatting will match the destination PowerPoint presentation.

Copying and Pasting While Keeping Original Formatting

The previous method set up a link to the data stored in the Excel workbook. However, all of the colors and effects used in the original chart were lost when you pasted to PowerPoint or Word.

There are times where you might want to keep the colors from the original workbook. The Paste Options menu offers the F shortcut – to Keep Source Formatting and Link Data.

Like the previous method, you still have the ability to keep the original data or to refresh the chart and get the new data.

Unlike the previous method, the original colors and effects stay with the chart in PowerPoint. The chart will not respond to Theme changes in PowerPoint.

You still have access to Chart Tools tabs in PowerPoint to change the colors in the chart.

> **TIP**
> You will be surprised to learn that like the previous method, refreshing the chart does not bring over any formatting changes that happened in the original workbook.

To copy the chart while keeping the original formatting, you follow these steps:

1. Open both PowerPoint and Excel.
2. In Excel, select the chart.
3. Press Ctrl+C or click the Copy icon on the Home tab.
4. Switch to PowerPoint by pressing Alt+Tab.

5. Open the Paste drop-down on the Home tab. Select the third icon for Keep Source Formatting and Link Data (F). The chart will be pasted with the original formatting.

> **TIP**
>
> Alternatively, for step 5, you can press Ctrl+V, then Ctrl alone, then the letter F (see Figure 12.6).

Figure 12.6
Set up a refreshable link to the data, but keep the formatting at the time of the paste.

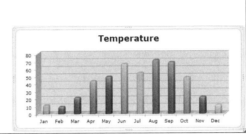

CAUTION

The source formatting options will copy the chart formatting at the time of the paste. If you later change formatting in the Excel file, those formatting changes will never show up in the PowerPoint version of the chart. If you need the PowerPoint chart to show formatting changes made in Excel, then you should use the steps in Pasting as a Link to Capture Future Excel Formatting Changes.

Pasting as Link to Capture Future Excel Formatting Changes

The default methods for pasting in Excel do not set up a link to the current formatting in the Excel workbook. If you want to be able to change formatting in Excel and have those formats carry through to PowerPoint or Word, you will want to use Paste Special and set up a Paste Link.

This method has the following pros and cons:

Con: You need to have access to the Excel file if you want to show the current formatting.

Con: You will be nagged about updating links every time you open the PowerPoint file.

Pro: This method works with files stored in compatibility mode.

Pro: Formatting changes to the original Excel file show up in the PowerPoint file.

Con: If you change the theme in the PowerPoint presentation, the formatting of the linked chart will not change.

To set up a linked chart, follow these steps:

1. Open both PowerPoint and Excel.
2. In Excel, select the chart.
3. Press Ctrl+C or click the Copy icon on the Home tab.
4. Switch to PowerPoint by pressing Alt+Tab.
5. On the Home tab, open the Paste drop-down. Select Paste Special. PowerPoint displays the Paste Special dialog.
6. On the left side of the dialog, select Paste Link. You now have only one option; Microsoft Excel Chart Object (see Figure 12.7). Click OK.

A copy of the original chart appears in PowerPoint. You do not have access to the Chart Tools, but you do have access to the Drawing Tools Format tab. You can use this tab to add a border around the chart.

The link set up with this option is the strongest link of any in this chapter. You can switch to Excel, change some data, and change some formatting. When you switch back to PowerPoint, the data and formatting changes will appear in the chart.

> **TIP**
> If you make changes to the Excel file while the PowerPoint workbook is closed, you will be prompted to update the links when you later open the PowerPoint presentation.

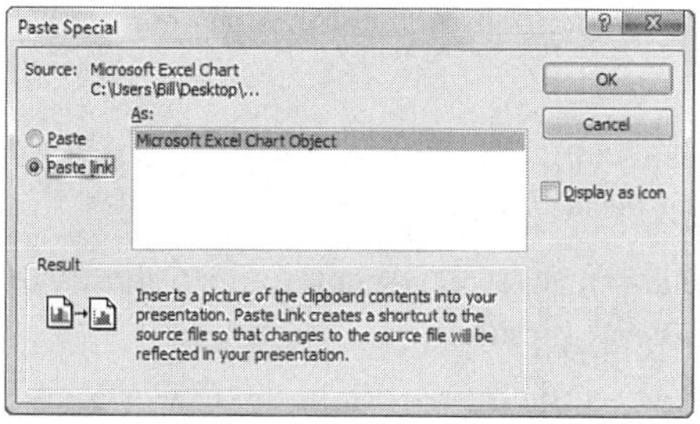

Figure 12.7
Bypass the Paste Options menu and go to Paste Special to set up the only link that can capture future formatting changes to the Excel chart.

Copying a Chart as a Live Chart Linked to a Copy of the Original Workbook

The problem with a straight copy and paste is that the PowerPoint slide and the original Excel workbook must remain on the same computer to maintain the link. If you plan to distribute the PowerPoint file to others, you can copy the chart along with the entire workbook.

To copy the chart, you follow these steps:

1. Open both PowerPoint and Excel.
2. In Excel, click the chart.
3. Press Ctrl+C or click the Copy icon on the Home tab.

4. Switch to PowerPoint by pressing Alt+Tab.

5. Paste by pressing Ctrl+V.

6. An icon appears at the lower-right corner of the pasted chart. Hover over the icon, and a drop-down arrow appears. Choose either the first icon for Keep Source Formatting and Embed Workbook or the second icon for Use Destination Theme and Embed Workbook.

One advantage of this method is that you can send the PowerPoint presentation to any recipient whose computer has Office 2007. The recipient can right-click the chart, select Edit, and see the entire Excel workbook. If that person makes changes to the assumptions in the workbook, the chart updates. The recipient also has full access to the Charting Tools tabs in PowerPoint.

However, the main advantage of this method is also a disadvantage. Even though you paste a single chart, Office 2010 embeds the entire workbook. This can create privacy concerns if the workbook contains sensitive data on other worksheets or file size concerns if you have millions of cells on other worksheets in the workbook.

Copying a Chart as a Picture

You can paste a picture of a chart in a PowerPoint slide. The picture is initially the same size as the chart in the Excel worksheet. Instead of having access to the Charting Tools tab, you only have access to the Picture Tools tab. The Picture Tools tab might allow you to change the chart to grayscale or a monochrome color, but you do not have access to the rich chart formatting tools.

To paste a chart as a picture, you copy the chart in Excel. On the PowerPoint slide, you can perform either of the following tasks:

- Press Ctrl+V to paste the chart. Press Ctrl again to open the Paste Options menu. Select the final icon to Paste as Picture.

- Select the drop-down arrow on the Paste icon in the PowerPoint Home tab. Select Paste Special and then those to paste the picture as PNG, GIF, JPEG, bitmap, Enhanced Metafile, or Windows Metafile.

- Show the Excel chart in Excel. Switch to PowerPoint. Use Insert, Screen Clipping and draw a rectangle around your chart in Excel.

The Paste Special dialog is shown in Figure 12.8.

After the chart is pasted as a picture, you can use any of the settings on the Picture Tools Format tab to apply a frame, bevel, shadow, or reflection to the chart. Figure 12.9 shows a bevel, a shadow, and a bit of perspective angle.

Figure 12.8
You can choose a picture format in the Paste Special dialog.

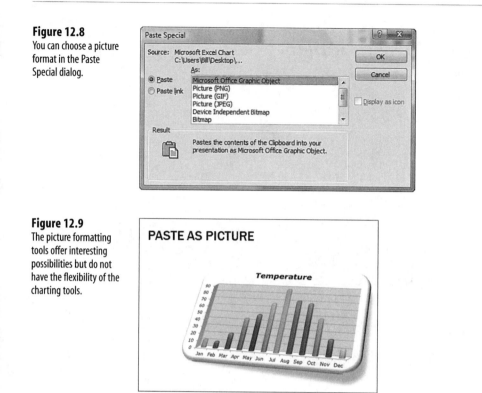

Figure 12.9
The picture formatting tools offer interesting possibilities but do not have the flexibility of the charting tools.

Creating a Chart in PowerPoint and Copying Data from Excel

Creating a chart in PowerPoint and copying data from Excel may seem to be the most tedious method, but it has the advantage of getting a completely editable chart into PowerPoint without the need to copy an entire workbook into the PowerPoint file.

You follow these steps to create the chart:

1. In PowerPoint, select New Slide from the Home tab. A new slide appears, with six icons in the center of the slide (see Figure 12.10).

2. Click the Chart icon in the center of the slide.

3. Choose a chart type and click OK. You see your PowerPoint slide on the left and a new Excel worksheet on the right. The worksheet is called Chart in Microsoft Office PowerPoint - Microsoft Excel (see Figure 12.11).

4. Click the original Excel workbook in the taskbar.

5. Highlight your source data and press Ctrl+C to copy it to the Clipboard.

6. Click the new workbook in the taskbar. Click in cell A1 and press Ctrl+V to paste the data. Your data will probably cover a smaller or larger range of data than the default dataset. If your dataset is smaller, remnants of the default dataset will appear outside your paste area, as shown in Figure 12.12.

Figure 12.10
When you insert a new slide in PowerPoint, six icons appear in the center of the slide.

Figure 12.11
PowerPoint creates a new workbook with default data.

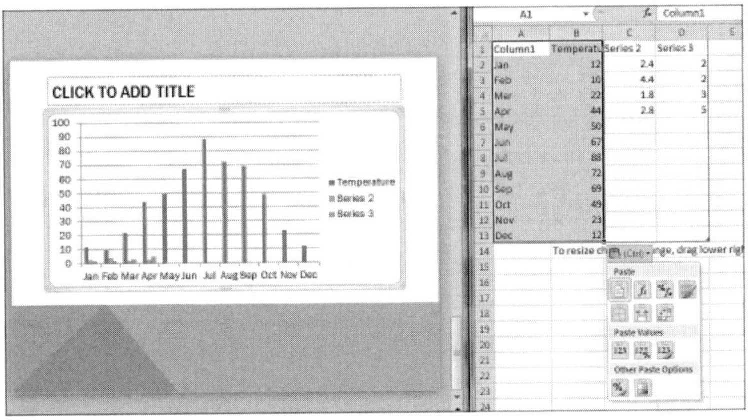

Figure 12.12
You paste your data over the default data.

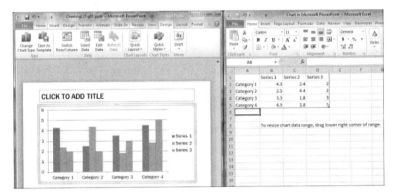

7. A blue outline appears around A1:D13. Grab the blue handle in the corner of Cell D13 and drag the handle to match the size of your pasted data.

8. Click the maximize button in the title bar of the PowerPoint application to return to PowerPoint.

You've now created a new chart in PowerPoint. The chart can be edited using the Chart Tools tabs. You've also minimized the size of the Excel data that must travel with the PowerPoint file.

Presenting Charts on the Web

You can export a chart to appear on a Web page. This technique is one way to make a PNG version of your chart.

You follow these steps to create an HTML page with a chart:

1. Save your Excel file as an Excel file.

2. If your chart is embedded on a worksheet, click the chart. On the Design tab, select Move Chart. Choose to move the chart to a new sheet.

3. Click the File menu to open the backstage view. Click Save As.

4. In the Save As dialog that appears, select Web Page (*.htm; *.html) from the Save As Type drop-down.

5. At the bottom of the Save As dialog, change Entire Workbook to Chart.

6. Specify a filename, such as `MyChart.html`.

7. Click Save. Excel displays the Publish as Web Page dialog, as shown in Figure 12.13. Click Publish.

Figure 12.13
Save the chart as HTML.

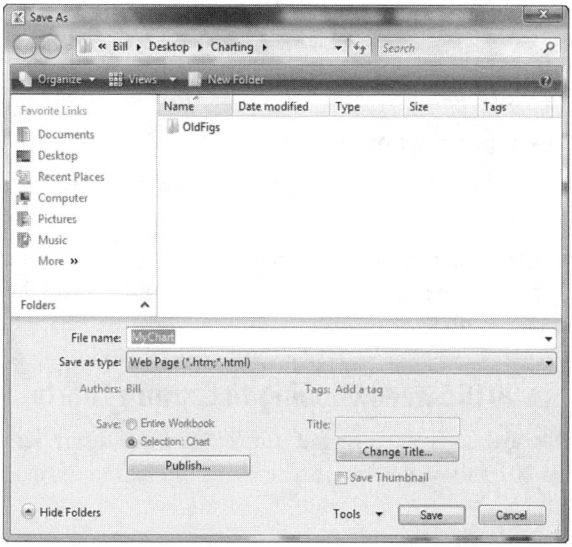

If you browse to the selected path, you will find your HTML file and also a new folder. In the preceding example, the folder would be called MyChart_files. This folder contains a PNG version of your chart.

Exporting Charts to Graphics

The steps in the preceding section are a convoluted way of creating a PNG version of a chart. If you don't mind typing a bit of VBA code, you can export the active chart quickly.

Using VBA to Export Charts as Images

VBA is the macro language behind Excel. Although Chapter 13, "Using Excel VBA to Create Charts," takes a more in-depth look at VBA, this section takes a quick peek into using VBA to convert charts to graphics files.

If you want to display the VBA Editor, try pressing Alt+F11.

> **NOTE** A few modern keyboards have repurposed the Function keys for other purposes, so Alt+F11 might not work for you.

If Alt+F11 doesn't get you to the VBA editor, you need to display the Developer tab in the Ribbon. If this tab is not on your computer, select the File menu to open the backstage view. Select Options from the left navigation. In the Excel Options dialog, select Customize Ribbon from the left navigation. In the right list box, select the Developer box. When the Developer tab is available, you can display the Visual Basic Editor using the Visual Basic icon on the Developer tab.

1. Switch to Excel.
2. Select a chart.
3. Switch back to Visual Basic.
4. Press Ctrl+G to display the Immediate window.
5. Type the following line of code and then press Enter: `ActiveChart.Export "C:\ MyChart.JPG", "JPG"`.

Of course, you can specify any path and filename instead of the name shown in the preceding code snippet. The file type can be GIF, JPG, or any other graphics filter installed on your computer's copy of Office.

Using Snag-It or Office 2010 Screen Clipping to Capture Charts

Screen capture tools such as Snag-It from Camtasia and the Insert Screen Clipping feature of Microsoft Office 2010 allow you to capture a specific region of the screen.

Snag-It allows you to specify an output file type of BMP, GIF, JPG, PCX, PNG, TGA, or TIF. You can also specify a higher resolution, suitable for printing using Snag-It.

The new Insert Screen Clipping feature in Office 2010 makes it easy to capture a region of a screen as a graphic in another application.

To grab a screen clipping using the Office 2010 Screen Clipping feature, follow these steps:

1. Open both Excel and PowerPoint or Word or OneNote.

2. In PowerPoint, navigate to the slide where you want the screen clipping to appear.

3. Switch to Excel. Make sure that the chart is visible in the screen. The screen clipping feature will grab from the most recent "other" application, so you want to make sure the chart is on the active worksheet of the Excel application immediately before switching back to PowerPoint.

4. Switch to PowerPoint. On the Insert tab, click the Screenshot drop-down. Ignore the thumbnails of the open applications and instead select the Screen Clipping menu item.

5. You should see a grayed-out version of the Excel window take up your whole screen. Using your mouse, draw a rectangle around the chart. When you release the mouse, you will switch back to PowerPoint and the chart will be inserted as a picture.

To see a demo of the screen clipping tool, search for "MrExcel Charts 12" at YouTube.

Converting to XPS or PDF

PDF is the ubiquitous Portable Document Format from Adobe. XML Paper Specification (XPS) is the newer open-source competitor from Microsoft.

To save a chart as a PDF file, follow these steps:

1. Select a chart in Excel.

2. Select the File menu to open Backstage View.

3. In the left navigation, select Share.

4. In the left panel of the Share Backstage View, select Create PDF/XPS Document.

5. In the right panel of the Backstage View, select Create a PDF/XPS.

6. In the Publish and PDF or XPS dialog, select PDF from the Save As Type list box.

7. Specify a filename.

8. Click Publish. The selected chart will be created as a single-page PDF file.

Next Steps

In Chapter 13, you will learn how to use VBA macros to automate the creation and formatting of charts. VBA is a macro language that has been in Excel for over a decade; you can use it to automate repetitive tasks.

Using Excel VBA to Create Charts

Introducing VBA

Version 5 of Excel introduced a powerful new macro language called Visual Basic for Applications (VBA). Every copy of Excel shipped since 1993 has had a copy of the powerful VBA language hiding behind the worksheets. VBA allows you to perform steps that you normally perform in Excel, but to perform them very quickly and flawlessly. A VBA program can turn a process that used to take days each month into a single button click and a minute of processing time. If you have a lot of charts to create, you can set up a macro to automatically produce a series of charts. This is appropriate if you regularly have to produce a similar set of charts every day, week, or month.

You shouldn't be intimidated by VBA. The VBA macro recorder tool gets you 80 percent of the way to a useful macro, and the examples in this chapter get you the rest of the way there.

Every example in this chapter is available for download from `http://www.mrexcel.com/chart2010data.html`.

> **NOTE**
>
> There is usually a nagging subset of features that work in the current version of Excel but do not work in legacy versions of Excel. However, all the good features in charting are new; consequently, hardly any of the code in this chapter is backward compatible with Excel 97–Excel 2003. If you need to write code to create Excel 2003 charts, you can use the examples from Chapter 10 of my book *VBA and Macros for Microsoft Excel* (ISBN 978-0789731296, Que Publishing). The project file from that chapter is available at `http://www.mrexcel.com/chartbookdata.html`.

Enabling VBA in Your Copy of Excel

By default, VBA is disabled in Office 2010. Before you can start using VBA, you need to enable macros in the Trust Center. Follow these steps:

1. From the File menu, select Options.
2. In the left navigation, select Trust Center.
3. On the right side of the Options dialog, click Trust Center Settings.
4. In the Trust Center left navigation, select Macro Settings.
5. Select Disable All Macros With Notification.

This will allow macros to run after you verify that you are expecting the macros to be in the file. New in Office 2010, for files stored on the local hard drive, you only need to confirm that you trust the macros once per workbook.

> **T I P**
> If you have previously displayed the Developer tab of the Ribbon, you can use the Macro Security icon on the Developer tab to jump quickly to the Trust Center dialog box.

Further, when you save your files, you have to save the files as Excel 2010 macro-enabled workbooks, with the .xlsm extension.

Enabling the Developer Tab

Most of the VBA tools are located on the Developer tab of the Excel 2010 Ribbon. By default, this tab is not displayed. To enable it, go to File, Options, Customize Ribbon. In the right list box, the Developer tab will be unchecked. Click to add a checkmark, and then click OK.

As shown in Figure 13.1, the Code group on the Developer tab of the Ribbon offers icons for accessing the Visual Basic Editor, the Macros dialog box, macro recording tools, and the Macro Security setting.

Figure 13.1
You need to enable the Developer tab to access the VBA tools.

The Visual Basic Editor

From Excel, you press Alt+F11 or, from the Developer tab, you select Visual Basic to open the Visual Basic Editor. The VBA Editor, shown in Figure 13.2, has three main sections:

Figure 13.2
The Visual Basic Editor window is lurking behind every copy of Excel shipped since 1993.

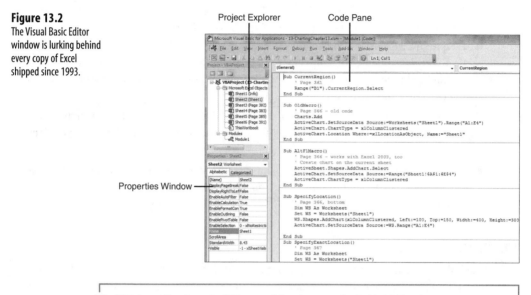

> **NOTE**
> If this is your first time using VBA, some of these items may be disabled. Follow the instructions given in the following list to make sure each is enabled.

- **Project Explorer**—This pane display
- **Properties window**—The Properties window is important when you begin to program user forms. It is also useful when you're writing normal code. You enable it by pressing F4.
- **Code window**—This is the area where you write your code. Code is stored in one or more code modules attached to the workbook. To add a code module to a workbook, you select Insert, Module from the application menu.

Visual Basic Tools

Visual Basic is a powerful development environment. Although this chapter cannot offer a complete course on VBA, if you are new to VBA, you should take advantage of the following:

- As you begin to type code, Excel usually offers a drop-down with valid choices. This feature, known as AutoComplete, allows you to type code faster and eliminate typing mistakes.

13

■ For assistance with any keyword, you can put the cursor in the keyword and press F1. You might need your installation CDs because the VBA Help file can be excluded from the installation of Office 2010.

■ Excel checks each line of code as you finish it. Lines in error appear in red. Comments appear in green. You can add a comment by typing a single apostrophe. You should use lots of comments so you can remember what each section of code is doing.

■ Despite the aforementioned error checking, Excel may still encounter errors at runtime. If this happens, you can click the Debug button. The line that caused the error is highlighted in yellow. You can then hover your mouse cursor over any variable to see the current value of the variable.

■ When you are in Debug mode, you can use the Debug menu to step through code line-by-line. You can toggle back and forth between Excel and VBA to see the effect of running a line of code on the worksheet.

■ Other great debugging tools are breakpoints, the Watch window, the Object Browser, and the Immediate window. You can read about these tools in the Excel VBA Help menu.

The Macro Recorder

Excel offers a macro recorder that is about 80 percent perfect for charts. Code that you record to work with one dataset is hard-coded to work only with that dataset. This behavior might work fine if your chart data occupies Cells A1:E7 every single day, but if you might have a different number of customers each day, it is unlikely that you will have the same number of rows each day. Given that you might need to work with other data, it would be a lot better if Excel could record your actions of selecting cells when you use the End key. This is one of the shortcomings of the macro recorder.

Excel pros often use the macro recorder to record code and expect to have to then clean up the recorded code. While the macro recorder in Excel 2007 was not finished for charting, it is now working well in Excel 2010.

Understanding Object-Oriented Code

If you took a class in BASIC a long time ago, the recorded code in VBA is going to appear rather foreign to you. Whereas BASIC is a procedural language, VBA is an object-oriented language. Most lines of VBA code follow the Noun.Verb, or Object.Method, syntax. Objects can be workbooks, worksheets, charts, cells, or ranges of cells. Methods can be typical Excel actions, such as Copy, Paste, and PasteSpecial.

Many methods allow adverbs—that is, parameters you use to specify how to perform a method. If you see a construction that includes a colon and an equal sign, it is an adverb, and you know that the macro recorder is describing how the method should work.

You might also see adjectives, or properties. If you set `ActiveCell.Font.ColorIndex = 3`, you are setting the font color (the property) of the active cell to red (the value).

Learning Tricks of the VBA Trade

You need to master a few simple techniques to be able to write efficient VBA code. These techniques will help you make the jump to writing effective code.

Writing Code to Handle a Data Range of Any Size

The macro recorder hard-codes the fact that your data is in a range, such as A1:E7. Although this hard-coding works for today's dataset, it may not work as you get new datasets. You need to write code that can deal with different sizes of datasets.

One method is to use the `CurrentRegion` property. If you specify one nonblank cell and ask for the current region, Excel extends the selection in each direction until it encounters the edge of the worksheet, a blank row, or a blank column. In Figure 13.3, for example, the following line of code selected A1:E4:

```
Range("B1").CurrentRegion.Select
```

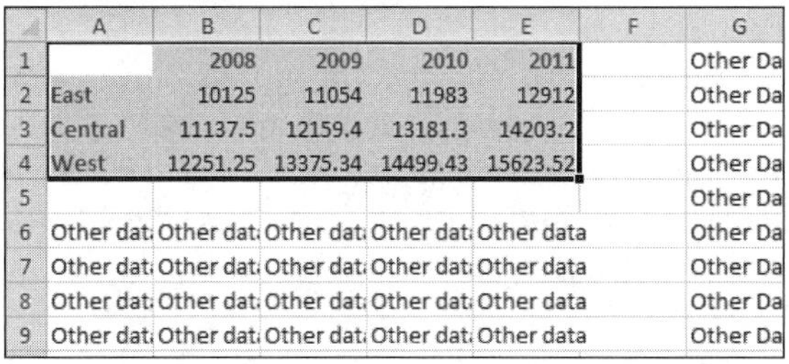

Figure 13.3
Selecting the current region extends the selection out until a blank row/column is encountered.

▲	A	B	C	D	E	F	G
1		2008	2009	2010	2011		Other Da
2	East	10125	11054	11983	12912		Other Da
3	Central	11137.5	12159.4	13181.3	14203.2		Other Da
4	West	12251.25	13375.34	14499.43	15623.52		Other Da
5							Other Da
6	Other dat	Other dat	Other dat	Other dat	Other data		Other Da
7	Other dat	Other dat	Other dat	Other dat	Other data		Other Da
8	Other dat	Other dat	Other dat	Other dat	Other data		Other Da
9	Other dat	Other dat	Other dat	Other dat	Other data		Other Da

If you are absolutely sure that Cell B1 is nonblank and that no other data touches your chart data, you could use the `CurrentRegion` approach to specify the data to a chart.

The macro recorder uses syntax such as `Range("H12")` to refer to a cell. However, it is more flexible to use `Cells(12, 8)` to refer to H12. Why (12, 8)? Because H12 is in Row 12, Column 8. Similarly, the macro recorder refers to a rectangular range using syntax such as `Range("A1:K415501")`. However, it is more flexible to use the `Cells` syntax to refer to the upper-left corner of the range and then use the `Resize()` syntax to refer to the number of rows and columns in the range:

```
Cells(1, 1).Resize(415501,11)
```

This approach is more flexible than using `Range("A1:K415501")` because you can replace any of the numbers with a variable. Rather than hard-coding Cells(12,8), you will frequently replace the numbers with variables such as Cells(i, j).

In the Excel user interface, you can use the End key on the keyboard to jump to the end of a range of data. If you move the cell pointer to the final row on the worksheet and press the End key and then the Up Arrow key, the cell pointer jumps to the last row that contains data. The equivalent of doing this in VBA is to use the following code:

```
Range("A1048576").End(xlUp).Select
```

You don't need to select this cell; you just need to find the row number that contains the last row. The following code locates this row and saves the row number to a variable named FinalRow:

```
FinalRow = Range("A1048576").End(xlUp).Row
```

There is nothing magical about the variable name FinalRow. You could call this variable x or y, or even give it your dog's name. However, because VBA allows you to use meaningful variable names, you should use something such as FinalRow to describe the final row.

> **NOTE**
>
> Excel 2010 offers 1,048,576 rows and 16,384 columns. Excel 97 through Excel 2003 offered 65,536 rows and 256 columns. To make your code flexible enough to handle any versions of Excel, you can use Rows.Count to learn the total number of rows in the currently running version of Excel. The preceding code could then be generalized like so:
>
> ```
> FinalRow = Cells(Rows.Count, 1).End(xlUp).Row
> ```

You can also find the final column in a dataset. If you are relatively sure that the dataset begins in Row 1, you can use the End key in combination with the left-arrow key to jump from cell XFD1 to the last column that contains data. To generalize for the possibility that the code is running in legacy versions of Excel, you can use the following code:

```
FinalCol = Cells(1, Columns.Count).End(xlToLeft).Column
```

End+Down Arrow Versus End+Up Arrow

You might be tempted to find the final row by starting in Cell A1 and using the End key in conjunction with the down-arrow key. You should avoid this approach. Data coming from another system is imperfect. If your program will import 500,000 rows from a legacy computer system every day for the next five years, a day will come when someone manages to key a null value into the data set. This value will cause a blank cell or even a blank row to appear in the middle of your data set. The formula Range("A1").End(xlDown) will then stop prematurely just before the blank cell instead of including all your data. This blank cell will cause that day's report to miss thousands of rows of data, a potential disaster that will call into question the credibility of your report. You should take the extra step of starting at the last row in the worksheet to greatly reduce the risk of problems.

Using Super-Variables: Object Variables

In typical programming languages, a variable holds a single value. You might use $x = 4$ to assign a value of 4 to the variable x.

Many properties describe a single cell in Excel. A cell might contain a value such as 4, and the cell also has a font size, a font color, a row, a column, possibly a formula, possibly a comment, a list of precedents, and more. It is possible to use VBA to create a super-variable that contains all the information about a cell or any other object. A statement to create a typical variable such as x = Range("A1") assigns the current value of Cell A1 to the variable *x*.

You can use the Set keyword to create an object variable:

```
Set x = Range("A1")
```

This formula creates a super-variable that contains all the properties of the cell. Instead of having a variable with only one value, you now have a variable in which you can access the value of many properties associated with that variable. You can reference x.Formula to learn the formula in Cell A1 or x.Font.ColorIndex to learn the color of the cell.

Using object variables can make it easier to write code. Instead of continuously referring to ThisWorkbook.Worksheets("Income Statement"), you can define an object variable and use that as shorthand. For example, the following code repeatedly refers to the same workbook:

```
ThisWorkbook.Worksheets("Income Statement").ChartObjects("Chart1").Chart _
    .SetSourceData Source:= ThisWorkbook.Worksheets("Income Statement") _
    .Range("A1:E4")
ThisWorkbook.Worksheets("Income Statement").ChartObjects("Chart1").Left = 10
ThisWorkbook.Worksheets("Income Statement").ChartObjects("Chart1").Top = 30
ThisWorkbook.Worksheets("Income Statement").ChartObjects("Chart1").Width = 300
ThisWorkbook.Worksheets("Income Statement").ChartObjects("Chart1").Height = 200
```

If you define an object variable first, the code becomes shorter and easier to write:

```
Dim WS as Worksheet
Set WS = ThisWorkbook.Worksheets("Income Statement")
WS.ChartObjects("Chart1").Chart.SetSourceData Source:= WS.Range("A1:E4")
WS.ChartObjects("Chart1").Left = 10
WS.ChartObjects("Chart1").Top = 30
WS.ChartObjects("Chart1").Width = 300
WS.ChartObjects("Chart1").Height = 200
```

If you define two object variables, you can simplify the code even further:

```
Dim WS as Worksheet
Dim ChtO as ChartObject
Set WS = ThisWorkbook.Worksheets("Income Statement")
Set ChtO = WS.ChartObjects("Chart 1")
ChtO.Chart.SetSourceData Source:= WS.Range("A1:E4")
ChtO.Left = 10
ChtO.Top = 30
ChtO.Width = 300

ChtO.Height = 200
```

13

> **NOTE** Provided that you do not type Option Explicit in the code window, VBA does not require you to declare your variables with the Dim statement. I tend not to declare regular variables. However, there is a benefit if you use Dim to declare your object variables; Excel will offer AutoComplete drop-downs showing all of the methods and properties available for the object variable. For this reason, I take the extra time to declare the object variables at the top of each macro.

Using With and End With When Referring to an Object

In the previous code, several lines all refer to the same chart object. Rather than reference this object on every line of code, you could specify the chart object once in a `With` statement. In each subsequent line, you could leave off the name of the chart and begin the line with a period. You would end the block of code with an `End With` statement. This is faster to write than typing the complete object name multiple times, and it executes faster because Excel only has to figure out what `WS.ChartObjects("Chart1")` means once. The following code uses the `With` syntax while setting five properties:

```
Dim WS as Worksheet
Set WS = ThisWorkbook.Worksheets("Income Statement")
With WS.ChartObjects("Chart1")
    .Chart.SetSourceData Source:= WS.Range("A1:E4")
    .Left = 10
    .Top = 30
    .Width = 300
    .Height = 200
End With
```

Continuing a Line

Some lines of code can get very long. To improve readability, you can break a line and continue it. To indicate that the current line is continued on the next line, you can type a space and then an underscore character. Typically, the convention is to then indent the continued line of code. This is not required by VBA, but improves readability. For example, the following two lines of code are really a single line of code:

```
FinalCol = Cells(1, Columns.Count). _
    End(xlToLeft).Column
```

> **NOTE**
>
> You are likely to break a line only when you reach the right edge of the code window, but the physical limitations of this book require lines to be broken into much smaller segments. Feel free to rejoin continued lines into a single line of code in your project.

> **CAUTION**
>
> Be careful to note that the continuation symbol is a space plus an underscore. If you forget the space, then VBA won't realize that you are trying to continue the line and you will get a compile error.

Adding Comments to Code

When you figure out an interesting technique in code, it's a good idea to add comments in the code. This will help you if you return to the code several months later, and it will help others who have to troubleshoot your code.

The comment character in VBA is a single apostrophe ('). You can use a single-line comment, a several-line comment, or a comment that takes up only the end of a line. The Visual Basic Editor changes the color of your comments to green to differentiate them from other code. The following macro has comments to document where you can turn to for more information:

```
Sub CommentsImproveReadability()
    Dim WS As Worksheet
    Set WS = Worksheets("Sheet1")
    ' Create a chart on a new sheet
    Charts.Add
    ' This technique is from chapter 13
    ' of the Excel Charting book
    ActiveChart.ChartType = xlColumnClustered
    ActiveChart.SetSourceData Source:=WS.Range("A1:B4")
    ActiveChart.Interior.ColorIndex = 4 ' Green
End Sub
```

Coding for New Charting Features in Excel 2010

Charts have been completely rewritten for Excel 2007. Most code from Excel 2003 will continue to work in Excel 2010. However, if you write code to take advantage of the new charting features, that code will not be backward compatible with Excel 2003.

The following are some of the methods and features that will not work in Excel 2003:

- ApplyLayout—This method applies one of the chart layouts available on the Design tab.

- SetElement—This method chooses any of the built-in element choices from the Layout tab.

- ChartFormat—This object allows you to change the fill, glow, line, reflection, shadow, soft edge, or 3-D format of most individual chart elements. This is similar to settings on the Format tab.

- AddChart—This method allows you to add a chart to an existing worksheet.

Referencing Charts and Chart Objects in VBA Code

If you go back far enough in Excel history, you find that all charts used to be created as their own chart sheets. Then, in the mid-1990s, Excel added the amazing capability to embed a chart right onto an existing worksheet. This allowed a report to be created with tables of numbers and charts all on the same page, something we take for granted today.

13

These two different ways of dealing with charts have made it necessary for us to deal with two separate object models for charts. When a chart is on its own standalone chart sheet, you are dealing with a Chart object. When a chart is embedded in a worksheet, you are dealing with a ChartObject object. Excel 2007 introduced a third evolutionary branch because objects on a worksheet are also a member of the Shapes collection.

In Excel 2003, to reference the color of the chart area for an embedded chart, you would have to refer to the chart in this manner:

```
Worksheets("Jan").ChartObjects("Chart 1").Chart.ChartArea.Interior. _
    ColorIndex = 4
```

In Excel 2010, you can instead use the Shapes collection:

```
Worksheets("Jan").Shapes("Chart 1").Chart.ChartArea.Interior.ColorIndex = 4
```

In any version of Excel, if a chart is on its own chart sheet, you don't have to specify the container; you can simply refer to the Chart object:

```
Sheets("Chart1").ChartArea.Interior.ColorIndex = 4
```

Creating a Chart

In legacy versions of Excel, you used the Charts.Add command to add a new chart. You then specified the source data, the type of chart, and if the chart should be on a new sheet or embedded on an existing worksheet. The first three lines of the following code create a clustered column chart on a new chart sheet. The fourth line moves the chart back to be an embedded object in Sheet1:

```
Charts.Add
ActiveChart.SetSourceData Source:=Worksheets("Sheet1").Range("A1:E4")
ActiveChart.ChartType = xlColumnClustered
ActiveChart.Location Where:=xlLocationAsObject, Name:="Sheet1"
```

If you plan to share your macros with people who still use Excel 2003, you should use the Charts.Add method. However, if your application will only be running in Excel 2010, you can use the new AddChart method. The code for the AddChart method can be as simple as the following:

```
' Create chart on the current sheet
ActiveSheet.Shapes.AddChart.Select
ActiveChart.SetSourceData Source:=Range("A1:E4")
ActiveChart.ChartType = xlColumnClustered
```

Alternatively, you can specify the chart type, size, and location as part of the AddChart method, as described in the next section.

Specifying the Size and Location of a Chart

The AddChart method has additional parameters you can use to specify the type of chart, the chart's location on the worksheet, and the size of the chart.

13

The location and size of a chart are specified in points (72 points = 1 inch). For example, the Top parameter requires the number of points from the top of row 1 to the top edge of the worksheet.

The following code creates a chart that roughly covers the range C11:J30:

```
Sub SpecifyLocation()
    Dim WS As Worksheet
    Set WS = Worksheets("Sheet1")
    WS.Shapes.AddChart(xlColumnClustered, _
        Left:=100, Top:=150, _
        Width:=400, Height:=300).Select
    ActiveChart.SetSourceData Source:=WS.Range("A1:E4")
End Sub
```

It would require a lot of trial and error to randomly figure out the exact distance in points to cause a chart to line up with a certain cell. Fortunately, you can ask VBA to tell you the distance in points to a certain cell. If you ask for the Left property of any cell, you find the distance to the top-left corner of that cell. You can also ask for the width of a range or the height of a range. For example, the following code creates a chart in exactly C11:J30:

```
Sub SpecifyExactLocation()
    Dim WS As Worksheet
    Set WS = Worksheets("Sheet1")
    WS.Shapes.AddChart(xlColumnClustered, _
        Left:=WS.Range("C11").Left, _
        Top:=WS.Range("C11").Top, _
        Width:=WS.Range("C11:J11").Width, _
        Height:=WS.Range("C11:C30").Height _
        ).Select
    ActiveChart.SetSourceData Source:=WS.Range("A1:E4")
End Sub
```

In this case, you are not moving the location of the Chart object; rather, you are moving the location of the container that contains the chart. In Excel 2010, it is either the ChartObject or the Shape object. If you try to change the actual location of the chart, you move it within the container. Because you can actually move the chart area a few points in either direction inside the container, the code will run, but you will not get the desired results.

To move a chart that has already been created, you can reference either ChartObject or the Shape and change the Top, Left, Width, and Height properties as shown in the following macro:

```
Sub MoveAfterTheFact()
    Dim WS As Worksheet
    Set WS = Worksheets("Sheet1")
    With WS.ChartObjects("Chart 9")
        .Left = WS.Range("C21").Left
        .Top = WS.Range("C21").Top
        .Width = WS.Range("C1:H1").Width
        .Height = WS.Range("C21:C25").Height
    End With
End Sub
```

Later Referring to a Specific Chart

When a new chart is created, it is given a sequential name, such as Chart 1. If you select a chart and then look in the name box, you see the name of the chart. In Figure 13.4, the name of the chart is Chart 14. This does not mean that there are 14 charts on the worksheet. In this particular case, many individual charts have been created and deleted.

Figure 13.4
You can select a chart and look in the name box to find the name of the chart.

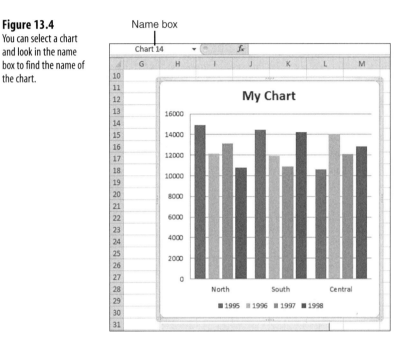

Name box

This means that on any given day that your macro runs, the Chart object might have a different name. If you need to reference the chart later in the macro, perhaps after you have selected other cells and the chart is no longer active, you might ask VBA for the name of the chart and store it in a variable for later use, as shown here:

```
Sub RememberTheName()
    Dim WS As Worksheet
    Set WS = Worksheets("Sheet1")
    WS.Shapes.AddChart(xlColumnClustered, _
        Left:=WS.Range("C11").Left, _
        Top:=WS.Range("C11").Top, _
        Width:=WS.Range("C11:J11").Width, _
        Height:=WS.Range("C11:C30").Height _
        ).Select
    ActiveChart.SetSourceData Source:=WS.Range("A1:E4")
    ' Remember the name in a variable
    ThisChartObjectName = ActiveChart.Parent.Name
    ' more lines of code...
    ' then later in the macro, you need to re-assign the chart
    With WS.Shapes(ThisChartObjectName)
```

```
        .Chart.SetSourceData Source:=WS.Range("A20:E24"), PlotBy:=xlColumns
        .Top = WS.Range("C26").Top
    End With
End Sub
```

In the preceding macro, the variable `ThisChartObjectName` contains the name of the chart object. This method works great if your changes will happen later in the same macro. However, after the macro finishes running, the variable will be out of scope, and you won't be able to access the name later.

If you want to be able to remember a chart name, you could store the name in an out-of-the way cell on the worksheet. The first macro here stores the name in Cell Z1, and the second macro then later modifies the chart using the name stored in Cell Z1:

```
Sub StoreTheName()
    Dim WS As Worksheet
    Set WS = Worksheets("Sheet1")
    WS.Shapes.AddChart(xlColumnClustered, _
        Left:=WS.Range("C11").Left, _
        Top:=WS.Range("C11").Top, _
        Width:=WS.Range("C11:J11").Width, _
        Height:=WS.Range("C11:C30").Height _
        ).Select
    ActiveChart.SetSourceData Source:=WS.Range("A1:E4")
    Range("Z1").Value = ActiveChart.Parent.Name
End Sub
```

After the previous macro stored the name in Cell Z1, the following macro will use the value in Z1 to figure out which macro to change:

```
Sub ChangeTheChartLater()
    Dim WS As Worksheet
    Set WS = Worksheets("Sheet1")
    MyName = WS.Range("Z1").Value
    With WS.Shapes(MyName)
        .Chart.SetSourceData Source:=WS.Range("A20:E24"), PlotBy:=xlColumns
        .Top = WS.Range("C26").Top
    End With

End Sub
```

If you need to modify a preexisting chart—such as a chart that you did not create—and there is only one chart on the worksheet, you can use this line of code:

```
WS.ChartObjects(1).Chart.Interior.ColorIndex = 4
```

If there are many charts and you need to find the one with the upper-left corner located in Cell A4, you could loop through all the chart objects until you find one in the correct location, like this:

```
For each Cht in ActiveSheet.ChartObjects
    If Cht.TopLeftCell.Address = "$A$4" then
        Cht.Interior.ColorIndex = 4
    End if
Next Cht
```

13

Coding Commands from the Design Tab

With charts in Excel 2010, there are three levels of chart changes that correspond to the three Chart Tools tabs. The global chart settings— chart type and style—are on the Design tab. Selections from the built-in element settings appear on the Layout tab. You make micro-changes by using the Format tab. This section deals with changes on the Design tab.

Specifying a Built-In Chart Type

There are 73 built-in chart types in Excel 2010. To change a chart to one of the 73 types, you use the ChartType property. This property can either be applied to a chart or to a series within a chart. Here's an example that changes the type for the entire chart:

```
ActiveChart.ChartType = xlBubble
```

To change the second series on a chart to a line chart, you use this:

```
ActiveChart.Series(2).ChartType = xlLine
```

Table 13.1 lists the 73 chart type constants that you can use to create various charts. The sequence of Table 13.1 matches the sequence of the charts in the Chart Type dialog.

Table 13.1   Chart Types for Use in VBA

Chart Type Constant	Chart TypeConstant
Clustered Column	xlColumnClustered
Stacked Column	xlColumnStacked
100% Stacked Column	xlColumnStacked100
3-D Clustered Column	xl3DColumnClustered
Stacked Column in 3-D	xl3DColumnStacked
100% Stacked Column in 3-D	xl3DColumn Stacked100
3-D Column	xl3DColumn
Clustered Cylinder	xlCylinder ColClustered
Stacked Cylinder	xlCylinderColStacked
100% Stacked Cylinder	xlCylinderColStacked100
3-D Cylinder	xlCylinderCol
Clustered Cone	xlConeColClustered
Stacked Cone	xlConeColStacked
100% Stacked Cone	xlConeColStacked100
3-D Cone	xlConeCol
Clustered Pyramid	xlPyramidColClustered
Stacked Pyramid	xlPyramidColStacked

Chart Type Constant	Chart TypeConstant
100% Stacked Pyramid	xlPyramidColStacked100
3-D Pyramid	xlPyramidCol
Line	xlLine
Stacked Line	xlLineStacked
100% Stacked Line	xlLineStacked100
Line with Markers	xlLineMarkers
Stacked Line with Markers	xlLineMarkersStacked
100% Stacked Line with Markers	xlLineMarkersStacked100
3-D Line	xl3DLine
Pie	xlPie
Pie in 3-D	xl3DPie
Pie of Pie	xlPieOfPie
Exploded Pie	xlPieExploded
Exploded Pie in 3-D	xl3DPieExploded
Bar of Pie	xlBarOfPie
Clustered Bar	xlBarClustered
Stacked Bar	xlBarStacked
100% Stacked Bar	xlBarStacked100
Clustered Bar in 3-D	xl3DBarClustered
Stacked Bar in 3-D	xl3DBarStacked
100% Stacked Bar in 3-D	xl3DBarStacked100
Clustered Horizontal Cylinder	xlCylinderBarClustered
Stacked Horizontal Cylinder	xlCylinderBarStacked
100% Stacked Horizontal Cylinder	xlCylinderBarStacked100
Clustered Horizontal Cone	xlConeBarClustered
Stacked Horizontal Cone	xlConeBarStacked
100% Stacked Horizontal Cone	xlConeBarStacked100
Clustered Horizontal Pyramid	xlPyramidBarClustered
Stacked Horizontal Pyramid	xlPyramidBarStacked
100% Stacked Horizontal Pyramid	xlPyramidBarStacked100
Area	xlArea
Stacked Area	xlAreaStacked
100% Stacked Area	xlAreaStacked100

13

Chart Type Constant	Chart TypeConstant
3-D Area	xl3DArea
Stacked Area in 3-D	xl3DAreaStacked
100% Stacked Area in 3-D	xl3DAreaStacked100
Scatter with Only Markers	xlXYScatter
Scatter with Smooth Lines and Markers	xlXYScatterSmooth
Scatter with Smooth Lines	xlXYScatterSmoothNoMarkers
Scatter with Straight Lines and Markers	xlXYScatterLines
Scatter with Straight Lines	xlXYScatterLinesNoMarkers
High-Low-Close	xlStockHLC
Open-High-Low-Close	xlStockOHLC
Volume-High-Low-Close	xlStockVHLC
Volume-Open-High-Low-Close	xlStockVOHLC
3-D Surface	xlSurface
Wireframe 3-D Surface	xlSurfaceWireframe
Contour	xlSurfaceTopView
Wireframe Contour	xlSurfaceTopViewWireframe
Doughnut	xlDoughnut
Exploded Doughnut	xlDoughnutExploded
Bubble	xlBubble
Bubble with a 3-D Effect	xlBubble3DEffect
Radar	xlRadar
Radar with Markers	xlRadarMarkers
Filled Radar	xlRadarFilled

Specifying a Template Chart Type

In "Creating a Chart Template" in Chapter 2, "Customizing Charts," you learned how to create a custom chart template. This is a great technique for saving time when you are creating a chart with a lot of custom formatting.

A VBA macro can make use of a custom chart template, provided that you plan on distributing the custom chart template to each person who will run your macro.

In Excel 2010, you save custom chart types as CRTX files and stored them in the %appdata%\Microsoft\Templates\Charts\ folder.

To apply a custom chart type, you use the following:

```
ActiveChart.ApplyChartTemplate "MyChart.crtx"
```

If the chart template does not exist, VBA returns an error. If you would like Excel to simply continue without displaying a debug error, you can turn on an error handler before the code and turn it back on when you are done. Here's how you do that:

```
On Error Resume Next
ActiveChart.ApplyChartTemplate ("MyChart.crtx")
On Error GoTo 0 ' that final character is a zero
```

Changing a Chart's Layout or Style

Two galleries—the Chart Layout gallery and the Styles gallery—make up the bulk of the Design tab.

The Chart Layout gallery offers from 4 to 12 combinations of chart elements. These combinations are different for various chart types. When you look at the gallery shown in Figure 13.5, the ToolTips for the layouts show that the layouts are imaginatively named Layout 1 through Layout 10.

Figure 13.5
The built-in layouts for bar charts are numbered 1 through 10. For other chart types, you might have 4 to 12 layouts.

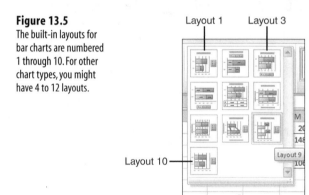

To apply one of the built-in layouts in a macro, you have to use the `ApplyLayout` method with a number from 1 through 12 to correspond to the built-in layouts. The following code will apply Layout 1 to the active chart:

```
ActiveChart.ApplyLayout 1
```

> **CAUTION**
>
> While line charts offer 12 built-in layouts, other types such as radar charts offer as few as four built-in layouts. If you attempt to specify apply a layout number that is larger than the layouts available for the current chart type, Excel will return a runtime error 5. Unless you just created the active chart in the same macro, there is always the possibility that the person running the macro changed your line charts to radar charts, so include some error handling before you use the `ApplyLayout` command.

13

Clearly, to effectively use a built-in layout, you must have actually built a chart by hand and found a layout that you actually like.

As shown in Figure 13.6, the Styles gallery contains 48 styles. These layouts are also numbered sequentially, with Styles 1 through 8 in Row 1, Styles 9 through 16 in Row 2, and so on. These styles actually follow a bit of a pattern:

Figure 13.6
The built-in styles are numbered 1 through 48.

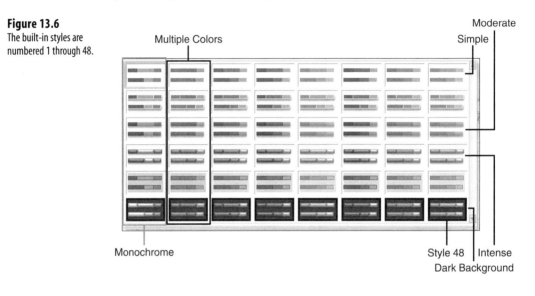

- Styles 1, 9, 17, 25, 33, and 41 (that is, the styles in column 1) are monochrome.
- Styles 2, 10, 18, 26, 34, and 42 (that is, the styles in column 2) use different colors for each point.
- All the other styles use hues of a particular theme color.
- Styles 1 through 8 use simple effects.
- Styles 9 through 17 use moderate effects.
- Styles 33 through 40 use intense effects.
- Styles 41 through 48 appear on a dark background.

If you are going to mix styles in a single workbook, you should consider staying within a single row or a single column of the gallery.

To apply a style to a chart, you use the `ChartStyle` property, assigning it a value from 1 to 48:

```
ActiveChart.ChartStyle = 1
```

The `ChartStyle` property changes the colors in the chart. However, a number of formatting changes from the Format tab do not get overwritten when you change the `ChartStyle` property. For example, in Figure 13.7, the second series previously had a glow applied and the third series had a clear glass bevel applied. Running the preceding code did not clear that formatting.

Figure 13.7
Setting the
`ChartStyle` property
does not override all
settings.

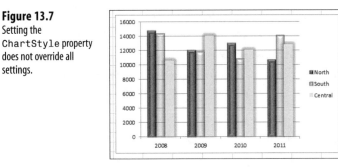

To clear any previous formatting, you use the `ClearToMatchStyle` method:

```
ActiveChart.ChartStyle = 1
ActiveChart.ClearToMatchStyle
```

Using SetElement to Emulate Changes on the Layout Tab

As discussed in Chapter 2, the Layout tab contains a number of built-in settings. Figure 13.8 shows a few of the built-in menu items for the Legend tab. There are similar menus for each of the icons in the figure.

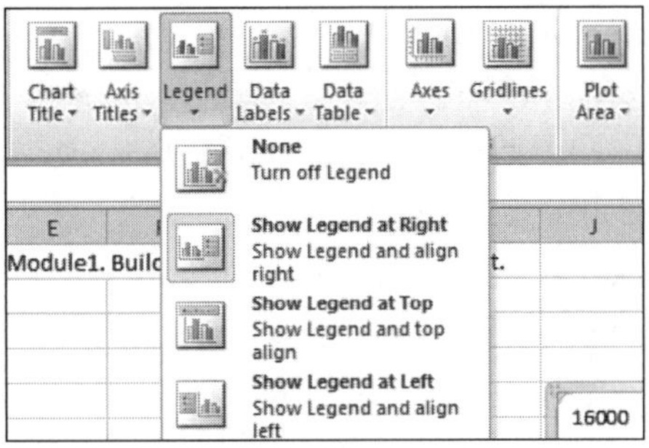

Figure 13.8
There are built-in menus similar to this one for each icon. If your choice is in the menu, the VBA code uses the `SetElement` method.

If you use a built-in menu item to change the titles, legend, labels, axes, gridlines, or background, it is probably handled in code that uses the `SetElement` method, which is new in Excel 2010.

`SetElement` does not work with the More choices at the bottom of each menu. It also does not work with the 3-D Rotation button. Other than that, you can use `SetElement` to change everything in the Labels, Axes, Background, and Analysis groups.

The macro recorder always works for the built-in settings on the Layout tab. If you don't feel like looking up the proper constant in this book, you can always quickly record a macro.

13

The `SetElement` method is followed by a constant that specifies which menu item to select. For example, if you want to choose Show Legend at Left, you can use this code:

```
ActiveChart.SetElement msoElementLegendLeft
```

Table 13.2 shows all the available constants that you can use with the `SetElement` method. These are in roughly the same order as they appear on the Layout tab.

Table 13.2   Constants Available with SetElement

Layout Tab Icon	Chart Element Constant
Chart Title	msoElementChartTitleNone
Chart Title	msoElementChartTitleCenteredOverlay
Chart Title	msoElementChartTitleAboveChart
Axis Titles	msoElementPrimaryCategoryAxisTitleNone
Axis Titles	msoElementPrimaryCategoryAxisTitleBelowAxis
Axis Titles	msoElementPrimaryCategoryAxisTitleAdjacentToAxis
Axis Titles	msoElementPrimaryCategoryAxisTitleHorizontal
Axis Titles	msoElementPrimaryCategoryAxisTitleVertical
Axis Titles	msoElementPrimaryCategoryAxisTitleRotated
Axis Titles	msoElementSecondaryCategoryAxisTitleAdjacentToAxis
Axis Titles	msoElementSecondaryCategoryAxisTitleBelowAxis
Axis Titles	msoElementSecondaryCategoryAxisTitleHorizontal
Axis Titles	msoElementSecondaryCategoryAxisTitleNone
Axis Titles	msoElementSecondaryCategoryAxisTitleRotated
Axis Titles	msoElementSecondaryCategoryAxisTitleVertical
Axis Titles	msoElementPrimaryValueAxisTitleAdjacentToAxis
Axis Titles	msoElementPrimaryValueAxisTitleBelowAxis
Axis Titles	msoElementPrimaryValueAxisTitleHorizontal
Axis Titles	msoElementPrimaryValueAxisTitleNone
Axis Titles	msoElementPrimaryValueAxisTitleRotated
Axis Titles	msoElementPrimaryValueAxisTitleVertical
Axis Titles	msoElementSecondaryValueAxisTitleBelowAxis
Axis Titles	msoElementSecondaryValueAxisTitleHorizontal
Axis Titles	msoElementSecondaryValueAxisTitleNone
Axis Titles	msoElementSecondaryValueAxisTitleRotated
Axis Titles	msoElementSecondaryValueAxisTitleVertical
Axis Titles	msoElementSeriesAxisTitleHorizontaI

Layout Tab Icon	Chart Element Constant
Axis Titles	`msoElementSeriesAxisTitleNone`
Axis Titles	`msoElementSeriesAxisTitleRotated`
Axis Titles	`msoElementSeriesAxisTitleVertical`
Axis Titles	`msoElementSecondaryValueAxisTitleAdjacentToAxis`
Legend	`msoElementLegendNone`
Legend	`msoElementLegendRight`
Legend	`msoElementLegendTop`
Legend	`msoElementLegendLeft`
Legend	`msoElementLegendBottom`
Legend	`msoElementLegendRightOverlay`
Legend	`msoElementLegendLeftOverlay`
Data Labels	`msoElementDataLabelCenter`
Data Labels	`msoElementDataLabelInsideEnd`
Data Labels	`msoElementDataLabelNone`
Data Labels	`msoElementDataLabelInsideBase`
Data Labels	`msoElementDataLabelOutSideEnd`
Data Labels	`msoElementDataLabelTop`
Data Labels	`msoElementDataLabelBottom`
Data Labels	`msoElementDataLabelRight`
Data Labels	`msoElementDataLabelLeft`
Data Labels	`msoElementDataLabelShow`
Data Labels	`msoElementDataLabelBestFit`
Data Labels	`msoElementDataTableNone`
Data Labels	`msoElementDataTableShow`
Data Labels	`msoElementDataTableWithLegendKeys`
Axis	`msoElementPrimaryCategoryAxisNone`
Axis	`msoElementPrimaryCategoryAxisShow`
Axis	`msoElementPrimaryCategoryAxisWithoutLabels`
Axis	`msoElementPrimaryCategoryAxisReverse`
Axis	`msoElementPrimaryCategoryAxisThousands`
Axis	`msoElementPrimaryCategoryAxisMillions`
Axis	`msoElementPrimaryCategoryAxisBillions`
Axis	`msoElementPrimaryCategoryAxisLogScale`

13

Layout Tab Icon	Chart Element Constant
Axis	msoElementSecondaryCategoryAxisNone
Axis	msoElementSecondaryCategoryAxisShow
Axis	msoElementSecondaryCategoryAxisWithoutLabels
Axis	msoElementSecondaryCategoryAxisReverse
Axis	msoElementSecondaryCategoryAxisThousands
Axis	msoElementSecondaryCategoryAxisMillions
Axis	msoElementSecondaryCategoryAxisBillions
Axis	msoElementSecondaryCategoryAxisLogScale
Axis	msoElementPrimaryValueAxisNone
Axis	msoElementPrimaryValueAxisShow
Axis	msoElementPrimaryValueAxisThousands
Axis	msoElementPrimaryValueAxisMillions
Axis	msoElementPrimaryValueAxisBillions
Axis	msoElementPrimaryValueAxisLogScale
Axis	msoElementSecondaryValueAxisNone
Axis	msoElementSecondaryValueAxisShow
Axis	msoElementSecondaryValueAxisThousands
Axis	msoElementSecondaryValueAxisMillions
Axis	msoElementSecondaryValueAxisBillions
Axis	msoElementSecondaryValueAxisLogScale
Axis	msoElementSeriesAxisNone
Axis	msoElementSeriesAxisShow
Axis	msoElementSeriesAxisReverse
Axis	msoElementSeriesAxisWithoutLabeling
GridLines	msoElementPrimaryCategoryGridLinesNone
GridLines	msoElementPrimaryCategoryGridLinesMajor
GridLines	msoElementPrimaryCategoryGridLinesMinor
GridLines	msoElementPrimaryCategoryGridLinesMinorMajor
GridLines	msoElementSecondaryCategoryGridLinesNone
GridLines	msoElementSecondaryCategoryGridLinesMajor
GridLines	msoElementSecondaryCategoryGridLinesMinor
GridLines	msoElementSecondaryCategoryGridLinesMinorMajor
GridLines	msoElementPrimaryValueGridLinesNone

13

Layout Tab Icon	Chart Element Constant
GridLines	`msoElementPrimaryValueGridLinesMajor`
GridLines	`msoElementPrimaryValueGridLinesMinor`
GridLines	`msoElementPrimaryValueGridLinesMinorMajor`
GridLines	`msoElementSecondaryValueGridLinesNone`
GridLines	`msoElementSecondaryValueGridLinesMajor`
GridLines	`msoElementSecondaryValueGridLinesMinor`
GridLines	`msoElementSecondaryValueGridLinesMinorMajor`
GridLines	`msoElementSeriesAxisGridLinesNone`
GridLines	`msoElementSeriesAxisGridLinesMajor`
GridLines	`msoElementSeriesAxisGridLinesMinor`
GridLines	`msoElementSeriesAxisGridLinesMinorMajor`
Plot Area	`msoElementPlotAreaNone`
Plot Area	`msoElementPlotAreaShow`
Chart Wall	`msoElementChartWallNone`
Chart Wall	`msoElementChartWallShow`
Chart Floor	`msoElementChartFloorNone`
Chart Floor	`msoElementChartFloorShow`
Trendline	`msoElementTrendlineNone`
Trendline	`msoElementTrendlineAddLinear`
Trendline	`msoElementTrendlineAddExponential`
Trendline	`msoElementTrendlineAddLinearForecast`
Trendline	`msoElementTrendlineAddTwoPeriodMovingAverage`
Lines	`msoElementLineNone`
Lines	`msoElementLineDropLine`
Lines	`msoElementLineHiLoLine`
Lines	`msoElementLineDropHiLoLine`
Lines	`msoElementLineSeriesLine`
Up/Down Bars	`msoElementUpDownBarsNone`
Up/Down Bars	`msoElementUpDownBarsShow`
Error Bar	`msoElementErrorBarNone`
Error Bar	`msoElementErrorBarStandardError`
Error Bar	`msoElementErrorBarPercentage`
Error Bar	`msoElementErrorBarStandardDeviation`

13

> ┌ C A U T I O N ───
> If you attempt to format an element that is not present, Excel returns a -2147467259 Method Failed
> error.

Changing a Chart Title Using VBA

The Layout tab's built-in menus let you add a title above a chart, but they don't offer you
the ability to change the characters in a chart title or axis title.

In the user interface, you can simply double-click the chart title text and type a new title to
change the title. Unfortunately, the macro recorder does not record this action.

To specify a chart title, you must type this code:

```
ActiveChart.ChartTitle.Caption = "My Chart"
```

Similarly, you can specify the axis titles by using the `Caption` property. The following code
will change the axis title along the category axis:

```
ActiveChart.Axes(xlCategory, xlPrimary).AxisTitle.Caption = "Months"
```

Emulating Changes on the Format Tab

The Format tab offers many new options for formatting such as Glow, Reflection, and
Soft Edge. To handle all of these new formats, Microsoft introduced the ChartFormat
object.

When the ChartFormat was introduced in Excel 2007, the macro recorder would not
record changes on the Format tab, making it tough to figure out how to write code to
implementthe new formatting. This gap in the macro recorder has been fixed in
Excel 2010.

Using the `Format` Method to Access New Formatting Options

Excel 2010 introduces a new object called the `ChartFormat` object. This object contains the
settings for `Fill`, `Glow`, `Line`, `PictureFormat`, `Shadow`, `SoftEdge`, `TextFrame2`, and `ThreeD`.
You can access the `ChartFormat` object by using the `Format` method on many chart elements. Table 13.3 lists a sampling of chart elements that can be formatted using the `Format`
method.

The `Format` method is the gateway to settings for `Fill`, `Glow`, and so on. Each of those
objects has different options. The following sections give examples of how to set up each
type of format.

Table 13.3 Chart Elements to Which Formatting Applies

Chart Element	VBA to Refer to This Chart Element
Chart Title	`ChartTitle`
Axis Title - Category	`Axes(xlCategory, xlPrimary).AxisTitle`
Axis Title - Value	`Axes(xlValue, xlPrimary).AxisTitle`
Legend Legend	
Data Labels for Series 1	`SeriesCollection(1).DataLabels`
Data Labels for Point 2	`SeriesCollection(1).DataLabel(2), or` `SeriesCollection(1).Points(2).DataLabels`
Data Table	`DataTable`
Axes - Horizontal	`Axes(xlCategory, xlPrimary)`
Axes - Vertical	`Axes(xlValue, xlPrimary)`
Axis - Series	`Axes(xlSeries, xlPrimary) (Surface Charts Only)`
Major Gridlines	`Axes(xlValue, xlPrimary).MajorGridlines`
Minor Gridlines	`Axes(xlValue, xlPrimary).MinorGridlines`
Plot Area	`PlotArea`
Chart Area	`ChartArea`
Chart Wall	`Walls`
Chart Back Wall	`BackWall`
Chart Side Wall	`SideWall`
Chart Floor	`Floor`
Trendline for Series 1	`SeriesCollection(1).TrendLines(1)`
Droplines	`ChartGroups(1).DropLines`
Up/Down Bars	`ChartGroups(1).UpBars`
Error Bars	`SeriesCollection(1).ErrorBars`
Series(1)	`SeriesCollection(1)`
Series(1)	`DataPoint SeriesCollection(1).Points(3)`

Changing an Object's Fill

As shown in Figure 13.9, the Shape Fill drop-down on the Format tab allows you to choose a single color, a gradient, a picture, or a texture for the fill.

To apply a specific color, you can use the RGB (red, green, blue) setting. To create a color, you specify a value from 0 to 255 for levels of red, green, and blue. The following code applies a simple blue fill:

```
Dim cht As Chart
```

13

Figure 13.9
Fill options include a
solid color, a gradient, a
texture, or a picture.

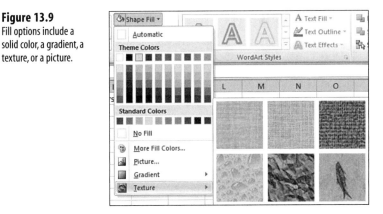

```
Dim upb As UpBars
Set cht = ActiveChart
Set upb = cht.ChartGroups(1).UpBars
upb.Format.Fill.ForeColor.RGB = RGB(0, 0, 255)
```

If you would like an object to pick up the color from a specific theme accent color, you use
the `ObjectThemeColor` property. The following code changes the bar color of the first series
to accent color 6 (which is an orange color in the Office theme but might be another color
if the workbook is using a different theme):

```
Sub ApplyThemeColor()
    Dim cht As Chart
    Dim ser As Series
    Set cht = ActiveChart
    Set ser = cht.SeriesCollection(1)
    ser.Format.Fill.ForeColor.ObjectThemeColor = msoThemeColorAccent6
End Sub
```

The standard color chooser drop-down in Excel offers six theme colors and then five variations of those colors ranging from light to dark. To lighten the theme color, use a positive
value between 0 and 1 for the `.TintAndShade` property:

```
ser.Format.Fill.ForeColor.ObjectThemeColor = msoThemeColorAccent6
ser.Format.Fill.ForeColor.TintAndShade = 0.2
```

To darken a color, choose a negative value between 0 and 1.

To apply a built-in texture, you use the `PresetTextured` method. The following code applies
a green marble texture to the second series, but there are 20 different textures that can be
applied:

```
Sub ApplyTexture()
    Dim cht As Chart
    Dim ser As Series
    Set cht = ActiveChart
    Set ser = cht.SeriesCollection(2)
    ser.Format.Fill.PresetTextured msoTextureGreenMarble
End Sub
```

To fill the bars of a data series with a picture, you use the `UserPicture` method and specify the path and filename of an image on the computer, as in the following example:

```
Sub FormatWithPicture()
    Dim cht As Chart
    Dim ser As Series
    Set cht = ActiveChart
    Set ser = cht.SeriesCollection(1)
    MyPic = "C:\dollarbills.jpg"
    ser.Format.Fill.UserPicture (MyPic)
End Sub
```

Microsoft had removed patterns as fills from Excel 2007. There was a lot of outcry from customers who used patterns to differentiate columns that were printed on monochrome printers. To apply a pattern, use the `.Patterned` method. Patterns have a type such as `msoPatternPlain` and also a foreground and background color. This code will create red dark vertical lines on a white background:

```
Sub FormatWithPicture()
    Dim cht As Chart
    Dim ser As Series
    Set cht = ActiveChart
    Set ser = cht.SeriesCollection(1)
    With ser.Format.Fill
        .Patterned msoPatternDarkVertical
        .BackColor.RGB = RGB(255,255,255)
        .ForeColor.RGB = RGB(255,0,0)
    End With
End Sub
```

CAUTION

Code that uses patterns will work in every version of Excel except Excel 2007. Do not use this code if you will be sharing the macro with co-workers who use Excel 2007.

Gradients are more difficult to specify than fills. Excel 2010 offers three methods that help you set up the common gradients. The `OneColorGradient` and `TwoColorGradient` methods require that you specify a gradient direction such as `msoGradientFromCorner`. You can then specify one of four styles, numbered 1 through 4, depending on whether you want the gradient to start at the top left, top right, bottom left, or bottom right. After using a gradient method, you need to specify the `ForeColor` and the `BackColor` settings for the object. The following macro sets up a two-color gradient using two theme colors:

```
Sub TwoColorGradient()
    Dim cht As Chart
    Dim ser As Series
    Set cht = ActiveChart
```

```
        Set ser = cht.SeriesCollection(1)
        MyPic = "C:\PodCastTitle1.jpg"
        ser.Format.Fill.TwoColorGradient msoGradientFromCorner, 3
        ser.Format.Fill.ForeColor.ObjectThemeColor = msoThemeColorAccent6
        ser.Format.Fill.BackColor.ObjectThemeColor = msoThemeColorAccent2
    End Sub
```

When using the `OneColorGradient` method, you specify a direction, a style (1 through 4), and a darkness value between 0 and 1 (0 for darker gradients or 1 for lighter gradients).

When using the `PresetGradient` method, you specify a direction, a style (1 through 4), and the type of gradient (for example, `msoGradientBrass`, `msoGradientLateSunset`, or `msoGradientRainbow`). Again, as you are typing this code in the VBA editor, the AutoComplete tool provides a complete list of the available preset gradient types.

Formatting Line Settings

The `LineFormat` object formats either a line or the border around an object. You can change numerous properties for a line, such as the color, arrows, dash style, and so on.

The following macro formats the trendline for the first series in a chart:

```
    Sub FormatLineOrBorders()
        Dim cht As Chart
        Set cht = ActiveChart
        With cht.SeriesCollection(1).Trendlines(1).Format.Line
            .DashStyle = msoLineLongDashDotDot
            .ForeColor.RGB = RGB(50, 0, 128)
            .BeginArrowheadLength = msoArrowheadShort
            .BeginArrowheadStyle = msoArrowheadOval
            .BeginArrowheadWidth = msoArrowheadNarrow
            .EndArrowheadLength = msoArrowheadLong
            .EndArrowheadStyle = msoArrowheadTriangle
            .EndArrowheadWidth = msoArrowheadWide
        End With
    End Sub
```

When you are formatting a border, the arrow settings are not relevant, so the code is shorter than the code for formatting a line. The following macro formats the border around a chart:

```
    Sub FormatBorder()
        Dim cht As Chart
        Set cht = ActiveChart
        With cht.ChartArea.Format.Line
            .DashStyle = msoLineLongDashDotDot
            .ForeColor.RGB = RGB(50, 0, 128)
        End With
    End Sub
```

Formatting Glow Settings

To create a glow, you have to specify a color and a radius. The radius value can be from 1 to 20. A radius of 1 is barely visible, and a radius of 20 is often way too thick.

A glow is actually applied to the shape outline. If you try to add a glow to an object where the outline is set to None, you cannot see the glow.

The following macro adds a line around the title and adds a glow around that line:

```
Sub AddGlowToTitle()
    Dim cht As Chart
    Set cht = ActiveChart
    cht.ChartTitle.Format.Line.ForeColor.RGB = RGB(255, 255, 255)
    cht.ChartTitle.Format.Line.DashStyle = msoLineSolid
    cht.ChartTitle.Format.Glow.Color.ObjectThemeColor = msoThemeColorAccent6
    cht.ChartTitle.Format.Glow.Radius = 8
End Sub
```

Formatting Shadow Settings

A shadow is composed of a color, a transparency, and the number of points by which the shadow should be offset from the object. If you increase the number of points, it appears that the object is farther from the surface of the chart. The horizontal offset is known as OffsetX, and the vertical offset is known as OffsetY.

The following macro adds a light blue shadow to the box surrounding a legend:

```
Sub FormatShadow()
    Dim cht As Chart
    Set cht = ActiveChart
    With cht.Legend.Format.Shadow
        .ForeColor.RGB = RGB(0, 0, 128)
        .OffsetX = 5
        .OffsetY = -3
        .Transparency = 0.5
        .Visible = True
    End With
End Sub
```

Formatting Reflection Settings

No chart elements can have reflections applied. The Reflection settings on the Format tab are constantly grayed out when a chart is selected. Similarly, the ChartFormat object does not have a reflection object.

Formatting Soft Edges

There are six levels of soft edge settings. The settings feather the edges by 1, 2.5, 5, 10, 25, or 50 points. The first setting is barely visible. The biggest settings are usually larger than most of the chart elements you are likely to format.

Microsoft says that the following is the proper syntax for SoftEdge:

```
Chart.Series(1).Points(i).Format.SoftEdge.Type = msoSoftEdgeType1
```

13

However, `msoSoftEdgeType1` and words like it are really variables defined by Excel. To try a cool trick, go to the VBA editor and open the Immediate pane by pressing Ctrl+G. In the Immediate pane, type `Print msoSoftEdgeType2` and press Enter. The Immediate window tells you that using this word is equivalent to typing 2. So, you could either use `msoSoftEdgeType2` or the value 2.

If you use `msoSoftEdgeType2`, your code will be slightly easier to understand than if you use simply 2. However, if you hope to format each point of a data series with a different format, you might want to use a loop such as this one, in which case it is far easier to use just the numbers 1 through 6 than `msoSoftEdgeType1` through `msoSoftEdgeType6`, as shown in this macro:

```
Sub FormatSoftEdgesWithLoop()
    Dim cht As Chart
    Dim ser As Series
    Set cht = ActiveChart
    Set ser = cht.SeriesCollection(1)
    For i = 1 To 6
        ser.Points(i).Format.SoftEdge.Type = i
    Next i
End Sub
```

> **CAUTION**
>
> It is a bit strange that the soft edges are defined as a fixed number of points. In a chart that is sized to fit an entire sheet of paper, a 10-point soft edge might work fine. However, if you resize the chart so that you can fit six charts on a page, a 10-point soft edge applied to all sides of a column might make the column completely disappear.

Formatting 3-D Rotation Settings

The 3-D settings handle three different menus on the Format tab. In the Shape Effects drop-down, settings under Preset, Bevel, and 3-D are all actually handled by the ThreeD object in the ChartFormat object. This section discusses settings that affect the 3-D rotation. The next section discusses settings that affect the bevel and 3-D format.

The methods and properties that can be set for the ThreeD object are very broad. In fact, the 3-D settings in VBA include more preset options than do the menus on the Format tab.

Figure 13.10 shows the presets available in the 3-D Rotation fly-out menu.

To apply one of the 3-D rotation presets to a chart element, you use the `SetPresetCamera` method, as shown here:

```
Sub Assign3DPreset()
    Dim cht As Chart
    Dim shp As Shape
    Set cht = ActiveChart
    Set shp = cht.Shapes(1)
    shp.ThreeD.SetPresetCamera msoCameraIsometricLeftDown
End Sub
```

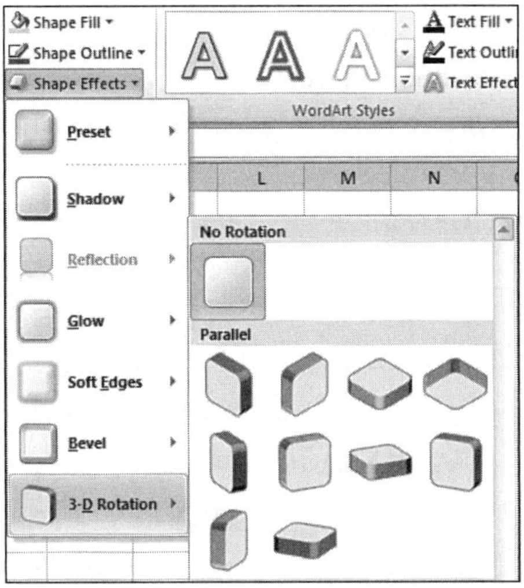

Figure 13.10
Whereas the 3-D Rotation menu offers 25 presets, VBA offers 62 presets.

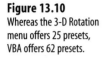

Table 13.4 lists all the possible SetPresetCamera values. If the first column indicates that it is a bonus or an Excel 2003 style, the value is a preset that is available in VBA but was not chosen by Microsoft to be included in the 3-D Rotation fly-out menu.

Table 13.4   3-D Preset Formats and Their VBA Constant Values

Menu Location	Description	VBA Value
Parallel group, row 1, column 1	Isometric Left Down	msoCameraIsometricLeftDown
Parallel group, row 1, column 2	Isometric Right Up	msoCameraIsometricRightUp
Parallel group, row 1, column 3	Isometric Top Up	msoCameraIsometricTopUp
Parallel group, row 1, column 4	Isometric Bottom Down	msoCameraIsometric BottomDown
Parallel group, row 2, column 1	Isometric OffAxis1 Left	msoCameraIsometric OffAxis1Left
Parallel group, row 2, column 2	Isometric OffAxis1 Right	msoCameraIsometric OffAxis1Right
Parallel group, row 2, column 3	Isometric OffAxis1 Top	msoCameraIsometric OffAxis1Top
Parallel group, row 2, column 4	Isometric OffAxis2 Left	msoCameraIsometric OffAxis2Left
Parallel group, row 3, column 1	Isometric OffAxis2 Right	msoCameraIsometric OffAxis2Right

13

Menu Location	Description	VBA Value
Parallel group, row 3, column 2	Isometric OffAxis2	`msoCameraIsometric`
	Top	`OffAxis2Top`
Parallel group, bonus selection	Isometric Bottom Up	`msoCameraIsometricBottomUp`
Parallel group, bonus selection	Isometric Left Up	`msoCameraIsometricLeftUp`
Parallel group, bonus selection	Isometric OffAxis3	`msoCameraIsometric`
	Bottom	`OffAxis3Bottom`
Parallel group, bonus selection	Isometric OffAxis3	`msoCameraIsometric`
	Left	`OffAxis3Left`
Parallel group, bonus selection	Isometric OffAxis3	`msoCameraIsometric`
	Right	`OffAxis3Right`
Parallel group, bonus selection	Isometric OffAxis4	`msoCameraIsometric`
	Bottom	`OffAxis4Bottom`
Parallel group, bonus selection	Isometric OffAxis4	`msoCameraIsometric`
	Left	`OffAxis4Left`
Parallel group, bonus selection	Isometric OffAxis4	`msoCameraIsometric`
	Right	`OffAxis4Right`
Parallel group, bonus selection	Isometric Right Down	`msoCameraIsometricRightDown`
Parallel group, bonus selection	Isometric Top Down	`msoCameraIsometricTopDown`
Perspective group, row 1, column 1	Perspective Front	`msoCameraPerspectiveFront`
Perspective group, row 1, column 2	Perspective Left	`msoCameraPerspectiveLeft`
Perspective group, row 1, column 3	Perspective Right	`msoCameraPerspectiveRight`
Perspective group, row 1, column 4	Perspective Below	`msoCameraPerspectiveBelow`
Perspective group, row 2, column 1	Perspective Above	`msoCameraPerspectiveAbove`
Perspective group, row 2, column 2	Perspective Relaxed	`msoCameraPerspective`
	Moderately	`RelaxedModerately`
Perspective group, row 2, column 3	Perspective Relaxed	`msoCameraPerspectiveRelaxed`
Perspective group, row 2, column 4	Perspective Contrasting	`msoCameraPerspective`
	Left Facing	`ContrastingLeftFacing`
Perspective group, row 3, column 1	Perspective Contrasting	`msoCameraPerspective`
	Right Facing	`ContrastingRightFacing`
Perspective group, row 3, column 2	Perspective Heroic	`msoCameraPerspective`
	Extreme Left Facing	`HeroicExtremeLeftFacing`
Perspective group, row 3, column 3	Perspective Heroic	`msoCameraPerspective`

13

Menu Location	Description	VBA Value
	Extreme Right Facing	HeroicExtremeRightFacing
Perspective group, bonus selection	Perspective Above	msoCameraPerspective
	Left Facing	AboveLeftFacing
Perspective group, bonus selection	Perspective Above	msoCameraPerspective
	Right Facing	AboveRightFacing
Perspective group, bonus selection	Perspective Heroic	msoCameraPerspective
	Left Facing	HeroicLeftFacing
Perspective group, bonus selection	Perspective Heroic	msoCameraPerspective
	Right Facing	HeroicRightFacing
Perspective group, Excel 2003 styles	Legacy Perspective	msoCameraLegacy
	Bottom	PerspectiveBottom
Perspective group, Excel 2003 styles	Legacy Perspective	msoCameraLegacy
	Lower Left	PerspectiveBottomLeft
Perspective group, Excel 2003 styles	Legacy Perspective	msoCameraLegacy
	Lower Right	PerspectiveBottomRight
Perspective group, Excel 2003 styles	Legacy Perspective	msoCameraLegacy
	Front	PerspectiveFront
Perspective group, Excel 2003 styles	Legacy Perspective Left	msoCameraLegacyPerspectiveLeft
Perspective group, Excel 2003 styles	Legacy Perspective	msoCameraLegacy
	Right	PerspectiveRight
Perspective group, Excel 2003 styles	Legacy Perspective Top	msoCameraLegacyPerspectiveTop
Perspective group, Excel 2003 styles	Legacy Perspective	msoCameraLegacy
	Upper Left	PerspectiveTopLeft
Perspective group, Excel 2003 styles	Legacy Perspective	msoCameraLegacy
	Upper Right	PerspectiveTopRight
Oblique group, row 1, column 1	Oblique Upper Left	msoCameraObliqueTopLeft
Oblique group, row 1, column 2	Oblique Upper Right	msoCameraObliqueTopRight
Oblique group, row 1, column 3	Oblique Lower Left	msoCameraObliqueBottomLeft
Oblique group, row 1, column 4	Oblique Lower Right	msoCameraObliqueBottomRight
Oblique group, bonus selection	Oblique Bottom	msoCameraObliqueBottom
Oblique group, bonus selection	Oblique Left	msoCameraObliqueLeft
Oblique group, bonus selection	Oblique Right	msoCameraObliqueRight
Oblique group, bonus selection	Oblique Top	msoCameraObliqueTop

13

Menu Location	Description	VBA Value
Oblique group, bonus selection	Orthographic Front	msoCameraOrthographicFront
Oblique group, Excel 2003 styles	Legacy Oblique Bottom	msoCameraLegacyObliqueBottom
Oblique group, Excel 2003 styles	Legacy Oblique	msoCameraLegacy
	Lower Left	ObliqueBottomLeft
Oblique group, Excel 2003 styles	Legacy Oblique	msoCameraLegacy
	Lower Right	ObliqueBottomRight
Oblique group, Excel 2003 styles	Legacy Oblique Front	msoCameraLegacyObliqueFront
Oblique group, Excel 2003 styles	Legacy Oblique Left	msoCameraLegacyObliqueLeft
Oblique group, Excel 2003 styles	Legacy Oblique Right	msoCameraLegacyObliqueRight
Oblique group, Excel 2003 styles	Legacy Oblique Top	msoCameraLegacyObliqueTop
Oblique group, Excel 2003 styles	Legacy Oblique	msoCameraLegacy
	Upper Left	ObliqueTopLeft
Oblique group, Excel 2003 styles	Legacy Oblique	msoCameraLegacy
	Upper Right	ObliqueTopRight

If you prefer not to use the presets, you can explicitly control the rotation around the x-, y-, or z-axis. You can use the following properties and methods to change the rotation of an object:

- RotationX—Returns or sets the rotation of the extruded shape around the x-axis, in degrees. This can be a value from -90 through 90. A positive value indicates upward rotation; a negative value indicates downward rotation.

- RotationY—Returns or sets the rotation of the extruded shape around the y-axis, in degrees. Can be a value from -90 through 90. A positive value indicates rotation to the left; a negative value indicates rotation to the right.

- RotationZ—Returns or sets the rotation of the extruded shape around the z-axis, in degrees. Can be a value from -90 through 90. A positive value indicates upward rotation; a negative value indicates downward rotation.

- IncrementRotationX—Changes the rotation of the specified shape around the x-axis by the specified number of degrees. You specify an increment from -90 to 90. Negative degrees tip the object down, and positive degrees tip the object up.

TIP   You can use the RotationX property to set the absolute rotation of the shape around the x-axis.

- `IncrementRotationY`—Changes the rotation of the specified shape around the y-axis by the specified number of degrees. A positive value tilts the object left, and a negative value tips the object right.

> **TIP** You can use the `RotationY` property to set the absolute rotation of the shape around the y-axis.

- `IncrementRotationZ`—Changes the rotation of the specified shape around the z-axis by the specified number of degrees. A positive value tilts the object left, and a negative value tips the object right.

> **TIP** You can use the `RotationZ` property to set the absolute rotation of the shape around the z-axis..

- `IncrementRotationHorizontal`—Changes the rotation of the specified shape horizontally by the specified number of degrees. You specify an increment from -90 to 90 to specify how much (in degrees) the rotation of the shape is to be changed horizontally. A positive value moves the shape left; a negative value moves it right.
- `IncrementRotationVertical`—Changes the rotation of the specified shape vertically by the specified number of degrees. You specify an increment from -90 to 90 to specify how much (in degrees) the rotation of the shape is to be changed horizontally. A positive value moves the shape left; a negative value moves it right.
- `ResetRotation`—Resets the extrusion rotation around the x-axis and the y-axis to 0 so that the front of the extrusion faces forward. This method doesn't reset the rotation around the z-axis.

Changing the Bevel and 3-D Format

There are 12 presets in the Bevel fly-out menu. These presets affect the bevel on the top face of the object. Usually in charts you see the top face; however, there are some bizarre rotations of a 3-D chart where you see the bottom face of charting elements.

The Format Data Series dialog contains the same 12 presets as the Bevel fly-out but allows you to apply the preset to the top or bottom face. You can also control the width and height of the bevel. The VBA properties and methods correspond to the settings on the 3-D Format category of the Format Data Series dialog (see Figure 13.11).

13

Figure 13.11
You can control the 3-D
Format settings, such
as bevel, surface, and
lighting.

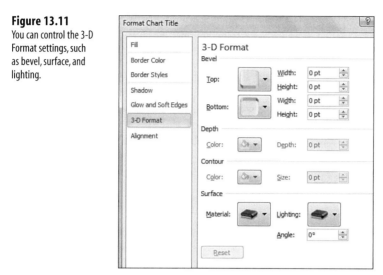

You set the type of bevel by using the `BevelTopType` and `BevelBottomType` properties. You can further modify the bevel type by setting the `BevelTopInset` value to set the width and the `BevelTopDepth` value to set the height. The following macro adds a bevel to the columns of Series 1:

```
Sub AssignBevel()
    Dim cht As Chart
    Dim ser As Series
    Set cht = ActiveChart
    Set ser = cht.SeriesCollection(1)
    ser.Format.ThreeD.Visible = True
    ser.Format.ThreeD.BevelTopType = msoBevelCircle
    ser.Format.ThreeD.BevelTopInset = 16
    ser.Format.ThreeD.BevelTopDepth = 6
End Sub
```

The 12 possible settings for the bevel type are shown in Table 13.5; these settings correspond to the thumbnails shown in Figure 13.12. To turn off the bevel, you use `msoBevel-None`.

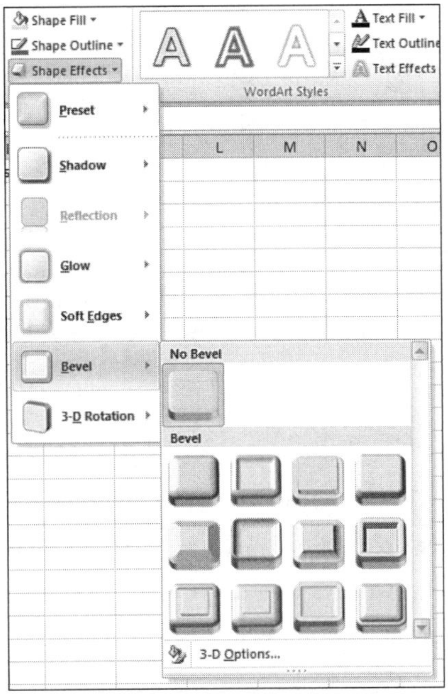

Figure 13.12
Samples of the 12 bevel types listed in Table 13.5.

Table 13.5 Bevel Types

Type	VBA Constant
Circle	msoBevelCircle
Relaxed Inset	msoBevelRelaxedInset
Cross	msoBevelCross
Cool Slant	msoBevelCoolSlant
Angle	msoBevelAngle
Soft Round	msoBevel1SoftRound
Convex	msoBevelConvex
Slope	msoBevelSlope
Divot	msoBevelDivot
Riblet	msoBevelRiblet
Hard Edge	msoBevelHardEdge
Art Deco	msoBevelArtDeco

13

Usually, the accent color used in a bevel is based on the color used to fill the object. If you would like control over the extrusion color, however, you first specify that the extrusion color type is custom and then specify either a theme accent color or an RGB color, as in the following example:

```
ser.Format.ThreeD.ExtrusionColorType = msoExtrusionColorCustom
' either use this:
ser.Format.ThreeD.ExtrusionColor.ObjectThemeColor = msoThemeColorAccent1
' or this:
ser.Format.ThreeD.ExtrusionColor.RGB = RGB(255, 0, 0)
```

You use the `Depth` property to control the amount of extrusion in the bevel, and you specify the depth in points. Here's an example:

```
ser.Format.ThreeD.Depth = 5
```

For the contour, you can specify either a color and a size of the contour or both. You can specify the color as an RGB value or a theme color. You specify the size in points, using the `ContourWidth` property. Here's an example:

```
ser.Format.ThreeD.ContourColor.RGB = RGB(0, 255, 0)
ser.Format.ThreeD.ContourWidth = 10
```

The Surface drop-downs are controlled by the following properties:

- `PresetMaterial`—This contains choices from the Material drop-down.
- `PresetLighting`—This contains choices from the Lighting drop-down.
- `LightAngle`—This controls the angle from which the light is shining on the object.

Figure 13.13 shows the Material drop-down menu from the 3-D category of the Format dialog box. Although the drop-down offers 11 settings, it appears that Microsoft designed a 12th setting in the object model. It is not clear why Microsoft does not offer the `SoftMetal` style in the dialog box, but you can use it in VBA. There are also three legacy styles in the object model that are not available in the Format dialog box. In theory, the new `Plastic2` material is better than the old `Plastic` material. The settings for each thumbnail are shown in Table 13.6.

Table 13.6   VBA Constants for Material Types

Type	VBA Constant	Value
Matte	msoMaterialMatte	25
Warm Matte	msoMaterialWarmMatte	8
Plastic	msoMaterialPlastic	26
Metal	msoMaterialMetal	27
Dark Edge	msoMaterialDarkEdge	11
Soft Edge	msoMaterialSoftEdge	12
Flat	msoMaterialFlat	14
Wire Frame	msoMaterialWireFrame	4

Type	VBA Constant	Value
Powder	msoMaterialPowder	10
Translucent Powder	msoMaterialTranslucentPowder	9
Clear	msoMaterialClear	13
Legacy	msoMaterialMatte	1
Legacy	msoMaterialPlastic	2
Legacy	msoMaterialMeta	13
Bonus	msoMaterialSoftMetal	15

Figure 13.13

Samples of the 11 material types shown in Table 13.6.

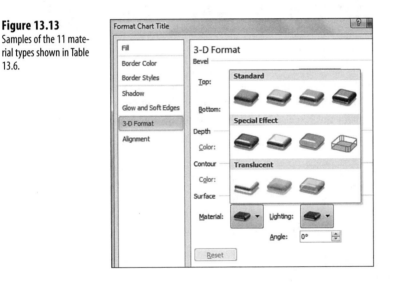

In Excel 2003, the material property was limited to matte, metal, plastic, and wire frame. Microsoft apparently was not happy with the old matte, metal, and plastic settings. It left those values in place to support legacy charts but created the new Matte2, Plastic2, and Metal2 settings. These settings are actually available in the dialog box.

In VBA, you are free to use either the old or the new settings. The columns in Figure 13.14 compare the new and old settings. The final column is for the SoftMetal setting that Microsoft left out of the Format dialog box. This was probably an aesthetic decision instead of an "oh no; this setting crashes the computer" decision. You can feel free to use msoMaterialSoftMetal to create a look that has a subtle difference from charts others create using the settings in the Format dialog box.

Figure 13.14
Comparison of some new
and old material presets.

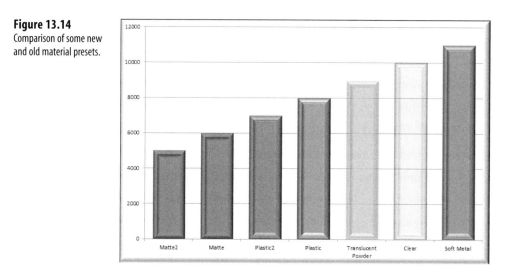

Figure 13.15 shows the Lighting drop-down menu from the 3-D category of the Format dialog box. The drop-down offers 15 settings. The Object Model offers these 15 settings, plus 13 legacy settings from the Excel 2003 Lighting toolbar. The settings for each of these thumbnails are shown in Table 13.7.

Figure 13.15
Samples of the 15 light-
ing types shown in Table
13.7.

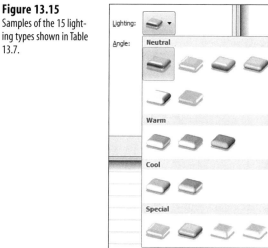

Table 13.7   VBA Constants for Lighting Types

Type	VBA Constant	Value
Neutral Category		
ThreePoint	msoLightRigThreePoint	13
Balanced	msoLightRigBalanced	14
Soft	msoLightRigSoft	15
Harsh	msoLightRigHarsh	16
Flood	msoLightRigFlood	17
Contrasting	msoLightRigContrasting	18
Warm Category		
Morning	msoLightRigMorning	19
Sunrise	msoLightRigSunrise	20
Sunset	msoLightRigSunset	21
Cool Category		
Chilly	msoLightRigChilly	22
Freezing	msoLightRigFreezing	23
Special Category		
Flat	msoLightRigFlat	24
TwoPoint	msoLightRigTwoPoint	25
Glow	msoLightRigGlow	26
BrightRoom	msoLightRigBrightRoom	27
Legacy Category		
Flat 1	msoLightRigLegacyFlat1	1
Flat 2	msoLightRigLegacyFlat2	2
Flat 3	msoLightRigLegacyFlat3	3
Flat 4	msoLightRigLegacyFlat4	4
Harsh 1	msoLightRigLegacyHarsh1	9
Harsh 2	msoLightRigLegacyHarsh2	10
Harsh 3	msoLightRigLegacyHarsh3	11
Harsh 4	msoLightRigLegacyHarsh4	12
Normal 1	msoLightRigLegacyNormal1	5
Normal 2	msoLightRigLegacyNormal2	6
Normal 3	msoLightRigLegacyNormal3	7
Normal 4	msoLightRigLegacyNormal4	8
Mixed	msoLightRigMixed	-2

13

Automating Changes in the Format Series Dialog

There is a huge gap in the Excel 2010 Ribbon interface. Somewhere between the global changes on the Design tab and the set element changes on the Layout tab, Microsoft offers no big icons to format the individual data series. Depending on the chart type, the Format Series dialog box holds special settings that can dramatically impact the look of your chart.

There are a few ways to access the Format Series dialog:

- Right-click a series in the chart and select Format Series from the context menu.

- From the first drop-down in either the Layout or Format tabs, choose the item that you want to format (for example, choose Series 1 from this drop-down to format Series 1). Then click the Format Selection button immediately below the drop-down.

The special settings appear in the Series Options category of the Format dialog box. The following are some of the settings you can control:

- **Gap Width and Separation**—Control whether the columns in a column chart should be touching each other, as in a histogram, or separated.

- **Plot on Second Axis**—Specifies that a series should be plotted on a secondary axis. This is useful when the magnitude of one series does not match the magnitude of another series.

- **Angle of First Slice**—Rotates pie and doughnut charts. Other settings for the round charts control features such as explosion and hole size.

- **Bar of Pie and Pie of Pie**—Control which categories appear in the secondary chart in these combination charts.

- **Bubble Size**—Controls how the bubbles are sized in a bubble chart.

- **Surface and Radar**—Control certain aspects of these chart types.

Understanding How Excel Groups Series into Chart Groups

Although you access many of the series settings in the Format Series dialog box, they actually apply globally to all the series in the chart that have the same chart type.

Say that you have built a chart where Series 1 and Series 2 are column charts and Series 3 is a line chart. If you format the gap width, the setting applies to both of the series that use the column chart type. In VBA, this object is represented by ChartGroup. Chart.ChartGroups(1) might apply to the column chart elements, and Chart. ChartGroups(2) might apply to the line chart elements. Because the groups can change when you change the chart type for a series, it is safer to use the built-in shortcut methods to select a particular group of series.

The macro recorder uses the relatively risky method of referring to the chart group by index number:

```
ActiveChart.ChartGroups(1).Overlap = 35
```

You could instead use the named shortcut method. Strangely, the shortcut still returns a collection of chart groups, so you still must specify the index number 1:

```
ActiveChart.ColumnGroups(1).Overlap = 35
```

This is inherently safer: Microsoft groups all the series that use column charts into a single chart group.

The shortcut methods available include `AreaGroups`, `BarGroups`, `ColumnGroups`, `DoughnutGroups`, `LineGroups`, and `PieGroups`.

The following sections discuss the various options you can control in the Series Options dialog.

Controlling Gap Width and Series Separation in Column and Bar Charts

Typically, the individual bars in a bar or column chart are separated by gaps. When scientists create histograms, they want to eliminate the gaps between bars.

Excel offers the `GapWidth` property, whose value can range from `0` to `500` to represent 0 percent to 500 percent. Figure 13.16 shows a typical chart and a chart where the gap width has been reduced to 25 percent.

Figure 13.16
In the bottom chart, the gap width has been reduced from the default to 25 percent.

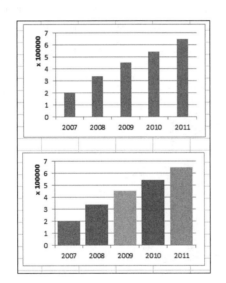

13

> **TIP**
> Note that reducing the gap size automatically makes the columns thicker. To keep the columns narrow, you should reduce the width of the chart.

The gap width setting applies to chart groups that contain bar or column markers. It can also be used to format the volume markers in volume-high-low-close charts or volume-open-high-low-close charts.

The following macro changes the gap width to 25 percent:

```
Sub FormatGapWidth()
    Dim cht As Chart
    Set cht = ActiveChart
    cht.ChartGroups(1).GapWidth = 25
    cht.ChartGroups(1).VaryByCategories = True
End Sub
```

> **TIP**
>
> The VaryByCategories property in the preceding code gives each column in a one-series chart a different color. This works for a pie, bar, or column chart with a single series. It is equivalent to selecting the Vary Colors By Point check box from the Fill category of the Format Data Series dialog.

When you create a clustered column chart with two series, the columns for each data point touch, as shown in the top chart in Figure 13.17. You can use the Overlap property to cause the columns to overlap. Values from 1 to 100 cause the columns to overlap anywhere from 1 percent to 100 percent. Values from -1 to -100 cause separations between the data points.

The middle chart in Figure 13.17 shows a 50 percent overlap. The bottom chart shows a −100 percent overlap.

Figure 13.17
The middle chart has an overlap, and the bottom chart has a negative overlap (that is, a separation).

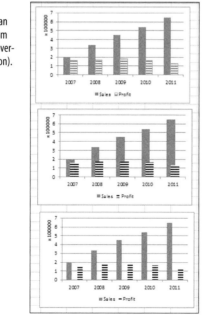

The following macro creates a 25 percent overlap between the series:

```
Sub FormatOverLap()
    Dim cht As Chart
    Set cht = ActiveChart
    cht.ChartGroups(1).Overlap = 25
End Sub
```

The `Overlap` property applies to clustered column and clustered bar charts. It should be set to 100 percent for the volume series in stock charts.

Moving a Series to a Secondary Axis

You might want to communicate data on a chart where the series are different orders of magnitude. In the top chart in Figure 13.18, the first two series represent sales and profit and show numbers in the hundreds of thousands. The third series is a profit percentage where the values are between 20 percent and 80 percent. When you plot these three series on a column chart, the columns for the profit percentage series will be so small that they will not be seen.

The solution is to plot the third series on a secondary axis. The left axis will continue to show hundreds of thousands, but the right axis scales to show percentages from 0 percent to 100 percent.

To move a series to the secondary axis, you use the `AxisGroup` property:

```
ActiveChart.SeriesCollection(3).AxisGroup = xlSecondary
```

Using a secondary axis solves one problem but introduces a new problem: How will the reader know that it is the profit percentage series which is plotted against the secondary axis? You can change the chart type of the third series from a column to a line. You can change the `ChartType` property for an individual series as follows:

```
ActiveChart.SeriesCollection(3).ChartType = xlLineMarkers
```

To further help the chart reader, you can change the font color of the tick labels for the secondary axis to match the line color of the third series. In the following macro, the font color for the secondary axis is changed to match the fill color of the third series (see the bottom chart in Figure 13.18):

```
Sub MoveToSecondaryAxis()
    Dim cht As Chart
    Dim ser As Series
    Dim ax As Axis
    Set cht = ActiveChart
    Set ser = cht.SeriesCollection(3)
    ser.AxisGroup = xlSecondary
    ser.ChartType = xlLineMarkers
    Set ax = cht.Axes(xlValue, xlSecondary)
    ax.TickLabels.Font.Color = ser.Format.Fill.ForeColor
End Sub
```

13

Unfortunately, this is a snapshot type of change. If you later change the theme or the color scheme of the chart, you have to change the tick label color to match the new Series 3 color.

Figure 13.18
In the top chart, the third series is too small to be seen. In the bottom chart, a secondary axis, a new chart type, and an axis font color solves many problems.

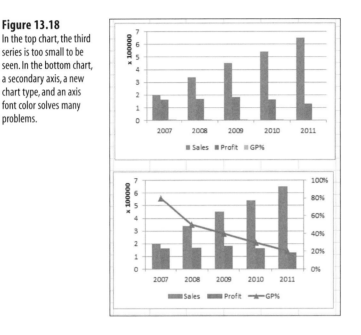

Spinning and Exploding Round Charts

Pie and doughnut charts have rotation and explosion properties. In a typical data series, there might be a few tiny pie slices at the end of the series. These pie slices typically appear in the back of the chart. If you move them around to the front of the chart, they are more visible, and there is more room for the data labels to appear outside the chart.

You control the angle of the first slice of a pie by using the `FirstSliceAngle` property of the `ChartGroup` object. Valid values range from `0` to `360`, representing rotations of 0 to 360 degrees. In the bottom-left chart in Figure 13.19, the original chart was rotated 159 degrees, using the following macro:

```
Sub RotateChart()
    ' Bottom Left Chart in Figure 13.19
    Dim cht As Chart
    Set cht = ActiveChart
    cht.ChartGroups(1).FirstSliceAngle = 159
End Sub
```

You can also explode pie and doughnut charts. In an exploded view, the individual wedges are separated from each other. You use the `Explosion` property to change the explosion effect. Valid values range from 0 to 400, representing 0 to 400 percent. With explosions, tiny values go a long way. The top-right chart in Figure 13.19 represents a 22 percent explosion and is created with this macro:

```
Sub ExplodeChart()
    ' Top Right Chart in Figure 13.19
    Dim cht As Chart
    Set cht = ActiveChart
    cht.ChartGroups(1).FirstSliceAngle = 159
    cht.ChartGroups(1).Explosion = 22
End Sub
```

Figure 13.19
You can rotate or explode pie charts to bring the small slices into view.

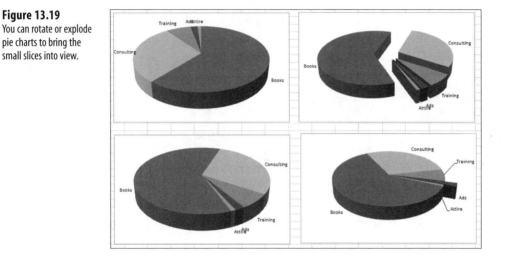

Sometimes, a better effect is to explode just a single slice of a pie. You can apply the Explosion property to a single data point. In the bottom-right chart in Figure 13.19, only the Ads slice is exploded. Note that the macro then adjusts the positioning of the adjoining data labels so that they can be seen around the exploded slice:

```
Sub ExplodeOneSlice()
    ' Bottom Right Chart in Figure 13.19
    Dim cht As Chart
    Dim ser As Series
    Dim poi As Point
    Dim dl As DataLabel
    Set cht = ActiveChart
    Set ser = cht.SeriesCollection(1)
    cht.ChartGroups(1).FirstSliceAngle = 114
    ' Explode one slice
    Set poi = ser.Points(4)
    poi.Explosion = 22
    ' fix the labels
    Set dl = ser.Points(3).DataLabel
    dl.Left = dl.Left + 30
    dl.Top = dl.Top - 50
    Set dl = ser.Points(5).DataLabel
    dl.Left = dl.Left + 10
    dl.Top = dl.Top + 20
End Sub
```

13

You can also control the hole size in the center of a doughnut chart. A typical doughnut chart starts out with a hole size that is 50 percent of the doughnut. You use the DoughnutHoleSize property to adjust this from 90 percent to 10 percent, using values of 90 to 10. The charts in Figure 13.20 show doughnut hole sizes of 70 percent on the top and 10 percent on the bottom. The following macro adjusts the doughnut hole size to 70 percent:

```
Sub ExplodeChart()
    Dim cht As Chart
    Set cht = ActiveChart
    cht.ChartGroups(1).DoughnutHoleSize = 70
End Sub
```

Figure 13.20
You can change the hole size in doughnut charts.

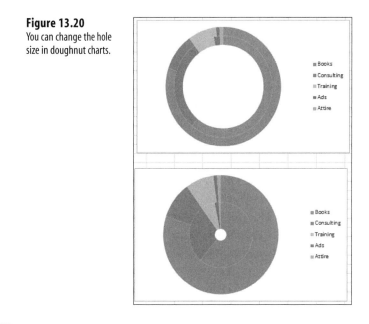

Controlling the Bar of Pie and Pie of Pie Charts

When your data contains many small pie slices and you care about the differences in those small slices, you can ask for the small slices to be plotted in a secondary pie or a secondary bar chart.

→ For complete details on these unique chart types, read "Using a Pie of Pie Chart" in Chapter 4. These chart types are found in the Pie category.

As these charts include two charts inside the chart area, Excel offers many additional settings for controlling the size and placement of each chart in relation to the other. There are also a myriad of ways to determine which pie wedges are represented in the secondary chart. You have complete control of these settings in VBA. You might consider the following:

- How do you decide which wedges are reported in the smaller pie? Excel offers choices to move the last *n* slices, move all slices smaller than *n* percent, or to move all slices smaller than a particular value. Excel also offers the custom method for moving the pie slices.

- Do you want leader lines from the "other" slice to the secondary plot? These are generally a good idea, but you can turn them off or even format them, if desired.

- How large should the secondary plot be compared to the first plot? Say that you are preparing charts for a meeting to discuss which product lines should be discontinued. In this case, the focus really is on the tiny wedges, and you might want to have the secondary plot be as large as or larger than the original pie.

- How wide should the gap be between the plots?

The following sections discuss how to adjust each of these settings with VBA.

Using a Rule to Determine Which Wedges Are in the Secondary Plot

Excel offers three built-in rules for determining which pie slices should be in the secondary plot. You can specify that all slices smaller than a certain percentage should be in the secondary plot, that all slices smaller than a certain value should be in the secondary plot, or even that the last n slices should be in the secondary plot.

You specify which of these rules to use with the `SplitType` property and then you specify a `SplitValue` setting to indicate where the split should occur.

In Figure 13.21, the top chart used Excel's defaults to show the last four points in the secondary plot. You could use any of these methods to create the bottom chart:

Figure 13.21
In the bottom chart, 80 percent of the slices appear in the secondary chart.

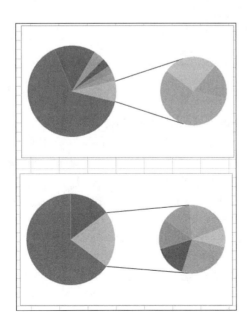

■ You could specify a split type of xlSplitByValue and then indicate that any values less than 10 should be in the secondary plot.

■ You could specify a split type of xlSplitByPercentValue and then indicate that any values less than 5 percent should be in the secondary plot.

■ You could specify a split type of xlSplitByPosition and then indicate that the last eight values should be in the secondary plot.

Any one of these three macros could be used to create the second chart in Figure 13.21:

```
Sub SmallerThan10ToPlot2()
    Dim cht As Chart
    Dim chtg As ChartGroup
    Set cht = ActiveChart
    Set chtg = cht.ChartGroups(1)
    ' Anything less than 10 to second group
    cht.ChartGroups(1).SplitType = xlSplitByValue
    ActiveChart.ChartGroups(1).SplitValue = 10
End Sub

Sub SmallerThan10PctToPlot2()
    Dim cht As Chart
    Dim chtg As ChartGroup
    Set cht = ActiveChart
    Set chtg = cht.ChartGroups(1)
    ' Anything less than 10% to 2nd plot
    chtg.SplitType = xlSplitByPercentValue
    chtg.SplitValue = 10
End Sub

Sub Last8ToPlot2()
    Dim cht As Chart
    Dim chtg As ChartGroup
    Set cht = ActiveChart
    Set chtg = cht.ChartGroups(1)
    ' Send last 8 slices to secondary plot
    chtg.SplitType = xlSplitByPosition
    chtg.SplitValue = 8
End Sub
```

Defining Specific Categories to Be in the Secondary Plot

You can choose to have complete control over which slices of a pie appear in a secondary chart. If you are trying to decide among three specific products to discontinue, for example, you can move all three of those products to the secondary pie.

To do this with a macro, you first set SplitType to xlSplitByCustomSplit. You can then use the SecondaryPlot property on individual data points. A value of 0 shows the data point in the left pie. A value of 1 sends the data point to the secondary pie.

Because you aren't sure how many items Excel will send to the secondary pie by default, you can write a macro such as the following to first loop through all data points and reset them to the primary pie, and then move three specific slices to the secondary pie:

```
Sub CustomPieofPie()
    Dim cht As Chart
    Dim chtg As ChartGroup
    Dim ser As Series
    Dim poi As Point
    Set cht = ActiveChart
    Set chtg = cht.ChartGroups(1)
    Set ser = cht.SeriesCollection(1)
    chtg.SplitType = xlSplitByCustomSplit
    ' Move all slices to first plot
    For Each poi In ser.Points
        poi.SecondaryPlot = 0
    Next poi
    ' Move points 1, 6, 10 to secondary plot
    ser.Points(2).SecondaryPlot = 1
    ser.Points(6).SecondaryPlot = 1
    ser.Points(10).SecondaryPlot = 1
End Sub
```

Figure 13.22 shows the results. This figure shows a bar of pie chart with three specific wedges moved to the secondary plot.

Figure 13.22
Instead of focusing on the smallest slices, this bar of pie chart focuses on three particular products.

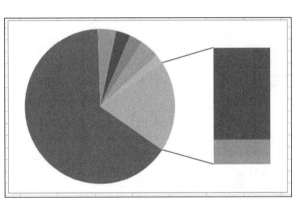

Controlling the Gap, Size, and Lines of a Secondary Plot

You adjust the gap between an original pie and a secondary plot by using the GapWidth property, whose values range from 0 to 500. In Figure 13.23, the bottom chart has a gap of 500, and the middle chart has a gap of 0.

You can turn on or off the two leader lines extending from the main pie to the secondary plot by setting the `HasSeriesLines` property to `True` or `False`. To format those lines, you use the `Format` property of the `SeriesLines` object. The following macro moves the secondary plot to the maximum distance and changes the series lines to a dash/dot style:

```
Sub MindTheGap()
    Dim chtg As ChartGroup
    Set chtg = ActiveChart.ChartGroups(1)
    chtg.GapWidth = 500
    chtg.HasSeriesLines = True
    chtg.SeriesLines.Format.Line.DashStyle = msoLineDashDot
End Sub
```

The size of the secondary plot usually starts off at 75 percent of the original pie. You can use the SecondPlotSize property to change the plot size from 5 to 200, representing 5 percent to 200 percent of the original pie chart. Figure 13.24 shows charts with secondary plot sizes of 75 percent, 5 percent, and 200 percent.

Figure 13.23
You use the GapWidth property to move the secondary plot closer to or farther from the main pie.

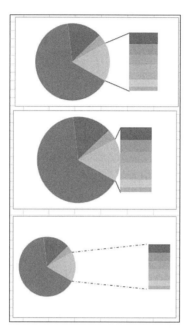

Figure 13.24
You can shift the focus toward or away from the secondary plot by adjusting its size.

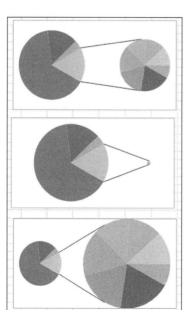

13

The following macro adjusts the size of the secondary plot to 50 percent of the size of the main pie:

```
Sub ChangeSize()
    Dim chtg As ChartGroup
    Set chtg = ActiveChart.ChartGroups(1)
    chtg.SecondPlotSize = 50
End Sub
```

Setting the Bubble Size

The bubble chart type includes an incredibly misleading setting that you should always avoid. A bubble chart places circles at particular x and y coordinates. The sizes of the circles are determined by the values specified in the third column of the data series.

By default, Excel scales the size of the circle so that the area of the circle is proportionate to the data. This is an appropriate choice. However, you can override this setting to say that the size represents the width of the circle. This always results in a misleading chart.

For example, in the upper-left chart in Figure 13.25, the smallest circle has a value of 1, and the largest circle has a value of 4. Because this chart uses the xlSizeIsArea setting, the bottom-left circle is four times larger than the top-right circle. The bottom-left chart plots the same data but uses the xlSizeIsWidth setting. With this setting, your circles will be completely out of scale.

Figure 13.25
The bottom-left chart uses xlSizeIsWidth and is misleading. The bottom-right chart shows a negative-sized circle, represented by a circle with no fill.

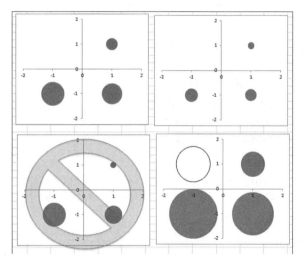

A circle with a width of 1 inch has an area of 0.785 square inches, according to =PI()*(1/2)^2. A circle with a width of 4 inches has an area of 12.56 square inches, according to =PI()*(4/2)^2. This means that with the xlSizeIsWidth setting, the bottom-left circle is 16 times larger than the top-right circle.

> **NOTE**
>
> It is strange that Excel even offers the `xlSizeIsWidth` setting. Microsoft makes sure to avoid the mistake of resizing markers in two dimensions when dealing with bar or column charts.

You can also choose to scale the circles from 0 to 300 percent by changing the `BubbleScale` property from `0` to `300`. The top-left chart in Figure 13.25 has a 100 percent scale. The top-right chart uses a 50 percent scale. The bottom-right chart uses a 300 percent scale.

Finally, you can specify whether Excel should show negative-sized circles on a chart. In the lower-right chart in Figure 13.25, the –2 in the upper quadrant is represented by a circle with a white fill instead of a circle with a blue fill.

The following macro demonstrates some of the settings available for bubble charts:

```
Sub BubbleSettings()
    Dim chtg As ChartGroup
    Set chtg = ActiveChart.ChartGroups(1)
    ' Never use the following setting
    ' chtg.SizeRepresents = xlSizeIsWidth
    chtg.SizeRepresents = xlSizeIsArea
    chtg.BubbleScale = 50
    chtg.ShowNegativeBubbles = True
End Sub
```

> **NOTE**
>
> You might not be able to see it in this monochrome book, but you can download the project files from http://www.mrexcel.com/chart2010data.html to see the effect in color.

Controlling Radar and Surface Charts

A couple minor settings affect surface charts and radar charts. A default surface chart uses contour shading within each color band to give a 3-D feeling. You can turn this off in a surface chart by using the `Has3DShading` property. In Figure 13.26, the bottom-left chart has the shading turned off.

Radar charts typically have the name of each category at the end of the axis. You can turn this off by setting the `HasRadarAxisLabels` property to `False`. The bottom-right chart in Figure 13.26 shows this setting.

The code for turning off the `Has3DShading` and `HasRadarAxisLabels` properties follows:

```
Sub FormatSurface()
    Dim chtg As ChartGroup
    Set chtg = ActiveChart.ChartGroups(1)
    chtg.Has3DShading = False
End Sub
Sub FormatRadar()
    Dim chtg As ChartGroup
    Set chtg = ActiveChart.ChartGroups(1)
    chtg.HasRadarAxisLabels = False
End Sub
```

Figure 13.26
The bottom charts reflect removing the 3-D contour (left) and radar axis labels (right).

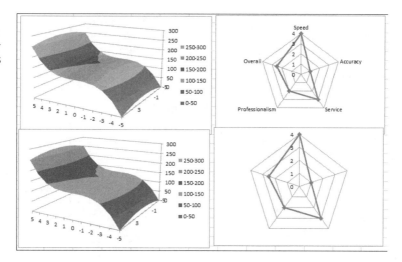

Exporting a Chart as a Graphic

You can export any chart to an image file on your hard drive. The ExportChart method requires you to specify a filename and a graphic type. The available graphic types depend on graphic file filters installed in your Registry. It is a safe bet that JPG, BMP, PNG, and GIF will work on most computers.

For example, the following code exports the active chart as a GIF file:

```
Sub ExportChart()
    Dim cht As Chart
    Set cht = ActiveChart
    cht.Export Filename:="C:\Chart.gif", Filtername:="GIF"
End Sub
```

> **CAUTION**
>
> Since Excel 2003, Microsoft has supported an Interactive argument in the Export method. Excel help indicates that if you set Interactive to TRUE, then Excel asks for additional settings depending on the file type. However, the dialog to ask for additional settings never appears, at least not for the four standard types of JPG, GIF, BMP, or PNG.

Creating a Dynamic Chart in a UserForm

With the ability to export a chart to a graphic file, you also have the ability to load a graphic file into an Image control in a UserForm. This means you can create a dialog box in which someone can dynamically control values used to plot a chart.

To create the dialog shown in Figure 13.27, you follow these steps:

Figure 13.27
This dialog box is a VBA UserForm displaying a chart. The chart redraws based on changes to the dialog controls.

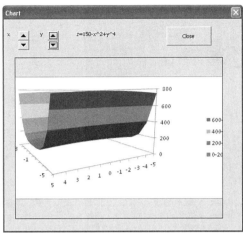

1. In the VBA window, select Insert, UserForm. In the Properties pane, rename the form `frmChart`.

2. Resize the UserForm.

3. Add a large `Image` control to the UserForm.

4. Add two spin buttons named `sbX` and `sbY`. Set them to have a minimum of 1 and a maximum of 5.

5. Add a `Label3` control to display the formula.

6. Add a command button labeled **Close**.

7. Enter this code in the code window behind the form:

```
Private Sub CommandButton1_Click()
    Unload Me
End Sub

Private Sub sbX_Change()
    MyPath = ThisWorkbook.Path & Application.PathSeparator & "Chart.gif"
    Worksheets("Surface").Range("O2").Value = Me.sbX.Value
    Worksheets("Surface").Shapes("Chart 1").Chart.Export MyPath
    Me.Label3.Caption = Worksheets("Surface").Range("O4").Value
    Me.Image1.Picture = LoadPicture(MyPath)
End Sub

Private Sub sbY_Change()
    MyPath = ThisWorkbook.Path & Application.PathSeparator & "Chart.gif"
    Worksheets("Surface").Range("O3").Value = Me.sbY.Value
    Worksheets("Surface").Shapes("Chart 1").Chart.Export MyPath
    Me.Label3.Caption = Worksheets("Surface").Range("O4").Value
    Me.Image1.Picture = LoadPicture(MyPath)
End Sub


Private Sub UserForm_Initialize()
    MyPath = ThisWorkbook.Path & Application.PathSeparator & "Chart.gif"
    Me.sbX = Worksheets("Surface").Range("O2").Value
```

```
    Me.sbY = Worksheets("Surface").Range("O3").Value
    Me.Label3.Caption = Worksheets("Surface").Range("O4").Value
    Worksheets("Surface").Shapes("Chart 1").Chart.Export MyPath
    Me.Image1.Picture = LoadPicture(MyPath)
End Sub
```

8. Use Insert, Module to add a `Module1` component with this code:

```
Sub ShowForm()
    frmChart.Show
End Sub
```

As someone changes the spin buttons in the UserForm, Excel writes new values to the worksheet. This causes the chart to update. The UserForm code then exports the chart and displays it in the UserForm (refer to Figure 13.27).

Creating Pivot Charts

A pivot chart is a chart that uses a pivot table as the underlying data source. As I lamented in Chapter 8, "Creating and Using Pivot Charts," pivot charts don't have the cool "show pages" functionality that regular pivot tables have. You can overcome this problem with a quick VBA macro that creates a pivot table and then a pivot chart based on the pivot table. The macro then adds the customer field to the page field of the pivot table. It then loops through each customer and exports the chart for each customer.

In Excel 2010, you first create a pivot cache by using the `PivotCache.Create` method. You can then define a pivot table based on the pivot cache. The usual procedure is to turn off pivot table updating while you add fields to the pivot table. Then you update the pivot table to have Excel perform the calculations.

It takes a bit of finesse to figure out the final range of the pivot table. If you have turned off the column and row totals, the chartable area of the pivot table starts one row below the `PivotTableRange1` area. You have to resize the area to include one fewer row to make your chart appear correctly.

After the pivot table is created, you can switch back to the `Charts.Add` code discussed earlier in this chapter. You can use any formatting code to get the chart formatted as you desire.

The following code creates a pivot table and a single pivot chart that summarize revenue by region and product:

```
Sub CreateSummaryReportUsingPivot()
    Dim WSD As Worksheet
    Dim PTCache As PivotCache
    Dim PT As PivotTable
    Dim PRange As Range
    Dim FinalRow As Long
    Dim ChartDataRange As Range
    Dim Cht As Chart
    Set WSD = Worksheets("Data")

    ' Delete any prior pivot tables
    For Each PT In WSD.PivotTables
```

13

```
        PT.TableRange2.Clear
Next PT
WSD.Range("I1:Z1").EntireColumn.Clear

' Define input area and set up a Pivot Cache
FinalRow = WSD.Cells(Application.Rows.Count, 1).End(xlUp).Row
FinalCol = WSD.Cells(1, Application.Columns.Count). _
    End(xlToLeft).Column
Set PRange = WSD.Cells(1, 1).Resize(FinalRow, FinalCol)

Set PTCache = ActiveWorkbook.PivotCaches.Create(SourceType:= _
    xlDatabase, SourceData:=PRange.Address)

' Create the Pivot Table from the Pivot Cache
Set PT = PTCache.CreatePivotTable(TableDestination:=WSD. _
    Cells(2, FinalCol + 2), TableName:="PivotTable1")

' Turn off updating while building the table
PT.ManualUpdate = True

' Set up the row fields
PT.AddFields RowFields:="Region", ColumnFields:="Product", _
    PageFields:="Customer"

' Set up the data fields
With PT.PivotFields("Revenue")
    .Orientation = xlDataField
    .Function = xlSum
    .Position = 1
End With

With PT
    .ColumnGrand = False
    .RowGrand = False
    .NullString = "0"
End With

' Calc the pivot table
PT.ManualUpdate = False
PT.ManualUpdate = True

' Define the Chart Data Range
Set ChartDataRange = _
    PT.TableRange1.Offset(1, 0).Resize(PT.TableRange1.Rows.Count - 1)

' Add the Chart
WSD.Shapes.AddChart.Select
Set Cht = ActiveChart
Cht.SetSourceData Source:=ChartDataRange
' Format the Chart
Cht.ChartType = xlColumnClustered
Cht.SetElement (msoElementChartTitleAboveChart)
Cht.ChartTitle.Caption = "All Customers"
Cht.SetElement msoElementPrimaryValueAxisThousands
' Hide the field buttons, Excel 2010 only
Cht.ShowAllFieldButtons = False
Cht.SeriesCollection(1).Fill.Patterned msoPattern50Percent
Cht.SeriesCollection(2).Fill.Patterned msoPatternLightHorizontal
```

```
        Cht.SeriesCollection(3).Fill.Patterned msoPatternLightVertical
        Cht.SeriesCollection(4).Fill.Patterned msoPatternDiagonalBrick
        Cht.SeriesCollection(5).Fill.Patterned msoPatternOutlinedDiamond

    End Sub
```

Figure 13.28 shows the resulting chart and pivot table.

Figure 13.28
VBA creates a pivot table and then a chart from the pivot table.

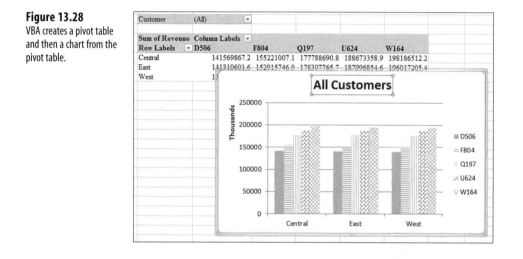

CASE STUDY: PRINTING A CHART FOR EACH CUSTOMER

In this case study, you'll use a pivot table and a pivot chart to summarize data from a pivot table. The goal is to create a pivot table with customers in the filter field area. The pivot table should summarize revenue by year and by product.

After this pivot table is created, you will add a chart with a chart title. You can then loop through each pivot item in the customer field. For each chart, you'll update the pivot table, change the chart title, and then export a chart with the name of the customer.

There is a bit more complexity in this macro than in the others shown so far in this chapter. The process of grouping daily dates up to yearly dates requires you to calculate the pivot table and then select one of the date fields. From TableRange1, you have to select a cell that is one row and one column from the top-left corner before you can group up to years.

After the first chart is created, you can loop through each pivot item in the customer pivot field. For each customer, you change the page field, recalculate the pivot table, change the title in the chart, and then export. To do all this, you use the following macro:

```
Sub CreateChartPerCustomer()
    Dim WSD As Worksheet
    Dim PTCache As PivotCache
    Dim PT As PivotTable
    Dim PRange As Range
    Dim FinalRow As Long
    Dim ChartDataRange As Range
```

13

```
                Dim Cht As Chart
                Dim PI As PivotItem
                Set WSD = Worksheets("Data")

                ' Delete any prior pivot tables
                For Each PT In WSD.PivotTables
                    PT.TableRange2.Clear
                Next PT
                WSD.Range("M1:Z1").EntireColumn.Clear

                ' Define input area and set up a Pivot Cache
                FinalRow = WSD.Cells(Application.Rows.Count, 1).End(xlUp).Row
                FinalCol = WSD.Cells(1, Application.Columns.Count). _
                    End(xlToLeft).Column
                Set PRange = WSD.Cells(1, 1).Resize(FinalRow, FinalCol)

                Set PTCache = ActiveWorkbook.PivotCaches.Create(SourceType:= _
                    xlDatabase, SourceData:=PRange.Address)

                ' Create the Pivot Table from the Pivot Cache
                Set PT = PTCache.CreatePivotTable(TableDestination:=WSD. _
                    Cells(2, FinalCol + 2), TableName:="PivotTable1")

                ' Turn off updating while building the table
                PT.ManualUpdate = True

                ' Set up the row fields
                PT.AddFields RowFields:="Product", ColumnFields:="Date", _
                    PageFields:="Customer"

                ' Set up the data fields
                With PT.PivotFields("Revenue")
                    .Orientation = xlDataField
                    .Function = xlSum
                    .Position = 1
                End With

                With PT
                    .ColumnGrand = False
                    .RowGrand = False
                    .NullString = "0"
                End With

                ' Calc the pivot table
                PT.ManualUpdate = False
                PT.ManualUpdate = True

                ' Find a date field & group by year

                PT.TableRange1.Offset(1, 1).Resize(1, 1).Group Start:=True, End:=True, _
                    Periods:=Array(False, False, False, False, False, False, True)

                ' Calc the pivot table
                PT.ManualUpdate = False
                PT.ManualUpdate = True
```

```
' CreateChart
Set ChartDataRange = _
    PT.TableRange1.Offset(1, 0).Resize(PT.TableRange1.Rows.Count - 1)

' Add the Chart
WSD.Shapes.AddChart.Select
Set Cht = ActiveChart
Cht.SetSourceData Source:=ChartDataRange
' Format the Chart
Cht.ChartType = xlColumnClustered
Cht.SetElement (msoElementChartTitleAboveChart)
Cht.ChartTitle.Caption = "All Customers"
Cht.SetElement msoElementPrimaryValueAxisThousands

' Loop through each customer
For Each PI In PT.PivotFields("Customer").PivotItems

    PT.PivotFields("Customer").ClearAllFilters
    PT.PivotFields("Customer").CurrentPage = PI.Name

    ' Calc the pivot table
    PT.ManualUpdate = False
    PT.ManualUpdate = True

    Cht.ChartTitle.Caption = PI.Name
    MyPath = ThisWorkbook.Path & Application.PathSeparator
    Cht.Export Filename:=MyPath & PI.Name & ".jpg", Filtername:="JPG"

Next PI
End Sub
```

Figure 13.29 shows one of the three dozen charts created by this macro in less than a minute.

Figure 13.29
The macro creates dozens of summary charts in under a minute.

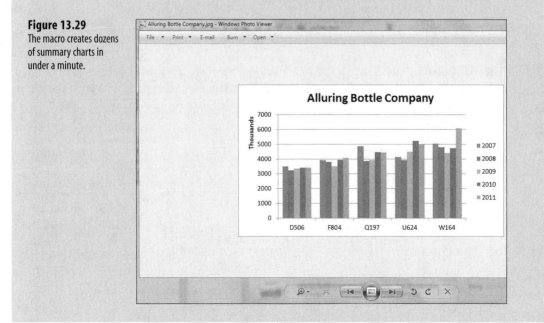

Creating Data Bars with VBA

The data bars in Excel 2010 now allow for negative values of a different color, solid or gradient fills, explicit min and max values, and even data bars that go right to left. The latter setting makes it easy to create comparative bar charts.

Figure 13.30 shows two sets of data bars created by VBA.

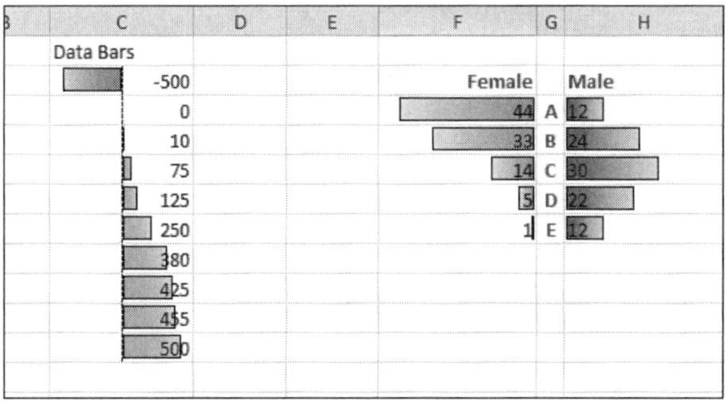

Figure 13.30
Two sets of data bars.

To add default data bars, use this code:

```
Range("C2:C11").FormatConditions.AddDataBar
```

You will want to customize the data bars by changing color, gradient, border color, and scale. Thus, it is easiest to assign the data bars to an object variable:

```
Dim DB As Databar
With Range("C2:C11")
    .FormatConditions.Delete
    ' Add the data bars
    Set DB = .FormatConditions.AddDatabar()
End With
```

The example in column C of Figure 13.30 includes negative data bars of a contrasting color, a horizontal axis in the center of the cell, a black border around the data bars, and a custom scale from -600 to +600. The code to create that data bar is as follows:

```
Sub DataBar()
' Add a Data bar
' Include negative data bars
' Control the min and max point
'
    Dim DB As Databar
    With Range("C2:C11")
        .FormatConditions.Delete
        ' Add the data bars
        Set DB = .FormatConditions.AddDatabar()
    End With

    ' Set the lower limit
    DB.MinPoint.Modify newtype:=xlConditionFormula, NewValue:="-600"
```

```
DB.MaxPoint.Modify newtype:=xlConditionValueFormula, NewValue:="600"

' Change the data bar to Green
With DB.BarColor
    .Color = RGB(0, 255, 0)
    .TintAndShade = -0.15
End With

' All of this is new in Excel 2010
With DB
    ' Use a gradiant
    .BarFillType = xlDataBarFillGradient
    ' Left to Right for direction of bars
    .Direction = xlLTR
    ' Assign a different color to negative bars
    .NegativeBarFormat.ColorType = xlDataBarColor
    ' Use a border around the bars
    .BarBorder.Type = xlDataBarBorderSolid
    ' Assign a different border color to negative
    .NegativeBarFormat.BorderColorType = xlDataBarSameAsPositive
    ' All borders are solid black
    With .BarBorder.Color
        .Color = RGB(0, 0, 0)
    End With
    ' Axis where it naturally would fall, in black
    .AxisPosition = xlDataBarAxisAutomatic
    With .AxisColor
        .Color = 0
        .TintAndShade = 0
    End With
    ' Negative bars in red
    With .NegativeBarFormat.Color
        .Color = 255
        .TintAndShade = 0
    End With
    ' Negative borders in red
End With

End Sub
```

The next macro creates two sets of simpler data bars. There is no need to format the axis or the negative bar color since these are not ever going to be present in this dataset.

The main difference is that the bars on the left have a `.Direction` property of xlRTL, which stands for right to left:

```
Sub DataBarCompare()
' Add two data bars. Right-to-Left for females
'
    Dim DB As Databar
    ' Create left-facing data bars for females
    With Range("F3:F7")
        .FormatConditions.Delete
        ' Add the data bars
        Set DB = .FormatConditions.AddDatabar()
    End With

    ' Set the lower limit
```

13

```
DB.MinPoint.Modify newtype:=xlConditionFormula, NewValue:="0"
DB.MaxPoint.Modify newtype:=xlConditionValueFormula, NewValue:="50"

' Change the data bar to Red, 15% lighter
With DB.BarColor
    .Color = RGB(255, 0, 0)
    .TintAndShade = 0.3
End With

' All of this is new in Excel 2010
With DB
    ' Use a gradiant
    .BarFillType = xlDataBarFillGradient
    ' Left to Right for direction of bars
    .Direction = xlRTL
    ' Use a border around the bars
    .BarBorder.Type = xlDataBarBorderSolid
    ' All borders are solid black
    With .BarBorder.Color
        .Color = RGB(0, 0, 0)
    End With
End With

' Create right-facing data bars for males
With Range("H3:H7")
    .FormatConditions.Delete
    ' Add the data bars
    Set DB = .FormatConditions.AddDatabar()
End With

' Set the lower limit
DB.MinPoint.Modify newtype:=xlConditionFormula, NewValue:="0"
DB.MaxPoint.Modify newtype:=xlConditionValueFormula, NewValue:="50"

' Change the data bar to Red, 15% lighter
With DB.BarColor
    .Color = RGB(0, 0, 255)
    .TintAndShade = 0.3
End With

' All of this is new in Excel 2010
With DB
    ' Use a gradiant
    .BarFillType = xlDataBarFillGradient
    ' Left to Right for direction of bars
    .Direction = xlLTR
    ' Use a border around the bars
    .BarBorder.Type = xlDataBarBorderSolid
    ' All borders are solid black
    With .BarBorder.Color
        .Color = RGB(0, 0, 0)
    End With
End With

End Sub
```

13

Creating Sparklines with VBA

Regular sparklines are relatively easy to create with VBA:

```
Dim SG as SparklineGroup
FinalRow = Cells(Rows.Count, 6).End(xlUp).Row
Set SG = WSL.Range("B2:D2").SparklineGroups.Add( _
    Type:=xlSparkLine, _
    SourceData:="Data!D2:F" & FinalRow
```

Figure 13.31 shows a set of simple sparklines created by VBA.

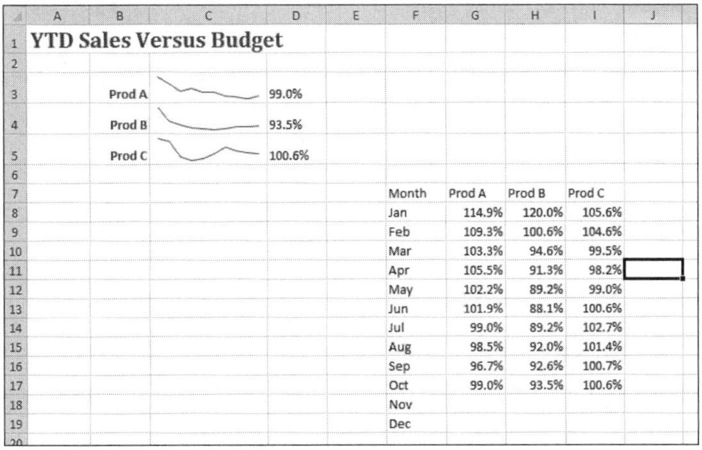
YTD Sales Versus Budget
Prod A 99.0%
Prod B 93.5%
Prod C 100.6%
Month Prod A Prod B Prod C
Jan 114.9% 120.0% 105.6%
Feb 109.3% 100.6% 104.6%
Mar 103.3% 94.6% 99.5%
Apr 105.5% 91.3% 98.2%
May 102.2% 89.2% 99.0%
Jun 101.9% 88.1% 100.6%
Jul 99.0% 89.2% 102.7%
Aug 98.5% 92.0% 101.4%
Sep 96.7% 92.6% 100.7%
Oct 99.0% 93.5% 100.6%
Nov
Dec

Figure 13.31
Simple sparklines don't communicate information about the min and max.

However, if you've read about sparklines in Edward Tufte's book, *Beautiful Evidence*, then you will want to go beyond the "regular" sparklines that are the default from Microsoft Excel.

Tufte's sparklines often have a gray band indicating the normal range for a variable. Sparklines don't support the gray band, but you can simulate it by using a transparent shape.

My idea of sparkline perfection involves these elements:

- The entire sparkline presentation requires three adjacent cells.
- The sparkline itself is in the center cell. The min and max of the sparkline are set to be the min and max of the data set. This causes the sparkline to fill 100 percent of the vertical height of the cell.
- The height of the cell is either 55 or 110. With 110, you can fit 10 lines of 8-point wrapped text.
- In the cell to the left of the sparkline, you would right-justify the maximum value, 8 line feeds, and then the minimum value. This communicates the highest and lowest point experienced in the data set.

- In the cell to the right of the sparkline, you would left-justify the final value. Depending on if the final value is in the top, middle, or bottom of the range, you would add sufficient number of line feeds before the value to get the label roughly adjacent to the endpoint.

- In the sparkline cell, center the title for the sparkline.

- In the sparkline cell, add a semi-transparent rectangle to show the acceptable values. It is incredibly difficult to position this manually. With VBA, though, you can get the box positioned nearly perfectly.

Figure 13.32 shows a set of four sparklines. Each line is showing readings from manufacturing lines taken every six minutes throughout one day. The min and max value are shown to the left of the cell. The final value is shown to the right of the cell. The colored band represents the acceptable range of 97 to 103.

Figure 13.32
VBA adds labels, titles, and an acceptable range to each sparkline.

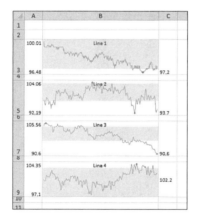

The code to create Figure 13.32 is shown here:

```
Sub ComplexSparklines()
Dim SG As SparklineGroup
Dim SL As Sparkline
Dim WSD As Worksheet ' Data worksheet
Dim WSL As Worksheet ' Dashboard
Dim Rg As Range
Dim Sh As Shape

    On Error Resume Next
    Application.DisplayAlerts = False
    Worksheets("Dashboard").Delete
    On Error GoTo 0

    Set WSD = Worksheets("Data")
    Set WSL = ActiveWorkbook.Worksheets.Add
    WSL.Name = "Dashboard"

    ' Set up the dashboard as alternating cells for sparkline then blank
```

```vba
WSL.Cells(1, 1).ColumnWidth = 5
WSL.Cells(1, 2).ColumnWidth = 35
WSL.Cells(1, 3).ColumnWidth = 5
For r = 3 To 9 Step 2
    WSL.Cells(r, 1).RowHeight = 55
    WSL.Cells(r + 1, 1).RowHeight = 9
Next r

NextRow = 3
NextCol = 2

FinalRow = WSD.Cells(Rows.Count, 1).End(xlUp).Row
Set AF = Application.WorksheetFunction

For i = 2 To 5
    If i > 6 Then Exit For
    ThisLine = WSD.Cells(1, i).Value
    ThisCol = Chr(64 + i)
    ThisSource = "Data!" & ThisCol & "2:" & ThisCol & FinalRow
    Set ThisRg = WSD.Cells(2, i).Resize(FinalRow - 1, 1)
    MyMax = AF.Max(ThisRg)
    MyMin = AF.Min(ThisRg)
    MyRg = MyMax - MyMin
    FinalVal = WSD.Cells(FinalRow, i).Value

    Set SG = WSL.Cells(NextRow, NextCol).SparklineGroups.Add( _
        Type:=xlSparkLine, _
        SourceData:=ThisSource)

    Set SL = SG.Item(1)

    SG.Axes.Horizontal.Axis.Visible = True
    With SG.Axes.Vertical
        .MinScaleType = xlSparkScaleCustom
        .MaxScaleType = xlSparkScaleCustom
        .CustomMinScaleValue = MyMin
        .CustomMaxScaleValue = MyMax
    End With

    ' Line in Green
    SG.SeriesColor.Color = RGB(0, 176, 80)

    ' If the high point is above range, in red
    If MyMax > 103 Then
        SG.Points.Highpoint.Visible = True
        SG.Points.Highpoint.Color.Color = 255
    End If
    If MyMin < 97 Then
        SG.Points.Lowpoint.Visible = True
        SG.Points.Lowpoint.Color.Color = 255
    End If

    ' Add a label to the sparkline cell
    With WSL.Cells(NextRow, NextCol)
        .Value = ThisLine
        .HorizontalAlignment = xlCenter
        .VerticalAlignment = xlTop
        .Font.Size = 8
```

13

```
        .WrapText = True
    End With

    ' Label the cell to the left with min and max
    With WSL.Cells(NextRow, NextCol - 1)
        .Value = Round(MyMax, 2) & vbLf & vbLf & vbLf & vbLf & _
        Round(MyMin, 2)
        .HorizontalAlignment = xlRight
        .VerticalAlignment = xlTop
        .Font.Size = 8
        .WrapText = True
    End With

    ' Calculate position for final point
    RtLabel = ""
    For j = MyMax To MyMin Step -(MyRg / 4)
        If j <= MyMin Then
            RtLabel = RtLabel & Round(FinalVal, 1)
            Exit For
        ElseIf j < FinalVal Then
            RtLabel = RtLabel & Round(FinalVal, 1)
            Exit For
        Else
            RtLabel = RtLabel & vbLf
        End If
    Next j

    With WSL.Cells(NextRow, NextCol + 1)
        .Value = RtLabel
        .HorizontalAlignment = xlLeft
        .VerticalAlignment = xlTop
        .Font.Size = 8
        .WrapText = True
    End With

    ' Color the cell
    ' if < 0.95, then red
    With WSL.Cells(NextRow, NextCol).Interior
        If FinalVal <= 95 Then
            .Color = 255
            .TintAndShade = 0.9
        ElseIf FinalVal > 105 Then
            .Color = RGB(0, 0, 255)
            .TintAndShade = 0.7
        End If
    End With

    ' Add a transparent rectangle to indicate the acceptable range
    celltop = WSL.Cells(NextRow, 2).Top
    cellht = WSL.Cells(NextRow, 2).Height
    CellLt = WSL.Cells(NextRow, 2).Left
    CellWid = WSL.Cells(NextRow, 2).Width
    ' The acceptable range is 97 - 103
    If MyMax <= 97 Then
        BandTop = celltop + cellht
    ElseIf MyMax <= 103 Then
        BandTop = celltop
    ElseIf MyMax > 103 Then
```

```
            DeltaTop = MyMax - 103
            BandTop = Round((DeltaTop / MyRg) * cellht, 0) + celltop
        End If

        If MyMin >= 103 Then
            BandBot = celltop
        ElseIf MyMin >= 97 Then
            BandBot = celltop + cellht
        Else
            DeltaBot = 97 - MyMin
            x = Round((DeltaBot / MyRg) * cellht, 0)
            BandBot = celltop + cellht - x
        End If

        BandHt = BandBot - BandTop

        If BandHt < 1 Then BandHt = 1

        Set Sh = WSL.Shapes.AddShape(Type:=msoShapeRectangle, _
            Left:=CellLt, _
            Top:=BandTop, _
            Width:=CellWid, _
            Height:=BandHt)
    '     Sh.ShapeStyle = msoShapeStylePreset23
        With Sh.Fill
            .Visible = msoTrue
            .ForeColor.RGB = RGB(102, 255, 255)
            .Transparency = 0.7294117212
    '        .Solid
        End With
        Sh.Line.Visible = msoFalse

        NextRow = NextRow + 2
    Next i

End Sub
```

Next Steps

While I hope this book has taught you how to create meaningful charts, the next chapter shows many examples of bad charts. People might try to use bad charts to mislead the reader intentionally or might just create a misleading chart because they think it looks cool. By knowing how to spot bad charts, you can prevent people from misleading you the next time you are sitting through a presentation.

13

Knowing When Someone Is Lying to You with a Chart

Several settings in Excel allow you to either inadvertently or intentionally create charts that are misleading. Many of the popular charting styles do a poor job of representing the underlying data. Don't get me wrong; the charts often look great, but they do not provide an accurate picture of the data.

This chapter illustrates many of the chart lies that are easy to incorporate into an Excel chart. My hope is not that you will use these to confuse the chart consumer. Instead, I hope you will avoid these types of charts. I also hope you learn to look with caution on charts created by others that use the techniques included in this chapter.

Lying with Perspective

Excel's 3-D charts attempts to show a two-dimensional object on a two-dimensional computer screen and give the perception that the objects are rendered in 3-D. Even though Excel provides a lot of support for the 3-D charts, they are not covered in great detail in this book because they often misrepresent your data. Instead, I hope you will resist the urge to use 3-D charts.

When I took a photography class, during the lesson on wide-angle lenses, the instructor pointed out that a wide-angle lens makes everything in the foreground look proportionally larger than it really is. If you are shooting a portrait of someone who has a big nose, you don't want to use a wide-angle lens for that portrait.

Similarly, with 3-D pie charts, any wedges at the front of the pie look much larger than wedges at the back of the pie. For example, in Figure 14.1, both charts show a labor component of 30 percent. If you want to impress the union during contract negotiations, you should use a 3-D chart where labor is in the front because the labor wedge in that chart is 2.8 times the size of the one in the top chart.

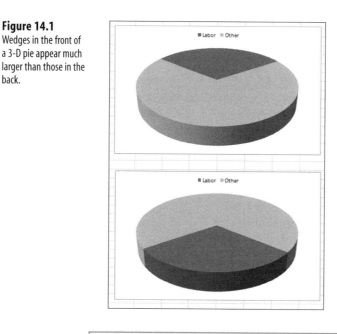

> **NOTE** If want to lie with a 3-D pie chart, you can accomplish that by changing the rotation of the pie. Right-click the pie, select Format Series, and then change the rotation angle.

In addition, perspective causes problems with 3-D column charts. For example, often the reader is not sure whether to look at the front or the back of the column.

Look in the top chart in Figure 14.2. Are any of the quarters over 3,000? Count the number of gridlines. The sixth line is 3,000. None of the bars ever touches the 3,000 line. However, in the bottom chart, both the Q3 and Q4 columns are over 3,000.

Lying with Shrinking Charts

The pyramid and cone charts should be banned from Excel. You could do without these 14 different charts, which inflate the data in the bottom series and deflate the data in the top series.

Consider a standard stacked bar chart like the top one in Figure 14.3. In this chart, a charity's administrative expenses are fairly high at 35 percent. If the charity wants to minimize its administrative expenses in a chart for its donors, it can change the chart to a cone or pyramid chart since this chart is naturally smaller at the top. In this example, the 35 percent wedge for administration in black looks like virtually nothing! This occurs because items at the top of the chart get significantly less pixels than items at the base of the chart.

Figure 14.2

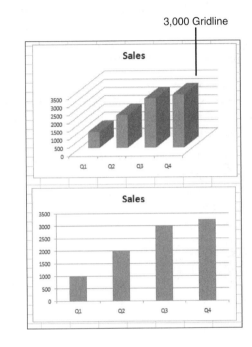

Figure 14.3
To misrepresent the 35 percent category in black at the top, you can put it in a cone chart.

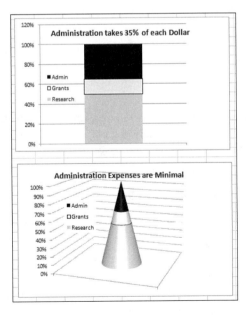

14

Lying with Scale

In various chapters of this book, you have seen how to change the minimum and maximum values for the scale along the vertical axis. Zooming in allows you to spot variability in tightly clustered values, such as shown in Figure 2.23 in Chapter 2, "Customizing Charts." Zooming out allows you to isolate data to a certain zone of the chart. In Figure 6.10, the volume scale was set two to three times larger than normal to keep the volumes in the lower third of the stock chart.

Although both of those concepts are valid reasons to change the scale, there are also consequences from changing the scale. Changing the scale allows you to paint a very different picture of the data. Figures 14.4 through Figure 14.6 show the same demand curve.

In Figure 14.4, the manufacturing plant zoomed the scale in to have a minimum of 4000 and a maximum of 7500. With a title proclaiming that sales are erratic, they can argue that the cost of staffing-up and staffing-down in order to meet the ripsaw demand for product is causing problems.

Figure 14.4
The chart produced by the manufacturing chart focus on the variability.

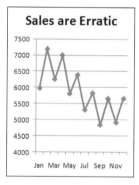

If the sales team presented their chart first, a different picture would have emerged. Figure 14.5 shows a chart where the scale has been zoomed out to have a minimum of 0 and a maximum of 20,000. With this chart, the demand looks almost constant.

Figure 14.5
By zooming out, the demand looks smooth.

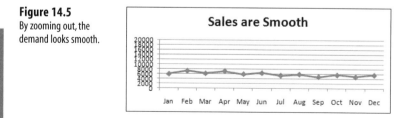

In addition, note that it is much less apparent in Figure 14.5 that the demand is trending down. Figure 14.6 attempts to hide this trend even more. By switching to a 3-D chart and adjusting the 3-D rotation settings, you can create a line that appears to be trending up at the end.

Figure 14.6
The downward trend appears to reverse.

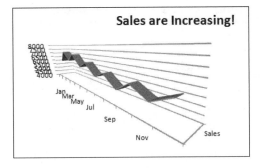

Lying Because Excel Will Not Cooperate

The chart in Figure 14.7 was presented at a board meeting. The treasurer intended to present the good news that a particular department produced a consistent profit for several years. Instead of showing one line with 42 months, he built a cross-tab table to show 12 months and a different line for each year.

Because the current year was not yet complete, data for July through December is blank in the original table. For this reason, it showed up as zeros in the chart data.

 Note that the subtitle in Figure 14.7 was not in the original chart. I penciled this editorial comment in as I was listening to the presentation.

The problem occurs from a clever formula in the charting data. This formula allowed the 48 rows of vertical monthly data to be presented in a 4-row by 12-column arrangement. The result is that the formula converts blank cells to zeroes for future months.

The solution shown in Figure 14.8 is to convert the zero results to NA(). Zeros are plotted on a chart, whereas #N/A errors are not plotted. By checking for a zero and then converting those results to #N/A errors, the future months are not plotted on the chart.

Zeros can be converted automatically to #N/A. Say that you are building a table with any formula such as =Formula. Edit that formula to be =IF(Formula=0,NA(),Formula).

14

Figure 14.7
Zeros in the future months make it look like all the money disappears.

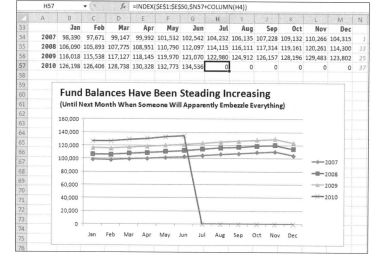

Figure 14.8
Convert the formula to show futures months as #N/A.

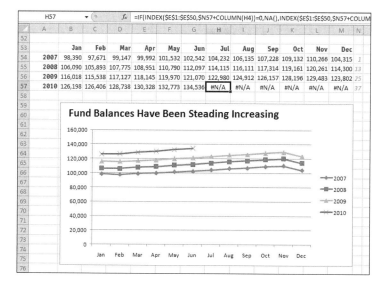

To see a demo of this chart problem and the solution, search for "MrExcel Charts 14" at YouTube.

Avoid Stacked Surface Charts

The message of the chart at the top of Figure 14.9 is that marketing costs more than tripled in three years. If the vice president of marketing wants to defend the marketing expenses, he might mix the marketing department in with other departments to show the marketing budget as a middle series in a stacked area chart.

In a stacked area chart, you can usually figure out what is happening with the numbers in the series at the base of the chart. However, after that first series, everything becomes difficult to judge.

In the chart at the bottom of Figure 14.9, the dramatic increase in marketing spending is not immediately apparent. Some people might see the downward slope at the top of the marketing region and incorrectly infer that marketing costs are decreasing.

Bottom line, don't use stacked area charts. Show the data as individual line charts instead.

Figure 14.9
Adding data obscures the marketing excesses.

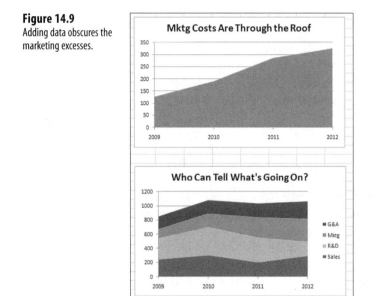

Asserting a Trend from Two Data Points

In the top chart in Figure 14.10, sales appear to be trending up. Even the automatic Excel trendline indicates this is occurring.

If you are presented with this chart, ask the presenter if they have more data. For example, it would be good to put those two data points in the context of a larger historical trend.

If you see more data, you might realize that the increase in the last year is actually the bottoming out of a six-year skid, as shown in the bottom chart in Figure 14.10.

14

Figure 14.10
Inferring a trend based on a two-point line is dangerous. You need to add more data points to tell the real story.

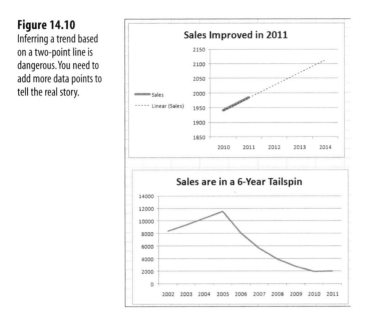

Deliberately Using Charts to Lie

Some people are just good at lying. For example, sales are increasing in Figure 14.11. Or are they? Notice that the chart author reversed the categories along the x-axis with the most recent year appearing at the left. Most people are conditioned that charts proceed from earliest to latest. If the presenter is flipping through slides in a PowerPoint presentation, the chances are no one will notice that sales are not trending up.

Figure 14.11
It appears that all is going well.

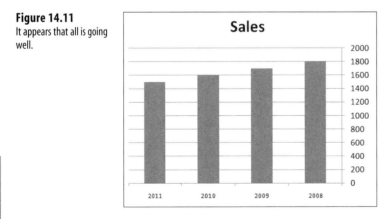

Excel makes it easy to create the chart in Figure 14.11. The Format Axis dialog for the chart offers a simple check box for Categories in Reverse Order, as shown in Figure 14.12.

Figure 14.12
The reversed years in Figure 14.11 come from this setting.

Categories in reverse

Format Axis

Axis Options	Axis Options
Number	Interval between tick marks: 1
Fill	Interval between labels:
Line Color	○ Automatic
Line Style	○ Specify interval unit: 1
Shadow	☑ Categories in reverse order
Glow and Soft Edges	Label distance from axis: 100
3-D Format	Axis Type:
	○ Automatically select based on data

Chart Something Else When Numbers Are Too Bad

As another example, in Figure 14.13, a city is drastically losing population. Jobs are scarce, education is bad, and people are moving out. The top chart paints a pretty bleak picture. The mayor, who has been around for 24 years, wants to put a happy spin on the message. His staff prepares the bottom chart, which shows how population growth has slowed.

Figure 14.13
When the absolute numbers are bleak, you plot the percentage rate of change.

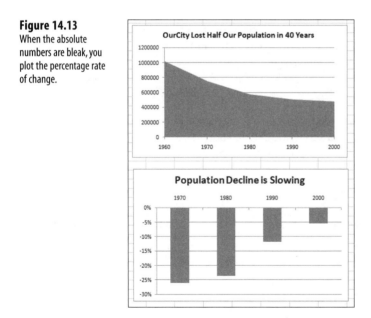

Beware of Pictographs That Do Not Follow the Rules

14

The next example is definitely a non-Excel lie. Even Excel is smart enough not to allow picture markers to change in both height and width. Someone had to make the markers invisible and use clip art to pull off the lie shown in Figure 14.14.

The image on the left is 100 pixels tall and 100 pixels wide. This seems like a reasonable way to represent $100 million in exports. When the chart designer scaled the picture up to 300 pixels for the March data, he allowed both the height and width to change. The size of the final image contains nine times the area of the first image, even though the exports increased by a factor of three.

Figure 14.14
The size of the images increased in both height and width. This causes a 200 percent increase to look like an 800 percent increase.

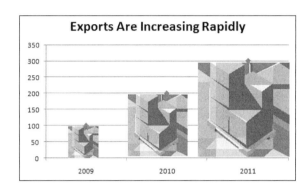

The rule for pictographs is that you should increase the height of the picture, but never the width. Even though Excel does this properly, charts in newspapers and magazines are frequently created in Photoshop. The designers try to create a pretty chart that does not distort the image by increasing the height and width of the marker. In the process, they create a misleading chart.

These are just a few of the many ways that people might try to lie to you with charts. Now that you have read this book, you should be able to spot a deception and call it out. You should also be able to use charts to represent data accurately.

Next Steps

Appendix A, "Charting References," lists several additional resources where you can find more information on charting.

Charting References

A

Other Charting Resources

If you enjoyed this book, there are many more resources for you to investigate. These are people, books, and websites that have had an influence on my charting life.

> **NOTE**
>
> Websites come and go. I will maintain a list of links to these references and any more that I find at `http://www.mrexcel.com/chartbook2010data.html`.

Gene Zelazny: The Guru of Business Charting

During a 40-year career at McKinsey & Company, Gene Zelazny has taught two generations of people how to effectively communicate with charts. I learned a lot about charting during a six-month stint on a McKinsey project team. The McKinsey consultants, such as Gino Picasso and Firoz Dosani, who taught me about charting, learned the craft from Gene Zelazny.

I enjoy Gene's work because he focuses on positive ways to effectively communicate by using charts and visuals. While Tufte spends a lot of ink showing why popular charts are bad, Gene cuts right to the chase and shows examples of effective charts.

Pick up anything that you find written by Gene. He first wrote Say It with Presentation. His best kit is The Say It with Charts Complete Toolkit. If you wonder where Microsoft got the idea for SmartArt graphics, you will see that Gene began advocating what Microsoft calls SmartArt long before Microsoft coined the name. The kit includes a book, images on CD-ROM, and more (see `http://www.zelazny.com/charts.html`).

PowerFrameworks.com

If you are the go-to person for charts in your company, then you need to subscribe to PowerFrameworks.com. The $249 annual subscription gives you access to hundreds of charting and presentation templates. Kathy Villella and Lisa Baker are constantly adding new, leading-edge elements to the site. For example, Kathy recently posted an umbrella chart element that you can import into PowerPoint. In addition to the element, Kathy provides several professionally designed ideas about how you could use the chart.

PowerFrameworks hires professional artists to bring its ideas to life. It makes sure that in a lock-and-key chart, the key actually fits in the lock. You can build brilliant-looking animated or still charts using these elements.

The company's ideas alone are worth the price of a PowerFrameworks subscription. Download the templates, label the charts, color with the Formatting tab, and you are ready to go.

A subscription to PowerFrameworks can help supercharge your career.

Books by Edward Tufte

I own everything that Professor Edward Tufte writes. He self-publishes his books and spares no expense in creating fantastic, full-color, beautiful books.

If Gene Zelazny was the source of Microsoft's ideas for SmartArt, then Edward Tufte is the source for Microsoft's ideas about sparklines. In his book *Beautiful Evidence*, Tuft demonstrated sparklines as "intense, word-sized graphics."

Zelazny's books are informative and filled with eye candy. I can spend an hour studying the beautiful Napoleon's March chart that manages to communicate seven different series with a single line. Tufte has found examples of good and bad charts throughout history. He coined the term *chartjunk*.

My only complaint is that Tufte comes off as a bit of a curmudgeon. He shows bad charts and explains why they are bad. I am sure that Tufte would skewer some of my charts in this book. After reading Tufte, I am filled with doubt and knowledge about what not to do. Zelazny counters this by only telling you what is effective.

Tufte has written the following books:

- The *Visual Display of Quantitative Information*, now in its second edition, contains 250 illustrations of the best and sometimes the worst ways of displaying information.
- *Envisioning Information* covers maps, charts, tables, timetables, and more. This book is aimed at those in the design profession.
- *Visual Explanations: Images and Quantities, Evidence and Narrative* is about the representation of verbs. This book talks about how to pack the most information into a small space and how to use visual information for making decisions.

■ *Beautiful Evidence* is a book in which Tufte introduces the concept of sparklines.

Tufte also maintains a website and forum at `http://www.EdwardTufte.com`.

Websites with Charting Tutorials

Excel gurus maintain numerous websites. A very few offer a better-than-usual concentration on charting and the process of creating unique charts:

■ **Jon Peltier**—Jon, a Microsoft MVP, has several excellent charting examples on his website. If I am Googling a particularly difficult chart problem, I end up at Jon's site more often than not. Visit his site at `http://www.PeltierTech.com`.

■ **Mike Alexander**—Mike runs a site with a funny name (DataPig Technologies) but great content. Many of his charting ideas made it into Chapter 7, "Using Advanced Chart Techniques." The benefit of Mike's site is that all the tutorials are five-minute videos that allow you to actually watch the charts being built. Visit `http://www.DataPigTechnologies.com`.

■ **Andy Pope**—Andy maintains a website with amazing chart examples. These examples run circles around even the advanced charts shown in Chapter 7 of this book. Andy is a Microsoft MVP. Visit his website, `http://www.andypope.info/charts.htm`.

■ **Tushar Mehta**—Tushar, a Microsoft MVP, has some nontraditional charting examples on his website, at `http://www.tushar-mehta.com/excel/charts/`.

■ **Tom Bunzel**—If you need to present your data with PowerPoint, check out Tom Bunzel's site, `http://www.professorppt.com`. Tom writes books about PowerPoint and numerous articles for InformIT.

Interactive Training

As I was working on the manuscript for this book, I also recorded an interactive DVD + Book that Que markets as LiveLessons Power Excel 2010. That product has over an hour of content on charting in Excel.

Live Training

If you are an MBA student at a business school, you might be lucky enough to catch Gene Zelazny as a guest speaker at your college. I highly recommend attending his seminar if he visits your town.

Edward Tufte provides a 1-day course on charting at various sites around the country. Check out `http://www.edwardtufte.com/tufte/courses` for a schedule.

Blogs About Charting

A few people are gracing the blogosphere with posts that often touch on charting:

- **Juice Analytics**—Zach and Chris Gemignani seem to be proponents of Edward Tufte. They often critique charts at their Juice Analytics blog, `http://www.juiceanalytics.com/weblog/`.

- **Daily Dose of Excel**—Many Excel MVPs contribute topics on various Excel topics to Dick Kusleika's Daily Dose of Excel blog. You can find an archive of the charting posts at `http://www.dailydoseofexcel.com/archives/category/charting/`.

- **Visual Business Intelligence**—Steven Few shows off new and innovative visual designs at his blog, `http://www.perceptualedge.com/blog/`.

- **Instant Cognition**—This wide-ranging blog has several excellent posts on visual report design. See `http://blog.instantcognition.com/category/visualization/charts/`.

- **Politikal Arithmetik**—Professor Charles Franklin's blog always has the latest political charts and analysis. Visit for inspiration on cool charting ideas: `http://politicalarithmetik.blogspot.com/`.

In addition, I produce a daily two-minute video podcast about Excel that occasionally dips into the charting realm. You can find a link to charting episodes at `http://www.mrexcel.com/chartbookdata.html`. I also maintain a blog for this book at `http://excelchartsgraphs@wordpress.com`

Visual Design Stores

If you are a fan of visual information and graphic design, then a must-see store on your next trip through Toronto is SWIPE. This store is dedicated to books on advertising and design.

David Michaelides has been running SWIPE for almost 20 years. If there is a book on advertising or design, he either has it or knows where to get it. The store is located at 477 Richmond Street West, Toronto. You can find more information at `http://www.swipe.com`. Plan to spend at least an hour browsing the store.

Professional Chart Designers

Well, I realize that if you are creating charts and getting paid for it, then you, the reader, are a professional chart designer. However, if you are in a pinch and need to find some outside help, check out the services of these designers:

- **Bob D'Amico**—Bob D'Amico is an illustrator and a designer. Although he drew the humorous charts in Chapters 4 and 6, he has a complete portfolio of serious charting designs he has completed for clients. Whether you need something serious or irreverent, contact Bob via e-mail at CartoonBob@mac.com.

■ **Andy Attiliis**—Andy Attiliis operates a professional charting design service at `http://www.ideasiteforbusiness.com/andy/dc.htm`.

Charting Utilities and Products

Some charts just aren't easy to create in Excel. The following are some of my favorite utilities for creating different charts:

■ **Speedometer Chart Creator**—Mala Singh provides an add-in that can generate speedometer charts in seconds instead of the hour it can take to draw a speedometer with AutoShapes. His charts show a current value plus yesterday's value, so you can get an idea of whether the value is trending up or down. Mala also offers the MacroEconomic Supply Curve Chart add-in, in which the width of the column indicates units sold and the height of the column indicates price. You can see these charts and more at `http://www.mrexcel.com/graphics.shtml`.

■ **Dashboard Reporting with Excel**—This is Charley Kyd's excellent kit about how to create dashboards in Excel. It features an e-book plus a dozen sample Excel files to get you started. Charley is the king of getting small charts readable in Excel; my favorite examples puts 112 readable postage stamp–size charts on a single letter-size sheet of paper. Visit `http://www.ExcelUser.com`.

■ **Xcelsius**—This product can use your Excel data to make interactive charts and output them to the Web or PowerPoint. Check it out at `http://www.businessobjects.com/xcelcius`.

> **NOTE**
>
> If you have resources that should be listed here, send them to the e-mail address listed at `http://www.mrexcel.com/chartbookdata.html`.

INDEX

Symbols

A

B

U

V

MrExcel
Library Series

Learn from Bill Jelen, Excel MVP, founder of MrExcel

VBA AND MACROS:
Microsoft Excel 2010

POWERPIVOT
FOR THE DATA ANALYST:
Microsoft Excel 2010

CHARTS AND GRAPHS:
Microsoft Excel 2010

PIVOT TABLE
DATA CRUNCHING:
Microsoft Excel 2010

Get to the Next Level in Excel Proficiency with Bill Jelen, Excel MVP and Best-Selling Author

Titles in the **MrExcel Library** are designed to launch readers to the next level in Excel proficiency by pinpointing a certain task and expanding on it—providing the reference material readers need to become more productive with advanced features of Excel.

Every book in the **MrExcel Library** pinpoints a specific set of crucial Excel skills, and presents focused tasks and examples for performing them rapidly and effectively. Selected by Bill Jelen, Microsoft Excel MVP and mastermind behind the leading Excel solutions website MrExcel.com, these books will:

- Dramatically increase your productivity—saving you 50 hours a year, or more
- Present proven, creative strategies for solving real-world problems
- Show you how to get great results, no matter how much data you have
- Help you avoid critical mistakes that even experienced users make

MrExcel LIBRARY   Visit **quepublishing.com/mrexcel**

que®

quepublishing.com | mrexcel.com

FREE Online Edition

Your purchase of **Charts and Graphs: Microsoft Excel 2010** includes access to a free online edition for 45 days through the Safari Books Online subscription service. Nearly every Que book is available online through Safari Books Online, along with more than 5,000 other technical books and videos from publishers such as Addison-Wesley Professional, Cisco Press, Exam Cram, IBM Press, O'Reilly, Prentice Hall, and Sams.

SAFARI BOOKS ONLINE allows you to search for a specific answer, cut and paste code, download chapters, and stay current with emerging technologies.

Activate your FREE Online Edition at
www.informit.com/safarifree

> **STEP 1:** Enter the coupon code: GAZFQGA.

> **STEP 2:** New Safari users, complete the brief registration form.
> Safari subscribers, just log in.

If you have difficulty registering on Safari or accessing the online edition, please e-mail customer-service@safaribooksonline.com